Pitt Series in Policy and Institutional Studies

POLITICAL LEADERSHIP
A Source Book

POLITICAL LEADERSHIP

A Source Book

Edited by
BARBARA KELLERMAN

University of Pittsburgh Press
Pittsburgh and London

Published by the University of Pittsburgh Press, Pittsburgh, Pa. 15260
Copyright © 1986, University of Pittsburgh Press
Manufactured in the United States of America
10 9 8 7 6 5 4 3 2

Library of Congress Cataloging-in-Publication Data

Main entry under title:

Political leadership.

(Pitt series in policy and institutional studies)
1. Political leadership—Addresses, essays,
lectures. 2. Political psychology—Addresses, essays,
lectures. I. Kellerman, Barbara. II. Series.
JA74.5.P625 1986   303.3'4   85-26436
ISBN 0-8229-3534-1
ISBN 0-8229-5382-X (pbk.)

A CIP catalogue record for this book is available
from the British Library.

Eurospan, London

For Cynthia L Macdonald

In the invisible writing of families, she is my sister

CONTENTS

INTRODUCTION

Perhaps no question is as central to political discourse as that of
political leadership. For if there is an "irreducible fact" of politics, it
is that in any political society some shall be the rulers and some the
ruled.[1]

A SOURCE book for the study of political leadership should begin with a
simple definition of what political leadership is. The trouble is that no
clear and widely agreed upon definition exists. Leadership is conceived of
as a power relation, or as a form of influence or persuasion; as a function
of group process, or as a function of individual personality. Sometimes
leadership is associated with a formal position in an organized system; at
others with an informal relationship between the individuals who make
things happen and those who lend them implicit or explicit support.

The word *political* is similarily problematical. Is political leadership
different from other forms of leadership? Generally, yes. Political leadership means control over policies that affect the public welfare, and political leaders may derive their power from the office they hold in a legally
sanctioned state government. The office bestows upon them the authority
to choose among alternative courses of action. However, not all political
leaders hold formal political office. Leaders of sociopolitical movements—Martin Luther King, Jr., for example—are empowered solely
by their ability to transform a strong public sentiment into a personal
crusade.[2]

There have been two main approaches to the study of political leadership: prescriptive and descriptive. The first has been the more common in
Western culture. Men and women great and small have always tendered
opinions on how leaders ought to lead. But there have been surprisingly
few careful descriptions of how leaders and followers actually behave.[3]
What we lack is a theory of political leadership that illuminates the
interaction between leaders and followers in different settings. Hence the
wry observation that leadership is one of the most observed and least
understood phenomena on earth.[4]

Perhaps the main reason for this situation is that the study of political leadership demands a broad-based, interdisciplinary approach. The contents of this book support this proposition. All the essays address some aspect of leadership, yet among the authors are philosophers, psychologists, sociologists, political scientists, historians, mythologists, literary figures, activists, and public officials. The collection is particularly rich in work in political psychology, work that explicitly connects political life to the psychology of individuals and groups.

Most of the selections in this book reflect their origins in Western culture. They were written over a span that ranges from ancient Greece to the late twentieth century and their subject is the big picture: how people organize themselves; the virtual inevitability of hierarchical relationships; the behavior of those in formal and informal leadership roles; and leaders as agents of change.

The essays, most of them fragments of longer works, are grouped around six key questions: Do leaders change history? Why do leaders lead? Why do followers follow? What are the types of leadership? How do leaders and followers relate? And, is there a leadership for all seasons? Finally, there is a section in which four extraordinary leaders—Wilson, Hitler, Lenin, and Gandhi—themselves address the subject at hand.

There is evidence of growing awareness in the academy and among the public in general that no question is "as central to political discourse as that of political leadership." The present compendium addresses this fresh interest by making available, in one volume, seminal writings on the topic. Some of the selections are fairly extensive; others are very brief excerpts that contain only the kernel of an argument. Together they forge a critical mass of literature on political leadership that testifies to the significant work already accomplished. My hope is that this critical mass will focus new attention on the role of political leadership in political life and also serve as a catalyst for the work that remains to be done.

Textual note. The excerpts in this book are reprinted without change, except that notes have been renumbered consecutively where necessary and in some cases have been somewhat altered to achieve greater clarity and consistency. The initials BK identify notes that I have added.

NOTES

1. Robert Dahl and Deane Neubauer, *Readings in Modern Political Analysis* (Englewood Cliffs, N.J.: Prentice-Hall, 1968), p. 251.

2. For further discussion of leadership as a political act, see my chapter in Barbara Kellerman, ed., *Leadership: Multidisciplinary Perspectives* (Englewood Cliffs, N.J.: Prentice-Hall, 1984), pp. 63–89.

3. Exceptions are biographies of leaders which, however, generally explore only a single case.

4. James MacGregor Burns, *Leadership* (New York: Harper & Row, 1978), p. 2.

POLITICAL LEADERSHIP
A Source Book

PART I

DO LEADERS CHANGE HISTORY?

THIS section explores whether and when leaders are agents of change. The issue is as old as the by now familiar "great man in history" debate, in which one side holds that history is shaped by a relatively few outstanding individuals, while the other insists that history constitutes a great tide of events that inevitably sweeps us all along in its wake.

Reality is surely more complex than either of these two positions suggests. Yet the persistence with which we view both past and present in terms of a very few prominent people suggests that a belief in the impact of key leaders is a relatively easy way for us to construct reality. Trying to understand history by studying both the major players and all the pertinent historical, political, economic, social, and cultural factors is an overwhelming task. To make life simple, we look to leaders to order our experiences.

Each of the six pieces in this section addresses the question of what role leaders actually play in the drama that is human history. The first entry, by Thomas Carlyle, presents the position that history is the story of what great men have accomplished. Carlyle argues heatedly that some men are manifestly superior to all others and that it is these supermen who, quite properly, become our leaders. Carlyle's is a Nietzschean view of history which sees the masses as led by an outstanding few who, in turn, account for "all things that we see standing accomplished in the world."

Herbert Spencer takes the opposite position entirely. For him, societies evolve in a uniform, gradual and progressive manner, and no single individual can alter the course of this development. Spencer posited three explanations for what he considered the misguided belief in the great man theory: the universal love of personalities; the "pleasant news" that to

3

understand history you have only to study the lives of great men; and the relative ease with which we can interpret events through the actions of a visable few. Spencer concludes that a close reading of history reveals that social and political change is the result "of the aggregate of conditions."

Although William James takes strong issue with Spencer in particular, in fact he falls somewhere between Carlyle and Spencer. James's approach is rational, scientific, Darwinian. He introduces the more modern idea that there must be a fit between the individual and the social environment for leadership and social evolution to occur. "Not every 'man' fits every 'hour,'" argues James. "Some incompatabilities there are. A given genius may come either too early or too late." James distinguishes between a necessary and a sufficient condition of history, arguing that when the evolutionary view of history (Spencer's) altogether denies the role of individual initiative, it is an "utterly vague and unscientific conception."

Sidney Hook joined the debate by distinguishing between the "eventful man" and the "event-making man." The eventful man is less important than the objective circumstance. "The possibility of dramatic action has already been prepared for by the direction of antecedent events." The event-making man, on the other hand, "finds a fork in the historical road [and] also helps, so to speak, to create it."

Fred Greenstein suggests that the great man advocates are right—and wrong. He makes a good case for the proposition that the question "How important is personality?" is not susceptible to a general answer. What we need instead is to examine the "terrain of politics in terms of the diverse ways in which 'the human element' comes into play."

Finally, Robert C. Tucker argues convincingly that at least in some cases, individuals certainly do have a profound impact on political outcomes. He claims that the Nazi and Soviet policies of domestic terror and foreign aggression during the thirties and forties were the direct result of Hitler's and Stalin's paranoid personalities and concludes that the early model of a totalitiarian polity was "seriously deficient" in its omission of the personal factor from the dynamics of totalitiarianism.

The responses to the question of whether leaders can, almost singlehandedly, change the course of history raise more questions than they answer. What is fascinating, in any case, is that the question of individual impact has remained to this day a subject of vigorous debate.

1

THOMAS CARLYLE

The Leader as Hero

W E have undertaken to discourse here for a little on Great Men, their manner of appearance in our world's business, how they have shaped themselves in the world's history, what ideas men formed of them, what work they did;—on Heroes, namely, and on their reception and perform-ance; what I call Hero-worship and the Heroic in human affairs. Too evidently this is a large topic; deserving quite other treatment than we can expect to give it at present. A large topic; indeed, an illimitable one; wide as Universal History itself. For, as I take it, Universal History, the history of what man has accomplished in this world, is at bottom the History of the Great Men who have worked here. They were the leaders of men, these great ones; the modellers, patterns, and in a wide sense creators, of whatsoever the general mass of men contrived to do or to attain; all things that we see standing accomplished in the world are properly the outer material result, the practical realisation and embodiment, of Thoughts that dwelt in the Great Men sent into the world: the soul of the whole world's history, it may justly be considered, were the history of these. Too clearly it is a topic we shall do no justice to in this place!

One comfort is, that Great Men, taken up in any way, are profitable company. We cannot look, however imperfectly, upon a great man, without gaining something by him. He is the living light-fountain, which it is good and pleasant to be near. The light which enlightens, which has enlightened the darkness of the world; and this not as a kindled lamp only, but rather as a natural luminary shining by the gift of Heaven; a flowing light-fountain, as I say, of native original insight, of manhood

From Thomas Carlyle, *On Heroes, Hero-Worship, and the Heroic in History* (Boston: Houghton Mifflin, 1907), lecture 1, pp. 1–2, 11–15. Written in 1840.

and heroic nobleness;—in whose radiance all souls feel that it is well with them. On any terms whatsoever, you will not grudge to wander in such neighborhood for a while. These Six classes of Heroes, chosen out of widely-distant countries and epochs, and in mere external figure differing altogether, ought, if we look faithfully at them, to illustrate several things for us. Could we see *them* well, we should get some glimpses into the very marrow of the world's history. How happy, could I but, in any measure, in such times as these, make manifest to you the meanings of Heroism; the divine relation (for I may well call it such) which in all times unites a Great Man to other men; and thus, as it were, not exhaust my subject, but so much as break ground on it! At all events, I must make the attempt. . . .

And now if worship even of a star had some meaning in it, how much more might that of a Hero! Worship of a Hero is transcendent admiration of a Great Man. I say great men are still admirable; I say there is, at bottom, nothing else admirable! No nobler feeling than this of admiration for one higher than himself dwells in the breast of man. It is to this hour, and at all hours, the vivifying influence in man's life. Religion I find stands upon it; not Paganism only, but far higher and truer religions, —all religion hitherto known. Hero-worship, heartfelt prostrate admiration, submission, burning, boundless, for a noblest godlike Form of Man, —is not that the germ of Christianity itself? The greatest of all Heroes is One—whom we do not name here! Let sacred silence meditate that sacred matter; you will find it the ultimate perfection of a principle extant throughout man's whole history on earth.

Or coming into lower, less *un*speakable provinces, is not all Loyalty akin to religious Faith also? Faith is loyalty to some inspired Teacher, some spiritual Hero. And what therefore is loyalty proper, the life-breath of all society, but an effluence of Hero-worship, submissive admiration for the truly great? Society is founded on Hero-worship. All dignities of rank, on which human association rests, are what we may call a *Hero-archy* (Government of Heroes), —or a Hierarchy, for it is "sacred" enough withal! The Duke means *Dux*, Leader; King is *Kön-ning, Kan-ning*, Man that *knows* or *cans*. Society everywhere is some representation, not *in*supportably inaccurate, of a graduated Worship of Heroes;— reverence and obedience done to men really great and wise. Not *insup-*portably inaccurate, I say! They are all as bank-notes, these social dignitaries, all representing gold;—and several of them, alas, always are *forged* notes. We can do with some forged false notes; with a good many even; but not with all, or the most of them forged! No: there have to come revolutions then; cries of Democracy, Liberty and Equality, and I know not what:—the notes being all false, and no gold to be had for *them*, people take to crying in their despair that there is no gold, that there never was any!—"Gold," Hero-worship, *is* nevertheless, as it was always and everywhere, and cannot cease till man himself ceases.

I am well aware that in these days Hero-worship, the thing I call Hero-worship, professes to have gone out, and finally ceased. This, for reasons which it will be worth while some time to inquire into, is an age that as it were denies the existence of great men; denies the desirableness of great men. Show our critics a great man, a Luther for example, they begin to what they call "account" for him; not to worship him, but take the dimensions of him—and bring him out to be a little kind of man! He was the "creature of the Time," they say; the Time called him forth, the Time did everything, he nothing—but what we the little critic could have done too! This seems to me but melancholy work. The Time call forth? Alas, we have known Times *call* loudly enough for their great man; but not find him when they called! He was not there; Providence had not sent him; the Time *calling* its loudest, had to go down to confusion and wreck because he would not come when called.

For if we will think of it, no Time need have gone to ruin, could it have *found* a man great enough, a man wise and good enough: wisdom to discern truly what the Time wanted, valour to lead it on the right road thither; these are the salvation of any Time. But I liken common languid Times, with their unbelief, distress, perplexity, with their languid doubting characters and embarrassed circumstances, impotently crumbling-down into ever worse distress towards final ruin;—all this I liken to dry dead fuel, waiting for the lightning out of Heaven that shall kindle it. The great man, with his free force direct out of God's own hand, is the lightning. His word is the wise healing word which all can believe in. All blazes round him now, when he has once struck on it, into fire like his own. The dry mouldering sticks are thought to have called him forth. They did want him greatly; but as to calling him forth—!—Those are critics of small vision, I think, who cry: "See, it is not the sticks that made the fire?" No sadder proof can be given by a man of his own littleness than disbelief in great men. There is no sadder symptom of a generation than such general blindness to the spiritual lightning, with faith only in the heap of barren dead fuel. It is the last con-summation of unbelief. In all epochs of the world's history, we shall find the Great Man to have been the indispensable saviour of his epoch;—the lightning, without which the fuel never would have burnt.

The History of the World, I said already, was the Biography of Great Men.

Such small critics do what they can to promote unbelief and universal spiritual paralysis: but happily they cannot always completely succeed. In all times it is possible for a man to arise great enough to feel that they and their doctrines are chimeras and cobwebs. And what is notable, in no time whatever can they entirely eradicate out of living men's hearts a certain altogether peculiar reverence for Great Men; genuine admiration, loyalty, adoration, however dim and perverted it may be. Hero-worship endures for ever while man endures. Boswell venerates his Johnson, right truly even in the Eighteenth century. The unbelieving French believe in their Voltaire; and burst-out round him into very curious Hero-worship, in that last act of his life when they "stifle him under roses." It has always seemed to me extremely curious this of Voltaire. Truly, if Christianity be the highest instance of Hero-worship, then we may find here in Voltaire-ism one of the lowest! He whose life was that of a kind of Antichrist, does again on this side exhibit a curious contrast. No people ever were so little prone to admire at all as those French of Voltaire. *Persiflage* was the character of their whole mind; adoration had nowhere a place in it. Yet see! The old man of Ferney comes up to Paris; an old, tottering, infirm man of eighty-four years. They feel that he too is a kind of Hero; that he has spent his life in opposing error and injustice, delivering Calases, unmasking hypocrites in high places;—in short that *he* too, though in a strange way, has fought like a valiant man. They feel withal that, if *persiflage* be the great thing, there never was such a *persifleur*. He is the realised ideal of every one of them; the thing they are all wanting to be: of all Frenchmen the most French. *He* is properly their god, —such god as they are fit for. Accordingly all persons, from the Queen Antoinette to the Douanier at the Porte St. Denis, do they not worship him? People of quality disguise themselves as tavern-waiters. The Maître de Poste, with a broad oath, orders his Postillion, "Va bon train; thou are driving M. de Voltaire." At Paris his carriage is "the nucleus of a comet, whose train fills whole streets." The ladies pluck a hair or two from his fur, to keep it as a sacred relic. There was nothing highest, beautifulest, noblest in all France, that did not feel this man to be higher, beautifuler, nobler.

Yes, from Norse Odin to English Samuel Johnson, from the divine Founder of Christianity to the withered Pontiff of Encyclopedism, in all times and places, the Hero has been worshipped. It will ever be so. We all love great men; love, venerate and bow down submissive before great men: nay can we honestly bow down to anything else? Ah, does not every true man feel that he is himself made higher by doing reverence to what is really above him? No nobler or more blessed feeling dwells in man's heart. And to me it is very cheering to consider that no sceptical logic, or general triviality, insincerity and aridity of any Time and its influences can destroy this noble inborn loyalty and worship that is in man. In times of unbelief, which soon have to become times of revolution, much down-rushing sorrowful decay and ruin is visible to everybody. For myself, in these days, I seem to see in this indestructibility of Hero-worship the everlasting adamant lower than which the confused wreck of revolutionary things cannot fall. The confused wreck of things crumbling and even crashing and tumbling all round us in these revolutionary ages, will get down so far; *no* farther. It is an eternal corner-stone, from which they can begin to build themselves up again. That man, in some sense or other worships Heroes; that we all of us reverence and must ever reverence Great Men: this is, to me, the living rock amid all rushings-down whatsoever;—the one fixed point in modern revolutionary history, otherwise as if bottomless and shoreless.

2

HERBERT SPENCER

The Great Man Theory Breaks Down

An allied class, equally unprepared to interpret sociological phenomena scientifically, is the class which sees in the course of civilization little else than a record of remarkable persons and their doings. One who is conspicuous as the exponent of this view writes:—"As I take it, universal history, the history of what man has accomplished in this world, is at bottom the history of the great men who have worked here." And this, not perhaps distinctly formulated, but everywhere implied, is the belief in which nearly all are brought up. Let us glance at the genesis of it.

Round their camp-fire assembled savages tell the events of the day's chase; and he among them who has done some feat of skill or agility is duly lauded. On a return from the war-path, the sagacity of the chief and the strength or courage of this or that warrior, are the all-absorbing themes. When the day, or the immediate past, affords no remarkable deed, the topic is the achievement of some noted leader lately dead, or some traditional founder of the tribe: accompanied, it may be, with a dance dramatically representing those victories which the chant recites. Such narratives, concerning, as they do, the prosperity and indeed the very existence of the tribe, are of the intensest interest; and in them we have the common root of music, of the drama, of poetry, of biography, of history, and of literature in general. Savage life furnishes little else worthy of note; and the chronicles of tribes contain scarcely anything more to be remembered. Early historic races show us the same thing. The Egyptian frescoes and the wall-sculptures of the Assyrians, represent the deeds of leading men; and inscriptions such as that on the Moabite stone, tell of

From Herbert Spencer, *The Study of Sociology* (New York: D. A. Appleton, 1884), pp. 30–37. First published in 1873.

nothing more than royal achievements: only by implication do these records, pictorial, hieroglyphic, or written, convey anything else. And similarly from the Greek epics, though we gather incidentally that there were towns, and war-vessels, and war-chariots, and sailors, and soldiers to be led and slain, yet the direct intention is to set forth the triumphs of Achilles, the prowess of Ajax, the wisdom of Ulysses, and the like. The lessons given to every civilized child tacitly imply, like the traditions of the uncivilized and semi-civilized, that throughout the past of the human race, the doings of conspicuous persons have been the only things worthy of remembrance. How Abraham girded up his loins and gat him to this place or that; how Samuel conveyed divine injunctions which Saul disobeyed; how David recounted his adventures as a shepherd, and was reproached for his misdeeds as a king—these, and personalities akin to these, are the facts about which the juvenile reader of the Bible is interested and respecting which he is catechized: such indications of Jewish institutions as have unavoidably got into the narrative, being regarded neither by him nor by his teacher as of moment. So too, when, with hands behind him, he stands to say his lesson out of *Pinnock*, we see that the things set down for him to learn, are—when and by whom England was invaded, what rulers opposed the invasions and how they were killed, what Alfred did and what Canute said, who fought at Agincourt and who conquered at Flodden, which king abdicated and which usurped, etc.; and if by some chance it comes out that there were serfs in those days, that barons were local rulers, some vassals of others, that subordination of them to a central power took place gradually, these are facts treated as relatively unimportant. Nay, the like happens when the boy passes into the hands of his classical master, at home or elsewhere. "Arms and the man" form the end of the story as they form its beginning. After the mythology, which of course is all-essential, come the achievements of rulers and soldiers from Agamemnon down to Caesar: what knowledge is gained of social organization, manners, ideas, morals, being little more than the biographical statements involve. And the value of the knowledge is so ranked that while it would be a disgrace to be wrong about the amours of Zeus, and while inability to name the commander at Marathon would be discreditable, it is excusable to know nothing of the social condition that preceded Lycurgus or of the origin and functions of the Areopagus.

Thus the great-man-theory of History finds everywhere a ready-prepared conception—is, indeed, but the definite expression of that which is latent in the thoughts of the savage, tacitly asserted in all early traditions, and taught to every child by multitudinous illustrations. The glad acceptance it meets with has sundry more special causes. There is, first, this universal love of personalities, which, active in the aboriginal man, dominates still—a love seen in the urchin who asks you to tell him a story, meaning, thereby, somebody's adventures; a love gratified in adults by police-reports, court-news, divorce-cases, accounts of accidents, and lists of births, marriages, and deaths; a love displayed even by conversations in the streets, where fragments of dialogue, heard in passing, show that mostly between men, and always between women, the personal pronouns recur every instant. If you want roughly to estimate any one's mental calibre, you cannot do it better than by observing the ratio of generalities to personalities in his talk—how far simple truths about individuals are replaced by truths abstracted from numerous experiences of men and things. And when you have thus measured many, you find but a scattered few likely to take anything more than a biographical view of human affairs. In the second place, this great-man-theory commends itself as promising instruction along with amusement. Being already fond of hearing about people's sayings and doings, it is pleasant news that, to understand the course of civilization, you have only to read diligently the lives of distinguished men. What can be a more acceptable doctrine than that while you are satisfying an instinct not very remotely allied to that of the village gossip—while you are receiving through print instead of orally, remarkable facts concerning notable persons, you are gaining that knowledge which will make clear to you why things have happened thus or thus in the world, and will prepare you for forming a right opinion on each question coming before you as a citizen. And then, in the third place, the interpretation of things thus given is so beautifully simple—seems so easy to comprehend. Providing you are content with conceptions that are out of focus, as most people's conceptions are, the solutions it yields appear quite satisfactory. Just as that theory of the Solar System which supposes the planets to have been launched into their orbits by the hand of the Almighty, looks feasible so long as you do not insist on knowing exactly what is meant by the hand of the Almighty; and just as the special creation of plants and animals seems a tenable hypothesis until you try and picture to yourself definitely the process by which one of them is brought into existence; so the genesis of societies by the actions of great men, may be comfortably believed so long as, resting in general notions, you do not ask for particulars.

But now, if, dissatisfied with vagueness, we demand that our ideas shall be brought into focus and exactly defined, we discover the hypothesis to be utterly incoherent. If, not stopping at the explanation of social progress as due to the great man, we go back a step and ask whence comes the great man, we find that the theory breaks down completely. The question has two conceivable answers: his origin is supernatural, or it is natural. Is his origin supernatural? Then he is a deputy-god, and we have Theocracy once removed—or, rather, not removed at all; for we must then agree with Mr. Schomberg, quoted above, that "the determination of Caesar to invade Britain" was divinely inspired, and that from him, down to "George III the GREAT and the GOOD," the successive rulers were appointed to carry out successive designs. Is this an unacceptable solution? Then the origin of the great man is natural; and immediately this is recognized he must be classed with all other phenomena in the society that gave him birth, as a product of its antecedents. Along with the whole generation of which he forms a minute part—along with its institutions, language, knowledge, manners, and its multitudinous arts and appliances, he is a resultant of an enormous aggregate of forces that have been co-operating for ages. True, if you please to ignore all that common observation, verified by physiology, teaches—if you assume that two European parents may produce a Negro child, or that from woolly-haired prognathous Papuans may come a fair, straight-haired infant of Caucasian type—you may assume that the advent of the great man can occur anywhere and under any conditions. If, disregarding those accumulated results of experience which current proverbs and the generalizations of psychologists alike express, you suppose that a Newton might be born in a Hottentot family, that a Milton might spring up among the Andamanese, that a Howard or a Clarkson might have Fiji parents, then you may proceed with facility to explain social progress as caused by the actions of the great man. But if all biological science, enforcing all popular belief, convinces you that by no possibility will an Aristotle come from a father and mother with facial angles of fifty degrees, and that out of a tribe of cannibals, whose chorus in preparation for a feast of human flesh is a kind of rhythmical roaring, there is not the remotest chance of a Beethoven arising; then you must admit that the genesis of the great man depends on the long series of complex influences which has produced the race in which he appears, and the social state into which that race has slowly grown. If it be a fact that the great man may modify his nation in its structure and actions, it is also a fact that there must have been those antecedent modifications constituting national progress before he could be evolved. Before he can re-make his society, his society must make him. So that all those changes of which he is the proximate initiator have their chief causes in the generations he descended from. If there is to be anything like a real explanation of these changes, it must be sought in that aggregate of conditions out of which both he and they have arisen.

Even were we to grant the absurd supposition that the genesis of the great man does not depend on the antecedents furnished by the society he is born in, there would still be the quite-sufficient facts that he is powerless in the absence of the material and mental accumulations which his society inherits from the past, and that he is powerless in the absence of the co-existing population, character, intelligence, and social arrangements. Given a Shakspeare, and what dramas could he have written without the multitudinous traditions of civilized life—without the various experiences which, descending to him from the past, gave wealth to his thought, and without the language which a hundred generations had developed and enriched by use? Suppose a Watt, with all his inventive power, living in a tribe ignorant of iron, or in a tribe that could get only as much iron as a fire blown by hand-bellows will smelt; or suppose him born among ourselves before lathes existed; what chance would there have been of the steam-engine? Imagine a Laplace unaided by that slowly-developed system of Mathematics which we trace back to its beginnings among the Egyptians; how far would he have got with the *Mécanique Céleste?* Nay, the like questions may be put and have like answers, even if we limit ourselves to those classes of great men on whose doings hero-worshippers more particularly dwell—the rulers and generals. Xenophon could not have achieved his celebrated feat had his Ten Thousand been feeble, or cowardly, or insubordinate. Caesar would never have made his conquests without disciplined troops, inheriting their *prestige* and tactics and organization from the Romans who lived before them. And, to take a recent instance, the strategical genius of Moltke would have triumphed in no great campaigns had there not been a nation of some forty millions to supply soldiers, and had not those soldiers been men of strong bodies, sturdy characters, obedient natures, and capable of carrying out orders intelligently.

Were any one to marvel over the potency of a grain of detonating powder, which explodes a cannon, propels the shell, and sinks a vessel hit—were he to enlarge on the transcendent virtues of this detonating powder, not mentioning the ignited charge, the shell, the cannon, and all that enormous aggregate of appliances by which these have severally been produced, detonating powder included; we should not regard his interpretation as very rational. But it would fairly compare in rationality with this interpretation of social phenomena which, dwelling on the important changes the great man works, ignores that vast pre-existing supply of latent power he unlocks, and that immeasurable accumulation of antecedents to which both he and this power are due.

Recognizing what truth there is in the great-man-theory, we may say that, if limited to early societies, the histories of which are histories of little else than endeavours to destroy or subjugate one another, it approximately expresses the fact in representing the capable leader as all-important; though even here it leaves out of sight too much the number and the quality of his followers. But its immense error lies in the assumption that what was once true is true for ever; and that a relation of ruler and ruled which was possible and good at one time is possible and good for all time. Just as fast as this predatory activity of early tribes diminishes, just as fast as larger aggregates are formed by conquest or otherwise, just as fast as war ceases to be the business of the whole male population, so fast do societies begin to develop, to show traces of structures and functions not before possible, to acquire increasing complexity along with increasing size, to give origin to new institutions, new activities, new ideas, sentiments, and habits: all of which unobtrusively make their appearance without the thought of any king or legislator. And if you wish to understand these phenomena of social evolution, you will not do it though you should read yourself blind over the biographies of all the great rulers on record, down to Frederick the Greedy and Napoleon the Treacherous.

3

WILLIAM JAMES

Great Men and Their Environment

AND this brings us at last to the heart of our subject. The causes of production of great men lie in a sphere wholly inaccessible to the social philosopher. He must simply accept geniuses as data, just as Darwin accepts his spontaneous variations. For him, as for Darwin, the only problem is, these data being given, how does the environment affect them, and how do they affect the environment? Now, I affirm that the relation of the visible environment to the great man is in the main exactly what it is to the "variation" in the Darwinian philosphy. It chiefly adopts or rejects, preserves or destroys, in short *selects* him.[1] And whenever it adopts and preserves the great man, it becomes modified by his influence in an entirely original and peculiar way. He acts as a ferment, and changes its constitution, just as the advent of a new zoological species changes the faunal and floral equilibrium of the region in which it appears. We all recollect Mr. Darwin's famous statement of the influence of cats on the growth of clover in their neighbourhood. We all have read of the effects of the European rabbit in New Zealand, and we have many of us taken part in the controversy about the English sparrow here—whether he kills most canker-worms or drives away most native birds. Just so the great man, whether he can be an importation from without like Clive in India or Agassiz here, or whether he spring from the soil like Mahomet or Franklin, brings about a rearrangement, on a large or small scale, of the pre-existing social relations.

The mutations of societies, then, from generation to generation, are in the main due directly or indirectly to the acts or the example of

From William James, *Selected Papers on Philosophy* (New York: E. P. Dutton, 1917), pp. 173–81, 188–89. First published in *Atlantic Monthly*, 1880.

16

individuals whose genius was so adapted to the receptivities of the moment, or whose accidental position of authority was so critical that they became ferments, initiators of movement, setters of precedent or fashion, centres of corruption, or destroyers of other persons, whose gifts, had they had free play, would have led society in another direction.

We see this power of individual initiative exemplified on a small scale all about us, and on a large scale in the case of the leaders of history. It is only following the commonsense method of a Lyell, a Darwin, and a Whitney to interpret the unknown by the known, and reckon up cumulatively the only causes of social change we can directly observe. Societies of men are just like individuals, in that both at any given moment offer ambiguous potentialities of development. Whether a young man enters business or the ministry may depend on a decision which has to be made before a certain day. He takes the place offered in the counting-house and is *committed*. Little by little, the habits, the knowledges, of the other career, which once lay so near, cease to be reckoned even among his possibilities. At first, he may sometimes doubt whether the self he murdered in that decisive hour might not have been the better of the two; but with the years such questions themselves expire, and the old alternative *ego*, once so vivid, fades into something less substantial than a dream. It is no otherwise with nations. They may be committed by kings and ministers to peace or war, by generals to victory or defeat, by prophets to this religion or to that, by various geniuses to fame in art, science, or industry. A war is a true point of bifurcation of future possibilities. Whether it fail or succeed, its declaration must be the starting-point of new policies. Just so does a revolution, or any great civic precedent, become a deflecting influence, whose operations widen with the course of time. Communities obey their ideals; and an accidental success fixes an ideal, as an accidental failure blights it.

Would England have to-day the "imperial" ideal which she now has if a certain boy named Bob Clive had shot himself, as he tried to do, at Madras? Would she be the drifting raft she is now in European affairs[2] if a Frederic the Great had inherited her throne instead of a Victoria, and if Messrs. Bentham, Mill, Cobden, and Bright had all been born in Prussia? England has, no doubt, to-day precisely the same intrinsic value relatively to the other nations that she ever had. There is no such fine accumulation of human material upon the globe. But in England the material has lost effective form, while in Germany it has found it. Leaders give the form. Would England be crying forward and backward at once, as she does now, "letting I will not wait upon I would," wishing to conquer but not to fight, if her ideal had in all these years been fixed by a succession of statesmen of supremely commanding personality, working in one direction? Certainly not. She would have espoused for better or worse, either one course or another. Had Bismarck died in his cradle, the Germans would still be satisfied with appearing to themselves as a race of spectacled *Gelehrten* and political herbivora, and to the French as *ces bons*, or *ces naïfs, Allemands*. Bismarck's will showed them, to their own great astonishment, that they could play a far livelier game. The lesson will not be forgotten. Germany may have many vicissitudes, but they—

> "will never do away, I ween,
> The marks of that which once hath been"—

of Bismarck's initiative, namely from 1860 to 1873.

The fermentative influence of geniuses must be admitted as, at any rate, one factor in the changes that constitute social evolution. The community *may* evolve in many ways. The accidental presence of this or that ferment decides in which way it *shall* evolve. Why, the very birds of the forest, the parrot, the mino, have the power of human speech, but never develop it of themselves; some one must be there to teach them. So with us individuals. Rembrandt must teach us to enjoy the struggle of light with darkness, Wagner to enjoy peculiar musical effects; Dickens give a twist to our sentimentality, Artemus Ward to our humour; Emerson kindles a new moral light within us. But it is like Columbus's egg. "All can raise the flowers now, for all have got the seed." But if this be true of the individuals in the community, how can it be false of the community as a whole? If shown a certain way, a community may take it; if not, it will never find it. And the ways are to a large extent indeterminate in advance. A nation may obey either of many alternative impulses given by different men of genius, and still live and be prosperous, just as a man may enter either of many businesses. Only, the prosperities may differ in their type.

But the indeterminism is not absolute. Not every "man" fits every "hour". Some incompatibilities there are. A given genius may come either too early or too late. Peter the Hermit would now be sent to a lunatic asylum. John Mill in the tenth century would have lived and died unknown. Cromwell and Napoleon need their revolutions, Grant his civil war. An Ajax gets no fame in the day of telescopic-sighted rifles; and, to express differently an instance which Spencer uses, what could a Watt have effected in a tribe which no precursive genius had taught to smelt iron or to turn a lathe?

Now, the important thing to notice is that what makes a certain genius now incompatible with his surroundings is usually the fact that some previous genius of a different strain has warped the community away from the sphere of his possible effectiveness. After Voltaire, no Peter the Hermit; after Charles IX. and Louis XIV., no general protestantization of France; after a Manchester school, a Beaconsfield's success is transient; after a Philip II., a Castelar makes little headway; and so on. Each bifurcation cuts off certain sides of the field altogether, and limits the future possible angles of deflection. A community is a living thing, and in words which I can do no better than quote from Professor Clifford,[3] "it is the peculiarity of living things not merely that they change under the influence of surrounding circumstances, but that any change which takes place in them is not lost but retained, and as it were built into the organism to serve as the foundation for future actions. If you cause any distortion in the growth of a tree and make it crooked, whatever you may do afterwards to make the tree straight the mark of your distortion is there; it is absolutely indelible; it has become part of the tree's nature. . . . Suppose, however, that you take a lump of gold, melt it, and let it cool. . . . No one can tell by examining a piece of gold how often it has been melted and cooled in geologic ages, or even in the last year by the hand of man. Any one who cuts down an oak can tell by the rings in its trunk how many times winter has frozen it into widowhood, and how many times summer has warmed it into life. A living being must always contain within itself the history, not merely of its own existence, but of all its ancestors."

Every painter can tell us how each added line deflects his picture in a certain sense. Whatever lines follow must be built on those first laid down. Every author who starts to rewrite a piece of work knows how impossible it becomes to use any of the first-written pages again. The new beginning has already excluded the possibility of those earlier phrases and transitions, while it has at the same time created the possibility of an indefinite set of new ones, no one of which, however, is completely determined in advance. Just so the social surroundings of the past and present hour exclude the possibility of accepting certain contributions from individuals; but they do not positively define what contributions shall be accepted, for in themselves they are powerless to fix what the nature of the individual offerings shall be.[4]

Thus social evolution is a resultant of the interaction of two wholly distinct factors—the individual, deriving his peculiar gifts from the play of the physiological and infrasocial forces, but bearing all the power of initiative and origination in his hands; and, second, the social environment, with its power of adopting or rejecting both him and his gifts. Both factors are essential to change. The community stagnates without the impulse of the individual. The impulse dies away without the sympathy of the community.

All this seems nothing more than common-sense. All who wish to see it developed by a man of genius should read that golden little work, Bagehot's *Physics and Politics*, in which (it seems to me) the complete sense of the way in which concrete things grow and change is as livingly present as the straining after a pseudo-philosophy of evolution is livingly absent. But there are never wanting minds to whom such views seem personal and contracted, and allied to an anthropomorphism long exploded in other fields of knowledge. "The individual withers, and the world is more and more," to these writers; and in a Buckle, a Draper, and a Taine we all know how much the "world" has come to be almost synonymous with the *climate*. We all know, too, how the controversy has been kept up between the partisans of a "science of history" and those who deny the existence of anything like necessary "laws" where human societies are concerned. Mr. Spencer, at the opening of his *Study of Sociology*, makes an onslaught on the "great-man theory" of history, from which a few passages may be quoted:—

"The genesis of societies by the action of great men may be comfortably believed so long as, resting in general notions, you do not ask for particulars. But now, if disatisfied with vagueness, we demand that our ideas shall be brought into focus and exactly defined, we discover the hypothesis to be utterly incoherent. If, not stopping at the explanation of social progress as due to the great man, we go back a step, and ask, Whence comes the great man? we find that the theory breaks down completely. The question has two conceivable answers: his origin is supernatural or it is natural. Is his origin supernatural? Then he is a deputy god, and we have theocracy once removed—or, rather, not removed at all. . . . Is this an unacceptable solution? Then the origin of the great man is natural; and immediately this is recognized, he must be classed with all other phenomena in the society that gave him birth as a product of its antecedents. Along with the whole generation of which he forms a minute part, along with its institutions, language, knowledge, manners, and its multitudinous arts and appliances, he is a *resultant*. . . . You must admit that the genesis of the great man depends on the long series of complex influences which has produced the race in which he appears, and the social state into which that race has slowly grown. . . . Before he can remake his society, his society must make him. All those changes of which he is the proximate initiator have their chief causes in the generations he descended from. If there is to be anything like a real explanation of those changes, it must be sought in that aggregate of conditions out of which both he and they have arisen."[5]

Now, it seems to me that there is something which one might almost call impudent in the attempt which Mr. Spencer makes, in the first sentence of this extract, to pin the reproach of vagueness upon those who believe in the power of initiative of the great man.

Suppose I say that the singular moderation which now distinguishes social, political, and religious discussion in England, and contrasts so strongly with the bigotry and dogmatism of sixty years ago, is largely due to J. S. Mill's example. I may possibly be wrong about the facts; but I am, at any rate, "asking for particulars," and not "resting in general notions." And if Mr. Spencer should tell me it started from no personal influence whatever, but from the "aggregate of conditions," the "generations," Mill and all his contemporaries "descended from," the whole past order of nature in short, surely he, not I, would be the person "satisfied with vagueness."

The fact is that Mr. Spencer's sociological method is identical with that of one who would invoke the zodiac to account for the fall of the sparrow, and the thirteen at table to explain the gentleman's death. It is of little more scientific value than the Oriental method of replying to whatever question arises by the unimpeachable truism, "God is Great." *Not* to fall back on the gods, where a proximate principle may be found, has with us Westerners long since become the sign of an efficient as distinguished from an inefficient intellect.

To believe that the cause of everthing is to be found in its antecedents is the starting-point, the initial postulate, not the goal and consummation, of science. If she is simply to lead us out of the labyrinth by the same hole we went in by three or four thousand years ago, it seems hardly worth while to have followed her through the darkness at all. If anything is humanly certain it is that the great man's society, property so-called, does *not* make him before he can remake it. Physiological forces, with which the social, political, geographical, and to a great extent anthropological conditions have just as much and just as little to do as the condition of the crater of Vesuvius has to do with the flickering of this gas by which I write, are what make him. Can it be that Mr. Spencer holds the convergence of sociological pressures to have so impinged on Stratford-upon-Avon about the 26th of April, 1564, that a W. Shakespeare, with all his mental peculiarities, had to be born there—as the pressure of water outside a certain boat will cause a stream of a certain form to ooze into a particular leak? And does he mean to say that if the aforesaid W. Shakespeare had died of cholera infantum, another mother at Stratford-upon-Avon would needs have engendered a duplicate copy of him, to restore the sociologic equilibrium—just as the same stream of water will reappear, no matter how often you pass a sponge over the leak, so long as the outside level remains unchanged? Or might the substitute arise at "Stratford-atte-Bowe"? Here, as elsewhere, it is very hard, in the midst of Mr. Spencer's vagueness, to tell that what he does mean at all. . . .

It is folly, then, to speak of the "laws of history" as of something inevitable, which science has only to discover and whose consequences any one can then foretell but do nothing to alter or avert. Why, the very laws of physics are conditional, and deal with *ifs*. The physicist does not say, "The water will boil anyhow;" he only says it will boil if a fire be kindled beneath it. And so the utmost the student of sociology can ever predict is that *if* a genius of a certain sort show the way, society will be sure to follow. It might long ago have been predicted with great confidence that both Italy and Germany would reach a stable unity if some one could but succeed in starting the process. It could not have been predicted, however, that the *modus operandi* in each case would be subordination to a paramount state rather than federation, because no historian could have calculated the freaks of birth and fortune which gave at the same moment such positions of authority to three such peculiar individuals as Napoleon III., Bismarck, and Cavour. So of our own politics. It is certain now that the movement of the independents, reformers, or whatever one please to call them, will triumph. But whether it do so by converting the Republican party to its ends, or by rearing a new party on the ruins of both our present factions, the historian cannot say. There can be no doubt that the reform movement would make more progress in one year with an adequate personal leader than as now in ten without one. Were there a great citizen, splendid with every civic gift, to be its candidate, who can doubt that he would lead us to victory? But, at present, we, his environment, who sigh for him and would so gladly preserve and adopt him if he came, can neither move without him, nor yet do anything to bring him forth.[6]

To conclude: The evolutionary view of history, when it denies the vital importnce of individual initiative, is, then, an utterly vague and unscientific conception, a lapse from modern scientific determinism into the most ancient oriental fatalism. The lesson of the analysis that we have made (even on the completely deterministic hypothesis with which we started) forms an appeal of the most stimulating sort to the energy of the individual. Even the dogged resistance of the reactionary conservative to changes which he cannot hope entirely to defeat is justified and shown to be effective. He retards the movement; deflects it a little by the concessions he extracts; gives it a resultant momentum, compounded of his inertia and his adversaries' speed; and keeps up, in short, a constant lateral pressure, which, to be sure, never heads it round about, but brings it up at last at a goal far to the right or left of that to which it would have drifted had he allowed it to drift alone.

NOTES

1. It is true that it remodels him, also, to some degree, by its educative influence, and that this constitutes a considerable difference between the social case and the zoological case. I neglect this aspect of the relation here, for the other is the more important. At the end of the article I will return to it incidentally.

2. The reader will remember when this was written.

3. *Lectures and Essays,* i. 82.

4. Mr. Grant Allen himself, in an article from which I shall presently quote, admits that a set of people who, if they had been exposed ages ago to the geographical agencies of Timbuctoo, would have developed into negroes might now, after a protracted exposure to the conditions of Hamburg, never become negroes if transplanted to Timbuctoo.

5. *Study of Sociology,* pp. 33–35.

6. Since this paper was written, President Cleveland has to a certain extent met the need. But who can doubt that if he had certain other qualities which he has not yet shown, his influence would have been still more decisive? (1896).

4

SIDNEY HOOK

The Eventful Man and the Event-Making Man

THROUGHOUT this book we have been using the word "hero" in the rather large and vague sense given to it in common usage. It is now necessary to make the term sufficiently precise to permit some check upon the position that will be subsequently developed.

Before proceeding to the main distinction upon which our thesis hangs, it will be helpful to introduce a few secondary distinctions that have been alluded to in earlier chapters. First of all, we must distinguish between the hero of historical action and the hero of thought. Popular estimates of "great" or "eminent" men rarely differentiate between the two. Thus in the well-known survey made by J. McKeen Cattell on the outstanding figures in western history, the ten who headed the list of a thousand names were: Napoleon, Shakespeare, Mohammed, Voltaire, Bacon, Aristotle, Goethe, Caesar, Luther, and Plato.[1] But as far as the records of historical events go, only four out of this group can be considered as candidates for the role of historical hero. No one can plausibly maintain that Shakespeare had any influence on the occurrence or non-occurrence of decisive historical events. It is not precluded that heroes of thought might also be great men of action or that the consequences of their ideas, as in the case of inventors, religious leaders, and social philosophers, might have impressive historical effects. But it is to the record of events that we must turn to evaluate their claims. In the history of the ancient world, it is Alexander, whose name does not appear on the list, who emerges as a historical hero rather than Aristotle. Only if it could be

From Sidney Hook, *The Hero in History* (Atlantic Highlands, N.J.: Humanities Press, 1943), chap. 9, pp. 151–70. Reprinted by permission of Humanities Press International, Inc., Atlantic Highlands, N.J.

shown that it was Aristotle's ideas that inspired Alexander in his march toward empire could the former be considered in this connection.

A second distinction must be recognized between historical figures who are famous, who can get themselves believed in, and individuals who have influenced events without achieving great popular fame. There is no reliable correlation between historical significance, measured by the effect of action on events, and historical fame, measured by acclaim or volume of eulogy. That is why the judgment of the scientific historian, who investigates specific causal connection, on the historical work of individuals, is always to be preferred to results of polls, comparative space allotments in standard works, and frequency of citation. The latter show enormous variation influenced by fashion, picturesqueness, *parti pris*, and very little by scientific findings. Particularly today, any "front" man can be built up into a "hero." From 1916 to 1933, Hindenberg was undoubtedly the most popular figure in Germany but one could mention half a dozen individuals who had greater influence on German history, including military history, during that period.

Finally, we must rule out as irrelevant the conception of the hero as a morally worthy man, not because ethical judgments are illegitimate in history, but because so much of it has been made by the wicked. Only the making of history concerns us here, not whether it has been made well or disastrously.

The hero in history is the individual to whom we can justifiably attribute preponderant influence in determining an issue or event whose consequences would have been profoundly different if he had not acted as he did. It is sometimes objected that there is no universal agreement about the "importance" of any issue, event, or consequences. Some individuals profess that it is not "important" to them whether India remains free or not, whether the war is lost or won, or whether the future world state is democratic or Fascist in form. All this is immaterial to the problem. No matter what *you* regard as important, the problem is inescapable. Would that which *you* regard as important have taken place anyhow no matter what individual figured in the events leading up to it? Or is it ever true to say that an individual was chiefly responsible for the occurrence or nonoccurrence of that important issue or event?

This brings us to the key distinction. This is the distinction between the hero as the *eventful man*[2] in history and the hero as the *event-making man* in history. The *eventful* man in history is any man whose actions influenced subsequent developments along a quite different course than would have been followed if these actions had not been taken. The *event-*

making man is an eventful man whose actions are the consequences of outstanding capacities of intelligence, will, and character rather than of accidents of position. This distinction tries to do justice to the general belief that a hero is great not merely in virtue of what he does but in virtue of what he is. From this point on, unless otherwise specified, when we speak of the hero or great man in history we shall mean the event-making man.

The merely eventful men in history play a role that may be compared to that of the little Dutch boy who kept his finger in the hole of the dikes and saved the town. Without meaning to strip the legend of its glamor, we can point out that almost anybody in the situation could have done it. All that was required was a boy, a finger, and the lucky chance of passing by. The event itself in the life of the community was of tremendous significance. It saved the town just as a little Dutch boy at Pearl Harbor might have saved the fleet if his alarm had been acted upon in time. But the qualities required to cope with the situation were of a fairly common distribution. Here, so to speak, one stumbles upon greatness just as one might stumble on a treasure that will ransom a town. Greatness, however, is something that must involve extraordinary talent of some kind and not merely the compounded luck of being born and of being present at the right place at a happy moment.

In the year 313, the Emperor Constantine, in the words of Gibbon, changed his status from that of "protector" to that of "proselyte" of the Church.[3] Few events have been more important in the development of western Europe than the reversal of previous Roman policy toward Christianity and its adoption by the official head of the Roman Empire. But not a single one of the qualities of Constantine's character, which enter into the disputed question of the reasons for his conversion, indicate that he was much more than a politician with an eye on the main chance. Whatever religious piety he had was not strong enough to prevent him from murdering his own son on a trumped-up charge. Constantine was an eventful man independently of whether Christianity would have become the official religion several centuries later, under quite different conditions and with different consequences, or whether, without him, the Roman Empire would never have been called Holy. But as decisive as Constantine's act was for his era, *he* was not a hero. The appellation of "great" was bestowed upon him in thanks by the grateful Christian minority. His later interference in church affairs gave them second thoughts about his greatness.

Although there is no evidence that any other Roman Emperor would have eased Christianity into its new status, it could have been done readily. The growth of Christianity, the position of the Emperor in Roman society, the decay in traditional belief manifested by the absence of a strong, fanatical opposition, made the adoption of Christianity an objective possibility, but neither a social nor political necessity. Constantine proselytized for Christianity for imperial reasons.[4] But there was no greater justification for believing that he could strengthen the state by using the church primarily as an instrument of public policy than by playing off Paganism and Christianity against each other. *After* Constantine and his work, and *because* of it, the effort to restore the pagan religion was doomed to fail. It is extremely unlikely that the Emperor Julian, despite his superior gifts, would have succeeded in depriving Christianity of its privileged status even if he had lived to a ripe age. But what he failed to do as a successor of Constantine—reduce Christianity to a religious sect contending on equal terms against other sects—he could easily have done in Constantine's stead. Constantine, therefore, must be regarded as an eventful rather than an event-making historical figure.

Both the eventful man and the event-making man appear at the forking points of history. The possibility of their action has already been prepared for by the direction of antecedent events. The difference is this. In the case of the eventful man, the preparation is at a very advanced stage. It requires a relatively simple act—a decree, a command, a common-sense decision—to make the decisive choice. He may "muff" his role or let someone steal it from him. But even if he doesn't, this does not prove him an exceptional creature. His virtue or vice is inferred from the happy or unhappy consequence of what he has done, not from the qualities he has displayed in the doing of it.

The event-making man, on the other hand, finds a fork in the historical road, but he also helps, so to speak, to create it. He increases the odds of success for the alternative he chooses by virtue of the extraordinary qualities he brings to bear to realize it. At the very least, like Caesar and Cromwell and Napoleon, he must free the path he has taken from opposition and, in so doing, display exceptional qualities of leadership. It is the hero as event-making man who leaves the positive imprint of his personality upon history—an imprint that is still observable after he has disappeared from the scene. The merely eventful man whose finger plugs a dike or fires the shot that starts a war is rarely aware of the nature of the alternative he faces and of the train of events his act sets off.

It is easy to make a sharp distinction in analysis between the eventful man and the event-making man, but there are few historical figures that will fit snugly into either classification. We must leave to historians the delicate task of ascertaining whether any particular "hero" of human history is, in respect to some significant happening, an event-making character—or merely lucky. That the classes defined by the distinction are not empty of members has been made apparent for eventful men and will be established for event-making men. Whether it is possible to treat these classes in terms of gradations or combinations of qualities common to both is doubtful. Yet the same historical personage may be eventful in one respect, event-making in another, and neither in a third.

It is not suggested that this approach is the only one that can be taken in evaluating the historical significance of individuals in history. For the nature of their influence may be expressed in ways so manifold that they sum up to a torrent, and yet at the same time in ways so indirect that it is difficult to trace their path.

The influence of Thomas Jefferson and Abraham Lincoln on American life, on the ways Americans have thought and acted, has been enormous. Yet it would be difficult, and perhaps irrelevant, to classify them either as eventful or event-making. Jefferson wished to be remembered after he was gone as "the author of the Declaration of Independence, the statute of Virginia for religious liberty, and father of the University of Virginia." Yet separately or together these achievements do not indicate that he was an eventful or event-making man. There is much in the contemporary rhetoric of democracy which would now be different had Jefferson not composed the Declaration of Independence, but the vision and faith to which he gave such felicitous phrasing were common to the distinguished company of whom he was one. The Statute on Religious Freedom gave formal expression to a movement of religious toleration already making its way through the states. The future of higher education in America, which already had a distinguished past before Jefferson, could hardly be said to have been profoundly influenced by him.

Oddly enough, from the point of view of narrow historical action, it is to something by which Jefferson himself set much less store that we must turn to find evidence for his event-making status. This is the Louisiana Purchase, in which he was the moving figure. He carried it through in the teeth of an opposition strong enough to have daunted a weaker man. And yet had this territory not been acquired from Napoleon when it was, England would probably have fallen heir to it at the Congress of Vienna if not sooner. Without the Louisiana territory—and the west to which it furnished access—the United States might have remained an Atlantic seaboard power. Its political history as well as its economic history might have been very different. There is no assurance that another incumbent of the presidency than Jefferson would have had the foresight and energy required to seize this golden opportunity to remove a foreign power and potential enemy from our borders, and at the same time to double the area under the American flag. But however we evaluate Jefferson's part in the territorial expansion of the United States, his stature as a man and thinker and his role as a historical force on American culture do not depend upon it. There is room for others besides those whom we call historical "heroes" in a democracy.

What shall we say of historical figures who enjoyed great political power and whose reigns, although outwardly uneventful, seem to be conspicuous for their peace and prosperity? This is the type of situation with which Wood was primarily concerned, and which he too easily set down to the credit of the ruling individuals. When can they be credited with it and when not? And if they are credited with it, when can they be regarded as eventful or event-making? Our illustration here will be drawn from a period that might be called "the golden age" of Roman history.

Gibbon gives it as a considered judgment that after the reign of Augustus the happiness of all the European peoples "depended on the character of a single man"—that is, on whoever happened to be the Roman Emperor. In an agricultural society, where people could find refuge and a living in the interstices of the economy, this could hardly have been the case. But in view of the immense powers for good or evil wielded by the Roman Emperors, we can appreciate the truth behind Gibbon's exaggeration. Yet historically, the most uneventful period of the Roman Empire from the point of view of wars, rebellions, palace revolutions, incursions of barbarians, was the forty-two-year reign of the two Antonines, Pius, and Marcus, in the second century of the Christian era. Of their united reigns Gibbon writes with positively un-English enthusiasm and unrestraint. They are "possibly the only period of history in which the happiness of a great people was the sole object of government." And not merely the object of government but the result! In one of the most extreme statements ever penned by any historian of note he asserts: "If a man were called to fix the period in the history of the world, during which the condition of the human race was happy and prosperous, he would, without hesitation, name that which elapsed from the death of Domitian to the accession of Commodus."[5]

A truly remarkable—and uneventful—period! At first glance it appears that our categories do not apply to it. Where nothing or little happens there is no call for eventful and event-making men. Yet we cannot resist the feeling if not only a tithe of what Gibbon says of them is true, the Antonines are historically just as significant as the Emperors who extended the boundaries of Rome, codified its laws, or altered its religion. But to be justified this feeling must rest on the belief, tacitly assumed by Gibbon, that the order, tranquillity, and the prosperity of an era are the *consequences of policies* adopted by these absolute rulers during their reign. That is to say, they *prevented* dire events that otherwise would have occurred. Certainly, if we hold the Roman Emperors responsible for the "crimes, follies and misfortunes" of their reigns, as Gibbon does, we must credit them for the peace, wisdom, and good fortune, too, even if their lives do not make as interesting reading as those of Nero, Caligula, and Commodus.

Whether the Roman Emperors were in fact responsible for the condition of the country to the extent assumed by Gibbon, who was unconsciously much addicted to the heroic interpretation of history, is highly disputable. Later historians are convinced that the state of Roman agriculture accounts for much more about Roman history and the happiness of its people than the character of the Roman Emperors. But this is hardly the place to settle the question. The main point is that the outwardly uneventful appearance of a period—its prosperity—is either the consequence of a policy adopted by the ruling individuals, or the consequence of social and economic conditions (together with other factors) whose development has not been appreciably influenced by policy. In the first case, those who are responsible for the policy may be eventful or event-making men depending upon what an analysis of the situation reveals. In the second case, the historical phenomenon can be adequately explained without introducing heroes in any of the senses previously considered. To the extent that political action can influence the prosperity of an era, the Antonines may have been largely responsible, as Gibbon believes, for this happy interlude in Roman history. But the prosperity of an era is never by itself sufficient evidence to warrant an inference about existing political leadership. No historian could reasonably maintain that we owe the postwar years of prosperity in the United States to the leadership of Harding and Coolidge.

The eventful man is a creature of events in that by a happy or unhappy conjunction of circumstances he finds himself in a position where action or abstention from action is decisive in a great issue. But he need not be aware of that issue and how his action or inaction affects it. The members of the Committee of Public Safety during the French

Revolution were, as a group, eventful men. But only Robespierre and St. Just were event-making in that they realized above all others what was at stake after Louis XVI had been deposed. Napoleon believed that if Robespierre had remained in power, France would have settled down to orderly processes of republican government and made Napoleon's accession to power impossible. But Robespierre was the architect of his own downfall and, despite all the politically motivated efforts to rehabilitate him, of the downfall of Republican France. Together with St. Just, he is responsible for carrying the Terror *beyond* the interests of national defense and public safety.[6]

Although Robespierre disapproved of the more barbaric excesses of indiscriminate executions and juridical frame-ups, it was his own policy that prepared the way for them. The Terror, to the point that Robespierre approved it, did not save France from the flames of counterrevolution. It supplied fuel to those flames. By terrorizing tens of thousands of Frenchmen who were genuinely hostile to despotism, it made easier Napoleon's usurpation. An incidental distinction of Robespierre is that by charging his opponents, even when they were as far apart as Danton and Anarchisis Cloots, with being spies in English pay, he set a fashion that was to be followed in the Russian Revolution. It was bad enough that Robespierre proclaimed: "The Republic owes its enemies nothing but death." It was historically fatal when he began to regard the enemies of Robespierre as the enemies of the Republic.

The disproportion between the ordinary capacities which the eventful man brings to history and the extraordinary effects of his actions is best illustrated by the personality of the Emperor Justinian and the place he fills in history. The great military achievements under his reign, won by Belisarius, the codification of Roman law, the closing of the philosophic schools at Athens, his intervention in theological affairs, his vast architectural works, had a profound influence on European culture. But at no point did Justinian rise above the level of mediocrity. Although he made the decisions that moved much abler men than himself into action, he showed no clear purpose in what he was doing or any conception of the effects his decisions would have on what he thought he was doing.

Justinian's most eventful act, according to Fisher, was the destruction of the heretical Arian Goths in Italy in the middle of the sixth century and the resulting desolation of the whole Italian peninsula. The rulers of the Goths had pursued a policy of strict religious tolerence toward the orthodox Christians in their realm. When Justinian ordered his generals to take the field against them, the Goths sued for peace again and again with offers of tribute of perpetual vassaldom. But the bigoted Justinian was adamant. Theodora, his beautiful, influential, and much wiser spouse, might have prevailed upon him to call off his generals, as she frequently did on other occasions, but for reasons of state she was more interested in protecting a different variety of heresy. The Goths were ultimately exterminated root and branch. "It was a profound error to destroy them. Had they been left in peace there might have been no Lombard invasions, no papal state, no revival of the Empire in the West, and the political unity which Italy so painfully achieved in the reign of Queen Victoria might have been realized in the reign of Ethelbert."[7]

Whether this event should be called an "error" depends, of course, on one's religious predilections. Those who accept the theology of the Council of Nicea call Justinian's crusade a blessing. But error or blessing, the act was fateful for the history of Europe.

At this point it is necessary to consider the relation between the hero and social interests. For one way of losing sight of the problem is to show that heroic action fits into the needs of a class already in power or of a class that comes into power after his work is done. Such an analysis, even when it is true, does not rule out the possibility that the class that remains in power and the class that comes to power do so in virtue of the unique qualities of the hero who serves their interests. But very often it is assumed that this possibility has been ruled out when all that has been established is that the hero must take note of social interests and find support among them.

The event-making figure in history obviously can achieve nothing by himself alone. He is dependent upon a narrow group of lieutenants or assistants who constitute a "machine," and upon a much broader group in the population whom we may call a social class. Both groups are tied to him by bonds of interest, but the nature of the interests is different. An oversimplified conception of the role of interests often presents the event-making figure as their servant, selected because of his capacity to further them and replaceable when he fails. The event-making figure is thus reduced once more to an instrument of historical or class Purpose, that is, the purposes of other men. The effect of his own purpose is regarded as a minor detail. That many, if not most, of the political personalities who stride the boards of history for a brief moment are instruments of other people's purposes may be granted. But it cannot be granted for those whom we have called event-making figures. We shall consider the relation of the hero, first to the social class that supports him, and then turn to his machine.

The dependence of the eventful figure on the support of a social class is much more in evidence before he accedes to power than when he is in possession of power and commands the state forces of coercion and education. A powerful social class which sees its vested position threatened, or which desires to use political power to break the vested position of another class, can usually arrange to give a candidate for the role of hero the *chance* to make good. But he may not be able to carry out all the tasks entrusted to him. His role may be that of a Bruening, a Schleicher, a von Papen, a Hoover, a Kerensky, or even a Leon Blum. But when he does make good, his very success if he is skillful enough, makes him independent of the class chiefly responsible for his selection. He may still serve its interests, but the decision to do so is his now and not theirs.

The independence of the event-making man, over and against the class whose interest he actually or presumably has been selected to serve, is achieved in various ways. First, he can build up other social interests in opposition to the class that has sponsored him. This is not difficult because in the demagogic preparation for power he has already promised much to other classes, except the national scapegoat. Since he always speaks in the name of the nation or people, he can justify his independence of the class that has originally supported him in terms of the very myths this class has helped to propagate. Secondly, the event-making man comes into control of the armed forces of the State. Not infrequently he already enjoys some military prestige and power before his advent to power. Third, he brings his machine into play to take over and administer social functions, pulverize opposition, and consolidate military influence. As far as possible the machine reduces all potential centers of resistance and draws into its periphery all independent institutions. In fact, it is the machine that makes possible the pursuit of the first two methods by which the event-making figure emancipates himself from dependence upon the class whose social need gave him his original opportunity.

It is to the machine then and not to the social class that we must look to uncover the chief dependence of the hero. Whether it be a political party, a Jesuit religious order, a military camarilla, the hero must bind it to himself with hoops stronger than steel. If he is to play the man of the hour and pay his debts to the social class that supported him, the machine is a convenient instrument. If he decides to take a course independent from the one he was expected to follow, its iron loyalty is all the more necessary. In either case the machine must become *his* machine if he is to triumph. How is this accomplished? In the main by giving its members certain material and psychological privileges that are sufficiently distinctive to mark them off as a separate social grouping. As a group they must be convinced that they are the senior partner in any political alliance with other social groups. They either supplant the existing bureaucracy or fuse with it in such a way that they occupy all the strategic posts.

The historical hero, however, cannot become merely the instrument of his machine and enjoy power long. For all his reliance upon it, he must remain its master. This he accomplishes by making it evident that he is indispensable to the continuation of its privileges, that his downfall is their downfall, but not necessarily that its downfall is his. Just as he uses the machine to bring other social groups in line, the hero uses these social groups, tamed but resentful over the privileges lost to the machine, to keep the latter in tow. The event-making figure in history wins the opportunity to move freely by skillfully playing off against each other the groups upon whom he is dependent. That is why he is more than an instrument of social class and more than a captain of a robber band. That is why he can be ruthless, if necessary, to the social class whose interests he claims to represent. That is why he can whirl his machine around into an abrupt spin in an opposite direction without consulting them or fearing defection. It goes without saying that he always strives to keep his machine in order, free of the grit and sand of dissidence and with an ample supply of spare parts at hand for necessary replacements.

Our conclusion then is that without meeting some social and group interests—economic, national, psychological—the hero cannot influence historical events; but he meets them in such a way that he always retains a considerable degree of freedom in choosing which interests to further and which to suppress or weaken. The behavior of most historical figures in relation to political and social issues can be explained in terms of the interests that speak through them. But there are individuals in history who not only talk back but react in such a way as to modify the original relations of social interest in a radical way.

The particular role that any historical character plays in relation to social interests may not be apparent from what he says about himself. He may claim to be serving the interests of a class when he is actually doing something quite different, or he may regard himself as completely independent of all social pressures when in fact he is merely a servant, sometimes even a contemptible tool, of special privilege.

NOTES

1. *Popular Science Monthly* 62 (1903); 359. This study was based on the comparative space allotted to a thousand pre-eminent men in standard biographical dictionaries and encyclopedias.

2. I owe the expression "eventful man" to Mr. Charles Haer, who is, however, in no way responsible for the position here developed.

3. Edward Gibbon, *History of the Decline and Fall of the Roman Empire*, Modern Library edition, vol. I, p. 636.

4. Cf. C. N. Cochrane, *Christianity and Classical Culture* (Oxford, 1940), p. 211.

5. Op. Cit., vol. I, p. 70. It is in this connection that his famous remark about history was made. Of the first Antonine he tells us: "His reign is marked by the rare advantage of furnishing very few materials for history: which is, indeed, little more than the register of the crimes, follies and misfortunes of mankind." As a historian Gibbon himself did not live up to this gloomy conception of history, i.e., his history registers much more.

6. Seven out of every ten persons guillotined or shot during the Frence terror were workers, peasants, and members of the lower middle class. The most recent studies show that of the approximately 17,000 victims, i.e., those sentenced after "trial," not counting those shot out of hand or those among the 500,000 political prisoners who succumbed to horrible prison conditions, 31¼ per cent were workers, 28 percent peasants, and 10½ per cent belonged to the lower middle class. See Donald Greer, *The Incidence of the Terror during the French Revolution: A Statistical Interpretation* (Cambridge, 1935), p. 166.

7. H. A. L. Fisher, *If or History Rewritten* (New York: 1911), vol. I, p. 131.

5

FRED GREENSTEIN

Personality and Politics

A bewildering variety of criticisms have been leveled at the hetero-geneous literature on personality and politics. The criticism has been so profuse that there is considerable accuracy to the sardonic observation of David Riesman and Nathan Glazer that the field of culture-and-personality research, within which many of the past accounts of personality and politics fall, has "more critics . . . than practitioners."[1] As we have seen, some of the criticisms are directed toward methodological difficulties of the existing research; but others are more fundamental, formal objections that would seem to apply even to methodologically sound inquiry. These objections typically seem to take the form of answers in the negative to the (often implicit) question: "Is personality important as a determinant of political behavior?"

The more intellectually challenging of the various formal objections—i.e., the assertions that *in principle* personality-and-politics research is not promising, even if one avoids the specific methodological pitfalls of case-study, typological, and aggregative inquiry—seem to fall under five headings. In each case, the objection is one that can be generalized to the study of how personality relates to any social phenomenon. And in each case, the objection proves on analysis to have certain positive implications for the study of the relationship between politics and "personality," in several senses of the latter term. Listed elliptically, the five objections are that:

From Fred Greenstein, *Personality and Politics* (Chicago: Markham, 1969), chap. 2, "Objections to the Study of Personality and Politics," pp. 33–46. Reprinted by permission of the author.

1. Personality characteristics tend to be randomly distributed in institutional roles. Personality, therefore, "cancels out" and can be ignored by analysts of political and other social phenomena.

2. People's personality characteristics are less important than their social characteristics in influencing behavior. This makes it unpromising to concentrate research energies on studying the impact of personality.

3. Personality is not of interest to political and other social analysts because individual actors (personalities) are severely limited in the impact they can have on events.

4. Personality is not an important determinant of behavior because individuals with varying personal characteristics will tend to behave similarly when placed in common situations. And if the ways that people vary do not affect their behavior, it is not useful to study personal variation.

5. Finally, there is a class of objections deprecating the relevance of personality to political analysis in which "personality" is equated with particular aspects of individual psychological functioning. We shall be concerned with one of the objections falling under this heading—viz., the assertion that deep psychological needs of the sort summarized by the term "ego-defensive" do not have an important impact on behavior and that, therefore, "personality" in this sense of the term need not be studied by the student of politics.

The first two of these objections seem to be based on fundamental misconceptions. Nevertheless, they do point to interesting problems for the student of political psychology. The final three objections are partially well-taken, but need to be rephrased in conditional form as "Under what circumstances?" questions. The remainder of this chapter consists of expanded accounts of each of the five objections and of the peremptory judgments I have just rendered on them.

Two Erroneous Objections

The Thesis That Personality "Cancels Out"

The assumption underlying the first objection seems to be, as Alex Inkeles points out, that "in 'real' groups and situations, the accidents of life history and factors other than personality which are responsible for recruitment [into institutional roles] will 'randomize' personality distribution in the major social statuses sufficiently so that taking systematic account of the influence of personality composition is unnecessary." As Inkeles easily shows, this assumption is false on two grounds.

First, "even if the personality composition of any group is randomly determined, random assortment would not in fact guarantee the *same* personality composition in the membership of all institutions of a given type. On the contrary, the very fact of randomness implies that the outcome would approximate a normal distribution. Consequently, some of the groups would by chance have a personality composition profoundly different from others, with possibly marked effects, on the functioning of the institutions involved." Secondly,

> there is no convincing evidence that randomness *does* consistently describe the assignment of personality types to major social statuses. On the contrary, there is a great deal of evidence to indicate that particular statuses often attract, or recruit preponderantly for, one or another personality characteristic and that fact has a substantial effect on individual adjustment to roles and the general quality of institutional functioning.[2]

The objection turns out, therefore, to be based on unwarranted empirical assumptions. It proves not to be an obstacle to research, but rather— once it is examined—an opening gambit for identifying a crucial topic of investigation for the political psychologist: How are personality types distributed in social roles and with what consequences?

The Thesis That Social Characteristics Are More Important Than Personality Characteristics

The second objection—assertng that individuals' social charac-teristics are "more important" than their personality characteristics— seems to result from a conceptual rather than empirical error. It appears to be an objection posing a pseudo-problem that needs to be dissolved analytically rather than resolved empirically.

. . . Let us consider the referents of "social characteristic" and "personality characteristic." By the latter we refer to some inner pre-disposition of the individual. The term "characteristic" applies to a state of the organism. Using the "environment→predispositions→response" paradigm, we assume that the environmental stimuli which elicit behav-ior are mediated through the individual's psychological predispositions.

But we also assume that the psychological predispositions (or "characteristics") are themselves to a considerable extent environmentally determined, largely by prior social experiences. It is to these prior environmental states, which may occur at any stage of the life cycle and which may or may not persist into the present, that we commonly refer when we use the expression "social characteristics." In this case, the term "characteristic" refers *not* to a state of the organism, but rather to the environment within which the organism has developed. This is made particularly clear by the common usage of *"objective* social characteristics."

It follows that social and psychological characteristics are in no way mutually exclusive. They do not compete as candidates for explanation of social behavior, but rather are complementary. Social characteristics can *cause* psychological characteristics; they are not substitutes for psychological characteristics. The erroneous assumption that social characteristics could even in principle be more important than psychological characteristics probably arises in part from the misleading impression of identity fostered by using the same noun in the two expressions.[3]

This confusion also very probably is contributed to by the standard procedures social scientists use to eliminate spurious correlations, namely, controlling for "third factors" and calculating partial correlations. When used indiscriminately and without reference to the theoretical standing of the variables that are being analyzed, control procedures can lead to the failure to recognize what Herbert Hyman once described as "the distinction between developmental sequences or configurations and problems of spuriousness."[4] An example of how the failure to recognize this distinction arises is provided by Urie Bronfenbrenner's interesting research report entitled "Personality and Participation: The Case of the Vanishing Variables."[5] Bronfenbrenner reports a study in which it was found that measures of personality were associated with participation in community affairs. However, as he notes, "it is a well-established fact that extent of participation varies as a function of social class position, with lower classes participating least." Bronfenbrenner therefore proceeds to measure the relationship between personality and participation, while controlling for social class (and certain other factors). The result: "Most of the earlier . . . significant relationships between personality measures and participation now disappear, leaving only two significant correlations, both of them quite low." One common interpretation of such a finding would be that Bronfenbrenner had shown the irrelevance of personality to participation; but his finding should not be so interpreted. Hyman's remarks, since they place the problem of relating social-background data to psychological data in its more general context, are worth quoting at some length.

. . . the concept of spuriousness cannot *logically* be intended to apply to antecedent conditions which are associated with that particular independent variable as part of a developmental sequence. Implicitly, the notion of an uncontrolled factor which was operating so as to produce a spurious finding involves the image of something *extrinsic* to the . . . apparent cause. Developmental sequences, by contrast, involve the image of a series of entities which are *intrinsically* united or substitutes for one another. All of them constitute a unity and merely involve different ways of stating the same variable as it changes over time. . . . Consequently, to institute procedures of control is to remove so-to-speak some of the very cause that one wishes to study. . . . How shall the analyst know what antecedent conditions are intrinsic parts of a developmental sequence? . . . One guide, for example, can be noted: instances where the "control" factor and the apparent explanation involve *levels of description from two different systems* are likely to be developmental sequences. For instance, an explanatory factor that was a personality trait and a control factor that was biological such as physique or glandular functions can be conceived as levels of description from different systems. Similarly, an explanatory factor that is *psychological* and a control factor that is sociological can be conceived as two different levels of description, i.e., one might regard an attitude as derivative of objective position or status or an objective position in society as leading to psychological processes such as attitudes. Thus, the concept of spuriousness would not be appropriate.[6]

In the Bronfenbrenner example, then, an individual's "objective" socioeconomic background—as opposed to such subjective concomitants as his sense of class consciousness—needs to be analyzed as a possible social determinant of the psychological correlates of participation. This enables the analyst to take account of the fact that, as Allport[7] puts it, "background factors never directly cause behavior; they cause attitudes [and other mental sets]" and the latter "in turn determine behavior." Allport's statement does not gainsay the use of controls. "I am not, of course, arguing against the use of breakdowns or matched groups," he adds. "They should, however, be used to show where attitudes come from and not to imply that social causation acts automatically apart from attitudes.

By suggesting the developmental source of a psychological state, a control often helps to explain the dynamics and functions of that state in the adult personality. A good example can be found in the well-known Hyman and Sheatsley critique of *The Authoritarian Personality*. At one point, Hyman and Sheatsley examine certain patterns of attitudes and certain typical ways of viewing the world which the authors of *The*

Authoritarian Personality tended to explain in terms of complex processes of personal psychopathology. Hyman and Sheatsley suggest that such attitudes (for example, highly punitive notions about how society should deal with sexual deviance) may be learned *cognitions* rather than manifestations of ego-defensiveness. They were able to suggest this by using controls to show that these attitudes are typical beliefs among lower socioeconomic-status strata and, therefore, may simply be conventionally learned orientations of individuals from such backgrounds. But what Hyman and Sheatsley do *not*—and on purely formal grounds *cannot*—show is that such attitudes are in some sense "social" or "cultural" *rather* than psychological.[8]

The more general lesson that emerges from our examination of the second objection is that students of personality and politics will often find it necessary to lay out developmental schemes of explanation placing social and psychological factors in the sequence in which they seem to have impinged upon each other.

THREE PARTIALLY CORRECT OBJECTIONS

The three remaining objections bear on (a) how much impact individual actors can have on political outcomes; (b) whether the situations in which political actors find themselves impose uniform behavior on individuals of varying personal characteristics, thus making it unprofitable for the political analyst to study variations in the actors' personal characteristics; and (c) the numerous questions that can be raised about the impact on behavior of particular classes of personal characteristics, including the so-called ego defensive personality dispositions that I shall be discussing. Once these objections are rephrased in conditional form, it becomes possible to state propositions indicating the circumstances under which each objection is or is not likely to be valid. But it must be emphasized that the propositions I shall be advancing in what follows are not hypotheses stated with sufficient precision to be testable. Given the appropriate theoretical interests, these propositions *can* be further specified so as to be testable—and falsifiable. But their present function is as sensitizers— that is, as general indications of the circumstances under which political analysts are and are not likely to find it desirable to study "personality" in the senses of the term implicit in the objections.

When Do Individual Actions Affect Events ("Action Dispensability")?

The objection to studies of personality and politics which emphasizes the limited capacity of single actors to shape events is similar in its essentials to the nineteenth- and early twentieth-century debates over social determinism—that is, over the role of individual actors (Great Men or otherwise) in history. In statements of this objection, emphasis is placed on the need for the times to be ripe in order for the historical actor to make his contribution. "What impact could Napoleon have had on history if he had been born in the Middle Ages?" is the type of question that is asked. Possibly because of the parlor-game aura of the issues it raises the problem of the impact of individuals on events has not had so much disciplined attention in recent decades as have the two remaining issues I shall be treating. Nevertheless, at one time or another it has received the attention of Tolstoy, Carlyle, William James, Plekhanov, and Trotsky (in his *History of the Russian Revolution*). The main attempt at a balanced general discussion seems to be Sidney Hook's vigorous, though unsystematic, 1943 essay *The Hero in History*.[9]

Since the degree to which actions are likely to have significant impacts is clearly variable, we can begin clarification by asking: *What are the circumstances under which the actions of single individuals are likely to have a greater or lesser effect on the course of events?* For shorthand purposes, this might be called the question of *action dispensability*. This is possibly not the only question that has arisen in hero-and-history debates, but it has the merit of presenting a discrete analytic problem. We can conceive of the actions performed in the political arena as being on a continuum, ranging from those that are indispensable for outcomes that concern us through those that are utterly dispensable. And we can make certain very general observatons about the circumstances which are likely to surround dispensable and indispensable actions.

This notion of action dispensability is, as we shall see, separable from the related notion of act*or* dispensability—that of whether we need to explain the action in terms of the actor's personal characteristics. The first is, as it were, the question of under what circumstances nations are likely to be saved (or lost) by the juxtaposition of the little Dutch boy's finger and the dike; the second is addressed to whether we must take account of the psychology of the little boy. In each case, there would be some advantage in speaking of "substitutability" rather than "dispensability," since the former term has the merit of suggesting a handy means of rough and ready reasoning about the *degree* of importance of an actor or of his personal characteristics: one may engage in the mental exercise of sub- stituting other possible acts (including inaction) and of hypothesizing the likely behavior of other historically available actors. But the antonym, "nonsubstitutability," is less successful than "indispensability" as a way of indicating the circumstances under which a particular act was a necessary link in some chain of events or under which the actor's personality qualities were a necessary antecedent of his act.

In rephrasing the actors-are-limited objection to the study of personality and politics in terms of action dispensability, we clarify the nature of the objection. What is at stake is more a social issue (concerning the influence of participants in decision-making processes) than a psychological issue. . . . Psychological data are only a part of what is needed for analyzing such effects, and analyses of them do not invariably raise important psychological issues.

The following three propositions suggest circumstances under which the actions of an individual are likely to be links in a chain of further events. The propositions are necessarily quite abstract because of the very great generality of the question "when do actions affect events?" But further specification can readily be introduced depending upon the context of investigation (e.g., the kinds of action being studied) and upon the concerns of investigators (e.g., the kinds of effects that are of interest). The likelihood of personal impact varies with (1) the degree to which the actions take place in an environment which admits of restructuring; (2) the location of the actor in the environment, and (3) the actor's peculiar strengths or weaknesses.

1. *The likelihood of personal impact increases to the degree that the environment admits of restructuring.* Technically speaking, we might describe situations or sequences of events in which modest interventions can produce disproportionately large results as "unstable." They are in a precarious equilibrium. The physical analogies are: massive rock formations at the side of a mountain which can be dislodged by the motion of a keystone, tinder-dry forest land, highly explosive compounds with properties like that of nitro-glycerine, and the weakened dikes of our little-Dutch-boy example.

Instability in this sense is by no means synonymous with what is loosely known as "political instability," a phrase commonly used to refer to a variety of unsettled phenomena, including political systems in which governments rise and fall with some frequency and systems in which violence is common. Many of the situations commonly referred to as unstable do not at all admit of restructuring. In the politics of many of the "unstable" Latin American nations, for example, most conceivable substitutions of actors and actions would lead to little change—at least in such "larger" political arrangements as the likelihood that officials will be changed by coup rather than by election. Thus, to return to physical analogy, an avalanche in motion down a mountainside is for the moment in stable equilibrium, since it cannot be influenced by modest interventions, just as the stationary rock formation that begot the avalanche was in unstable equilibrium.

The situation which does not admit readily of restructuring appears typically to be one in which a variety of factors press toward the same outcome so that the outcome can be expected to occur even if some of the contributing factors are eliminated.[10] The outcome that can be expected to occur "no matter what happens" can in fact be a *non*-outcome, as in the numerous instances of pattern maintenance involving the persistence of timeworn institutional arrangements. Or it may be the sort of highly likely occurrence to which such vague notions as "historical inevitability" are applied: a chain of events that is decisively under way and almost certain to arrive at a particular conclusion. In situations that do not readily admit of restructuring, a key variable is likely to be the self-fulfilling prophesies generated by the actors' own perceptions of the degrees and ways in which the situation is manipulable, and by whom.

Hook, in *The Hero in History*, offers the outbreak of World War I and of the February Revolution as instances of historical sequences which, if not "inevitable," probably could not have been averted by the actions of any single individual. In the first case, the vast admixture of multiple conflicting interests and intertwined alliances and, in the second case, the powerful groundswell of discontent were such as to leave the impression that no action by any single individual—excluding the farfetched hypothetical instances that invariably can be imagined—would have averted the outcome. On the other hand, Hook attempts to show in detail that without the specific actions of Lenin the October Revolution might well not have occurred. By implication, he suggests that Lenin was operating in an especially unstable environment. A similar argument might be advanced about the degree to which key leaders (notably Hitler) could exercise leverage over the political environment of Europe just prior to the outbreak of World War II, on the basis of the various accounts at our disposal of the state of affairs that preceded the invasion of Poland in 1939. In defending such an argument, however, it would be vital to avoid taking the circular route of simply showing that the environment *had* been manipulated by a single actor.[11]

2. *Likelihood of personal impact varies with the actor's location in the environment.* To shape events, an action must be performed not only in an unstable environment, but also by an actor who is strategically placed

in that environment. It is, for example, a commonplace that actors in the middle and lower ranks of many bureaucracies are unable to accomplish much singly, since they are restrained or inhibited by others. Robert C. Tucker points out what may almost be a limiting case on the other end of the continuum in an essay on the lack of restraint on Russian policy-makers, both under the czars and since the Revolution. He quotes with approval Nikolai Turgenev's mid-nineteenth-century statement that, "in all countries ruled by an unlimited power there has always been and is some class, estate, some traditional institutions which in certain instances compel the sovereign to act in a certain way and set limits to his caprice; nothing of the sort exists in Russia."[12] Tucker also has pointed to the tendency in totalitarian states for the political machinery to become "a conduit of the dictatorial psychology"[13]—that is, for there to be a relatively unimpeded conversion of whims of the dictator into governmental actions as a consequence of his authoritarian control of the bureaucratic apparatus.

3. *The likelihood of personal impact varies with the personal strengths of weaknesses of the actor.* My two previous observations can be recapitulated with an analogy from the poolroom. In the game of pocket billiards, the aim of the player is to clear as many balls as possible from the table. The initial distribution of balls parallels my first observation about the manipulability of the environment. With some arrays a good many shots are possible; perhaps the table can even be cleared. With other arrays no successful shots are likely. The analogy to point two—the strategic location of the actor—is, of course, the location of the cue ball. As a final point, we may note the political actor's peculiar strengths or weaknesses. In the poolroom, these are paralleled by the player's skill or lack of skill. Skill is of the utmost importance, since the greater the actor's skill, the less his initial need for a favorable position or a manipulable environment, and the greater the likelihood that *he himself* will contribute to making his subsequent position favorable and his environment manipulable. By the same token, a singularly inept politician may reduce the manipulability of his environment.[14]

The variable of skill is emphasized in Hook's detailed examination of Lenin's contribution to the events leading up to the October Revolution. Hook concludes that Lenin's vigorous, persistent, imaginative participation in that sequence was a necessary (though certainly not sufficient) condition for the outcome. Hook's interest, of course, is in lending precision to the notion of the Great Man. Therefore, he is concerned with the individual who, because of especially great talents, is able to alter the course of events. For our purposes, the Great Failure is equally significant: an actor's capabilities may be relevant to an outcome in a negative as well as positive sense. In each case, what presumably concerns us is a personal input—including again the failure to take available courses of action—that diverts the course of events from what would have been expected if the actor's personal capacities had been more typical.[15]

NOTES

1. David Riesman and Nathan Glazer, "The Lonely Crowd: A Reconsideration in 1960," in Seymour M. Lipset and Leo Lowenthal, eds., *Culture and Social Character* (New York: Free Press of Glencoe, 1961), p. 437. For examples of discussions that are in varying degrees critical of personality and politics writings, see Edward A. Shils, "Authoritarianism: 'Right' and 'Left,'" in Richard Christie and Marie Jahoda, eds., *Studies in the Scope and Method of "The Authoritarian Personality"* (Glencoe, Ill.: Free Press, 1954), pp. 24–49; Sidney Verba, "Assumptions of Rationality and Non-Rationality in Models of the International System," *World Politics* 14 (1961): 93–117; Reinhard Bendix, "Compliant Behavior and Individual Personality," *American Journal of Sociology* 58 (1952): 292–303; and David Spitz, "Power and Personality: The Appeal to the 'Right Man' in Democratic States," *American Political Science Review* 52 (1958): 84–97.

2. Alex Inkeles, "Sociology and Psychology," in Sigmund Koch, ed., *Psychology: A Study of a Science*, 6 (New York: McGraw-Hill, 1963), p. 354.

3. My criticism of the second objection would, of course, not stand in any instance where some acquired inner characteristic (such as a sense of class consciousness) was being defined as a social characteristic, and in which it was being argued that this "social" characteristic was "more important" than a "personality" characteristic. In terms of my usage, this would imply an empirical assertion about the relative influence of two types of psychological, or "personality," variables. By now, it should be clear that my remarks on the meaning of terms are simply short-handed approaches to clarify the underlying issue; at no point do I want to engage in the quixotic enterprise of attempting to establish "correct" usage.

4. Herbert Hyman, *Survey Design and Analysis* (Glencoe, Ill.: Free Press, 1955), pp. 254–74. The phrase in quotation marks is the heading of a section in which Hyman discusses this matter and is at p. 254.

5. Urie Bronfenbrenner, "Personality and Participation: The Case of the Vanishing Variables," *Journal of Social Issues* 16 (1960): 54–63. For an alternative, and I think more useful, approach to analyzing the effects of personality on participation, see David Horton Smith, "A Psychological Model of Individual Participation in Voluntary Organizations: Applications to Some Chilean Data, " *American Journal of Sociology* 72 (1966): 249–66.

6. Herbert Hyman, op. cit., pp. 254–57 (italics in the original). Also see Hubert Blalock, "controlling for Background Factors: Spuriousness Versus Developmental Sequences," *Sociological Inquiry* 34 (1964): 28–39, for a discussion of the rather complex implications of this distinction for data analysis.

7. Gordon Allport, "Review of *The American Soldier*," *Journal of Abnormal and Social Psychology* 45 (1950): 172.

8. Herbert Hyman and Paul B. Sheatsley, "'The Authoritarian Personality'—a Methodological Critique," in Richard Christie and Marie Jahoda, eds., op. cit., pp. 50–122. As M. Brewster Smith has pointed out to me, the tendency of some sociologists to "control away" psychological variables inappropriately is paralleled by "a näive application of the analysis of variance model" on the part of some psychologists who "fail to realize that prior conceptual decisions are required before it can be interpreted causally." Smith comments that "for practical prediction in a *stable* political system, one can often ignore the psychological mediation. In an unstable one it is risky to do so. In any case, theoretical understanding requires spelling out the mediation." Cf. the discussion by Angus Campbell and his associates of "the funnel of causality," in *The American Voter* (New York: Wiley, 1960), chap. 2.

9. Sidney Hook, *The Hero in History* (New York: John Day, 1943).

10. I take this point from Wassily Leontief's interesting essay "When Should History Be Written Backwards?" *The Economic History Review* 16 (1963): 1–8.

11. But such an argument, based on an account of the properties of the environment, ought to be possible. In order to find indicators of "manipulability" (compare the indicators of other dispositional concepts, such as "fragility"), it is not necessary to bring about the end-state to which the concept points. It *would*, however, be appropriate (and non-tautological) to collect trend-data on the circumstances under which environments had changed in response to individual actors. For an account of the outbreak of World War II which parallels Hook's analysis of Lenin and the October Revolution, see Alan Bullock, *Hitler: A Study in Tyranny*, rev. ed. (New York: Harper, 1960).

12. Robert C. Tucker, *The Soviet Political Mind* (New York: Praeger, 1963), pp. 145–65; quotation from Turgenev at p. 147.

13. Robert C. Tucker, "The Dictator and Totalitarianism," *World Politics* 17 (1965): 583.

14. Putting it a bit more formally, the skill (or ineptness) of the actor at t_1 may be a key determinant of the manipulability of his environment at t_2. To the degree that we take environmental conditions as given (i.e., considering them statically at a single point in time), we underestimate the impact of individuals on politics. For examples of political actors shaping their own roles and environments, see Hans H. Gerth and C. Wright Mills, *Character and Social Structure* (New York: Harcourt, Brace, 1953), chap. 14.

15. Without getting into the bog of technical philosophical debate about testing counter-factuals (propositions taking the form: "if x had not occurred, then . . . "), this observation suggests a means of empirical leverage on action dispensability—and it is also relevant to the discussion which follows of actor dispensability. When we say that in some single instance an action or actor was indispensable, we are evidently stating a covert, multi-instance proposition about likely outcomes, under a series of circumstances in which the only variation consists of acts or actors like the ones to which we are imputing indispensability. For a highly imaginative study of political leadership which brings this point home, see Donald B. Rosenthal and Robert L. Crain, "Executive Leadership and Community Innovation: The Fluoridation Experience," *Urban Affairs Quarterly*" 1 (1966): 39–57. Rosenthal and Crain show that the position taken by mayors on water

fluoridation is an extraordinarily good predictor of the outcome of community fluoridation decisions. The point that analyses of the single instance often involves thinking in
multiple-case terms emerges again in my remarks in chapter three on single case
analysis.

For a classical discussion of how to reason about the "what-would-have-happened-if?"
questions raised by analyses of action dispensability, see Max Weber, *The Methodology of
the Social Sciences* (Glencoe, Ill.: Free Press, 1949), pp. 172ff.

6

ROBERT C. TUCKER

The Dictator and Totalitarianism

A sense of the theoretical inadequacy of the conception of totalitarianism seems to have been growing in American political science in the 1960s. Increasingly the complaint is heard that this construct is too narrow and limited to serve as a useful basic category for comparative analysis of contemporary one-party systems. It leaves out of view the nationalist single-party systems that share very many significant characteristics with the Fascist and Communist systems. It does not fare well in the face of the recent growth of diversity among Communist systems themselves. Furthermore, the politics of post-Stalin Russia have become more and more difficult to analyze in terms of the theory of totalitarianism, the fall of Khrushchev being only one in a long series of events that do not easily find places in the model of a totalitarian polity; and efforts to modify the model so that it will fit contemporary Soviet communism—e.g., by introducing the idea of a "rationalist totalitarianism"—seem of little avail. And owing to the tendency to see totalitarian systems as examples of what might be called government without politics, with a unitary elite controlling an atomized population by organization and terror, the theory of totalitarianism has obstructed rather than facilitated awareness of the intra-elite politics of factional conflict and policy debates that rage constantly behind the scenes of the Soviet and other Communist systems, despite their official pretensions to monolithic unity and their claims that factions are forbidden. For these and other reasons, some students of the comparative politics of modern authoritarianism

From "The Dictator and Totalitarianism," *World Politics* 17, no. 4 (July 1965): 565–73. Copyright © by Princeton University Press. Reprinted by permission of Princeton University Press.

have become dissatisfied with the concept of totalitarianism and have begun to formulate alternative basic categories, such as "movement-regimes," "mobilization systems," and the like.[1]

But are we now to discard the concept of totalitarianism as an obsolete or obsolescent category in modern political science? Considering it an essential part of our theoretical equipment, I for one would not like to see this happen. In order to prevent it from happening, however, it appears necessary to carry out a more radical critique of the theory of totalitarianism than has yet been made, rather as medicine may have to resort to a more radical form of treatment in order to save a patient. So far criticism has concentrated upon the deficiencies of the theory in application to systems or situations that were not in view or in existence at the time the theory was devised. The more radical critique must address itself to a different question: How valid was the theory as a representation of political reality in the two historical cases that it was particularly devised to explain—Hitler's Germany and Stalin's Russia? The time is now especially propitious for pursuing this question, since we have far more documentary and other information on the two cases than was available in earlier years. Here the question will be considered only in the aspect relating to the role of the dictator in the system.

When we confront the theoretical model of a totalitarian polity with what we now know about the factual situation in Hitler's Germany and Stalin's Russia, it appears that the model was seriously deficient in its omission of the personal factor from the dynamics of totalitarianism, its obliviousness to the impact of the dictator's personality upon the political system and process. For not only do Hitler and Stalin turn out to have been, as already indicated, autocrats who at many crucial points individually dominated the decision-making process and behavior of their governments, but the factual evidence likewise supports the further conclusions that (1) in both instances we have to do with individuals whose personalities would be classified somewhere on the continuum of psychiatric conditions designated as paranoid; and (2) in both instances the needs of the paranoidal personality were a powerful motivating factor in the dictatorial decision-making. The dictator did not, so to speak, confine the expression of his psychopathological needs to his private life while functioning "normally" in his public political capacity. Rather, he found a prime outlet for those needs in political ideology and political activity. In terms of Lasswell's formula, his psychopathological "private affects" were displaced onto "public objects." As a result, the dynamics of totalitarianism in Hitler's Germany and Stalin's Russia were profoundly influenced by the psychodynamics of the totalitarian dictator. The Soviet case is particularly instructive in this regard. For while our factual knowledge is less complete, we have here a system that survived the totalitarian dictator and thus some possibility of assessing the impact of his personality by studying the difference that his death made.

Before coming to power Hitler set forth in *Mein Kampf*, with its doctrine about a world-wide Jewish conspiracy to subvert the master race, a private vision of reality showing very strong parallels with psychiatric descriptions of a paranoid delusional system. Subsequently the vision began to be acted out inside Germany in the anti-Jewish terror, of which Hitler himself was the single most powerful driving force. Still later, when World War II was precipitated by the German invasion of Poland in 1939, it was Hitler's furiously insistent determination to (as he put it) "annihilate my enemies" that drove him, in the face of widespread apathy toward war in his own society and even in his own government, to push the world over the brink; and the story of his actions and reactions on the eve and in the uncertain early days of the conflict is like a page out a case history of paranoia, save that this was likewise a page of world history. During the war the internal terror continued, now on the scale of occupied Europe as a whole. It was Hitler's own will to genocide that generated the relentless pressure under which Himmler's terror machine proceeded during the war to carry out the murder of European Jewry: "Himmler organized the extermination of the Jews, but the man in whose mind so grotesque a plan had been conceived was Hitler. Without Hitler's authority, Himmler, a man solely of subordinate virtues, would never have dared to act on his own."[2]

Stalin's career differed from Hitler's, among other ways, in that he did not come to power as the recognized leader of his own movement but gradually took over from above a movement that had come to power much earlier under other leadership, mainly Lenin's. Certain other differences flowed from this. Whereas Hitler's personal dictatorship was established rather easily through the blood purge of June 1934, which took no more than a few hundred lives, Stalin's arose through the veritable conquest of the Communist party and Soviet state in the Great Purge of 1936–1938, in which an estimated five to nine million persons were arrested on charges of participation in an imaginary great anti-Soviet counterrevolutionary conspiracy. In this case the dictator's private vision of reality was not set forth in advance in a bible of the movement, but was woven into the preexisting Marxist-Leninist ideology during the show trials of 1936–1938, which for Stalin were a dramatization of his conspir-

acy view of Soviet and contemporary world history. The original party
ideology was thus transformed according to Stalin's own dictates into the
highly "personalized" new version of Soviet ideology that was expressed in
the Moscow trials and in Stalin's *Short Course* of party history published
in 1938. Contrary to the above-reviewed theory of totalitarianism, the
Great Purge of 1936–1938 was not a product of the needs of Soviet
totalitarianism as a system. Apart from the fact that it was only in the
course of this purge that the Soviet state finally became a fully totalitarian
one, especially in the sense of being the scene of permanent and pervasive
terror, we have it now on highest Soviet authority that the purge was
extremely dysfunctional for the Soviet state since it greatly weakened the
ability of the country to withstand the coming test of total war. Not
system-needs but the needs of Stalin, both political and psychopathological, underlay to a decisive degree the terror of 1936–1938.[3]

As in Hitler's case, we see in Stalin's the repetitive pattern, the subsequent reenactment in foreign relations of psychopathological themes and
tendencies expressed earlier in the internal sphere. It was mainly in the
postwar era of Soviet cold war against the West, against Tito, and so
forth, that Stalin's psychological needs and drives found relatively unin-
hibited outlet in the field of external relations. Contributing factors
included, on the one hand, the fact that an older and more deeply
disordered Stalin was now less able to exercise restraint save in the face of
very grave external danger, and, on the other hand, the capacity of a
relatively more strong and less threatened Soviet Union to make its
weight felt internationally with a large degree of impunity. We have the
testimony of Khrushchev in the 1956 secret report that now "The
willfulness of Stalin showed itself not only in decisions concerning
the internal life of the country but also in the international relations of
the Soviet Union," and that Stalin "demonstrated his suspicion and
haughtiness not only in relation to individuals in the U.S.S.R., but in
relation to whole parties and nations." The latter point is illustrated with a
vivid recollection of Stalin in 1948 deciding on the break with Tito in a
state of blind fury, exclaiming: "I will shake my little finger—and there
will be no more Tito. He will fall."[4] Other postwar Soviet acts or policies
that were influenced, if not directly caused, by Stalin's psychological
needs include the imperious demands upon Turkey in 1945; the shutting
down of cultural contacts and general isolationism of the 1947–1953
period; the extension of blood purges and show trials to Soviet-dominated
Eastern Europe; the suspicion shown toward nationalist revolutions in
Asia and elsewhere; and the unprecedentedly extreme Soviet psychologi-

cal warfare of 1949–1953 against the West as manifested, in particular, in the savage propaganda campaign about alleged American germ warfare in Korea. There was, finally, the extraordinarily significant affair of the Kremlin doctors in January–February 1953, which had a vital bearing upon Soviet foreign policy as well as upon internal affairs. The way in which Stalin's psychopathology found expression in this final episode of his career will be discussed below.

In both Germany and Russia, then, the dictatorial personality exerted its impact originally in ideology and the internal life of the country, and later found a major field of expression in foreign relations as well. The internal impact was felt, among other ways, in the form of terror; the external, in a special sort of aggressiveness that may best be described, perhaps, as an externalization of the terror. In other words, domestic terror, which may be viewed under the aspect of "internal aggression" against elements of the population, was followed by foreign aggression, which may be viewed as a turning of the terror outward upon the world. Parenthetically, since this temporal order of priority was and generally would be conditioned by objective factors in the situation (e.g., the necessity for the dictator to capture control of his own society before he can channel his personality needs into foreign policy), there may be a basis for relatively early identification of a rising totalitarian dictator of the type of Stalin or Hitler. This suggests, moreover, that the international community might possibly develop a politics of prevention based on stopping the dictatorial personality at the stage of "internal aggression." However, this would necessitate a modification of the traditional doctrine of nonintervention insofar as it sanctions the unlimited right of a nation-state to deal with its own population as the ruler or regime sees fit, provided only that it continues to observe the accepted norms of international law in relations with other states. Upon the willingness and ability of the international community to recognize this problem, and to institute means of preventing individuals of paranoid tendency from gaining or long retaining control of states, may hang the human future. Were Hitler and Stalin, for example, dictators of their respective countries in the 1960s instead of the 1930s, the probability-coefficient of civilization's survival would be very low.[5]

The evidence disclosed by the Stalin and Hitler cases on the connection between dictatorial psychopathology and the politics of totalitarianism strongly suggests that the personal factor should be included in the theoretical model of a totalitarian system. On the basis of the factual record in these cases, as just summarized, the contribution of the dictator's personality to the dynamics of totalitarianism should be recognized as one of the regular and important components in the "syndrome." Such a conclusion appears all the more compelling in view of the extremely heavy emphasis that the theory has placed, as noted earlier, upon pervasive and permanent terror as the very essence of totalitarianism. For in the Soviet and Nazi cases, the dictators themselves, driven by pathological hatred and fear of what they perceived as insidiously conspiratorial enemy forces operating at home and abroad, were responsible to a very significant extent for the totalitarian terror that did in fact exist in Hitler's Germany and Stalin's Russia. The Soviet case is especially instructive since it reflects the relation of Stalin to the Stalinist terror, not only positively in the form of direct evidence of his determining role, but also negatively in the form of the decline of terror that began to be felt almost immediately after his death and has since continued. As late as January–February 1953, it may be said on the basis of the present writer's personal observations in Russia at that time, Soviet society was almost paralyzed with terror as preparations for another great purge developed to the accompaniment of ominous official charges that an anti-Soviet conspiracy, with threads leading to foreign intelligence services, was or had been abroad in the land. Stalin's death at that time not only cut short the purge operation but inaugurated the subsiding of the internal terror that had developed in a wavelike movement of advance and partial retreat ever since his rise to supreme power in 1929. Soviet citizens insistently refer to the subsiding of the terror as perhaps the most significant single expression of change they have experienced in post-Stalin Russia; and most foreign observers and scholars specializing in Soviet studies appear to agree with them on this point. Insofar as terror has continued to exist in post-Stalin Soviet society, it has become, to use Arendt's distinction, terror of the "dictatorial" rather than the "totalitarian" variety.

Given these facts and the premises of the theory of totalitarianism, certain conclusions concerning both Russia and totalitarianism would seem to follow. First, if total terror is the essence of totalitarianism, then a Soviet political system in which such terror has ceased to exist and in which terror generally has greatly subsided over a substantial period of years should be pronounced, at least provisionally, post-totalitarian. Second, if the terror in Hitler's Germany was connected in considerable degree with Hitler as a personality, and that in Stalin's Russia with Stalin as a personality, then the explanations of totalitarian terror in terms of functional requisites of totalitarianism as a system or a general ideological fanaticism in the ruling elite would appear to have been basically erroneous—a conclusion which derives further strength from the fact that the ruling elite in post-Stalin Russia remains committed to the Communist ideology. Third, the theory of totalitarianism should not only bring the dictator and his personality into the "syndrome," but also should give specific recognition to the role of the dictatorial personality in the dynamics of totalitarian terror.

The theory of totalitarianism has not, however, moved in this direction. The indicated critical post-mortem on earlier interpretations of the dynamics of totalitarian terror has not appeared. The evidence from Hitler's Germany and Stalin's Russia in the relation of the dictator as a terroristic personality to the practice of totalitarian terror, and for such peculiarly totalitarian characteristics of it as its tendency to grow over time, has been generally disregarded. And instead of provisionally pronouncing post-Stalin Russia to be post-totalitarian on the ground that the terror has subsided, some theorists specializing in Soviet studies have taken the very different path of eliminating terror from the definition of totalitarianism. This leads to the thesis that what we see in Russia after Stalin is a system of "totalitarianism without terror." Thus Brzezinski, who had earlier viewed terror as the "most universal characteristic" of totalitarianism, writes that we seem to be witnessing the emergence in post-Stalin Russia of a "voluntarist totalitarian system" and that terror must now be seen not as something essential to a totalitarian system but only "as a manifestation of a particular stage in the development of the system." In explanation of this point he states further: "Terror and violence may be necessary to change a primitive, uneducated, and traditional society rapidly. Persuasion, indoctrination, and social control can work more effectively in relatively developed societies."[6]

But such a view of the causation of the terror is open both to the objections already leveled against explanations running in terms of system-needs, and to others in addition. It is debatable, and nowadays increasingly being debated, whether the terrorism of forced collectivization and industrialization in 1929–1933 was a necessity for Soviet communism in achieving its goals of modernization. Such a prominent Communist theorist and politician as Nikolai Bukharin was profoundly convinced that there was no such necessity, and many others in Russia at that time shared his view. Moreover, some western specialists on Russia and even, apparently, certain people in present-day Soviet Russia are increasingly of the opinion that his view was correct on the whole.[7] But even if we leave this question open, allowing for the possibility that terror and violence were in fact necessities of the modernization process in the

Soviet case, the heightened terror by purge that was directed against the Communist party and Soviet managerial elite between 1934 and 1939 and was mounting again in 1949–1953 cannot be explained by the need to "change a primitive, uneducated, and traditional society rapidly." By 1934 collectivization was a *fait accompli* and generally accepted as such even by the peasantry, the pace and rigors of industrialization had slackened, and there was no serious resistance among the population or within the ruling Party to the continuing process of modernization. Certainly there was no opposition to it on such a scale that it required to be quelled by terroristic means. And just at this time, when any need for terror and violence for modernization purposes had subsided, a vast new intensification of it occurred on Stalin's initiative and under his personal direction. Moreover, terror rose again in a post-war Soviet Union which, despite the devastation visited upon it by the Second World War, was basically the urbanized and industrialized country that we know in our time. These facts do not square with the thesis that the terror was a manifestation of a particular stage in the development of the Soviet system connected with forced modernization. Nor does this thesis explain why the postulated stage in the development of the system should have lasted as long as Stalin lived and ended with his death or very soon after. In actuality, what this fact and other positive evidence indicate is that the Stalinist terror was in large part an expression of the needs of the dictatorial personality of Stalin, and that these needs continued to generate the terror as long as he lived. In my view, the instinct that originally led the theorists of totalitarianism to treat total terror as belonging to the very essence of this phenomenon was a sound one. But if their insight is to be salvaged, it will be necessary to reckon in a new way with the personal factor in the totalitarian terror and the dynamics of totalitarianism in general.

NOTES

1. For the concept of a "rationalist totalitarianism," see Z. Brzezinski, "Totalitarianism and Rationality," *American Political Science Review* 50 (September 1956): 751–63. Examples of recent criticisms of the concept of totalitarianism are A. Z. Groth, "The 'Isms' in Totalitarianism," ibid. 58 (December 1964): 888–901; and this writer's "Towards a Comparative Politics of Movement-Regimes," ibid. 55 (June 1961): 281–89.

2. Alan Bullock, *Hitler: A Study in Tyranny* (New York, 1962), p. 703. On Hitler's hysterical outbrust on the eve of the war about annihilating his enemies, see Birger

Dahlerus, *The Last Attempt* (London, 1948), chap. 6; also G. M. Gilbert, *The Psychology of Dictatorship* (New York, 1950), p. 301. For a full account of Hitler's actions and reactions during the entire crucial period of the war's beginning, see Bullock, chap. 9, esp. pp. 536–39. Also of interest in this general connection is Ivone Kirkpatrick's account of the psychological motivations underlying Mussolini's decision to embark upon the Abyssinian war (*Mussolini: A Study in Power* [New York, 1964], p. 320.

3. For a detailed elaboration of this argument, along with an analysis of the ideology of the purge trials in terms of the analogy with a paranoid system, see the introduction to R. C. Tucker and S. F. Cohen, eds., *The Great Purge Trial* (New York, 1965). It is significant that the conspiracy themes that Stalin incorporated into Marxist-Leninist ideology have largely lapsed or subsided in post-Stalin Russia.

4. Nikita Khrushchev, *Crimes of the Stalin Era* (New York, 1956), p. 48.

5. The menace of the paranoid in the nuclear age has been strongly emphasized by Lasswell. Pointing out that "All mankind might be destroyed by a single paranoid in a position of power who could imagine no grander exit than using the globe as a gigantic funeral pyre," he goes on: "Even a modicum of security under present-day conditions calls for the discovery, neutralization and eventual prevention of the paranoid. And this calls for the overhauling of our whole inheritance of social institutions for the purpose of disclosing and eliminating the social factors that create these destructive types" (*Power and Personality* [New York, 1948], p. 184). My own remarks above are meant to suggest that, pending the requisite systematic attack upon the problem, it may be possible to devise interim means of dealing with developing situations of this kind before it is too late.

6. *Ideology and Power in Soviet Politics* (New York, 1962), pp. 80, 88–89. Merle Fainsod, who in the 1953 first edition of his study of Soviet government had called terror the "linchpin of modern totalitarianism," in the 1963 edition revises this sentence to read: "Every totalitarian regime makes some place for terror in its system of controls" (*How Russia Is Ruled*, 2d ed., p. 421). See also Allen Kassof, "The Administered Society: Totalitarianism Without Terror," *World Politics* 16 (July 1964), 558–75.

7. See, for example, "Was Stalin Really Necessary?" in Alec Nove's, *Economic Rationality and Soviet Politics* (New York, 1964). Soviet second thoughts have been expressed, albeit very cautiously, in the form of criticism of unnecessary "excesses" in the implementation of the collectivization policy by Stalin.

PART II

WHY DO LEADERS LEAD?

THE literature of Western culture reveals that the question of what motivates people to behave as they do has always intrigued us. But only in the last hundred years did we start to generate theories about the underlying reasons for individual and group behavior. More than anyone else, Sigmund Freud prompted this line of inquiry. His investigation of the unconscious was a brilliantly creative attempt to uncover what, at the deepest level, determines our life choices.

The three authors represented in this section are all clearly in the Freudian tradition. They stress the significance of the individual actor; they argue for the explanatory power of unconscious motives; and they believe that these motives are rooted in early childhood.

Harold Lasswell, who originally published *Psychopathology and Politics* in 1930, was the first American social scientist to apply Freudian theory to political life. He described the "political man," one who turns to public life to realize his private motives. To the extent that political man is successful in politics, he becomes perforce a leader although, according to Lasswell, the nature of this leadership can vary considerably. (In *Psychopathology and Politics* three different types of leaders are posited: agitators, administrators, and reformers.) Lasswell's deceptively simple formula, which explains why for some people public life holds such a powerful attraction, is generally considered an enduring contribution to our understanding of political leaders.

Indeed, Alexander L. George refers in the first paragraph of his article on "Power As a Compensatory Value for Political Leaders" to Lasswell's seminal work. His purpose in this article is to apply Lasswell's general hypotheses on the "power seeker" (a person who "pursues power as a means of compensation against deprivation") to a specific political leader: Woodrow Wilson. To this end, George first examines the concepts of self-esteem and the power motive, and then the quest for power as compensation for low-esteem. George finds evidence to support Lasswell's formulation, but on the basis of the data on Wilson, he concludes that the original hypothesis should be expanded to include consideration of the "'field of power' within which the individual will strive for compensation and the types of situations in which the individual's power-need will be aroused."

E. Victor Wolfenstein's book, *The Revolutionary Personality*, postulates that all political revolutionaries have childhood and adolescent experiences that are somehow similar. This profoundly Freudian notion obviously downplays the importance of historical context and immediate circumstance. At center stage is the revolutionary figure—and his mother and father. Thus, Wolfenstein freely compares Lenin, Trotsky, and Gandhi, even though the latter exercised leadership in a completely different context.

Wolfenstein's group psychobiography is successful because the raw material is of such unusual interest, he applies the psychoanalytic theories of Freud and Erik Erikson deftly, and there is something inherently fascinating in the idea that people who appear to be so different can be motivated by impulses so similar. To be sure, psychobiographers have proved themselves easy targets. Their craft is regarded with suspicion by many who think it silly to consider the great events of history in the light of any single individual's successful passing through the oral, anal, and genital phases. Yet when carefully employed, psychoanalytic theory provides provocative explanations of why some individuals will go through so much in order to exert power over others.

7

HAROLD D. LASSWELL

The Development of Political Man

IT will be remembered that Freud's search for signs of the traumatic situation led him to uncover the contemporaneous functioning of all sorts of unconscious motivations in both the diseased and the healthy personality. The quest led him farther. Freud felt impelled to set up a schematic representation of the typical genetic development of the human personality. This grew out of the comparative study of very thoroughly analyzed cases and was rooted in empirical observation. Freud has always kept close to his data; and no matter how far his imagination soared, actual clinical experience was the starting-place and the landing-field for the flight.

The energy of a developed personality can be treated as dispersed in three directions: in the affirmative expression of socialized impulses, in unsocialized impulses, and in the maintenance of resistance charges against unsocialized impulses. The original forms of energy expression which are available to the infant are in many ways incompatible with the demands of human intercourse. The infant must surrender many primitive forms of gratification, if he is to be loved, and to avoid discomfort and pain. He must build up a self which represents the demands of society. The surrounding adults coerce and wheedle him into taking their commands for his own laws. The conscience is the introjected environment which imposes limitations upon the antisocial impulses. As the infant and child grows, he avoids conflicts with the environment by removing the locus of the conflict within himself, and plays nurse, mother, and

From Harold D. Lasswell, *Psychopathology and Politics* (New York: Viking, 1960), chap. 65, pp. 65–77. Reprinted with permission of The Free Press, a division of Macmillan, Inc. Copyright © 1960 by The Free Press. First published in 1930.

father to himself. He learns to control his own excretions and to chasten his own murderous rages. He achieves individuality of emphasis by accepting the socialization of his major impulses.

But this incorporation of the requirements of the social order into the personality does not proceed smoothly, nor does it abolish the primitive psychological structures which have been developed and apparently discarded at each step of the way toward adulthood. Much of the energy of the personality is spent in blocking the entry of the unadjusted impulses of the self into consciousness and into overt expression. Careful scrutiny of individual behavior over a twenty-four-hour period strikingly shows the extent to which the personality is controlled by very elementary psychological structures. Moments of fatigue, moments of deprivation, moments of irresponsible reverie, all betray the presence of tendencies which are unassimilated to the world of adult reality.

Freud began to build up his conception of personality development by the gradual universalization of phenomena which he encountered in actual clinical work, and which he first described in relatively modest and restricted terms. He began his original psychological contributions by stressing the role of sexuality in the etiology of certain neuroses. He found that all sorts of pathological conditions and developmental abnormalities were apparently due to some shortcoming in sexual integration. This emphasis upon sexual adjustment as a necessary prerequisite of healthy adulthood met with so much opposition that Freud's energies were taken up with defending and elaborating his position. Now the sexual function is essentially a species function and stresses the biological uniformities of man at the expense of individuality. A topic like "personality development" requires a comprehensive theory of individuality, and this Freud did not develop until the split with Adler, who insisted upon the role of a drive toward individualization and who denied that the much neglected "ego instincts" of Freud were enough to support a comprehensive theory.

The story of Freud's neurosis-sexuality-personality theories begins with his earliest independent psychological contributions. Many clinicians before Freud had been abundantly impressed by the frequency with which sexual troubles seemed to beget "nervous" troubles. In his hypnotic work, Freud was especially struck by the frequency with which specifically sexual episodes were involved in the pathogenic experiences. Freud now proceeded to generalize about the sexual element in neurosis, and announced that neurosis was a function of deviated sexual life.

Freud armed in defense of his generalization with two new weapons. The first was his experience in letting patients talk it out and in treating most of their productions as symbolic of something else. He acquired facility in interpreting what other people took literally as being a disguised representation of something else. So, when Freud was confronted with cases which were not manifestly sexual, he felt able to treat the non-sexual elements as symbolic representations of sexuality and to justify himself by claiming that his more intensive research procedure supplied him with the sustaining facts. Needless to say, those who had not them-selves experienced the shift in standpoint which Freud had achieved were alienated by his seeming arbitrariness.

Freud's second reliance was on an inclusive theory of sexuality. Undaunted by the ridicule heaped upon his sexual theory of the neurosis, he carried the war into enemy territory by extending the whole concept of sexuality backward from puberty through the life of the growing child to infancy.

At first glance this might appear to be a cheap, dialectical trick to confound his critics by telling them that "sex" meant all the things they had called by other names. Freud's *Three Contributions to Sexual Theory* was saved from being a rhetorical quibble by the virtuosity of his imagina-tion and by the apparent definiteness of the connections which he traced between the various features of childhood development and the patterns of healthy and perverse adult sexuality. Careful analysis of biologically efficacious intercourse shows that it is a complex integration of many acts. It involves a partner of the opposite sex. Its essential feature is an increasing tension until the point of explosive release, followed by perfect relaxation. The male must be sadistic enough to run the risk of hurting the female by injecting the penis in the vagina. The participants must be willing to indulge in all sorts of preliminary play for the sake of heighten-ing the critical tension, involving tongue, lips, nipples, and all the eroge-nous zones of the body.

Comparing the details of this completed pattern of the unam-biguously sexual act with the earlier activities of the infant and child, Freud drew a host of analogies. Children indulge in play in sexual pos-tures, exhibit their sexual parts to one another, and take pleasure in sexual peeping; but Freud carried his analysis of the sexuality of children much farther. Child specialists had often remarked that the nursing male child frequently exhibits the phenomenon of an erect penis and a desire to suckle for some time after hunger contractions cease. The general pattern of the sequence hunger-nursing-peaceful relaxation follows the characteristic curve of the sexual act. Freud suggested that inspection of the nursing pattern reveals that the pleasure derived by the child goes far beyond immediate biological necessities. This excess gratification Freud treats as a primitive outcropping of the sexual instinct, which need not be supposed to appear suddenly with the maturation of the glandular apparatus, but may be thought of as growing like the usual biological process by integrating partial components into one complex synthesis.

Sexual differentiation arises gradually, for at first distinctions of sex are not recognized by the child. The human animal is bisexual, a concept which Freud took over with some reservations from Wilhelm Fliess. Distinctions are acheived within the world of family experience. The child is attracted sexually toward the parent of the opposite sex but is too weak to compete for the loved object. Thus the father, who is too mighty to be killed and put out of the way, is copied by the son, who seeks to absorb his power into his own personality. The repression of the father-hostility, mother-love sentiments produces the Oedipus complex. The child achieves a socialized self by playing the role of the father in relation to his own impulses. The "latency period" rises from four to six, according to Freud, when the early sexual struggle against the father is given up. The fear of the father (the "castration complex") leads to the passing of the Oedipus phase of growth.

Now Freud specified a variety of difficulties which arise whenever there is failure to achieve successful integration of the partial components of the sexual instinct. He connected homosexuality, psychological frigidity, and impotence, exhibitionism, sadism, masochism, voyeurism, and a variety of other abnormalities with definite failures in integration. Sometimes the individual becomes obsessed by ideas which have a disguised sexual meaning, and sometimes he indulges in physical symptoms which possess a similar unconscious significance. The first is an obsessional neurosis, and the second is hysteria.

The stress which Freud laid upon the sexuality of the child, and upon socialization by intimidation, broke with revolutionary violence in a culture which swaddled its infants in sentimentality. The child of the poets was like this:

> Not in entire forgetfulness,
> and not in utter nakedness,
> But trailing clouds of glory we do come
> From God, who is our home:
> Heaven lies about us in our infancy!
> —William Wordsworth

The child of the Freudians was like this:

The child, at one time or another in its life, is, in a sense, autoerotic, narcissistic, exhibitionistic, inclined to play the role of "Jack the Peeper," incestuous, patricidal, or matricidal, homosexual, fetichistic, masochistic and sadistic. (G. V. Hamilton, *An Introduction to Objective Psychopathology*, p. 301)

As early as 1898 Freud had begun to elaborate the idea that sexuality begins at birth. But as late as 1900, when the *Interpretation of Dreams* appeared, he wrote in a footnote that "childhood knows nothing, as yet, of sexual desire." With the elaboration of his sexual theory, Freud became less preoccupied in defending himself against his psychiatric colleagues than in perfecting defenses aganst his friends. Freud began to build up a circle in 1903. Of the original group, Alfred Adler and Wilhelm Stekel were the two who were destined to achieve the most subsequent attention. By 1906 Ferenczi of Budapest and the Zurich contingent—the eminent Bleuler and his assistants—became cordial and interested. In 1908 a conference was held at Salzburg; and in 1909 G. Stanley Hall invited Freud to lecture at Clark University. In 1910 an international society was organized at Nuremberg, and the institutionalization of the psychoanalytic trend was well launched.

The first cleavage came about when Freud and Adler finally broke in 1911. In and out of season Adler stressed the "masculine protest," the drive of the human being to master every situation in which he finds himself. The individual specializes in overcoming his short stature, his enuresis, his ugliness, and his other defects; his principal drive is to differentiate himself rather than to perform his species function.

Adler represented several other currents of dissent from Freud. Freud had felt compelled to stress the antisocial drives of human nature, and Adler held a less Hobbesian view. The "social-feelings" component of human nature was accorded a place in the Adlerian system; and when the "socially useful" norms of individual adjustment were violated by the individual, "inferiority feelings" ensued. Therapy consisted in bringing this interpretation home to the maladapted person, leading him to relinquish his socially useless means of mastery and to allow his "social feelings" to express themselves more freely. Adler's therapy showed that he represented a pedagogical-ethical reaction against Freud's denial of the training function of the scientific analyst. Freud said repeatedly that the business of the analyst is to expose the patient to himself, and to leave it to the patient to work out his particular modes of adaptation to reality. Adler wants to give the patient a general scheme of thinking and to let him have some practice in indulging the "social feelings" of his nature.

Adler likewise represented a protest against the complexities of Freud's style of thought. The distinction can be drawn best, perhaps, by saying that Freud proceeded from symptoms to meanings, and from meanings to other meanings and from other meanings to conditions. The analysis consists in uncovering lifelong chains of meaning attached to particular objects. Janet never achieved this process, and Adler short-circuited it. Adler begins with the symptom and proceeds as directly as possible to the condition. His books abound in succinct characterizations of cases, and "symbolic" material is at a minimum. Employing his orienting principle, he directs attention to a sympathetic reconstruction of the social relationships of the patient and selects those problems which the individual has tried to master by antisocial or personally crippling devices. The "common-sense" simplicity of Adler's observations commends his doctrines in circles which are repelled by the alien terminology and the elaborate interpretative machinery of Freud.

Under the perpetual hammering of Adler, Freud undertook to expand upon his sketchy theory of the ego. At first Freud was inclined to say that Adler had nothing to add because he had himself spoken of the ego instincts as well as the sexual instincts. Such a solution was hardly satisfying, and the self did not find a suitable resting-place in Freud's theoretical system until the role of narcissism (love of the self) was taken up and set forth at length. This "saved" the sexual theory, and it made the analysis of ego processes a problem of major interest to psychoanalysis. Stress was laid upon the fact that when the individual's libido flows outward toward objects, and when obstacles or deprivations are imposed upon this outward reaching, the libido turns back upon the self. This excessive libidinization of the self rendered subsequent adjustment to reality very difficult, and many personality deformations and formations are traceable to this developmental warp.

The break between Freud and Jung in 1913 had less immediate importance for personality theory than the previous schism. Like Adler, Jung undertook to subordinate the role of sexuality; but Jung accomplished his purpose less by postulating concurrent ego-instincts than by invoking an inclusive energy concept which would embrace sexuality, ego-drives, and many other accessory manifestations. Jung, paralleling Adler again, came to the rescue of human nature, postulating a moral trend in the unconscious. And Jung, like Adler, frankly advises and trains his patients. Jung's two distinctive lines of innovation were concerned with dream interpretations and ethnological applications. Jung expanded dream interpretations for the sake of laying bare the "racial unconscious." Using saga material and dream material, Jung undertook to deflate the claims of sexuality and to demonstrate the limited applicability of the Oedipus idea.

Freud was assailed at a vital spot and rallied to defend himself in *Totem and Taboo*. He scored a point over Jung, who had relied on saga material, by drawing heavily on the ethnological summaries of Frazer in the *Golden Bough* to justify the universality of the Oedipus complex. This was Freud's first contribution to systematic social theory, and will come up for consideration in that connection. From the standpoint of personality theory, perhaps the most valuable passages are those which describe the infant's overvaluation of thought—the "omnipotence of thought," as it was phrased by a patient.

Some years later Jung, now on his own for some time, devised his classification of personality types and vastly increased popular and technical interest in the subject. This in turn has stimulated the group around Freud to develop a formal psychoanalytic characterology. In this task they were assisted by some early communications of Freud, wherein he took note of some of the character types met with in his practice. . . .

The other schisms between Freud and his pupils (involving Stekel and Rank) have been less significant for personality theory thus far, although Rank's sociological interests may germinate now that he is away from the immediate presence of the master.

Freud, who had obstinately clung to the phraseology of sex, rejecting every proposal for an overmastering set of terms which would carry less restricted connotations, executed a brilliant maneuver in 1926 and proposed to regard human activity as manifestations of two principles, the life and death instincts. Life consists in accumulation and the release of tension; and, generalizing this phenomenon, we have the life and death drives.[1]

Suppose we put aside further exposition of the analytical personality theories, and in the light of these conceptions set up a general formula which describes the developmental history of the political man. The most general formula would employ three terms. The first component, stands for the private motives of the individual as they are nurtured and organized in relation to the family constellation and the early self. We shall have occasion to see that primitive psychological structures continue to function within the personality long after the epochs of infancy and childhood have been chronologically left behind. The prominence of

hate in politics suggests that we may find that the most important private
motive is a repressed and powerful hatred of authority, a hatred which has
come to partial expression and repression in relation to the father, at least
in patrilineal society, where the male combines the function of biological
progenitor and sociological father.

The second term, *d*, in such a formula describes the displacement of
private motives from family objects to public objects. The repressed
father-hatred may be turned against kings or capitalists, which are social
objects playing a role before and within the community. Harmonious
relations with the father of the family may actually depend upon the
successful deflection of hatred from private to public objects.

The third symbol, *r*, signifies the rationalization of the displacement
in terms of public interests. The merciless exploitation of the toolless
proletariat by the capitalists may be the rational justification of the
attitude taken up by the individual toward capitalism.

The most general formula which expresses the developmental facts
about the fully developed political man reads thus:

$$p \} d \} r = P,$$

where *p* equals private motives; *d* equals displacement onto a public
object; *r* equals rationalization in terms of public interest; *P* equals the
political man; and } equals transformed into.

The *p* is shared by the political man with every human being. Differentiation rises first in the displacement of affects on to public objects, and
in the molding of the life in such a way as to give an opportunity for the
expression of these affects. The non-political man may feel himself
aggrieved against a brother and against every fellow-worker with whom he
comes in contact. His mind may be taken up with personal fantasies of
love or hate for specific people, and his ideological world (his attitudes
toward the state, the church, the destiny of man) may be very poorly
elaborated. He is a fly in the meshes of his immediate environment, and
his struggles are fought in terms of the world of face-to-face reality. When
such a man displaces his affects upon a person who happens to be a
public object, this does not make him a political man. Impulsively killing
a king who happens to insult one's sister does not make a politician of the
regicide; there must be a secondary elaboration of the displacement in
terms of general interest. It is the rationalization which finally transmutes
the operation from the plane of private to the plane of public acts.
Indeed, the private motives may be entirely lost from the consciousness of

the political man, and he may succeed in achieving a high degree of objective validation for his point of view. In the "ideal" case this has gone so far that the private motives which led to the original commitment are of feeble current importance.

Upon what does the displacement and the rationalization depend? No doubt the general answer is that the selection of certain public objects depends upon the "historical" accident of the patterns offered by the personal environment of the individual at critical phases of growth. It is safe to predict that more politicians rise from families with political traditions than without them. But this very broad conclusion requires no technique of intensive investigation of individual instances to support it. If the psychopathological approach to the individual is worth the trouble, it must disclose a variety of relatively novel circumstances which dispose individuals to adopt, reject, or modify the patterns of act and phrase which are offered in the environment. Provisionally, we may assume that the puberty phase of biological growth, which coincides with increasing social demands, may be the period in which the attitudes toward the invisible environment most rapidly crystallize.

NOTE

1. *Beyond the Pleasure Principle.*

8

ALEXANDER L. GEORGE

Power as a Compensatory Value

SOME years ago, Harold D. Lasswell drew upon the findings of theories of various schools of dynamic psychology in formulating a general hypothesis about the "power seeker" as a person who "pursues power as a means of compensation against deprivation. *Power is expected to overcome low estimates of the self,* by changing either the traits of the self or the environment in which it functions" (Lasswell 1948, 39 and 53 [italics in the original]). The pervasiveness of power strivings as compensation for organic or imagined defects was given early emphasis by Alfred Adler. The fruitfulness of Adler's theories for subsequent social psychological approaches to personality is now widely recognized (Murphy 1947, ch. 24, "Compensation for Inferiority").

LASSWELL'S POWER SEEKER

Lasswell deliberately formulated the hypothesis about the "power seeker" in such general terms in order to encompass a great variety of more detailed findings and hypotheses about such matters. As a result, his hypothesis provides a relatively "shallow" account of the origins of a need for power, forgoing explanations having greater depth. There are resulting advantages, however, that should not be minimized. The hypothesis provides an alternative explanation of the need for power in terms (i.e., compensation for low self-estimates) that are easier to establish than a more detailed account of its earlier and deeper origins. The problems of interest to the political scientist generally do not require the same level of

From the *Journal of Social Issues* 24, no. 3 (July 1968): 29–49. Reprinted by permission of the Society for the Psychological Study of Social Issues.

explanation in matters of this kind that the psychoanalyst is interested in. Moreover, the political scientist lacks the data, observational opportunities and diagnostic skills for making fuller in-depth reconstructions. Under these circumstances, attempts to do so are likely to be difficult, frustrating and unduly speculative—as well as often being unnecessary.

By linking the emergence of an individual's high valuation of, or need for power to low self-estimates, Lasswell's hypothesis usefully orients research on "power-oriented" political leaders to findings emerging from research on childhood development and socialization and to ego psychology. Attention is directed to the development of the "self" component of the ego, beliefs about the self, the extent and quality of self-esteem and its implications for behavior. In this context, attention is also directed to the emergence of the individual's personal values. Thus, the hypothesis holds that some individuals develop an unusually strong need or striving for power (and/or for other personal values such as affection, deference, rectitude) as a means of seeking compensation for damaged or inadequate self-esteem. Personal "values" or needs of this kind—which may be regarded as "ego motives" since they are part of the ego subsystem of the personality—are an important part of the individual's motivational structure. The operation of these "values" in the individual's behavior can be related not merely to deeper unconscious motives but also to the sphere of the "autonomous" functioning of the ego. In addition to utilizing various devices for dealing with unconscious motives (the classical ego defenses), the ego is also capable of employing various adjustive and constructive strategies in efforts to secure satisfaction for personal "values" such as the need for power, affection, deference, etc., thereby maintaining personality equilibrium. The emergence of these adjustive and constructive strategies, and their operation in the individual's choice, definition and performance of political roles constitute a useful focus for studying the interaction of personality and political behavior in political leaders.

The "shallowness" of Lasswell's hypothesis—i.e., the fact that it refers only to that layer of unconscious needs present in the ego self-system (i.e., the personal "values" referred to), does not rule out the possibility of exploring deeper levels of motivation and psychodynamic processes. Rather, far from cutting off this possibility, assessment of an individual's personal needs or values can provide a useful stepping stone to efforts to probe deeper, more complex dimensions of motivational structure and dynamics. Inferences can be made from the strength and operation of these personal needs to deeper levels of motivation. Psycho-analytic and related theories provide hypotheses linking personal needs that are part of the ego's self-system with the arcane recesses of motivation and its psychodynamics. These "ego motives" also have a linkage with psychogenetic, developmental hypotheses: many hypotheses of this kind are available concerning the origins of damaged self-esteem which, in turn, creates strong needs for power or other values.[1]

Another merit of Lasswell's general hypothesis about the "power-seeker," or *homo politicus*, is that it encourages the political scientist to move beyond the question of the detailed psychogenetic origins of the need for power to focus on fuller study of the development of the power seeker's interest in politics. How does the individual who emerges from childhood and into adolescence with this kind of subjective need for power go about developing a knowledge of politics, selecting one or another political role, acquiring relevant political skills, creating or utilizing opportunities to become a leader of organized groups? There are central questions concerning the socialization of political leaders, and they have important linkages with the emphasis in Lasswell's hypothesis on the compensatory character of some leaders' interest in power.

LASSWELL'S HYPOTHESIS IN POLITICAL BIOGRAPHY . . .

This paper attempts to broaden the theoretical framework of Lasswell's general hypothesis and suggests a method for employing it in research on political leaders. It is hoped that this will encourage those who want to use Lasswell's hypothesis in psychological biography to pay greater attention to data requirements implicit in the hypothesis and to employ more explicit standards of inference in such studies.

Additional research in this direction seems highly desirable. While it is by no means the case that all political leaders are "power seekers," those whose interest in politics is of the kind postulated in Lasswell's hypothesis are of particular interest to political scientists and historians. As in the case of Woodrow Wilson, political personalities of this kind often emerge as reformers and innovators if successful in obtaining political office. Once in power, they often attempt to recast political institutions, reinterpret and expand the functions of existing political roles or create new ones which fit their needs, political style and aspirations. A better understanding of this kind of political personality, therefore, may throw light on the nature of psychodynamics of "role-determining" as against "role-determined" political leadership. Of course, the creation or reinterpretation of leadership roles can only be understood in the context of social-historical dynamics and the institutional setting. However, as

Gerth and Mills observe (1953, ch. 14, "The Sociology of Leadership"), the "great leader" has often been a man who successfully managed such institutional dynamics and created new roles of leadership.

Lasswell's general hypothesis has had some influence on subsequent studies of political leadership and political behavior more generally (Barber 1965; Edinger 1965; Hargrove 1966; Lane 1959). Some years ago I found it particularly valuable for understanding the development of Woodrow Wilson's interest in political power and some of the dynamics of his political behavior. In the belief that Lasswell's hypothesis is of wider application in the study of political leadership, I will try to show how it can be utilized in a relatively systematic manner for purposes of data collection and data interpretation. This requires that meaningful operational definitions be given to the key terms in the hypothesis: "low self-estimates," "power," "compensation." I will indicate some of the problems encountered in doing so, present a set of provisional operational definitions, and illustrate their application with materials available to the biographer on Woodrow Wilson. [2]

LOW SELF-ESTEEM

Let us begin with that portion of the hypothesis that postulates the presence of low self-estimates in the subject of study. Many life experiences can produce damaged self-esteem in the basic personality. We need not delve deeply here into the question of the psychogensis of low self-estimates, either generally or for a specific person or the origins of other related personality dynamisms. [3]

For our purposes an answer to the causal question—on which there are a variety of theories—is not essential; we can draw upon and utilize descriptions of the dynamics of such behavior, about which there tends to be less disagreement in the literature of dynamic psychology. Whatever creates a given personality dynamism in a particular individual, such as low self-estimates, it is the presence of that dynamism itself that is directly relevant to most of the questions we want to ask about his interest in leadership, his behavior in seeking political office and his performance in office.

The existence and operation of a dynamism such as low self-estimates often can be readily identified in the kinds of historical materials about a political leader (or aspirant to leadership) that are usually available to biographers. In addition, materials of this kind can sometimes be elicited by the investigator from the subject himself or from others who have known him.[4]

THE CASE OF WILSON

In Wilson's case, the importance of childhood experiences in this respect is richly suggested in materials collected by the official biographer (Baker 1927). These suggest that some of the critical experiences leading to damaged self-esteem lay in the character of Wilson's relations with his father, a Presbyterian minister.

Dr. Joseph Wilson, a man of handsome and distinguished appearance, was an accomplished preacher. He was also a strict disciplinarian. He placed on young "Tommy," his first son, the burden of living up to his very high expectations for moral and intellectual attainments. Dr. Wilson undertook to supervise the boy's early schooling. A harder taskmaster it would be difficult to find. To illustrate: Dr. Wilson, who had at one time been a professor of rhetoric, had a passion for the correct use of the English language. "Tommy" was not permitted the use of an incorrect word or an unpolished phrase. His compositions had to be rewritten, sometimes four or five times, before the elder Wilson was satisfied. This instruction, continued over a period of years, was of the most intensive, exacting kind and demanded severe and conscientious application.

The father dealt with his son's imperfections with that caustic wit for which he was noted among all who knew him. In this tension-producing situation the child never openly rebelled. It is significant, however, that he was slow in achieving the usual intellectual skills. He did not learn his letters until he was nine. He could not read until he was eleven.[5]

"Low self-estimates" can be given detailed operational content for purposes of data collection by specifying some of the subjective feelings of which it may be comprised. For example: (a) feelings of unimportance; (b) feelings of moral inferiority; (c) feelings of weakness; (d) feelings of mediocrity; (e) feelings of intellectual inadequacy. Many of these, and others, were present in Wilson;s case. He felt eternally inferior to his father, in appearance as well as in accomplishment. His own recollections of his youth indicate early fears that he was stupid, ugly, worthless and unlovable. These feelings apparently had rich opportunities for elaboration in his religious convictions concerning the fundamental wickedness of human nature. Data on subjective feelings of this kind, of course, may not always be available to the investigator. It would be useful, therefore, to supplement this operational definition of low self-estimates with items of behavior that are perhaps more easily observed.

THE POWER MOTIVE

We turn now to the term "power" in Lasswell's general hypothesis. Several difficulties arise in attempting to give it a relevant operational definition. We must remind ourselves that "power" here is a value or need for the possession or exercise of sanctions or the means for influencing others. Accordingly, we do not seek to define "power" in order to measure objectively its presence or use. Rather, we define "power need" as the desire for the enjoyment of power, the high valuation or cathexis of power. And we want to find ways of identifying the presence of such a power need.

The character and content of an individual's "power" motive may be shaped by the conditions that gave rise to low self-estimates and its accompanying psychodynamics. One possibility is that the ensuing demand for power may be reactive-formative against the fear of passivity, of weakness, of being dominated. Another possibility is that the demand for power may be aggressive or destructive. Power, then, may be desired for various reasons in different power-demanding persons and perhaps at different times in the same individual. That is, power may be desired for one or more of these reasons: (a) so as to dominate and/or deprive others; (b) so as not to be dominated, or interfered with, by other political actors; (c) so as to produce political achievements. (It may be useful on future occasions to specify additional variants of the power need, or to restate these differently.)

As the third of these possible components of a "power need" implies, it may be *instrumental* at times rather than primary in persons who seek compensation thereby. Thus power may be desired and exercised in order to satisfy other personal needs, such as a need for achievement, for respect, for security, for rectitude. In some instances, one of the components of a power motive we have postulated—the desire not to be dominated by others—may seem to be an end in itself, more highly valued than other needs. In other cases, the desire for, pursuit and exercise of power may be clearly or predominantly instrumental for gaining satisfaction of other needs and values.

Two other conclusions about the status of the "power" motive have emerged from our effort to apply Lasswell's general hypothesis to Wilson. First, the demand or need for "power" in compensation-seeking political types does not operate uniformly in the subject's political motivation under all conditions. Rather, the presence and/or strength of the "power demand" (or of some components of it) in the individual's motivation varies, being subject to special arousal conditions (see below, pp. 81–82). A second conclusion is that an individual's striving for "power" in the context of compensation may either be reinforced by, or in conflict with other strong needs—such as the need for affection, approval, respect, achievement, rectitude, etc. —that he may also be pursuing in the political arena.

In the case of a *multi*-valued political personality like Wilson, it is a complex task to establish the underlying motivational structure of different needs, and especially, to gauge the shifting interrelationship and priority of these needs. In attempting to determine the role of personality in the subject's political behavior it becomes necessary, therefore, to assess not merely the relative strength of individual needs or motives in the personality system generally but, more important, the ways in which the subject reconciles competing or conflicting needs in choosing his goals, and the conditions under which one or another need or pattern of needs has primacy in his behavior. For the importance and operative role of different needs in specific situations depends not only on their relative strength but may vary with the subject's shifting expectations as to the possibility of satisfying them in each situation. As the above suggests, I recognize that damaged self-esteem can create unusually strong needs for several values, not merely for power or another single value. In Wilson's case, we inferred a strong need also for affection, respect, rectitude and enlightenment. The interrelationship of these strong, at times competing values in Wilson's motivation and political behavior is depicted in *Woodrow Wilson and Colonel House* (George and George 1956; for a brief summary see 319–22). I should add that in my initial study of Wilson (unpublished paper, 1941), I attempted to estimate from available historical data Wilson's high or low demand for most of the eight values Harold Lasswell has listed and described on a number of occasions. . . . I do indeed agree with his emphasis on the importance of characterizing the subject's position with respect to all eight values. In the present paper, however, I have focused more narrowly than in the full-length study on the need for power and the problems of operationalizing it.

POWER-STRIVING FOR COMPENSATION

Let us turn now to the compensatory process mentioned in Lasswell's formulation about the "power-seeking" type. If this hypothesis is correct and applicable to political leaders like Wilson, we would expect that in acquiring and exercising power the subject experiences not merely reduction of tension but also euphoric feelings of a kind that serve to counter some of the low self-estimates from which he suffers. The problem of establishing and tracing such a compensatory process empirically requires close examination of the relationship between (a) low self-estimates, (b) specific items of behavior that express the individual's power demand and satisfy it to some extent, and (c) the substantive content of the ensuing compensatory gratifications, if any. In this respect, however, it is well to heed to the warning of clinical psychologists who have observed that uniform regularities cannot be expected between particular items of manifest behavior and their tension-reducing, equilibrium-restoring functions for the personality. The complexity of the dynamics of behavior in this respect adds to the difficulty of devising operational indicators of manifest behavior that can be taken as giving expression to the demand for "power" in persons striving thereby for compensation. For, evidently, the same item of manifest behavior may fulfill different functions for different personalities and, at different times, for the same individual.

We must be satisfied for the time being, therefore, with cataloguing various items of political behavior that may or may not express an individual's striving to gratify one or another component of his power need. In constructing such a catalogue we have drawn upon the syndrome of behavior associated with the so-called "compulsive" character in Freudian psychoanalytic accounts (Freud 1950, 45–50; and Fenichel 1945, 278–84). We list six items of behavior that serve as possible indicators of a striving for power gratification on the part of a compensation-seeking personality:

- *Unwillingness to permit others to share* in his actual or assumed field of power.[6]
- *Unwillingness to take advice* regarding his proper functioning in his actual or assumed field of power.
- *Unwillingness to delegate* to others tasks that are believed to belong to his regularly constituted field of power.
- *Unwillingness to consult* with others, who have a claim to share power, regarding his functioning in the actual or assumed field of power.
- *Unwillingness to inform* others with respect to his functioning in his actual or assumed field of power.
- *Desire to devise and impose orderly systems* upon others in the political arena.

Before leaving this topic, we remind ourselves that these items are only *possible* indicators of a power need in the personality. Depending on the context, behavior of this kind may serve other functions for the personality as well as its power need; or it may be entirely divorced from the individual's striving for power gratification.

Occurrences of these items of behavior in the leader's political activity may indeed be solely role-determined, being called for by his assessment of the way in which role expectations should be interpreted in the light of the requirements of the situation. On the other hand, personality needs may reinforce or conflict with role requirements and may either improve or distort his assessment of the situation and his choice of action alternatives.

In more general terms we are asserting the possibility that personality needs and motives of an unconscious character may influence an individual's *selection* and *definition* of political roles for himself; further, these needs may infuse themselves into his *performance* of these roles and help account either for unusually skillful or inexpedient behavior on behalf of the policy objectives to which he has ostensibly committed himself in the political arena. The fact that a person's behavior *can* be interpreted in terms of role demands, therefore, does not relieve the investigator from considering the possibility that aspects of basic personality are also expressing themselves and shaping such behavior. It is incorrect, therefore, to define the problem as some proponents of role theory tend to do in terms of "role versus personality." Rather, the interplay of role and personality needs to be considered.[7]

THE PRESENCE OF CONFLICTING EVIDENCE

There are many striking instances of these six items of behavior in Wilson's career. But, at the same time, there are also numerous examples and testimonials to the fact that in exercising the powers of his office Wilson did consult and inform others, took advice and delegated authority. Faced with apparently conflicting evidence of this kind, we found it fruitful to examine the behavior in question more closely. We found that different observers reporting on this aspect of his political behavior seemed to mean different things when asserting that he did or did not "consult." Some of the disagreement among observers on this score could be reduced to a language problem—that is, the absence of a rigorous standard language used scrupulously by all observers reporting on his behavior. (This can be dealt with by defining terms like "consultation" more precisely and translating reports by participant observers accordingly.)

The apparently conflicting evidence was reconciled also by analyzing the *conditions* under which Wilson did and did not consult, etc. This led to the formulation of a more selective statement of Lasswell's general hypothesis that has already been implied by including the phrase "in his actual or assumed field of power" in listing above the possible behavioral indicators of a power need. Let us clarify the phrase.

In order to overcome or compensate for low self-estimates, the power-seeking personality attempts to carve out a sphere of activity in which he can demonstrate his competence and worth. The importance of such a developmental process to a personality suffering from damaged self-esteem is obvious.[8] Achievement of competence in a given sphere of activity, however narrow or specialized it may be, provides the personality with a "field" in which it can function productively, possibly with considerable autonomy (freedom from "interference" from others), perhaps aggressively and self-righteously on occasion and more generally in a manner as to reach a personality equilibrium otherwise lacking for someone who suffers from low self-estimates.

Lasswell's general hypothesis is transformed in this way into a more selective one which helps to resolve the apparent inconsistency or contradictory behavior of the subject with regard to some of the six behavioral indicators listed above. Thus, the selective version of the hypothesis holds that manifestations of power-striving are not encountered throughout the entire range of the subject's political behavior but operate more selectively, that is, only when he is performing in his actual or assumed field of power. Even this formulation, we shall note shortly, does not sufficiently identify and restrict for a particular individual the conditions under which his power need manifests itself directly.

We may recall that Lasswell's general hypothesis about *homo politicus* confines itself to explaining a need for power in terms of compensation for low self-estimates, without venturing to push the explanation further in order to account also for the origins of low self-estimates. While the study of a power-oriented leader's career and political behavior may benefit from hypotheses as to the origins of his low self-estimates, the investigator need not feel hobbled by an inability to provide more specific, in-depth hypotheses of this kind (or to demonstrate such hypotheses). Rather, if he can demonstrate the applicability of Lasswell's general hypothesis to his subject, this should suffice by way of explaining his need for power. The investigator can then proceed to the essential, and more rewarding task of relating the subject's compensatory interest in power to his emerging expectations and orientations to the future, i.e., what he wants the state of affairs to be like in the near and more distant future, and how he proposes to help bring about these desired changes.

In Wilson's Case . . .

In Wilson's case, we find him engaged from early adolescence to early maturity in carving out or creating what we here have called a "field aim" and a "sphere of competence." An interest in politics manifested itself early. In his fourteenth year, Wilson organized a group of boys into a club and composed a constitution for it. Two years later his political interests had become more sharply defined. We find him sitting at his desk under a picture of Gladstone. When his little cousin asked who it was, Wilson replied: "That is Gladstone, the greatest statesman that ever lived. I intend to be a statesman, too." He settled his ambition upon a political career in his sophomore year in college. Thereafter, we find him defining his political ambition in terms of available political roles and striving to acquire knowledge and skills relevant to successful perform- ance of the preferred political roles selected for himself. Thus, in his sophomore year at Princeton, Wilson read a series of articles on the relationship between oratory and political leadership. These articles, the official biographer notes, were "the precipitate that clarified the mind of the eager youth. They discovered to him the field which he loved. They made him suddenly aware of his own powers. . . . *He* could debate, he could lead"! Wilson sat down at once to write his father that he had discovered he had a mind. It is clear that oratory recommended itself to him as a means of achieving influence and control over others. At the close of his sophomore year, he wrote an article for the *Princetonian* which reveals his own ambitions: "What is the object of oratory? Its object is persuasion and conviction—the control of other minds by a strange personal influence and power."

Even before he became a teacher, Wilson had a clear idea of the use to which he would put his talent for oratory and a clear conception of the political role which he wished to play, should the opportunity arise. After the publication of his first book, *Congressional Government*, in 1885, he wrote his fiancée confessing that his heart's first ambition lay elsewhere:

> . . . I have a strong instinct of leadership, an unmistakably oratorical tempera- ment, and the keenest possible delight in affairs; and it has required very

constant and stringent schooling to content me with the sober methods of the scholar and the man of letters. I have no patience for the tedious toil of what is known as 'research'; *I have a passion for interpreting great thoughts to the world; I should be complete if I could inspire a great movement of opinion*, if I could read the experiences of the past into the practical life of the men of today and so communicate the thought to the minds of the great mass of the people as to impel them to great political achievements. . . . My feeling has been . . . that *my power to write was meant to be a handmaiden to my power to speak and to organize action*. . . . (Italics supplied)[9]

When Wilson Consulted . . .

Even within his "actual or assumed field of power" a leader who pursues power as a compensatory value does not invariably refuse to consult and take advice, to inform others and to delegate, etc. I will briefly summarize some of the more discriminating observations regarding Wilson's willingness or unwillingness to permit others to share in the powers of his office that emerged from an analysis of the conditions in which he acted one way or the other: (a) He typically consulted more readily in order to obtain facts rather than opinions; (b) he consulted and took advice more readily from those whose approval and affection he could count on;[10] (c) he could delegate power in matters in which he was little interested, matters which did not engage his aspiration for great achievement.[11]

When Wilson Cooperated . . .

Wilson's expressed willingness to consult and cooperate with legislators was always a complicated matter. We found it necessary to distinguish two types of situations in analyzing Wilson's relationship with legislative bodies.

First, as long as the possibility existed of getting what he wanted from the legislature, Wilson could operate with considerable skill in order to mobilize potential support. He could be, as in the first year of the Governorship and in the "honeymoon" period of the Presidency, extremely cordial, if firm; gracious, if determined; and generally willing to go through the motions of consulting and granting deference to legislators whose support he needed. It is this phase of his "party leadership" that excited the admiration of contemporaries and historians alike. However, these skillful tactics of leadership were predicated on the expectation that he would be able to push through his proposed legislation in essentially unadulterated form. As Wilson often put it, he was willing to accept alterations of "detail," but not of the "principles" of his legislative proposals.

Second, once opposition crystallized sufficiently to threaten the defeat or marked alteration of his legislative proposals, Wilson was faced with a different type of situation. Skillful political behavior—the logic of the situation—now demanded genuine consultation with opponents to explore the basis of disagreement and to arrive at mutual concessions, bargains and formulas to assure passage of needed legislation. In this type of situation Wilson was unable to function expediently and proved singularly gauche as a politician. Once faced with strong opposition to a legislative proposal to which he had committed his leadership aspirations, Wilson became rigidly stubborn and tried to force through his proposal without compromising it.

In these situations, the desire to succeed in achieving a worthwhile political objective, in part or in essence if not fully and exactly as he preferred, became of less importance than to maintain the equilibrium of his personality system. He seems to have experienced opposition to his will in such situations as an unbearable threat to his self-esteem. The ensuing struggle for his self-esteem led, on the political level, to stubborn self-defeating behavior on his part. For to compromise in such situations was to submit to domination in the very sphere of power which he had carved out for himself to repair his damaged self-esteem. Opposition to his will, therefore, set into motion disruptive anxieties and brought to the surface long-smouldering aggressive feelings which, as a child, he had not dared to express.

Thus, for example, when the possibility of rejection of the Treaty by the Senate was mentioned to him, Wilson snapped: "Anyone who opposes me in that, I'll crush"! When the French Ambassador told Wilson that the Allies would be glad to accept American membership in the League even with a set of reservations that would satisfy influential Republican Senators, Wilson curtly replied: "Mr. Ambassador, I shall consent to nothing. The Senate must take its medicine." When the acting Senate Democratic minority leader, Hitchcock, suggested concessions to win over enough Republican Senators, Wilson replied: "Let Lodge hold out the olive branch." Earlier, upon returning from the Paris Peace Conference in February 1919 Wilson publicly announced his determination to strike back at Senatorial critics of the Treaty: "I have fighting blood in me," he boasted, "and it is sometimes a delight to let it have scope . . ." (George and George 1956, 235, 289, 301, 311).

We have noted a cyclical pattern of this kind in Wilson's career, a repetition of this maladaptive self-defeating behavior as President of Princeton, Governor of New Jersey and as President of the United States. This was not an area in which he was able to learn from his earlier difficulties and failures, a fact which testifies indirectly to the presence and operation of strong unconscious motives.

EVIDENCE OF COMPENSATION

Let us take up now another problem encountered in attempting to make relatively systematic applications of Lasswell's general hypothesis. The hypothesis requires evidence that the exercise of power over others does indeed yield the individual compensatory gratifications. For the hypothesis to hold, and to be applicable to a given individual, it is not sufficient that he find it generally pleasant to exercise power; its exercise must provide him with satisfactions of a special kind appropriate to his low self-estimates.

The prospect for obtaining systematic evidence of subjective feelings of this kind from materials conventionally available to the biographer or to the student of political leadership must be viewed soberly. Yet, even episodic and fragmentary evidence of this kind—and perhaps that is all that can be realistically expected—will serve to give insight into the compensatory dynamics of the subject's involvement in various areas of his political behavior.

The next step in operationalizing the general hypothesis is to formulate a catalogue, however tentative or incomplete, of the *types of euphoric feelings* a personality of this kind might be expected to experience if, indeed, the hypothesis is correct regarding the compensatory character of his interest in power.

A first approximation of this kind was derived from psychoanalytic literature in which several types of euphoric feelings associated with power-striving and gratification are described. The listing of these feelings was then elaborated and structured more systematically by identifying the logical counterparts to the low self-estimates identified and listed above. From this emerged the following list of five low self-estimates and the corresponding euphoric feelngs to be expected in cases when power was exercised in a manner that the subject could represent to himself as being successful:

Low Estimates of Self	*Euphoric Feeling*
	(from successful functioning in actual or assumed sphere or power)
Feelings of unimportance:	*Sense of uniqueness*, the subjective experiencing of which may be paraphrased as follows: "If what should be done is to be accomplished, I must do it since no one else will undertake it or is in a position to do it." (Note the realtion to the feeling that one is the "chosen instrument," the feeling of being "indispensable" for a certain task, the feeling of having a "mission.")
Feelings of moral inferiority:	*Sense of superior virtue:* "I know best what is right (moral) in this matter."
Feelings of weakness:	*Sense of superior strength:* "No one can tell *me* what to do in this sphere; others, not I, must yield."
Feelings of Mediocrity:	*Sense of superior ability:* "No one else can do this (whatever the subject is doing in his field of power) so well."
Feelings of intellectual inadequacy:	*Sense of intellectual superiority* (in sphere of competence and power functioning): "My judgment is infallible; I never make mistakes; I can rely upon my own reasoning."

Wilson's Euphoric Feelings . . .

We did not expect that euphoric feelings of the kind listed above would be explicitly and fully articulated very often in the kinds of historical materials available for the study. Perhaps the most that could be expected were occasional hints or expressions of such feelings. In the end, however, a surprising amount of relevant data of this kind was turned up indicating that Wilson had experienced many of these euphoric feelings from the exercise of his power. Some of this material has already been presented. A few additional examples of the kind of historical material we have regarded as evidence in this respect will be cited here.

After rewriting the constitution of the Johns Hopkins debating society, thereby transforming it into a "House of Commons," Wilson reported to his fiancée the great pleasure he had derived from the project: "It is characteristic of my whole self that I take so much pleasure in these proceedings of this society. . . . I have a sense of power in dealing with men collectively which I do not feel always in dealing with them singly." Indeed, all his life long, Wilson was rewriting constitutions, deriving satisfaction from reordering the relations of men along what he considered to be more fruitful lines. That constitution-writing had a deep personal meaning for Wilson is further suggested by the fact that such activities were always also instrumental to his desire to exercise strong leadership.

As a youth, he revamped the constitution of every club and organization to which he belonged in order to transform it into a miniature House of Commons. Indeed, he often renamed it thus. In these model Houses of Common in which Wilson, as the outstanding debater, usually became Prime Minister, independent leadership was possible and the orator could make his will prevail. Thus, rewriting constitutions was for Wilson a means of restructuring those institutional environments in which he wanted to exercise strong leadership by means of oratory, a skill in which he was already adept as an adolescent and to the perfection of which he assiduously labored for years. From an early age Wilson's scholarly interest in the workings of American political institutions was an adjunct of his ambition to become a great statesman.

When Wilson's career is studied from this standpoint considerable light is thrown on the intriguing question of the role of personal motivations in political inventiveness and creativity (George and George 1956, 144–48, 321–22). Political psychologists have hypothesized that a compulsive interest in order and power is often to be found in strong political leaders who were great institution-builders and who made it their task to transform society. The case study of Wilson lends support to this hypothesis.[12]

When Carving Out a Sphere of Competence . . .

The process of carving out a sphere of competence, already referred to, is marked by a tendency to shift from one extreme of subjective feelings to the other: that is, from lack of self-confidence to high self-estimates and self-assurance in the actual or assumed field of power.

Wilson could establish a sphere of competence for himself only by meeting very high standards. He went through painstaking, conscientious study and practice in order to acquire the necessary knowledge and skills, and in order to legitimize in his own eyes his right to a sphere of competence in which to function autonomously and as a leader of other men. But once having established it, he could not permit himself or others to question it. Within this sphere of competence, he felt free—almost defiantly—to assert a sense of intellectual superiority.

One of his friends, Mrs. Edith G. Reid, cites a letter he wrote at the age of thirty to a former classmate:

> Hiram, I have—as I hope you have not discovered, but as you doubtless have—an intellectual selfconfidence, possibly out of all proportion to my intellectual strength, which has made me feel that in matters in which I have qualified myself to speak I could never be any man's follower. . . .

To this Mrs. Reid comments:

> Such confidence in himself might at this time seem merely youth's bravado, but it was part of the essence of his nature—the quality which made people so often exclaim, "Do you never think yourself wrong"? And the answer would always be the same. "Not in matters where I have qualified myself to speak."

This type of see-saw process, from great uncertainty to extreme certainty, can be noted not only in Wilson's development but also in his decision process in specific situations. Many of his decisions reflect the characteristics of the compulsively conscientious person who passes from pronounced subjective doubt to extreme subjective certainty. Once Wilson emerged with a decision on an issue, especially one which mobilized his aspirations for high achievement, his mind snapped shut. He felt his decision was the only possible one morally as well as intellectually. Having conscientiously put himself through a laborious examination of relevant facts, he categorically identified his view of the matter with righteousness and would not permit himself or anyone else to question it. Thus, a dogmatic insistence on a particular viewpoint frequently followed a protracted period of indecision on the question. Once he had evolved his own position, he was typically impatient of any delay on the part of others, even those who might still be committed to ideas which he himself only shortly before had held with equal tenacity.

For years, for example, he opposed federal action to establish women's suffrage. When at last, during the war, he was converted to the cause, he began at once to deride Senators who did not instantly respond to his plea that the Senate concur in a constitutional amendment to enfranchise women:

> "When my conversion to this idea came," he told a group of suffragettes on October 3, 1918, "it came with an overwhelming command that made it necessary that I should omit nothing and use the position I occupied to enforce it, if I could possibly do so. I pride myself on only one feature of it, that I did understand when circumstances instructed me. There are some men who, I am sorry to say, have recently illustrated the fact that they would not learn. Their minds are provincial. They do not know a great influence when it is abroad. . . . . I have to restrain myself sometimes from intellectual contempt.

Unfortunately, this was a typical attitude, often openly expressed, toward those who also shared in the power of decision and who disagreed with him.

Again, after a period of agonized uncertainty about whether or not to lead the nation into World War I, he convinced himself of its necessity and ever afterwards vehemently denounced those whose doubts persisted. For, as he wrote Arthur Brisbane on September 4, 1917, the issues had assumed in his mind "a great simplicity" (George and George 1956, 120–21).

In Conclusion . . .

The provisional operationalization of the key terms in Lasswell's hypothesis that has been presented and illustrated in this paper with reference to Wilson may have to be revised or supplemented if other leaders are also studied in some detail. Hopefully, these operational definitions and lists of possible indicators will be useful even for those leaders who, as I would expect, express their power need in ways different from Wilson's. From this standpoint, the question is: Are the operational definitions sufficiently general and comprehensive to permit somewhat different findings for different leaders, i.e., different results expressed within the framework of a standardized set of operational definitions of "low self-estimates," "power need," "power striving," "compensation"?

It will be seen that I distinguish between the question of the "generality" of the operational definitions (which I hope can be obtained) and the question of the "generality" or uniformity of the *behavioral manifestations* of power-as-a-compensatory value (where I expect to find interesting variations among different leaders who fall under Lasswell's general hypothesis about the power-seeker but possess different kinds of multi-valued personalities and/or operate in different political contexts).

Another problem can be anticipated if Lasswell's hypothesis is applied to a larger sample of political leaders. This concerns the matter of the observational approach the investigator needs to take in order to establish whether adult political leaders who apparently possess high self-esteem suffered earlier in life from low self-estimates and, hence, whether their self-esteem is importantly "compensatory." To employ or test Lasswell's hypothesis does require a *developmental* study of the individual. Cross-sectional observations and measurements of the self-esteem status of an adult political leader may, if of a superficial character, fail to turn up indicators of the earlier low self-estimates problem experienced by the personality; hence, that individual may be incorrectly placed outside of Lasswell's hypothesis.

Operationalization of Lasswell's general hypothesis is, in any case, necessary if it is to be applied systematically in empirical research on political personality and behavior. These operational definitions must be valid, of course, from the standpoint of the findings and theory of dynamic psychology; but at the same time, they have been selected and formulated so as to provide links to the kind of empirical data about political behavior that is available to political scientists.

We are, as a result, in a better position to organize collection of relevant and critical data for application and assessment of the hypothesis. If these operational definitions are adequate and defensible, they provide specific links to relevant empirical data that is already available about the subject or that, possibly, can be acquired from him or from others who know him. The presence of behavioral data of this kind, properly analyzed and interpreted, provides a demonstrable basis for inferring the applicability of the general hypothesis to the political personality of the subject in question—i.e., his interest in power as a means of compensation for low self-estimates—and, of course, for additional analysis of the role this dynamism plays in his political behavior: in his choice of political roles, the character and skillfulness of his performance of those roles. Conversely, the absence of such behavioral data on low self-estimates, on a subjective interest in power, and on compensatory gratifications from its exercise can be taken as an empirical basis for rejecting the applicability of the general hypothesis to a given political leader.

The effort to apply Lasswell's hypothesis to Woodrow Wilson, it should be noted, led to the formulation of a more selective version of the hypothesis, one which identified the special conditions under which the kind of personal need for power postulated by the hypothesis was present in Wilson's political behavior. This highlights the importance in such studies of identifying the "field of power" within which the individual will strive for compensation and the types of situations in which the individual's power need will be aroused.

If we may generalize provisionally from this one case, the demand or need for power in compensation-seeking personalities does not operate uniformly in the individual's political motivation under all conditions. The presence or strength of the power demand (or of some components of it) may be expected to vary, being subject to special arousal conditions. Finally, our study calls attention to the fact that *homo politicus* is likely to be a multi-valued personality; his striving for power as compensation may be reinforced by, or conflict with strong personal needs for other values that he may also pursue in the political arena. It is a complex but necessary task to establish not only general motivational patterns in multivalued leaders but also the conditions under which one or another need or pattern of needs has primacy in the subject's political behavior.

NOTES

This article draws on an unpublished paper given together with Juliette L. George at the annual meeting of the American Political Science Association in September 1956. Opportunity for additional research was provided by a research grant from the Foundations' Fund for Research in Psychiatry whose support is gratefully acknowledged.

1. I plan to develop these observations more fully in work in progress.

2. I will necessarily have to be selective in citing illustrative materials from Woodrow Wilson's career. Fuller documentation will be found in *Woodrow Wilson and Colonel House* (George and George 1956, particularly 114–21). In preparing the biography, published in 1956, we learned of the existence of the Freud-Bullitt study of Wilson but it was unavailable to us.

3. In 1948 Lasswell drew upon studies of personality development available at that time to present a generalized account of the causal conditions and psychodynamic processes whereby extreme cravings for power, respect and related deference values or needs come into being (Lasswell 1948, 44–54). It may be noted that Lasswell's earlier treatment of this question is quite compatible with Erik Erikson's more recent and somewhat more specific tracing of the origins of such personality dynamisms to special characteristics of

the child's conflict relationship with his father and the way in which it is eventually resolved. In this respect, Erikson (1964, 202–03) finds important common features in the childhood and adolescent development experiences of a number of reformers and innovators who have been studied: Luther, Gandhi, Kierkegaard, Woodrow Wilson, Eleanor Roosevelt. Of particular interest to our discussion of Lasswell's general hypothesis is Erikson's observation that in their early years all of these five reformers and ideaological innovators exhibited low self-estimates, a strong conscience, precocious attention to "ultimate concerns" and a sense of responsibility for a segment of mankind. (In recent years Victor Wolfenstein [1967] has explored in detail and on a comparative basis the question of psychogenetic origins in developing a model of the revolutionary personality.)

4. Lewis Edinger (1965, 275–81) reports that he found useful for structuring his interviews and search for data on Kurt Schumacher the earlier version of the operational definition of this hypothesis presented in our unpublished 1956 paper.

5. For a fuller account of this and other materials on Wilson, see George and George 1956, chap. 1, which also indicates some of the father's positive contributions to the development of his son.

6. What is meant by "actual or assumed field of power" will be clarified shortly.

7. A particularly useful statement of this is provided by Daniel J. Levinson (1959). A fuller discussion of these points with reference to Wilson's interest in writing constitutions (interpreted as manifesting and satisfying a desire to devise and impose orderly systems on others) appears in my unpublished paper (1960).

8. The present discussion of "compensation" as emerging from a developmental process in which the individual suffering from low self-estimates carves out a "sphere of competence" and a "field of power" can be usefully related to Erik Erikson's concept of the adolescent identity crisis. The fruitfulness of a synthesis of Lasswell's hypothesis about power as compensatory for low self-estimates with Erickson's model of adolescent identity crisis is demonstrated, I believe for the first time, in James D. Barber, "Classifying and Predicting Presidential Styles: Two 'Weak' Presidents," *Journal of Social Issues* 24, no. 3 (July 1968): 51–80.

Among ego psychologists, Robert W. White (1963) has particularly emphasized the importance of the emergence in the individual of a sense of competency and efficacy.

9. For documentation and elaboration see George and George 1956, 23.

10. Persons like Senator Glass, Joseph Tumulty (his secretary), and especially Colonel House could serve Wilson as advisers either because they would not push their disagreements with him once they saw that his mind was made up, or because they were so deferential to him that they would accept his point of view when he finally formulated a position.

11. Thus the official biographer, Baker (1927), could correctly observe that it was difficult for Wilson to delegate authority, "especially in matters which profoundly engaged his interest or awakened his emotions." And at the same time, Josephus Daniels, Wilson's Secretary of the Navy, could remark also with justice that "From the inception Mr. Wilson gave the members of his Cabinet free rein in the management of the affairs of their department. No President refrained so much from hampering them by naming their subordinates. Holding them responsible, he gave them liberty, confidence and cooperation."

12. It should be noted, as James D. Barber has emphasized (1965, and in a personal communication), that political institutions also "compensate." In order to survive and to

act, institutions also develop adaptive strategies and ways of handling conflict. It is the interplay of these institutional adaptive strategies and habits with those of individual incumbents that has important implications for the stability and effectiveness of government.

REFERENCES

Baker, Ray Stannard. *Woodrow Wilson: Life and Letters*. Vol. I. New York: Doubleday, Page and Co., 1927.

Barber, James D. *The Lawmakers*. New Haven and London: Yale University Press, 1965.

Edinger, Lewis J. *Kurt Schumacher: A Study in Personality and Political Behavior.* Stanford and London: Stanford University Press and Oxford University Press, 1965.

Erikson, Erik H. *Insight and Responsibility*. New York: W. W. Norton, 1964,

George, Alexander L. "Some Uses of Dynamic Psychology in Political Biography." Unpublished paper, 1960.

George, Alexander L., and George, Juliette L. *Woodrow Wilson and Colonel House: A Personality Study*. New York: John Day, 1956. (Paperback edition with new preface, Dover Press, 1964.)

George, Alexander L., and George, Juliette L. "Woodrow Wilson: Personality and Political Behavior." Unpublished paper prepared for annual meeting of The American Political Science Association, 1956.

Lasswell, Harold D. *Power and Personality*. New York: W. W. Norton, 1948.

Levinson, Daniel J. "Role, Personality, and Social Structure in the Organizational Setting." *Journal of Abnormal and Social Psychology* 58 (1959): 170–80; reprinted in N. J. Smelser and W. T. Smelser, *Personality and Social Systems*. New York: Wiley, 1963.

White, Robert W. *Ego and Reality in Psychoanalytic Theory*. Monograph No. 11 of *Psychological Issues* 3 (3), New York: International Universities Press, 1963.

Wolfenstein, Victor. *The Revolutionary Personality*. Princeton, N.J.: Princeton University Press, 1967.

9

E. VICTOR WOLFENSTEIN

The Revolutionary Personality

W E [began] by asking the question of why a man becomes a revolutionist. In attempting to answer it, we examined the existing materials on our
three men [Lenin, Trotsky, and Gandhi] covering the period from earliest
childhood through young manhood, by which time all three had
embarked upon revolutionary activity as a vocation. Using Erikson's formulation of the stages of psycho-sexual development as a guide, the
following picture emerged. For the oral phase, when trust and mistrust
are at issue, there is no consistent pattern for revolutionists. Lenin apparently was very mistrustful from an early age, Trotsky and Gandhi seemed
to have had considerable faith in the underlying benevolence of their
environments. Thus in later life Lenin was difficult to betray, but also
pessimistic—so that, for example, in the summer of 1917 he beat a rather
too hasty retreat in the face of relatively negligible force. Trotsky, on the
other hand, was constantly surprised by antagonistic responses from others—he did not expect to be punished for school pranks or struck down
by his "enemies" for his revolutionary activity. Nor was he able to see the
world in the kill-or-be-killed terms which was a necessary component of
one's political orientation in post-Lenin Russia. During those times when
boldness and daring yielded returns, however, such as during the Revolution itself and the Civil War, his optimism allowed him to act in ways
that added greatly to his prestige and power. The contrast between Lenin
and Trotsky is clearly seen in their attitudes toward the Germans at Brest-

From E. Victor Wolfenstein, *The Revolutionary Personality: Lenin, Trotsky, Gandhi* (Princeton:
Princeton University Press, 1971), chap. 6, "Summary," pp. 303–13. Copyright © 1967 by Princeton
University Press. Reprinted with permission of Princeton University Press.

Litovsk; Trotsky felt the Germans would not attack even if a peace treaty were not signed and that if they did the results would not be disastrous. Lenin was convinced that the Germans *would* attack and that the very life of the Revolution was being endangered.

Gandhi, with a personality combining basic trust with great needs to suffer punishment, resembled Trotsky in his response to his circumstances. He expected others to react to his nonviolent provocations with restraint, although toward the end of his life expectations about the imminence of death developed. Thus in 1930 he was able to lead the Salt March, fully expecting that the British would allow him to carry on as if he were their friend; and in 1930 he was largely right. In 1942, however, when he adopted the same approach, based on the same confidence in his foes, the result was immediate arrest and failure.

For the anal phase, as for the oral, considerable variability exists for revolutionists. Lenin developed a firm sense of autonomy and of his own worth, so that in adult life he seldom found it necessary to react, to insult or to insist on personal prerogatives. Trotsky and Gandhi, by contrast, both had severe problems with shame, which they mastered in contrasting ways. During his school days Trotsky was able to develop a talent, namely an ability to manipulate the tools of intellect, which he used as a lever against those who had formerly humiliated him (such as his father and the peasants on the estate at Yanovka). It was a lever he continued to use throughout his life. With it he demonstrated to others their manifest inferiority and with it he was able to assert his right to center stage during the climax of the revolutionary drama. But it also contributed to the creation of the antipathies and jealousies which help to account for his isolation from 1905 through 1917 and his downfall after Lenin's death.

Gandhi also was plagued by great feelings of shame, but he did not find in his school work or anywhere else in his early life sufficient support for his shaky feelings of self-respect. It was not until his arrival in South Africa that he found that, in this new context, his gifts and training provided him with the kind of esteem Trotsky had been able to win as a schoolboy. By that time Gandhi had already developed too strong a feeling of lowliness to transform himself into a man of selfless confidence like Lenin or powerful arrogance like Trotsky. Instead he viewed himself as the most humble of the humble and took upon his shoulders the abuse directed against all Indians in South Africa. He escaped from his personal shame by asserting the autonomy and dignity of the lowly.

The genital phase we treated together with adolescence, for in all men, but in the present cases especially, the problems of the latter phase are the problems of the former—with complications. The intervening period is latency, in which feelings of inferiority must be warded off so that industriousness can emerge. All three men had substantial success during this period, and hence we suppose that the capacity for sublimation which is the hallmark of competent management of the Oedipal conflict is also a prerequisite of the successful revolutionist.[1] The sustained capacity for work which all three developed was to be of great value to them later on. Lenin's ability to give almost pedantic attention to the most minute details of organization, communication, and policy helped him to maintain his control of the Bolshevik Party both before and after the seizure of power; and Trotsky's sustained intellectual creativity in adulthood, which won him Lenin's respect and thus in part accounts for his position as co-leader of the party before Lenin's death, was largely a continuation of the behavior patterns of the brilliant schoolboy. Gandhi, who performed dutifully but not excitingly during latency, never relished intellectual achievement as the other two did. Where Lenin and Trotsky found a basis for superiority in this kind of activity, Gandhi found his in other areas. In the Indian context, however, intellectual prominence was not as essential an attribute of leadership as it was in the Russian, especially, in the latter case, as it was during the period of the exile to western Europe before 1917. Among the Russians one had to be an accomplished Marxist to gain the respect of others, in the Indian case there was no such universally agreed upon canon of intellectual legitimacy.

Turning then to adolescence, we found the following situation to be common to all three men. Each had an unusually ambivalent relationship with his father. In Lenin's case there was a sturdy identification with his father, combined with a residue of strained feelings resulting from his father's frequent and prolonged absences combined with his loving attention when he was with the family. Trotsky admired his father greatly and considered him to be a superior to his mother in many ways, but resented his monopolization of his mother's time and affection and was irked by his inability to emulate his father successfully in the performance of those tasks which gained respect from others at Yanovka. Moreover he had been separated from the family during latency, when he went to Odessa to school, and thus the talents which he did develop were not immediately relevant to his familial competition: his ability to write a brilliant theme did not help him to cut wheat. At the same time this separation meant that he carried with him a more infantile view of his father than did Lenin or Gandhi—and hence one more awe-inspiring and difficult to combat.

Gandhi, whose masculine self-assurance was tenuous in any case, found his emotional life enormously complicated by his early marriage. He was forced to act like a man in the most basic way when he was still unsure of what it meant—or required—to be a man. He was haunted by fears and struggling to solidify his masculinity through, for example, the eating of meat as well as through the assertion of his prerogatives vis-à-vis his wife. All three men were thus forced to come to grips with the problem of forming a masculine identity under tense and difficult circumstances.

Although perhaps without quite the same intensity, this kind of ambivalence is far from uncommon during adolescence. For it to be transformed into revolutionary energy it must be accentuated rather than diminished as adolescence progresses. In Lenin's case the successive deaths of his father and his brother, the latter indirectly at the hands of the Tsar, created a great burden of guilt—and at the same time a way out from under that load. The death of Gandhi's father at the very moment when Gandhi was in bed with his wife also radically intensified feelings of guilt and precipitated a flight from India and his family. In Trotsky the trauma was neither as great nor as clear-cut. Rather there was an increasing alienation from his father and his father's way of life which resulted in a rather sharp break with the family when he had finished high school. But in all three cases contact with the father was cut off when the emotional involvement with him was still extremely high, so that the feelings of guilt that accompany the adolescent break with paternal authority, and which in the present cases were already so strong, were kept alive and problematical.

Because late adolescence and young manhood is not only the period of separation from the family but also the time when the individual must turn his attention to creating an occupation for himself, the psychosexual conflicts of adolescence are an important part of the context of vocational choice.[2] Thus when the nature of the youth's relation to paternal authority is very much at issue, it is extremely likely that the individual will be responsive to occupations, of which revolutionary activity is one, which allow him to work through his conflicts and hopefully resolve them. This was in fact what happened here, and thus we hypothesized that the revolutionist is one who escapes from the burdens of Oedipal guilt and ambivalence by carrying his conflict with authority into the political realm. For this to happen two conditions must exist: the conflict with paternal authority must be alive and unresolvable in the family context as adolescence draws to a close, and there must exist a political context in terms of which the conflict can be expressed. The former condition was met in the cases of Lenin and Gandhi by the death of the father, which made it impossible to outgrow him and difficult to learn to live with the memories of him. Surrogate fathers had to be found in terms of which the issue could be resolved if neurotic involvements were to be avoided. For Trotsky the break was not as sharp—hence he had a lingering desire to be the favorite son until after the deaths of his father and Lenin in the 1920s.

The second condition, the existence of an appropriate precipitant, was also met in all three cases. The death of his brother as the result of a revolutionary action provided both a partial model for political action and the enemy against whom Lenin was to fight. In Gandhi's case the insult from the British political agent in Kathiawad and the subsequent experiences during his confrontation with himself at the Maritzburg station were the occasions for what was to become his revolutionary response (although it was to take many more years before he was ready to call for a change in the nature of government and social structure). For Trotsky his arrest and the strains of imprisonment as the result of his relatively playful "revolutionary" activity with the Southern Russian Workers' Union changed him from a rather aimless adolescent to a confirmed enemy of tsarism.

In this way, then, a man becomes a revolutionist; but until he has defined his relations with other men much more specifically he is not ready to be an effective advocate of his cause—in fact, at this juncture, he is still uncertain of the nature of his cause. But the event which activates the revolutionary potential of the individual, along with his previous experiences which resulted in that potential, provide the material out of which the revolutionary personality is built. The basic attribute of this personality is that it is based on opposition to governmental authority; this is the result of the individual's continuing need to express his aggressive impulses vis-à-vis his father and the repressive action of governmental officials. The latter permits the individual to externalize his feelings of hatred—previously he had been tormenting himself because his feelings of antipathy toward his father were balanced by feelings of love, respect, and the desire to emulate him. Now the situation is much less ambivalent; governmental authority is clearly malevolent, unlike one's father who served as the basis for one's standards of morality, and hence can be fought with a clear conscience. And because, at least in the three cases studied, the aggressive governmental action came as a consequence of individual actions which were representative, rather than personal, the individual finds a cause to defend. Sasha, with whom Lenin identified, had been fighting for the Russian people, Trotsky had been defending the rights and dignity of the working class, and Gandhi was insisting that Indians be treated as men. Thus far the cause is crudely conceived and unelaborated; with time an ideological superstructure is based upon it so that the individual can fulfill his needs for self-justification.

In this manner the revolutionist dichotomizes his world, and with it the emotional complex of his ambivalent feelings toward his father. As a consequence his feelings of guilt are substantially reduced, so that in all three cases we saw the men turning from introspection and inaction to vigorous pursuance of their revolutionary vocations. Lenin read his brother's books and sought out exiled populist terrorists in order to learn from them of his brother's cause and the techniques of revolutionary struggle; Trotsky composed revolutionary songs in prison and undertook a Marxist study of freemasonry; and Gandhi set about organizing the Indian community in South Africa. In addition each man turned his attention to creating or subscribing to some system of justification which would complement the aggressive aspect of his personality, each sought a benevolent father, concretely and abstractly, to set up in opposition to the evil father that was tsarism or the British raj. This is necessary for the revolutionist for two reasons. First, it satisfies his need to feel that he is not betraying his father's moral standards, which formed the basis of his superego and which therefore can be flaunted only with great strain. Second, in this manner he can assure himself that he is fighting under the aegis of a strong, protective, and righteous paternal authority who guarantees victory over his powerful foes. Thus Lenin could not simply subscribe to his brother's Narodism, for that was only the creed of a rebellious son and had not safeguarded Sasha, and therefore could not safeguard him, from the blows of avenging tsarism. Hence he evolved into a Marxist, finding in its doctrine of the inevitable victory of the working class and in the confident and assertive personality of Plekhanov both justification and protection. The identification with his brother was very strong, however, and hence Lenin's Marxism was really a blend of Russian voluntaristic populism and scientific socialism.

Trotsky, of course, was also a Marxist, although he fought against it for several months before he discovered that it satisfied his need for a total explanatory and justificatory system better than his amorphous and not very deeply held populism. Later in London he was to find in the editorial board of *Iskra* that concrete embodiment of Marxism that Lenin at first found in Plekhanov. In contrast to the two Russians, Gandhi had no intellectual resource like Marxism available to him, but he gradually evolved the idea of *Hind Swaraj*, which contained or implied some of the core attributes of revolutionary Marxism. Although it differed from Marxism in many ways, it shared with it a dichotomized view of the world (between spirituality and materialism, truth and *maya*), a justification of the rebellion of the lowly and an image of a utopian society which was to result from the revolutionary struggle. In sum, all three men met their personal crises by adopting a revolutionary political stance and an ideological justification for their actions.

The next question the inquiry was directed to was why a revolutionist does or does not become a leader. The answer was formulated in terms of the individual's attitudes toward his fellow revolutionists (superiors, peers, and inferiors) and toward governmental authority. For each of these I attempted to analyze both the individual's relations with these other actors and his rationalized view of these relationships.

We found that Lenin and Gandhi, who maintained greater control over their followers—and who had more followers—found it possible to do away with a leader mediating between them and their gods, while Trotsky, who was not as successful as a leader, did not. Lenin broke with Plekhanov as soon as he had any extensive contact with him and Gandhi, while acknowledging Gokhale as his political guru, never accepted the authority of another man as binding. Both men claimed to be in direct contact with their respective truths and each claimed that at any given juncture the alternative that he chose was the only correct one. Each found subservience to others unbearable. As long as there was a living man to whom they owed the respect and obedience they formerly owed their fathers, the strains of the earlier relationships would be perpetuated; because the constant tendency of these men was to act in such a way as to reduce psychic strain, followership was exceedingly difficult for them. Trotsky, whose father's death had not been involved in his choice of revolution as a career, and who consequently was not bearing as large a burden of guilt as were the other two, found it less difficult, although not easy, to work under others. He eventually came to accept Lenin's authority and to see in him the father to whom he could be the favorite son.

The inability to be a follower, of course, does not account for the ability to be a leader. For this something more is needed, namely a firm identification with parental authority, an underlying feeling of connection with the moral standards and behavior of one parent or the other.

Thus Lenin, who identified with his father as he did with Sasha (that is, as a result of childhood emulation of him and in order to ward off the feelings of loss and guilt at his death), was able to play the political father's role naturally and effectively. Gandhi, through his incorporation of many of his mother's characteristics, was also able to make decisions without recourse to any higher earthly authority. But Trotsky found much less that was useful in the model his father provided. Moreover, he was separated from his father, except for summer vacations, from the age of eight on and thus had less of an opportunity to emulate him. Hence Trotsky was not able to envisage himself in the role of *the* leader until very late in his life.

Just as the leader casts off all superiors, so he eliminates all peers. Lenin began as one of three "brothers," Potresov and Martov being the other two, but soon found that his brothers were ineffective or "soft." Gandhi worked with others without insisting on that clear demarcation of relations which was a hallmark of Leninism, but his self-proclaimed status of the most humble of men—but one to whom God spoke— insured him against serious rivalry. Trotsky found it difficult to work with peers (his conflicts with party members during the Civil War is just one example), but he was never able to achieve a position of uniqueness which would save him from having to deal with men who considered themselves his equal and whom he viewed as brothers. Thus while Lenin and Gandhi lived in an emotional world populated only by followers and enemies, Trotsky had to live with superiors and peers as well. The lower intensity of his original familial conflicts enabled him to live a more normal life, to allow his relations with others to be somewhat more jumbled—and hence it prevented him from ascending to the top rung of leadership. For, as Erikson says, the psychological requisites of leadership include the mastery of great personal conflict:

> Still others, although suffering and deviating dangerously through what appears to be a prolonged adolescence, eventually come to contribute an original bit to an emerging style of life; the very danger which they have sensed has forced them to mobilize capacities to see and say, to dream and plan, to design and construct, in new ways.[3]

Although the leader eliminates superiors and peers in terms of personal relations, he maintains both in abstract form. Lenin does not follow Plekhanov, therefore he follows Marx all the more fervently; Gandhi has no guru but follows absolutely the dictates of his inner voice. At the same time, the idea of a political brotherhood and of the brotherhood of man (or the working class) is exalted while, for example, Lenin willingly split the party and Gandhi withdrew from political life to the confines of his *ashram*.

The leader needs and is able to bear the responsibility of having followers. At a minimum he will accept those who acknowledge his leadership, who come to him as children needing protection and guidance. In his followers the leader sees the child he once was; and he can therefore relieve somewhat his residual burden of guilt about his feelings toward his father by showing the latter (that is, the remnants of his father preserved in his superego) that, not only has he become like him, but he has become an even better father in the process. He tries to take care of his children, his followers, better than he feels his father took care of him.[4] As a result, he expects them to be grateful and, what is more, because he sees himself in them he expects betrayal from them—just as he feels he has betrayed his father. Thus Lenin was always suspicious of the intentions of his followers and Gandhi took any failure of his followers to be his own.

NOTES

1. As has been stressed earlier, and as is emphasized below, the ability to manage the problems of guilt which result from the Oedipal phase does not connote that the problems were minimal. Far from it. For all three men the conflict was unusually intense and was much aggravated by the events of adolescence; but all three found the resources, both within themselves and in their environments, to master it. And in that mastery lay the origins both of their commitment to revolutionary activity and, especially in the cases of Lenin and Gandhi, of their ability to assume leadership roles.

2. Erik Erikson, *Young Man Luther* (New York: Norton, 1958), pp. 17–18.

3. Ibid., pp. 14–15.

4. There is also, and might be mentioned, an important maternal theme here, but one which I have not had opportunity to explore systematically in this study. Gandhi, of course, reflects this theme most clearly.

PART III

WHY DO FOLLOWERS FOLLOW?

THE rewards of leadership are more obvious than those of followership. Power, status, and money all provide what are generally considered good reasons for wanting to become a leader. But why is it that followers are willing to accept the authority of political leaders?

The responses to this question fall into two broad categories. Leaders satisfy some of our individual needs and some of our collective needs as well. Exactly which benefits are being provided at a given moment depends, of course, on the nature of the leader, the followers, the tasks at hand, and the more general historical circumstance. In the event, leadership will generally not take place unless followers in some way stand to gain. (Sometimes this "gain" will amount to no more than the avoidance of pain. The willingness to submit to dictators, for example, can simply stem from fear of punishment for refusing to obey.)

INDIVIDUAL NEEDS

The first two pieces in this section explore the very essence of the human spirit. In his book, *The Hero with a Thousand Faces*, Joseph Campbell draws on both ancient hero myths and contemporary psychology to explore our deep wish to transcend the ordinary. His analysis of hero tales from throughout history and across cultures reveals an archetype: the hero whose fantastic exploits lend meaning to our otherwise meaningless lives. Campbell moves skillfully from the ancient past to the twentieth century, arguing that "Freud, Jung and their followers have demonstrated irrefutably that the logic, the heroes, and the deeds of myth survive into modern times."

101

In *Moses and Monotheism* Freud explores the place in history, especially in the history of religion, of the great man. Inevitably this brings him to the question of why great men can, frequently, exert power over others. The reason, he argues, is that the large majority of people actually want an authority figure whom they can "admire" and to whom they can "submit." Such a person enables them to fullfill the "longing for the father that lives in each of us from [our] childhood days." The strong leader, then, provides us with fatherlike protection, and in that analogue "lies the essence . . . of the great man."

The next three selections are classics of modern social science. Each was spawned by the Holocaust. The authors were challenged to explain the inexplicable: how Hitler could have led the German people to the point of becoming his partners in crime.

The authors of the 1950 research report *The Authoritarian Personality* sought to uncover the origins of anti-Semitism. Their investigation was guided by the hypothesis that "the political, economic, and social convictions of an individual often form a broad and coherent pattern, as if bound together by a 'mentality' or 'spirit,' and that this pattern is an expression of deep-lying trends in his personality." Adorno and his colleagues postulated a type that came to be known as the "authoritarian personality" characterized by, among other things, an exaggerated need to submit to authority which, in turn, makes it a prime target for dictators such as Hitler. It should be noted that Adorno et al. also followed in the Freudian tradition: they concluded that the authoritarian personality originates in early childhood and that it cannot, therefore, be "cured." Only by preventing its development can we have any assurance that a genocidal catastrope such as the Holocaust will never be repeated.

The excerpt from Erich Fromm's bestselling volume *Escape from Freedom* contains the kernel of his argument that people are attracted to authoritarianism because it provides them with a sense of belonging and protection. Freedom and democracy, on the other hand, are inevitably accompanied by feelings of anxiety and loneliness, which then tempt us to "completely submerge" ourselves in the "world outside." (Incidentally, the genesis of this process also occurs in very early childhood.) It should be noted that Fromm by no means confines his analysis to history. His discussion constitutes a warning for present and future generations as well. "There is no greater mistake and no graver danger," he writes, "than not to see that in our own society we are faced with the same phenomenon that is fertile soil for the rise of fascism anywhere: the insignificance and powerlessness of the individual."

When the results of Stanley Milgram's experiments on obedience to authority became known to members of the academic community, there was dismay and disbelief. How could ordinary residents of New Haven, Connecticut, continue to administer electric shocks to people even after they cried that they could no longer stand the pain? Like Adorno et al. and Fromm, Milgram undertook his study as a response to the Nazi atrocities. He began his experiments shortly after the trial of Adolph Eichmann, whose defense was based on the claim that he could not be held responsible for the murder of thousands of concentration camp inmates because he was merely acting on orders from superiors. The key to Milgram's work was the experimenter in the lab coat who was perceived by his subjects to be a figure of legitimate power. They did what he ordered them to do. Thus, like Eichmann, most of Milgram's subjects obeyed the instructions of the authority figure, even though he was instructing them to inflict pain for reasons neither fully clear nor justified. Milgram concluded that the potential for unquestioning obedience to authority is in all of us, which means, in turn, that under certain circumstances, it *can* happen here.

COLLECTIVE NEEDS

Fred H. Willhoite looks at group life from the biobehavioral perspective. His exploration of patterns of dominance and deference among primates presents strong evidence for the proposition that the stratification evident in groups of monkeys, chimpanzees, baboons, and gorillas has an analogue in groups of humans. The main functions of social organization among primates are to ensure relative stability and order within the group and maximum protection against threats from those outside it. The biobehavioral approach suggests that humans, like other primates, are programmed to follow their leaders because it is in their collective interest to do so. Willhoite concludes his article with a discussion of the normative implications of dominance structures among humans.[1]

As indicated above, in *Moses and Monotheism* Freud speculates on why individuals follow great men. He concludes that our longing for a father figure makes us willing to follow someone extraordinary enough to tap into that longing. In the excerpt from *Group Psychology and the Analysis of the Ego*, Freud puts forth a quite different, though not contradictory, explanation for why we follow our leaders. The reasoning here is rooted not in our needs as individuals, but in our needs as members of the groups to which most of us—for reasons Freud also explores—belong. Freud declares that groups are inevitably "led by a chief" because they, like individuals, need and long for a primal father.[2] Moreover this primal father serves as the collective ideal. That is, he is the focal point of the group, the incarnation of the group's identity. Hence the leader is indispensable; indeed, without him there is no group.

On one level, Robert Michels's *Political Parties* is simply an examination of leadership and followership in German socialist parties during the early years of the twentieth century. But on another level, his work is no less than a theory of organization and social order. His "iron law of oligarchy" argues that organizations are inevitably divided into "a minority of directors and a majority of directed. Who says organization says oligarchy." In other words, even groups committed to democracy cannot have large institutions such as nation-states, unions, parties, or churches without turning power over to the few who are at the summit of these institutions. Seymour Martin Lipset has noted that the iron law of oligarchy inevitably creates its own momentum. As power accrues to the top, rank and file have less. And as rank and file have less, the leadership cadre acquires resources such as information and expertise which, in turn, makes it still more powerful.

The selection from Michels's book, which argues so convincingly for the "mechanical and technical impossiblity of direct government by the masses," implicitly takes issue with the equation between political democracy and political participation. For Michels writes not about any collective *need* for leadership, but rather about the *inevitability* of a political elite in all groups save those with a very simple social structure.

NOTES

1. For a further expostion of Willhoite's ideas on this subject, see his chapter, "Political Evolution and Legitimacy: The Biocultural Origins of Hierarchical Organization," in *Biology and Bureaucracy*, ed. Elliott White (Lanham, Md.: University Press of America, 1985).

2. For a more complete version of this argument, also see chapter 9 of Sigmund Freud, *Group Psychology and the Analysis of the Ego* (New York: Norton, 1954), pp. 49–53.

10

JOSEPH CAMPBELL

The Hero in Myth and Dream

Whether we listen with aloof amusement to the dreamlike mumbo jumbo of some red-eyed witch doctor of the Congo, or read with cultivated rapture thin translations from the sonnets of the mystic Lao-tse; now and again crack the hard nutshell of an argument of Aquinas, or catch suddenly the shining meaning of a bizarre Eskimo fairy tale: it will be always the one, shape-shifting yet marvelously constant story that we find, together with a challengingly persistent suggestion of more remaining to be experienced than will ever be known or told.

Throughout the inhabited world, in all times and under every circumstance, the myths of man have flourished; and they have been the living inspiration of whatever else may have appeared out of the activities of the human body and mind. It would not be too much to say that myth is the secret opening through which the inexhaustible energies of the cosmos pour into human cultural manifestation. Religions, philosophies, arts, the social forms of primitive and historic man, prime discoveries in science and technology, the very dreams that blister sleep, boil up from the basic, magic ring of myth.

The wonder is that the characteristic efficacy to touch and inspire deep creative centers dwells in the smallest nursery fairy tale—as the flavor of the ocean is contained in a droplet or the whole mystery of life within the egg of a flea. For the symbols of mythology are not manufactured; they cannot be ordered, invented, or permanently suppressed.

From Joseph Campbell, *The Hero with a Thousand Faces*, Bollingen Series 17 (Princeton: Princeton University Press, 1949), chap. 1, pp. 3–4, 12–20. Copyright © 1949, renewed 1976 by Princeton University Press. Reprinted with permission of Princeton University Press and Routledge & Kegan Paul.

They are spontaneous productions of the psyche, and each bears within it, undamaged, the germ power of its source.

What is the secret of the timeless vision? From what profundity of the mind does it derive? Why is mythology everywhere the same, beneath its varieties of costume? And what does it teach?

Today many sciences are contributing to the analysis of the riddle. Archaeologists are probing the ruins of Iraq, Honan, Crete, and Yucatan. Ethnologists are questioning the Ostiaks of the river Ob, the Boobies of Fernando Po. A generation of orientalists has recently thrown open to us the sacred writings of the East, as well as the pre-Hebrew sources of our own Holy Writ. And meanwhile another host of scholars, pressing researches begun last century in the field of folk psychology, has been seeking to establish the psychological bases of language, myth, religion, art development, and moral codes.

Most remarkable of all, however, are the revelations that have emerged from the mental clinic. The bold and truly epoch-making writings of the psychoanalysts are indispensable to the student of mythology; for, whatever may be thought of the detailed and sometimes contradictory interpretations of specific cases and problems, Freud, Jung, and their followers have demonstrated irrefutably that the logic, the heroes, and the deeds of myth survive into modern times. In the absence of an effective general mythology, each of us has his private, unrecognized, rudimentary, yet secretly potent pantheon of dream. The latest incarnation of Oedipus, the continued romance of Beauty and the Beast, stand this afternoon on the corner of Forty-second Street and Fifth Avenue, waiting for the traffic light to change. . . .

Sigmund Freud stresses in his writings the passages and difficulties of the first half of the human cycle of life—those of our infancy and adolescence, when our sun is mounting toward its zenith. C. G. Jung, on the other hand, has emphasized the crises of the second portion—when, in order to advance, the shining sphere must submit to descend and disappear, at last, into the night-womb of the grave. The normal symbols of our desires and fears become converted, in this afternoon of the biography, into their opposites; for it is then no longer life but death that is the challenge. What is difficult to leave, then, is not the womb but the phallus—unless, indeed, the life-weariness has already seized the heart, when it will be death that calls with the promise of bliss that formerly was the lure of love. Full circle, from the tomb of the womb to the womb of the tomb, we come: an ambiguous, enigmatical incursion into a world of solid matter that is soon to melt from us, like the substance of a dream. And, looking back at what had promised to be our own unique, unpredictable, and dangerous adventure, all we find in the end is such a series of standard metamorphoses as men and women have undergone in every quarter of the world, in all recorded centuries, and under every odd disguise of civilization.

The story is told, for example, of the great Minos, king of the island-empire of Crete in the period of its commercial supremacy: how he hired the celebrated artist-craftsman Daedalus to invent and construct for him a labyrinth, in which to hide something of which the palace was at once ashamed and afraid. For there was a monster on the premises—which had been born to Pasiphaë, the queen. Minos, the king, had been busy, it is said, with important wars to protect the trade routes; and meanwhile Pasiphaë had been seduced by a magnificent, snow-white, sea-born bull. It had been nothing worse, really, than what Minos' own mother had allowed to happen: Minos' mother was Europa, and it is well known that she was carried by a bull to Crete. The bull had been the god Zeus, and the honored son of that sacred union was Minos himself—now everywhere respected and gladly served. How then could Pasiphaë have known that the fruit of her own indiscretion would be a monster: this little son with human body but the head and tail of a bull?

Society has blamed the queen greatly; but the king was not unconscious of his own share of guilt. The bull in question had been sent by the god Poseidon, long ago, when Minos was contending with his brothers for the throne. Minos had asserted that the throne was his, by divine right, and had prayed the god to send up a bull out of the sea, as a sign; and he had sealed the prayer with a vow to sacrifice the animal immediately, as an offering and symbol of service. The bull had appeared, and Minos took the throne; but when he beheld the majesty of the beast that had been sent and thought what an advantage it would be to possess such a specimen, he determined to risk a merchant's subtution— of which he supposed the god would take no great account. Offering on Poseidon's altar the finest white bull that he owned, he added the other to his herd.

The Cretan empire had greatly prospered under the sensible jurisdiction of this celebrated lawgiver and model of public virtue. Knossos, the capital city, became the luxurious, elegant center of the leading commercial power of the civilized world. The Cretan fleets went out to every isle and harbor of the Mediterranean; Cretan ware was prized in Babylonia and Egypt. The bold little ships even broke through the Gates of Hercules to the open ocean, coasting then northward to take the gold of Ireland and the tin of Cornwall,[1] as well as southward, around the bulge of Senegal, to remote Yorubaland and the distant marts of ivory, gold, and slaves.[2]

But at home, the queen had been inspired by Poseidon with an ungovernable passion for the bull. And she had prevailed upon her husband's artist-craftsman, the peerless Daedalus, to frame for her a wooden cow that would deceive the bull—into which she eagerly entered; and the bull was deceived. She bore her monster, which, in due time, began to become a danger. And so Daedalus again was summoned, this time by the king, to construct a tremendous labyrinthine enclosure, with blind passages, in which to hide the thing away. So deceptive was the invention, that Daedalus himself, when he had finished it, was scarcely able to find his way back to the entrance. Therein the Minotaur was settled: and he was fed, thereafter, on groups of living youths and maidens, carried as tribute from the conquered nations within the Cretan domain.[3]

Thus according to the ancient legend, the primary fault was not the queen's but the king's; and he could not really blame her, for he knew what he had done. He had converted a public event to personal gain, whereas the whole sense of his investiture as king had been that he was no longer a mere private person. The return of the bull should have symbolized his absolutely selfless submission to the functions of his role. The retaining of it represented, on the other hand, an impulse to egocentric self-aggrandizement. And so the king "by the grace of God" became the dangerous tyrant Holdfast—out for himself. Just as the traditional rites of passage used to teach the individual to die to the past and be reborn to the future, so the great ceremonials of investiture divested him of his private character and clothed him in the mantle of his vocation. Such was the ideal, whether the man was a craftsman or a king. By the sacrilege of the refusal of the rite, however, the individual cut himself as a unit off from the larger unit of the whole community: and so the One was broken into the many, and these then battled each other—each out for himself— and could be governed only by force.

The figure of the tyrant-monster is known to the mythologies, folk traditions, legends, and even nightmares, of the world; and his characteristics are everywhere essentially the same. He is the hoarder of the general benefit. He is the monster avid for the greedy rights of "my and mine." The havoc wrought by him is described in mythology and fairy tale as being universal throughout his domain. This may be no more than his household, his own tortured psyche, or the lives that he blights with the touch of his friendship and assistance; or it may amount to the extent of his civilization. The inflated ego of the tyrant is a curse to himself and his world—no matter how his affairs may seem to prosper. Self-terrorized, fear-haunted, alert at every hand to meet and battle back the anticipated aggressions of his environment, which are primarily the reflections of the uncontrollable impulses to acquisition within himself, the giant of self-achieved independence is the world's messenger of disaster, even though, in his mind, he may entertain himself with humane intentions. Wherever he sets his hand there is a cry (if not from the housetops, then—more miserably—within every heart): a cry for the redeeming hero, the carrier of the shining blade, whose blow, whose touch, whose existence, will liberate the land. . . .

The hero is the man of self-achieved submission. But submission to what? That precisely is the riddle that today we have to ask ourselves and that it is everywhere the primary virtue and historic deed of the hero to have solved. As Professor Arnold J. Toynbee indicates in his six-volume study of the laws of the rise and disintegration of civilizations,[4] schism in the soul, schism in the body social, will not be resolved by any scheme of return to the good old days (archaism), or by programs guaranteed to render an ideal projected future (futurism), or even by the most realistic, hardheaded work to weld together again the deteriorating elements. Only birth can conquer death—the birth, not of the old thing again, but of something new. Within the soul, within the body social, there must be— if we are to experience long survival—a continuous "recurrence of birth" (*palingensia*) to nullify the unremitting recurrences of death. For it is by means of our own victories, if we are not regenerated, that the work of Nemesis is wrought: doom breaks from the shell of our very virtue. Peace then is a snare; war is a snare; change is a snare; permanence a snare. When our day is come for the victory of death, death closes in; there is nothing we can do, except be crucified—and resurrected; dismembered totally, and then reborn.

Theseus, the hero-slayer of the Minotaur, entered Crete from without, as the symbol and arm of the rising civilization of the Greeks. That was the new and living thing. But it is possible also for the principle of regeneration to be sought and found within the very walls of the tyrant's empire itself. Professor Toynbee uses the terms "detachment" and "transfiguration" to describe the crisis by which the higher spiritual dimension is attained that makes possible the resumption of the work of creation. The first step, detachment or withdrawal, consists in a radical transfer of emphasis from the external to the internal world, macro- to microcosm, a retreat from the desperations of the waste land to the peace of the everlasting realm that is within. But this realm, as we know from psychoanalysis, is precisely the infantile unconscious. It is the realm that we enter in sleep. We carry it within ourselves forever. All the ogres and secret helpers of our nursery are there, all the magic of childhood. And more important, all the life-potentialities that we never managed to bring to adult realization, those other portions of ourself, are there; for such golden seeds do not die. If only a portion of that lost totality could be dredged up into the light of day, we should experience a marvelous expansion of our powers, a vivid renewal of life. We should tower in stature. Moreover, if we could dredge up something forgotten not only by ourselves but by our whole generation or our entire civilization, we should become indeed the boon-bringer, the culture hero of the day—a personage of not only local but world historical moment. In a word: the first work of the hero is to retreat from the world scene of secondary effects to those causal zones of the psyche where the difficulties really reside, and there to clarify the difficulties, eradicate them in his own case (i.e., give battle to the nursery demons of his local culture) and break through to the undistorted, direct experience and assimilation of what C. G. Jung has called "the archetypal images."[5] This is the process known to Hindu and Buddhist philosophy as *viveka,* "discrimination."

The archetypes to be discovered and assimilated are precisely those that have inspired, throughout the annals of human culture, the basic images of ritual, mythology, and vision. These "Eternal Ones of the Dream"[6] are not to be confused with the personally modified symbolic figures that appear in nightmare and madness to the still tormented individual. Dream is the personalized myth, myth the depersonalized ream; both myth and dream are symbolic in the same general way of the dynamics of the psyche. But in the dream the forms are quirked by the peculiar troubles of the dreamer, whereas in myth the problems and solutions shown are directly valid for all mankind.

The hero, therefore, is the man or woman who has been able to battle past his personal and local historical limitations to the generally valid, normally human forms. Such a one's visions, ideas, and inspirations come pristine from the primary springs of human life and thought. Hence they are eloquent, not of the present, disintegrating society and psyche, but of the unquenched source through which society is reborn. The hero has died as a modern man; but as eternal man—perfected, unspecific, universal man—he has been reborn. His second solemn task and deed therefore (as Toynbee declares and as all the mythologies of mankind indicate) is to return then to us, transfigured, and teach the lesson he has learned of life renewed.[7]

NOTES

1. Harold Peake and Herbert John Fleure, *The Way of the Sea* and *Merchant Venturers in Bronze* (Yale University Press, 1929 and 1931).

2. Leo Frobenius, *Das unbekannte Afrika* (Munich: Oskar Beck, 1923), pp. 10–11.

3. Ovid, *Metamorphoses*, VIII, 132ff.; IX, 736ff.

4. Arnold J. Toynbee, *A Study of History* (Oxford University Press, 1934), vol. VI, pp. 169–75.

5. "Forms or images of a collective nature which occur practically all over the earth as constituents of myths and at the same time as autochthonous, individual products of unconscious origin" (C. G. Jung, *Psychology and Religion* [Collected Works, vol. 11; New York and London, 1958], par. 88. Orig. written in English 1937. See also his *Psychological Types*, index.)

As Dr. Jung points out (*Psychology and Religion*, par. 89), the theory of the archetypes is by no means his own invention. Compare Nietzsche:

"In our sleep and in our dreams we pass through the whole thought of earlier humanity. I mean, in the same way that man reasons in his dreams, he reasoned when in the waking state many thousands of years. . . . The dream carries us back into earlier states of human culture, and affords us a means of understanding it better" (Friedrich Nietzsche, *Human all too Human*, vol. I, p. 13; cited by Jung, *Psychology and Religion*, par. 89, n. 17).

Compare Adolf Bastian's theory of the ethnic "Elementary Ideas," which, in their primal psychic character (corresponding to the Stoic *Logoi spermatikoi*), should be regarded as "the spiritual (or psychic) germinal dispositions out of which the whole social structure has been developed organically," and, as such, should serve as bases of inductive research (*Ethnische Elementargedanken in der Lehre vom Menchen* [Berlin, 1895], vol. I, p. ix).

Compare Franz Boas: "Since Waitz's thorough discussion of the question of the unity of the human species, there can be no doubt that in the main the mental characteristics of man are the same all over the world" (*The Mind of Primitive Man*, p. 104. Copyright, 1911 by The Macmillan Company and used with their permission). "Bastian was led to speak of the appalling monotony of the fundamental ideas of mankind all over the globe" (ibid., p. 155). "Certain patterns of associated ideas may be recognized in all types of culture" (ibid., p. 228).

Compare Sir James G. Frazer: "We need not, with some enquirers in ancient and modern times, suppose that the Western peoples borrowed from the older civilization of the Orient the conception of the Dying and Reviving God, together with the solemn ritual, in which that conception was dramatically set forth before the eyes of the worshippers. More probably the resemblance which may be traced in this respect between the religions of the East and West is no more than what we commonly, though incorrectly, call a fortuitous coincidence, the effect of similar causes acting alike on the similar constitution of the human mind in different countries and under different skies" (*The Golden Bough*, one-volume edition, p. 386. Copyright, 1922 by The Macmillan Company and used with their permission).

Compare Sigmund Freud: "I recognized the presence of symbolism in dreams from the very beginning. But it was only by degrees and as my experience increased that I arrived at a full appreciation of its extent and significance, and I did so under the influence of . . . Wilhelm Stekel. . . . Stekel arrived at his interpretations of symbols by way of intuition, thanks to a peculiar gift for the direct understanding of them. . . . Advances in psycho-analytic experience have brought to our notice patients who have shown a direct understanding of dream-symbolism of this kind to a surprising extent. . . . This symbolism is not peculiar to dreams, but is characteristic of unconscious ideation, in particular among the people, and it is to be found in folklore, and in popular myths, legends, linguistic idioms, proverbial wisdom and current jokes, to a more complete extent than in dreams." (*The Interpretation of Dreams,* translated by James Strachey, Standard Edition, vol. V, pp. 350–351).

Dr. Jung points out that he has borrowed his term *archetype* from classic sources: Cicero, Pliny, the *Corpus Hermeticum,* Augustine, etc. (*Psychology and Religion,* par. 89). Bastian notes the correspondence of his own theory of "Elementary Ideas" with the Stoic concept of the *Logoi spermatikoi.* The tradition of the "subjectively known forms" (Sanskrit: *antarjñeyarūpa*) is, in fact, coextensive with the tradition of myth, and is the key to the understanding and use of mythological images—as will appear abundantly in the following chapters.

6. This is Géza Róheim's translation of an Australian Aranda term, *altjiranga mitjina,* which refers to the mythical ancestors who wandered on the earth in the time called *altjiranga nakala,* "ancestor was." The word *altjira* means: (a) a dream, (b) ancestor, beings who appear in the dream, (c) a story (Róheim, *The Eternal Ones of the Dream* [New York: International Universities Press, 1945], pp. 210–211).

7. It must be noted against Professor Toynbee, however, that he seriously misrepresents the mythological scene when he advertises Christianity as the only religion teaching this second task. *All* religions teach it, as do all mythologies and folk traditions everywhere. Professor Toynbee arrives at his misconstruction by way of a trite and incorrect interpretation of the Oriental ideas of Nirvana, Buddha, and Bodhisattva; then contrasting these ideals, as he misinterprets them, with a very sophisticated rereading of the Christian idea of the City of God. This is what leads him to the error of supposing that the salvation of the present world-situation might lie in a return to the arms of the Roman Catholic church.

11

SIGMUND FREUD

The Great Man

H OW is it possible that one single man can develop such extraordinary effectiveness, that he can create out of indifferent individuals and families *one* people, can stamp this people with its definite character and determine its fate for millennia to come? Is not such an assumption a retrogression to the manner of thinking that produced creation myths and hero-worship, to times in which historical writing exhausted itself in narrating the dates and life-histories of certain individuals—sovereigns or conquerors? The inclination of modern times tends rather to trace back the events of human history to more hidden, general, and impersonal factors—the forcible influence of economic circumstances, changes in food supply, progress in the use of materials and tools, migrations caused by increase in population and change of climate. In these factors individuals play no other part than that of exponents or representatives of mass tendencies which must come to expression and which found that expression as it were by chance in such persons.

These are quite legitimate points of view, but they remind us of a significant discrepancy between the nature of our thinking-apparatus and the organization of the world which we are trying to apprehend. Our imperative need for cause and effect is satisfied when each process has *one* demonstrable cause. In reality, outside us this is hardly so; each event seems to be over-determined and turns out to be the effect of several converging causes. Intimidated by the countless complications of events, research takes the part of one chain of events against another, stipulates

From Sigmund Freud, *Moses and Monotheism*, trans. Katherine Jones (New York: Knopf, 1939), pp. 136–42. Copyright 1939 by Alfred A. Knopf, Inc. and renewed 1967 by Ernst L. Freud and Anna Freud. Reprinted by permission of Alfred A. Knopf, Inc., Sigmund Freud Copyrights Ltd., The Institute of Psychoanalysis, and The Hogarth Press. First published in 1939.

contrasts that do not exist and that are created merely through tearing apart more comprehensive relations.[1]

If, therefore, the investigation of one particular case demonstrates the outstanding influence of a single human personality, our conscience need not reproach us that through accepting this conclusion we have dealt a blow at the doctrine of the significance of those general impersonal factors. In point of fact there is without doubt room for both. In the genesis of monotheism we cannot, it is true, point to any other external factor than those I have already mentioned: namely, that this development has to do with the establishing of closer connections among different nations and the existence of a great empire.

We will keep, therefore, a place for "the great man" in the chain, or rather in the network, of determining causes. It may not be quite useless, however, to ask under what condition we bestow this title of honour. We may be surprised to find that it is not so easy to answer this question. A first formulation which would define as great a human being specially endowed with qualities we value highly is obviously in all respects unsuitable. Beauty, for instance, and muscular strength, much as they may be envied, do not establish a claim to "greatness." There should perhaps be mental qualities present, psychical and intellectual distinction. In the latter respect we have misgivings: a man who has an outstanding knowledge in one particular field would not be called a great man without any further reason. We should certainly not apply the term to a master of chess or to a virtuoso on a musical instrument, and not necessarily to a distinguished artist or a man of science. In such a case we should be content to say he is a great writer, painter, mathematician, or physicist, a pioneer in this field or that, but we should pause before pronouncing him a great man. When we declare, for instance Goethe, Leonardo da Vinci, and Beethoven to be great men, then something else must move us to do so beyond the admiration of their grandiose creations. If it were not for just such examples one might very well conceive the idea that the title "a great man" is reserved by preference for men of action—that is to say, conquerors, generals, and rulers—and was intended as a recognition of the greatness of their achievements and the strength of the influence that emanated from them. However, this, too, is unsatisfying, and is fully contradicted by our condemnation of so many worthless people of whom one cannot deny that they exercised a great influence on their own and later times. Nor can success be chosen as a distinguishing feature of greatness, if one thinks of the vast number of great men who, instead of being successful, perished after being dogged by misfortune.

We should therefore, tentatively, incline to the conclusion that it is hardly worth while to search for an unequivocal definition of the concept: "a great man." It seems to be a rather loosely used term, one bestowed without due consideration and given to the supernormal development of certain human qualities; in doing so we keep close to the original literal sense of the word "greatness." We may also remember that it is not so much the nature of the great man that arouses our interest as the question of what are the qualities by virtue of which he influences his contemporaries. I propose to shorten this investigation, however, since it threatens to lead us far from our goal.

Let us agree, therefore, that the great man influences his contemporaries in two ways: through his personality and through the idea for which he stands. This idea may lay stress on an old group of wishes in the masses, or point to a new aim for their wishes, or, again, lure the masses by other means. Sometimes—and this is surely the more primitive effect—the personality alone exerts its influence, and the idea plays a decidedly subordinate part. Why the great man should rise to significance at all we have no doubt whatever. We know that the great majority of people have a strong need for authority which they can admire, to which they can submit, and which dominates and sometimes even ill-treats them. We have learned from the psychology of the individual whence comes this need of masses. It is the longing for the father that lives in each of us from his childhood days, for the same father whom the hero of legend boasts of having overcome. And now it begins to dawn on us that all the features with which we furnish the great man are traits of the father, that in this similarity lies the essence, which so far has eluded us, of the great man. The decisiveness of thought, the strength of will, the forcefulness of his deeds, belong to the picture of the father; above all other things, however, the self-reliance and independence of the great man, his divine conviction of doing the right thing, which may pass into ruthlessness. He must be admired, he may be trusted, but one cannot help also being afraid of him. We should have taken a cue from the word itself; who else but the father should in childhood have been the great man?

Without doubt it must have been a tremendous father image that stooped in the person of Moses to tell the poor Jewish labourers that they were his dear children. And the conception of a unique, eternal, omnipotent God could not have been less overwhelming for them; he who thought them worthy to make a bond with him promised to take care of them if only they remained faithful to his worship. Probably they did not find it easy to separate the image of the man Moses from that of his God, and their instinct was right in this, since Moses might very well have incorporated into the character of his God some of his own traits, such as his irascibility and implacability. And when they killed this great man they only repeated an evil deed which in primeval times had been a law directed against the divine king, and which, as we know, derives from a still older prototype.[2]

When, on the one hand, the figure of the great man has grown into a divine one, it is time to remember, on the other hand, that the father also was once a child. The great religious idea for which the man Moses stood was, as I have stated, not his own; he had taken it over from his king Ikhnaton. And the latter—whose greatness as a founder of religion is proved without a doubt—perhaps followed intimations which through his mother or by other ways had reached him from the Near or the Far East.

We cannot trace the network any further. If the present argument, however, is correct so far, the idea of monotheism must have returned in the fashion of a boomerang into the country of its origin. It appears fruitless to attempt to ascertain what merit attaches to an individual in a new idea. Obviously many have taken part in its development and made contributions to it. On the other hand it would be wrong to break off the chain of causation with Moses and to neglect what his successors, the Jewish Prophets, achieved. Monotheism had not taken root in Egypt. The same failure might have happened in Israel after the people had thrown off the inconvenient and pretentious religion imposed on them. From the mass of Jewish people, however, there arose again and again men who lent new colour to the fading tradition, renewed the admonishments and demands of Moses, and did not rest until the lost cause was once more regained. In the constant endeavour of centuries, and last but not least through two great reforms—the one before, the other after the Babylonian exile—there took place the change of the popular God Jahve into the God whose worship Moses had forced upon the Jews. And it is the proof of a special psychical fitness in the mass which had become the Jewish people that it could bring forth so many persons who were ready to take upon themselves the burden of the Mosaic religion for the reward of believing that their people was a chosen one and perhaps for other benefits of a similar order.

NOTES

1. I would guard myself, however, against a possible misunderstanding. I do not mean to say that the world is so complicated that every assertion must hit the truth somewhere. No, our thinking has preserved the liberty of inventing dependencies and connections that have no equivalent in reality. It obviously prizes this gift very highly, since it makes such ample use of it—inside as well as outside of science.

2. Sir James G. Frazer, *The Golden Bough* (London: Macmillan, 1911), p. 192.

12

T. W. ADORNO, ELSE FRENKEL-BRUNSWIK, DANIEL J. LEVINSON, R. NEVITT SANFORD

The "Authoritarian" Syndrome

T HIS syndrome comes closest to the over-all picture of the high scorer as it stands out throughout our study. If follows the "classic" psychoanalytic pattern involving a sadomasochistic resolution of the Oedipus complex, and it has been pointed out by Erich Fromm under the title of the "sadomasochistic" character.[1] According to Max Horkheimer's theory in the collective work of which he wrote the sociopsychological part, external social repression is concomitant with the internal repression of impulses. In order to achieve "internalization" of social control which never gives as much to the individual as it takes, the latter's attitude toward authority and its psychological agency, the superego, assumes an irrational aspect. The subject achieves his own social adjustment only by taking pleasure in obedience and subordination. This brings into play the sadomasochistic impulse structure both as a condition and as a result of social adjustment. In our form of society, sadistic as well as masochistic tendencies actually find gratification. The pattern for the translation of such gratifications into character traits is a specific resolution of the Oedipus complex which defines the formation of the syndrome here in question. Love for the mother, in its primary form, comes under a severe taboo. The resulting hatred against the father is transformed by reaction-formation into love. This transformation leads to a particular kind of superego. The transformation of hatred into love, the most difficult task an individual has to perform in his early development, never succeeds completely. In the psychodynamics of the "authoritarian character," part of the preceding aggressiveness is absorbed and turned into masochism, while another part is left over as sadism, which seeks an outlet in those with whom the subject does not identify himself: ultimately the outgroup. The Jew frequently becomes a substitute for the hated father, often assuming, on a fantasy level, the very same qualities against which the subject revolted in the father, such as being practical, cold, domineering, and even a sexual rival. Ambivalence is all-persuasive, being evidenced mainly by the simultaneity of blind belief in authority and readiness to attack those who are deemed weak and who are socially acceptable as "victims." Stereotypy, in this syndrome, is not only a means of social identification, but has a truly "economic" function in the subject's own psychology: it helps to canalize his libidinous energy according to the demands of his overstrict superego. Thus stereotypy itself tends to become heavily libidinized and plays a large role in the subject's inner household. He develops deep "compulsive" character traits, partly by retrogression to the anal-sadistic phase of development. Sociologically, this syndrome used to be, in Europe, highly characteristic of the lower middle-class. In this country, we may expect it among people whose actual status differs from that to which they aspire. This is in marked contrast to the social contentment and lack of conflict that is more characteristic of the "Conventional" syndrome, with which the "Authoritarian" one shares the conformist aspect.

Interview M352 begins as follows:

(Satisfaction?) "Well, I'm the head operator—shift foreman—rotating schedules. . . . (Subject emphasizes "head" position)—small department—5 in department—5 in a shift—I get personal satisfaction . . . that I have 5 people working for me, who come to me for advice in handlng the production that we make, and that the ultimate decision . . . is mine, and in the fact that in the ultimate decision, I should be *right*—and am usually, and the knowledge that I am correct gives me personal satisfaction. The fact that I earn a living doesn't give me any personal satisfaction. It's these things that I have mentioned . . . knowing that I am pleasing someone else also gives me satisfaction."

The denial of material gratifications, indicative of a restrictive superego, is no less characteristic than the twofold pleasure in being obeyed and giving pleasure to the boss.

His upward social mobility is expressed in terms of overt identification with those who are higher in the hierarchy of authority:

(What would more money make possible?) "Would raise our standard, automobile; move into better residential section; associations with business and fraternal, etc., would be raised . . . to those in a bracket higher, except for a few staunch friends which you keep always; and naturally, associate with people on a higher level—with more education and more experience. After you get there, and associate with those people . . . that fires you on to the next step higher. . . ."

His religious belief has something compulsive and highly punitive:

"My belief is that, just according to the Bible, there is a God—the world has gone along and needed a Savior, and there was one born—lived, died, risen again, and will come back some time; and the person who has lived according to Christianity will live forever—those who have not will perish at that time."

This overt rigidity of conscience, however, shows strong traces of ambivalence: what is forbidden may be acceptable if it does not lead to social conflict. The over-rigid superego is not really integrated, but remains external.

"Adultery, as long as never found out, is o.k. —if found out, then it's wrong— since some of the most respected people do it, it must be all right."

The subject's concept of God is plainly identical with such an externalized superego or, to use Freud's original term, with the "ego ideal," with all the traits of a strong, but "helpful" father:

"Well, when it comes down to the fundamentals, everybody has an idea of some sort: may not call Him God, but an ideal that they live up to and strive to be like. . . . Heathens or anybody else has some sort of religion, but it is something that they put their faith in that can do things for them—can help them."

The genetic relation between the Authoritarian" syndrome and the sadomasochistic resolution of the Oedipus complex is borne out by some statements of the subject about his own childhood:

"Well, my father was a very strict man. He wasn't religious, but strict in raising the youngsters. His word was law, and whenever he was disobeyed, there was punishment. When I was 12, my father beat me practically every day for getting into the tool chest in the back yard and not putting everything away . . . finally he explained that those things cost money, and I must learn to put it back." . . . (Subject explains that his carelessness led to a beating everyday, as promised by the father, and finally after several weeks, he simply quit using the tools altogether, because "I just couldn't get 'em all back") . . . "But, you know, I never hold that against my father—I had it coming. He laid the law down, and if I broke it, there was punishment, but never in uncontrolled anger. My father was a good man—no doubt about that. Always interested in boys' activities.

"My father was a great fraternal man; was out practically every night. Took an active part always on committees—a good mixer, everybody liked him . . . a good provider. We always had everything we needed, but no unnecessary luxuries . . . no whims provided for. . . . Father felt they were luxuries that probably—felt they were unnecessary. . . . Yes, rather austere. . . . (Which parent closest to?) I think my father. Although he beat the life out of me, I could talk to him about anything." . . . (Subject emphasizes that his father always gave everyone, including himself, a square deal.)

The subject has been "broken" by the father: he has been overadjusted. It is exactly this aspect which bears the main emphasis in his anti-Semitism. He who admires brute force blames the Jews for their recklessness in practical matters.

"The Jews seem to be taking advantage of the present-day situation, I think. Now, they want to—they're bringing these Jews in from Europe, and they seem to click together, somehow, and they seem to be able to corner capital. They're a peculiar people—no conscience about anything except money." (Subject apparently meant, here, no conscience about money, although maybe about other things.) "If you stand in the way of their making money, they'll brush you aside."

Rigidity of the image of the Jew, visible already in the "Conventional" syndrome, tends to become absolute and highly vindictive:

"To me a Jew is just like a foreigner in the same class as—say, oh, I was gonna say a Filipino. You would be pointed out . . . they observe all these different religious days that's completely foreign to me—and they stick to it—they don't completely Americanize. . . . (What if there were less prejudice aganst them?) I don't know—I can't help but feel that a Jew is meant to be just the way he is—no change possible—a sort of instinct that will never lose—stay Jewish right straight through. (What ought to be done?) They have the ability to get control—now, how we're gonna stop 'em . . . probably have to pass some regulation prohibiting them."

Again the idea of authority is the focal point: the Jews appear dangerous to him as usurpers of "control."

One last feature of the "Authoritarian" syndrome should be mentioned. It is the psychological equivalent of the "no-pity-for-the-poor" ideology discussed in Chapter XVII. The identification of the "authoritarian" character with strength is concomitant with rejection of everything that is "down." Even where social conditions have to be recognized as the reason for the depressed situation of a group, a twist is applied in order to transform this situation into some kind of well-deserved punishment. This is accompanied by moralistic invectives indicative of strict repression of several desires:

> He went on to emphasize that you should segregate Negroes and whites, that by all means give equal opportunities and everything instead of "evading the problem" as he called it. He refers to high prevalence of venereal disease among Negroes, which he blames on their low morals and, under further questioning by the interviewer, he finally attributes it to "congested conditions of living" and tries very hard to explain what he means. This leads to a lack of modesty and respect for privacy—everybody's thrown together—"lose the distance that is supposed to be between people," etc., etc.

The emphasis on "distance," the fear of "close physical contacts" may be interpreted as corroborative of our thesis that, for this syndrome, the ingroup-outgroup dichotomy absorbs large quantities of psychological energy. Identification with the familial structure and ultimately with the whole ingroup becomes, to this kind of individual, one of the main mechanisms by which they can impose authoritarian discipline upon themselves and avoid "breaking away"—a temptation nourished continuously by their underlying ambivalence.

NOTE

1. Institute of Social Research, *Studien über Autorität und familie*, M. Horkheimer, ed. (Paris: Felix Alcan, 1936).

13

ERICH FROMM

The Emergence of the Individual
and the Ambiguity of Freedom

BEFORE we come to our main topic—the question of what freedom means to modern man, and why and how he tries to escape from it—we must first discuss a concept which may seem to be somewhat removed from actuality. It is, however, a premise necessary for the understanding of the analysis of freedom in modern society. I mean the concept that freedom characterizes human existence as such, and furthermore that its meaning changes according to the degree of man's awareness and conception of himself as an independent and separate being.

The social history of man started with his emerging from a state of oneness with the natural world to an awareness of himself as an entity separate from surrounding nature and men. Yet this awareness remained very dim over long periods of history. The individual continued to be closely tied to the natural and social world from which he emerged; while being partly aware of himself as a separate entity, he felt also part of the world around him. The growing process of the emergence of the individual from his original ties, a process which we may call "individuation," seems to have reached its peak in modern history in the centuries between the Reformation and the present.

In the life history of an individual we find the same process. A child is born when it is no longer one with its mother and becomes a biological entity separate from her. Yet, while this biological separation is the beginning of individual human existence, the child remains functionally one with its mother for a considerable period.

From Erich Fromm, *Escape from Freedom* (New York: Avon, 1965), pp. 39–47. Copyright © 1941, 1969 by Erich Fromm. Reprinted by permission of Henry Holt & Co., Inc.

To the degree to which the individual, figuratively speaking, has not yet completely severed the umbilical cord which fastens him to the outside world, he lacks freedom: but these ties give him security and a feeling of belonging and of being rooted somewhere. I wish to call these ties that exist before the process of individuation has resulted in the complete emergence of an individual "primary ties." They are organic in the sense that they are a part of normal human development; they imply a lack of individuality, but they also give security and orientation to the individual. They are the ties that connect the child with its mother, the member of a primitive community with his clan and nature, or the medieval man with the Church and his social caste. Once the stage of complete individuation is reached and the individual is free from these primary ties, he is confronted with a new task: to orient and root himself in the world and to find security in other ways than those which were characteristic of his preindividualistic existence. Freedom then has a different meaning from the one it had before this stage of evolution is reached. It is necessary to stop here and to clarify these concepts by discussing them more concretely in connection with individual and social development.

The comparatively sudden change from foetal into human existence and the cutting off of the umbilical cord mark the independence of the infant from the mother's body. But this independence is only real in the crude sense of the separation of the two bodies. In a functional sense, the infant remains part of the mother. It is fed, carried, and taken care of in every vital respect by the mother. Slowly the child comes to regard the mother and other objects as entities apart from itself. One factor in this process is the neurological and the general physical development of the child, its ability to grasp objects—physically and mentally—and to master them. Through its own activity it experiences a world outside of itself. The process of individuation is furthered by that of education. This process entails a number of frustrations and prohibitions, which change the role of the mother into that of a person with different aims which conflict with the child's wishes, and often into that of a hostile and dangerous person.[1] This antagonism, which is one part of the educational process though by no means the whole, is an important factor in sharpening the distinction between the "I" and the "thou."

A few months elapse after birth before the child even recognizes another person as such and is able to react with a smile, and it is years before the child ceases to confuse itself with the universe.[2] Until then it shows the particular kind of egocentricity typical of children, an egocentricity which does not exclude tenderness for and interest in others, since "others" are not yet definitely experienced as really separate from itself. For the same reason the child's leaning on authority in these first years has also a different meaning from the leaning on authority later on. The parents, or whoever the authority may be, are not yet regarded as being a fundamentally separate entity; they are part of the child's universe, and this universe is still part of the child; submission to them, therefore, has a different quality from the kind of submission that exists once two individuals have become really separate.

A remarkably keen description of a ten-year-old child's sudden awareness of its own individuality is given by R. Hughes in A *High Wind in Jamaica*:

"And then an event did occur, to Emily, of considerable importance. She suddenly realised who she was. There is little reason that one can see why it should not have happened to her five years earlier, or even five years later; and none, why it should have come that particular afternoon. She had been playing house in a nook right in the bows, behind the windlass (on which she had hung a devil's-claw as a door knocker); and tiring of it was walking rather aimlessly aft, thinking vaguely about some bees and a fairy queen, when it suddenly flashed into her mind that she was *she*. She stopped dead, and began looking over all of her person which came within the range of her eyes. She could not see much, except a fore-shortened view of the front of her frock, and her hands when she lifted them for inspection; but it was enough for her to form a rough idea of a little body she suddenly realised to be hers.

"She began to laugh, rather mockingly. 'Well!' she thought, in effect: 'Fancy *you*, of all people, going and getting caught like this!—You can't get out of it now, not for a very long time: you'll have to go through with being a child, and growing up, and getting old, before you'll be quit of this mad prank!'

"Determined to avoid any interruption of this highly important occasion, she began to climb the ratlines, on her way to her favorite perch at the masthead. Each time she moved an arm or a leg in this simple action, however, it struck her with fresh amazement to find them obeying her so readily. Memory told her, of course, that they had always done so before: but before, she had never realised how surprising this was. Once settled on her perch, she began examining the skin of her hands with the utmost care: for it was *hers*. She slipped a shoulder out of the top of her frock; and having peeped in to make sure she really was continuous under her clothes, she shrugged it up to touch her cheek. The contact of her face and the warm bare hollow of her shoulder gave her a comfortable thrill, as if it was the caress of some kind of friend. But whether her feeling came to her through her cheek or her shoulder, which was the caresser and which the caressed, that no analysis could tell her.

"Once fully convinced of this astonishing fact, that she was now Emily Bas-Thornton (why she inserted the 'now' she did not know, for she certainly imagined no transmigrational nonsense of having been any-one else before), she began seriously to reckon its implications."

The more the child grows and to the extent to which primary ties are cut off, the more it develops a quest for freedom and independence. But the fate of this quest can only be fully understood if we realize the dialectic quality in this process of growing individuation.

This process has two aspects: one is that the child grows stronger physically, emotionally, and mentally. In each of these spheres intensity and activity grow. At the same time, these spheres become more and more integrated. An organized structure guided by the individual's will and reason develops. If we call this organized and integrated whole of the personality the self, we can also say that the *one side of the growing process of individuation is the growth of self-strength*. The limits of the growth of individuation and the self are set, partly by individual conditions, but essentially by social conditions. For although the differences between individuals in this respect appear to be great, every society is characterized by a certain level of individuation beyond which the normal individual cannot go.

The other aspect of the process of individuation is *growing aloneness*. The primary ties offer security and basic unity with the world outside of oneself. To the extent to which the child emerges from that world it becomes aware of being alone, of being an entity separate from all others. This separation from a world, which in comparison with one's own individual existence is overwhelmingly strong and powerful, and often threatening and dangerous, creates a feeling of powerlessness and anxiety. As long as one was an integral part of that world, unaware of the pos-sibilities and responsibilities of individual action, one did not need to be afraid of it. When one has become an individual, one stands alone and faces the world in all its perilous and overpowering aspects.

Impulses arise to give up one's individuality, to overcome the feeling of aloneness and powerlessness by completely submerging oneself in the world outside. These impulses, however, and the new ties arising from them, are not identical with the primary ties which have been cut off in the process of growth itself. Just as a child can never return to the mother's womb physically, so it can never reverse, psychically, the process of individuation. Attempts to do so necessarily assume the character of submission, in which the basic contradiction between the authority and the child who submits to it is never eliminated. Consciously the child may feel secure and satisfied, but unconsciously it realizes that the price it pays is giving up strength and the integrity of its self. Thus the result of submission is the very opposite of what it was to be: submission increases the child's insecurity and at the same time creates hostility and rebelliousness, which is the more frightening since it is directed against the very persons on whom the child has remained—or become—dependent.

However, submission is not the only way of avoiding aloneness and anxiety. The other way, the only one which is productive and does not end in a insoluble conflict, is that of *spontaneous relationship to man and nature*, a relationship that connects the individual with the world without eliminating his individuality. This kind of relationship—the foremost expressions of which are love and productive work—are rooted in the integration and strength of the total personality and are therefore subject to the very limits that exist for the growth of the self.

The problem of submission and of spontaneous activity as two possible results of growing individuation will be discussed later on in great detail; here I only wish to point to the general principle, the dialectic process which results from growing individuation and from growing freedom of the individual. The child becomes more free to develop and express its own individual self unhampered by those ties which were limiting it. But the child also becomes more free *from* a world which gave it security and reassurance. The process of individuation is one of growing strength and integration of its individual personality, but it is at the same time a process in which the original identity with others is lost and in which the child becomes more separate from them. This growing separation may result in an isolation that has the quality of desolation and creates intense anxiety and insecurity; it may result in a new kind of closeness and a solidarity with others if the child has been able to develop the inner strength and productivity which are the premise of this new kind of relatedness to the world.

If every step in the direction of separation and individuation were matched by corresponding growth of the self, the development of the child would be harmonious. This does not occur, however. While the process of individuation takes place automatically, the growth of the self is hampered for a number of individual and social reasons. The lag between these two trends results in an unbearable feelng of isolation and powerlessness, and this in its turn leads to psychic mechanisms, which later on are described as *mechanisms of escape*.

NOTES

1. It should be noted here that instinctual frustration *per se* does not arouse hostility. It is the thwarting of expansiveness, the breaking of the child's attempt to assert himself, the hostility radiating from parents—in short, the atmosphere of suppression—which create in the child the feeling of powerlessness and the hostility springing from it.

2. Jean Piaget, *The Moral Judgment of the Child* (New York: Harcourt, Brace & Co., 1932), p. 407. Cf. H. S. Sullivan, "Conceptions of Modern Psychiatry: The First William Alanson White Lectures," *Psychiatry* 3, no. 1 (1940).

14

STANLEY MILGRIM

The Dilemma of Obedience

OBEDIENCE is as basic an element in the structure of social life as one can point to. Some system of authority is a requirement of all communal living, and it is only the man dwelling in isolation who is not forced to respond, through defiance or submission, to the commands of others. Obedience, as a determinant of behavior, is of particular relevance to our time. It has been reliably established that from 1933 to 1945 millions of innocent people were systematically slaughtered on command. Gas chambers were built, death camps were guarded, daily quotas of corpses were produced with the same efficiency as the manufacture of appliances. These inhumane policies may have originated in the mind of a single person, but they could only have been carried out on a massive scale if a very large number of people obeyed orders.

Obedience is the psychological mechanism that links individual action to political purpose. It is the dispositional cement that binds men to systems of authority. Facts of recent history and observation in daily life suggest that for many people obedience may be a deeply ingrained behavior tendency, indeed, a prepotent impulse overriding training in ethics, sympathy, and moral conduct. C. P. Snow (1961) points to its importance when he writes:

> When you think of the long and gloomy history of man, you will find more hideous crimes have been committed in the name of obedience than have ever been committed in the name of rebellion. If you doubt that, read William

Shirer's 'Rise and Fall of the Third Reich.' The German Officer Corps were brought up in the most rigorous code of obedience . . . in the name of obedience they were party to, and assisted in, the most wicked large scale actions in the history of the world. (p. 24)[1]

The Nazi extermination of European Jews is the most extreme instance of abhorrent immoral acts carried out by thousands of people in the name of obedience. Yet in lesser degree this type of thing is constantly recurring: ordinary citizens are ordered to destroy other people, and they do so because they consider it their duty to obey orders. Thus, obedience to authority, long praised as a virtue, takes on a new aspect when it serves a malevolent cause; far from appearing as a virtue, it is transformed into a heinous sin. Or is it?

The moral question of whether one should obey when commands conflict with conscience was argued by Plato, dramatized in *Antigone*, and treated to philosophic analysis in every historical epoch. Conservative philosophers argue that the very fabric of society is threatened by disobedience, and even when the act prescribed by an authority is an evil one, it is better to carry out the act than to wrench at the structure of authority. Hobbes stated further that an act so executed is in no sense the responsibility of the person who carries it out but only of the authority that orders it. But humanists argue for the primacy of individual conscience in such matters, insisting that the moral judgments of the individual must override authority when the two are in conflict.

The legal and philosophic aspects of obedience are of enormous import, but an empirically grounded scientist eventually comes to the point where he wishes to move from abstract discourse to the careful observation of concrete instances. In order to take a close look at the act of obeying, I set up a simple experiment at Yale University. Eventually, the experiment was to involve more than a thousand participants and would be repeated at several universities, but at the beginning, the conception was simple. A person comes to a psychological laboratory and is told to carry out a series of acts that come increasingly into conflict with conscience. The main question is how far the participant will comply with the experimenter's instructions before refusing to carry out the actions required of him.

But the reader needs to know a little more detail about the experiment. Two people come to a psychology laboratory to take part in a study of memory and learning. One of them is designated as a "teacher" and the other a "learner." The experimenter explains that the study is concerned with the effects of punishment on learning. The learner is conducted into a room, seated in a chair, his arms strapped to prevent excessive movement, and an electrode attached to his wrist. He is told that he is to learn a list of word pairs; whenever he makes an error, he will receive electric shocks of increasing intensity.

The real focus of the experiment is the teacher. After watching the learner being strapped into place, he is taken into the main experimental room and seated before an impressive shock generator. Its main feature is a horizontal line of thirty switches, ranging from 15 volts to 450 volts, in 15-volt increments. There are also verbal designations which range from SLIGHT SHOCK to DANGER—SEVERE SHOCK. The teacher is told that he is to administer the learning test to the man in the other room. When the learner responds correctly, the teacher moves on to the next item; when the other man gives an incorrect answer, the teacher is to give him an electric shock. He is to start at the lowest shock level (15 volts) and to increase the level each time the man makes an error, going through 30 volts, 45 volts, and so on.

The "teacher" is a genuinely naïve subject who has come to the laboratory to participate in an experiment. The learner, or victim, is an actor who actually receives no shock at all. The point of the experiment is to see how far a person will proceed in a concrete and measurable situation in which he is ordered to inflict increasing pain on a protesting victim. At what point will the subject refuse to obey the experimenter?

Conflict arises when the man receiving the shock begins to indicate that he is experiencing discomfort. At 75 volts, the "learner" grunts. At 120 volts he complains verbally; at 150 he demands to be released from the experiment. His protests continue as the shocks escalate, growing increasingly vehement and emotional. At 285 volts his response can only be described as an agonized scream.

Observers of the experiment agree that its gripping quality is somewhat obscured in print. For the subject, the situation is not a game; conflict is intense and obvious. On one hand, the manifest suffering of the learner presses him to quit. On the other, the experimenter, a legitimate authority to whom the subject feels some commitment, enjoins him to continue. Each time the subject hesitates to administer shock, the experimenter orders him to continue. To extricate himself from the situation, the subject must make a clear break with authority. The aim of this investigation was to find when and how people would defy authority in the face of a clear moral imperative.

There are, of course, enormous differences between carrying out the orders of a commanding officer during times of war and carrying out the orders of an experimenter. Yet the essence of certain relationships remain, for one may ask in a general way: How does a man behave when he is told by a legitimate authority to act against a third individual? If anything, we may expect the experimenter's power to be considerably less than that of the general, since he has no power to enforce his imperatives, and participation in a psychological experiment scarcely evokes the sense of urgency and dedication engendered by participation in war. Despite these limitations, I thought it worthwhile to start careful observation of obedience even in this modest situation, in the hope that it would stimulate insights and yield general propositions applicable to a variety of circumstances.

A reader's initial reaction to the experiment may be to wonder why anyone in his right mind would administer even the first shocks. Would he not simply refuse and walk out of the laboratory? But the fact is that no one ever does. Since the subject has come to the laboratory to aid the experimenter, he is quite willing to start off with the procedure. There is nothing very extraordinary in this, particularly since the person who is to receive the shocks seems initially cooperative, if somewhat apprehensive. What is surprising is how far ordinary individuals will go in complying with the experimenter's instructions. Indeed, the results of the experiment are both surprising and dismaying. Despite the fact that many subjects experience stress, despite the fact that many protest to the experimenter, a substantial proportion continue to the last shock on the generator.

Many subjects will obey the experimenter no matter how vehement the pleading of the person being shocked, no matter how painful the shocks seem to be, and no matter how much the victim pleads to be let out. This was seen time and again in our studies and has been observed in several universities where the experiment was repeated. It is the extreme willingness of adults to go to almost any lengths on the command of an authority that constitutes the chief finding of the study and the fact most urgently demanding explanation.

A commonly offered explanation is that those who shocked the victim at the most severe level were monsters, the sadistic fringe of society. But if one considers that almost two-thirds of the participants fall into the category of "obedient" subjects, and that they represented ordinary people drawn from working, managerial, and professional classes, the argument becomes very shaky. Indeed, it is highly reminiscent of the issue that arose in connection with Hannah Arendt's 1963 book, *Eichmann in*

Jerusalem. Arendt contended that the prosecution's effort to depict Eichmann as a sadistic monster was fundamentally wrong, that he came closer to being an uninspired bureaucrat who simply sat at his desk and did his job. For asserting these views, Arendt became the object of considerable scorn, even calumny. Somehow, it was felt that the monstrous deeds carried out by Eichmann required a brutal, twisted, and sadistic personality, evil incarnate. After witnessing hundreds of ordinary people submit to the authority in our own experiments, I must conclude that Arendt's conception of the *banality of evil* comes closer to the truth than one might dare imagine. The ordinary person who shocked the victim did so out of a sense of obligation—a conception of his duties as a subject— and not from any peculiarly aggressive tendencies.

This is, perhaps, the most fundamental lesson of our study: ordinary people, simply doing their jobs, and without any particular hostility on their part, can become agents in a terrible destructive process. Moreover, even when the destructive effects of their work become patently clear, and they are asked to carry out actions incompatible with fundamental standards of morality, relatively few people have the resources needed to resist authority. A variety of inhibitions against disobeying authority come into play and successfully keep the person in his place.

Sitting back in one's armchair, it is easy to condemn the actions of the obedient subjects. But those who condemn the subjects measure them against the standard of their own ability to formulate high-minded moral prescriptions. That is hardly a fair standard. Many of the subjects, at the level of stated opinion, feel quite as strongly as any of us about the moral requirement of refraining from action against a helpless victim. They, too, in general terms know what ought to be done and can state their values when the occasion arises. This has little, if anything, to do with their actual behavior under the pressure of circumstances.

If people are asked to render a moral judgment on what constitutes appropriate behavior in this situation, they unfailingly see disobedience as proper. But values are not the only forces at work in an actual, ongoing situation. They are but one narrow band of causes in the total spectrum of forces impinging on a person. Many people were unable to realize their values in action and found themselves continuing in the experiment even though they disagreed with what they were doing.

The force exerted by the moral sense of the individual is less effective than social myth would have us believe. Though such prescriptions as "Thou shalt not kill" occupy a pre-eminent place in the moral order, they do not occupy a correspondingly intractable position in human psychic structure. A few changes in newspaper headlines, a call from the draft board, orders from a man with epaulets, and men are led to kill with little difficulty. Even the forces mustered in a psychology experiment will go a long way toward removing the individual from moral controls. Moral factors can be shunted aside with relative ease by a calculated restructuring of the informational and social field.

What, then, keeps the person obeying the experimenter? First, there is a set of "binding factors" that lock the subject into the situation. They include such factors as politeness on his part, his desire to uphold his initial promise of aid to the experimenter, and the awkwardness of withdrawal. Second, a number of adjustments in the subject's thinking occur that undermine his resolve to break with authority. The adjustments help the subject maintain his relationship with the experimenter, while at the same time reducing the strain brought about by the experimental conflict. They are typical of thinking that comes about in obedient persons when they are instructed by authority to act against helpless individuals.

One such mechanism is the tendency of the individual to become so absorbed in the narrow technical aspects of the task that he loses sight of its broader consequences. The film *Dr. Strangelove* brilliantly satirized the absorption of a bomber crew in the exacting technical procedure of dropping nuclear weapons on a country. Similarly, in this experiment, subjects become immersed in the procedures, reading the word pairs with exquisite articulation and pressing the switches with great care. They want to put on a competent performance, but they show an accompanying narrowing of moral concern. The subject entrusts the broader tasks of setting goals and assessing morality to the experimental authority he is serving.

The most common adjustment of thought in the obedient subject is for him to see himself as not responsible for his own actions. He divests himself of responsibility by attributing all initiative to the experimenter, a legitimate authority. He sees himself not as a person acting in a morally accountable way but as the agent of external authority. In the postexperimental interview, when subjects were asked why they had gone on, a typical reply was: "I wouldn't have done it by myself. I was just doing what I was told." Unable to defy the authority of the experimenter, they attribute all responsibility to him. It is the old story of "just doing one's duty" that was heard time and time again in the defense statements of those accused at Nuremberg. But it would be wrong to think of it as a thin alibi concocted for the occasion. Rather, it is a fundamental mode of thinking for a great many people once they are locked into a subordinate position in a structure of authority. The disappearance of a sense of responsibility is the most far-reaching consequence of submission to authority.

Although a person acting under authority performs actions that seem to violate standards of conscience, it would not be true to say that he loses his moral sense. Instead, it acquires a radically different focus. He does not respond with a moral sentiment to the actions he performs. Rather, his moral concern now shifts to a consideration of how well he is living up to the expectations that the authority has of him. In wartime, a soldier does not ask whether it is good or bad to bomb a hamlet; he does not experience shame or guilt in the destruction of a village: rather he feels pride or shame depending on how well he has performed the mission assigned to him.

Another psychological force at work in this situation may be termed "counteranthropomorphism." For decades psychologists have discussed the primitive tendency among men to attribute to inanimate objects and forces the qualities of the human species. A countervailing tendency, however, is that of attributing an impersonal quality to forces that are essentially human in origin and maintenance. Some people treat systems of human origin as if they existed above and beyond any human agent, beyond the control of whim or human feeling. The human element behind agencies and institutions is denied. Thus, when the experimenter says, "The experiment *requires* that you continue," the subject feels this to be an imperative that goes beyond any merely human command. He does not ask the seemingly obvious question, "Whose experiment? Why should the designer be served while the victim suffers?" The wishes of a man—the designer of the experiment—have become part of a schema which exerts on the subject's mind a force that transcends the personal. "It's *got* to go on. It's *got* to go on," repeated one subject. He failed to realize that a man like himself wanted it to go on. For him the human agent had faded from the picture, and "The Experiment" had acquired an impersonal momentum of its own.

No action of itself has an unchangeable psychological quality. Its meaning can be altered by placing it in particular contexts. An American newspaper recently quoted a pilot who conceded that Americans were bombing Vietnamese men, women, and children but felt that the bombing was for a "noble cause" and thus was justified. Similarly, most subjects in the experiment see their behavior in a larger context that is benevolent and useful to society—the pursuit of scientific truth. The psychological laboratory has a strong claim to legitimacy and evokes trust and confidence in those who come to perform there. An action such as shocking a victim, which in isolation appears evil, acquires a totally different meaning when placed in this setting. But allowing an act to be dominated by its context, while neglecting its human consequences, can be dangerous in the extreme.

At least one essential feature of the situation in Germany was not studied here—namely, the intense devaluation of the victim prior to action against him. For a decade and more, vehement anti-Jewish propaganda systematically prepared the German population to accept the destruction of the Jews. Step by step the Jews were excluded from the category of citizen and national, and finally were denied the status of human beings. Systematic devaluation of the victim provides a measure of psychological justification for brutal treatment of the victim and has been the constant accompaniment of massacres, pogroms, and wars. In all likelihood, our subjects would have experienced greater ease in shocking the victim had he been convincingly portrayed as a brutal criminal or a pervert.

Of considerable interest, however, is the fact that many subjects harshly devalue the victim *as a consequence* of acting against him. Such comments as, "He was so stupid and stubborn he deserved to get shocked," were common. Once having acted against the victim, these subjects found it necessary to view him as an unworthy individual, whose punishment was made inevitable by his own deficiencies of intellect and character.

Many of the people studied in the experiment were in some sense against what they did to the learner, and many protested even while they obeyed. But between thoughts, words, and the critical step of disobeying a malevolent authority lies another ingredient, the capacity for transforming beliefs and values into action. Some subjects were totally convinced of the wrongness of what they were doing but could not bring themselves to make an open break with authority. Some derived satisfaction from their thoughts and felt that—within themselves, at least—they had been on the side of the angels. What they failed to realize is that subjective feelings are largely irrelevant to the moral issue at hand so long as they are not transformed into action. Political control is effected through action. The attitudes of the guards at a concentration camp are of no consequence when in fact they are allowing the slaughter of innocent men to take place before them. Similarly, so-called "intellectual resistance" in occupied Europe—in which persons by a twist of thought felt that they had defied the invader—was merely indulgence in a consoling psychological mechanism. Tyrannies are perpetuated by diffident men who do not possess the courage to act out their beliefs. Time and again in the experiment people disvalued what they were doing but could not muster the inner resources to translate their values into action.

A variation of the basic experiment depicts a dilemma more common than the one outlined above: the subject was not ordered to push the trigger that shocked the victim, but merely to perform a subsidiary act (administering the word-pair test) before another subject actually delivered the shock. In this situation, 37 of 40 adults from the New Haven area continued to the highest shock level on the generator. Predictably, subjects excused their behavior by saying that the responsibility belonged to the man who actually pulled the switch. This may illustrate a dangerously typical situation in complex society: it is psychologically easy to ignore responsibility when one is only an intermediate link in a chain of evil action but is far from the final consequences of the action. Even Eichmann was sickened when he toured the concentration camps, but to participate in mass murder he had only to sit at a desk and shuffle papers. At the same time the man in the camp who actually dropped Cyclon-B into the gas chambers was able to justify *his* behavior on the grounds that he was only following orders from above. Thus there is a fragmentation of the total human act; no one man decides to carry out the evil act and is confronted with its consequences. The person who assumes full responsibility for the act has evaporated. Perhaps this is the most common characteristic of socially organized evil in modern society.

The problem of obedience, therefore, is not wholly psychological. The form and shape of society and the way it is developing have much to do with it. There was a time, perhaps, when men were able to give a fully human response to any situation because they were fully absorbed in it as human beings. But as soon as there was a division of labor among men, things changed. Beyond a certain point, the breaking up of society into people carrying out narrow and very special jobs takes away from the human quality of work and life. A person does not get to see the whole situation but only a small part of it, and is thus unable to act without some kind of over-all direction. He yields to authority but in doing so is alienated from his own actions.

George Orwell caught the essence of the situation when he wrote:

As I write, highly civilized human beings are flying overhead, trying to kill me. They do not feel any enmity against me as an individual, nor I against them. They are only "doing their duty," as the saying goes. Most of them, I have no doubt, are kind-hearted law abiding men who would never dream of committing murder in private life. On the other hand, if one of them succeeds in blowing me to pieces with a well-placed bomb, he will never sleep any the worse for it.

NOTE

1. "Either-Or," *Progressive*, February 1961.

15

FRED H. WILLHOITE, JR.

Primates and Political Authority

M Y central argument: There seem to be good reasons to believe that man's biological nature incorporates strong propensities to establish and sustain dominance-deference heirarchies within his social groupings; that is, the stratification of political authority, power, and influence may be *by nature* intrinsic to human social existence. If this hypothesis is tenable, a presupposition common to both liberal and radical political thought must be critically reconsidered and perhaps drastically revised.

The validity and utility of evolutionary-biological (or biobehavioral) analysis of political behavior are almost certainly not widely assumed, accepted, or even thought about very much, so far, by the great majority of political scientists. Nevertheless, this is a mode of analysis of human behavior that, in a variety of forms, is increasingly utilized by zoologists (especially ethologists, who study animal behavior), psychologists, anthropologists, and even a few sociologists.[1] Furthermore, there has been some writing along these lines by political scientists.[2]

Because numerous explanations and justifications of the basic premises of an evolutionary-biological perspective on human behavior appear in the sources which have been cited so far, I shall not present here any elaborate statement and defense of this approach.[3] Put very briefly, it involves assuming as the fundamental paradigm for the study of all living things (including man) the modern "neo-Darwinian" theory of evolution: species diverge and evolve as a result of the interactions of genetic variability, mutation, genetic recombination, and natural selection for fitness in given environments.[4] Since not merely the physical structure of an

From Fred H. Willhoite, Jr., "Primates and Political Authority: A Biobehavioral Perspective," *American Political Science Review* 70 (December 1976): 1110–26. Reprinted by permission.

animal but also its behavior determines its evolutionary fitness, natural selection shapes the behavioral capabilities and propensities of every species and every individual.[5] Although in the hominid (prehuman and human species) line, generalized learning ability and intelligent adaptability have been strongly selected for, it is legitimate to infer that we have inherited both cognitive and affective biases which significantly and differentially influence our learning processes.[6] That is, because we are the products of an evolutionary history, we are genetically "programmed" to learn and persist in certain kinds of behaviors much more readily than is the case with other possible behaviors (and probably also, to a limited degree, to respond in stereotyped ways to certain types of stimuli). This does not necessarily mean that a particular behavior is *inevitable*, rather that heredity significantly affects the *probability* of its development.[7]

Setting out from these premises, how might we discover what kinds of evolved behavioral propensities in man may be relevant to comprehending and theorizing about political behavior? This effort invariably requires speculation about the nature of man's evolution, given the paucity, so far, of knowledge of the human behavioral genotype. Speculation can be, of course, more or less well grounded in and consistent with available evidence. The principal types of data used thus far in efforts to reconstruct the course of hominid evolution are studies of the behavior of other animal species (especially subhuman primates), interpretations of prehominid and hominid fossils, and observations of the behavior of contemporary Stone Age peoples. There are major problems in the evolutionary interpretation of each of these catagories of data, but new discoveries of considerable significance and suggestiveness are constantly being reported—especially in the areas of primate behavior and hominid fossil-hunting. Reconstructions based on scientifically conscientious speculation seem at least deserving of serious consideration by all students of human behavior.

RELEVANCE OF PRIMATE STUDIES

So far as scientific evidence is concerned, I shall focus primarily upon studies and intepretations of subhuman primate behavior, a field which has developed rapidly only in the past fifteen years. Carefully drawn analogies (and, to some degree, perhaps, homologies)[8] between behavior patterns in monkeys and apes and human behaviors are both legitimate and enlightening. A leading primate behavior theorist and an anthropologist conclude: " . . . to understand human societies, one needs to discover the lineaments of them in subhuman primate societies. This now seems possible."[9]

Monkeys and apes are considered to be of great significance for the study of man primarily because they are our nearest evolutionary relatives. Among the major primate groups, divergences from common ancestors occurred, probably, from about ten to fifty million years ago. Most recently on this time scale predecessors of present-day great apes (chimpanzees, gorillas, orangutans) and of hominids diverged; next most recently, precursors of Old World monkeys (e.g., macaques, baboons) diverged from the primate line that eventually led to man; and long before that time, the New World monkeys (e.g., spider monkeys, squirrel monkeys) had differentiated from the primate line which ultimately produced Old World monkeys, apes, and hominids. An eminent primatologist points out that man shares a considerable degree of genetic potential with apes and monkeys and that anthropoid primates have been very conservative species which have departed little from the ancestral pattern of primate structure. Thus, he concludes, it is quite reasonable to assume that studies of ape and monkey behavior can provide indirect evidence for the impact of evolution on man's behavior. Especially is this the case if the species studied lives in an environment similar to that which early man probably inhabited (presumably because in different ecological settings differing phenotypical behaviors will be manifested by separate populations of the same species—if the genotypical behavioral range of a species is relatively broad.[10]

In regard to my central argument, then, what might we learn from primate behavior studies that may help us to comprehend a behavioral pattern ubiquitously noted in human societies—the differential distribution of authority, power, and influence (political stratification)? Essentially, I agree that "political institutions, and particularly high ranking political roles, seem functionally analogous to dominance hierarchies such as those found among many primates."[11] But further, this question must be considered: how likely does it seem that these functional similarities stem, in part, from evolved behavioral propensities common to man and other primate species?

Difficulties and complications immediately arise in attempting to discern the behavioral referents of "dominance" in various studies of primate behavior. (Other terms which are sometimes used, apparently as synonyms of "dominance," are "status hierarchy" and "rank order.") Frequently the direction and outcome of agonistic encounters (threats and attacks) are used as indicators of dominance; in other cases a primary measure is differential access to incentives (e.g., food, estrous females, favored resting places); and sometimes a study focuses on leadership (or "forefronting") of group movement. These—and other proposed measures of rank order—are not invariably intercorrelated in every group of every primate species that has been studied.[12] Despite formidable methodological difficulties and, sometimes, conceptual ambiguity, almost every study of primate social groupings among a wide variety of species has discerned definite rank differentiations among group members. Very frequently these relationships have been more clearly evidenced in deferential and submissive behaviors than in assertive and intrusive activities. This point is emphasized by Hans Kummer, a leading student—both in field and in laboratory settings—of baboon behavior; Kummer asserts that it is the general rule among primate species that younger and weaker individuals defer to older and stronger ones and that males rank higher than females of the same age. Each group member learns its own rank of dominance. Fighting to determine or clarify rank order is relatively infrequent (but can be decisive when it does occur). The dominance order within a group seems to result primarily from some individuals learning—through experience—automatic deference to certain others, with respect to agonistic encounters or access to incentives.[13]

FOUR PRIMATE SPECIES

Credence may more readily attach to these generalizations if the nature and structure of dominance hierarchies in some particular primate groups are succinctly reviewed. I have singled out for this treatment studies of rhesus macaques, savanna-dwelling baboons, gorillas, and chimpanzees—primarily because one or more of these species has been commonly treated as the primate from which we might draw the most nearly valid analogies concerning the behavior of our prehominid and early hominid ancestors.[14]

The rhesus macaque is a primarily terrestrial monkey native to India and some neighboring areas of southern Asia. The representatives of this species whose behavior has been most intensively studied, however, live on Cayo Santiago, a small island off the east coast of Puerto Rico; these are descendants of a breeding stock transplanted to this location by a primatologist in 1938.[15]

In his study, Kaufmann found in a troop of about 150 monkeys a clear-cut linear dominance hierarchy among the adult males, as determined by physical displacements of one animal by another and by the direction of aggressive and submissive signals. There appeared to be distinct rank orders both for different groups of males and for individuals within those groupings. Most dominant were mature adult males in a "central hierarchy." Next in line were young adult males who tended to act together as a group to defend against attacks on one of them by other males; some of these young males were beginning to infiltrate the central hierarchy. Lowest in the male rank order were animals that were mainly orphans or sons of females in other bands; because of their usual location in relation to the rest of the band, these are referred to as "peripheral males." (In the study of macaques in India, a similar band structure was found. There was, however, less clear-cut ranking of every individual male, because two males who ranked lower than another individual would frequently team up to become dominant over him.[16] This kind of "coalition behavior" will be noted as significant also for savanna-dwelling baboons and chimpanzees.)

What are the social functions of the dominance hierarchy in the rhesus band? The "alpha" (most dominant individual) male was usually followed by the females in the band who had young infants. Although he infrequently initiated group movement, an initiative was seldom successful unless he participated in it. When the band was on the move, the males in the central hierarchy tended to remain in the center of its ranks, along with most of the females and infants. These dominant males also intervened to stop nearly every fight that was observed to break out between any other members of the band; this was done usually by running toward the combatants and threatening them visually or vocally. Finally, a positive correlation was noted between males' ranks and the extent of their mating behavior; presumably the higher ranking males were most successful in fathering offspring.[17]

Savanna-dwelling baboons live in numerous areas of southern and eastern Africa, and their behavior has been studied fairly extensively in the field.[18] These monkeys are close evolutionary kin to the macaques, and are similar to them behaviorally in many ways. Thus a type of male dominance hierarchy found among some baboon troops appears to be a linear rank order with one adult male clearly and consistently in the alpha position.[19] But in other troops the dominance hierarchy involves a more complex form of the "teaming" or "coalition" behavior observed among macaques in India. (In these studies, dominance was determined by noting relatively stereotyped aggressive sequences among males and, to a lesser degree, by differential access to incentives such as estrous females and food provided by human observers.)[20]

Usually (though not invariably), if there are three or more adult males in the troop, the more complex kind of hierarchy develops. For example, in one troop there were six fully adult males. Three of these animals frequently teamed with one another to defend against challenges or attacks from other adult males. None of the other three males in the band was ever seen to co-operate with any other individual. Thus, although one of these latter was individually the most dominant male in the band, any two or all three of the "co-operators" together were dominant over him. The latter trio were therefore considered to be the "central hierarchy" of the band. In another band, the significance of "coalition behavior" for dominance structure became clearly evident when one member of a two-male central hierarchy disappeared. Almost at once a formerly subordinate male displaced the remaining member of the central hierarchy and was soon joined in a new coalition of that type by a male that had only recently joined the band.[21] Membership in the troop's central hierarchy seemed to facilitate a male's success in copulating with females at the peak of estrus (when they are most likely to conceive), even as compared to individually *more* dominant males outside the central hierarchy.[22]

The social functions of the dominance hierarchy appear to be quite similar to those discerned in bands of macaques. Troops members ordinarily orient their attention to and follow the cues of the most dominant males. Thus, in troop movements, even though less dominant males usually go ahead of the troop, these animals sometimes get temporarily separated from the body of the troop because the central hierarchy males have taken another direction. As with the macaques, the most dominant males ordinarily remain in the center of the troop on the move, along with females and their infants. As soon as any strange or predatory animal is sighted (usually signalled by a barking sound from one of the peripheral males ahead, behind, or at the side of the troop), the central hierarchy males rush to confront in concert whatever danger may be present. Also like macaques, dominant male baboons—and almost exclusively the most dominant—frequently intervene to break up fights among other members of the troop, usually by means of noisy and menacing agonistic threats which seldom result in actual fighting. In sum, "the main characteristics of baboon social organization . . . are derived from a complex dominance pattern among adult males that usually ensures stability and comparative peacefulness within the group, maximum protection for mothers with infants, and the highest probability that offspring will be fathered by the most dominant males."[23]

The primate species which are phylogenetically nearest to man are the African great apes—the gorilla and the chimpanzee.[24] The gorilla is an endangered species now confined to certain lowland and mountainous rainforest areas of central Africa. Only the mountain gorilla has thus far been studied in the wild, but considerable attention has been given to its dominance-oriented behavior.[25]

Gorillas live in relatively permanent groups of from two to thirty individuals. They wander daily over large home ranges, feeding on relatively abundant types of plants. A typical group consists of one or more fully mature ("silver-backed") males, several females, half a dozen juveniles and infants, and one or more less mature ("black-backed") males. Also some "lone males" were observed (though no lone females); these animals seemed to associate freely with certain groups but never remained with any group for an extended period of time.

Group organization is quite cohesive. It features a central core composed of a dominant silver-backed male and all the females and young. All other males, both silver-backed and black-backed, tend to assume peripheral positions as the group spreads out over a relatively small area (rarely exceeding two hundred square feet) to feed. Rank order largely correlates with body size; silver-backed males are dominant over all black-backed males, females, and young. If there are two or more silver-backed males in a group, they are arranged in linear dominance hierarchy.

Dominance is most often expressed with respect to positions along narrow trails or in favored sitting places. A subordinate animal ordinarily moves aside to be supplanted by a dominant individual; the latter's mere approach or brief stare at the subordinate is usually a sufficient stimulus to effect this change. Occasionally the dominant animal gives the lower-ranking one a light tap with the back of the hand, which always produces movement by the subordinate.

The dominant male in a gorilla group functions as its leader. Every group member seems to be constantly aware of the activity of the "alpha" male, and cues reflecting a change in the activity of the group are taken from him. Every part of the daily routine—travel, location of rest stops and feeding places, time and place of nesting—appears to be largely determined by the leader. In one case of a perceived external threat (the human observer), the leader dropped behind the fleeing group to face the intruder. When the group is moving rapidly, the leader is at or near the front of it; when its movements are slow, he is often located in the center or near the end of the group. Maintenance of order does not appear to be a significant function of the dominant male-leader—primarily because intragroup aggressiveness is confined to staring, snapping at, or bluff-charging another group member. Even these kinds of interactions were extremely rare.[26]

The final species included in this brief survey is the chimpanzee, which lives in rainforest and woodland areas of central Africa.[27] Until very recently, it was believed that chimpanzees do not live in closed, permanent groups, as do savanna baboons and macaques. Jane Goodall reported that, within a large home range, chimpanzees move about in small temporary groups which may consist of any combination of age and sex classes: "The only group that may be stable over a period of several years is a mother with her infant and young juvenile offspring."[28]

But in 1971, dramatic changes began to occur in the life of the Gombe Reserve (Tanzania) chimpanzee population which Goodall and her colleagues have been observing for a decade and a half. The whole large group suddenly divided into two separate groups, which occupied distinct territories and became overtly aggressive toward each other. Young males now "patrol" the boundaries between their group's territory and their "enemy's." These terms may seem overly anthropomorphic, but when such "patrols" sight a lone chimp not belonging to their group, they are likely to chase that individual and attack viciously if the outsider is caught. Several all-out bloody fights between members of these two groups have been witnessed, and at least three infants and three adults have been fatally wounded since early 1974.[29]

The early field reports on chimpanzee behavior[30] also reported such a paucity of dominance-submission interactions that Goodall questioned the feasibility of applying the dominance concept to a local chimpanzee population as a whole. Further study has persuaded her, however, that hierarchy and dominance are central features of chimpanzee group life. Although the hierarchy is not a neat and rigid progression of linear dominance, both high- and low-ranking individuals usually have clear-cut statuses. An individual's rank may vary, depending upon the social-behavioral context (e.g., the presence or absence of other family members), an individual's current motivation level, or the animal's "mood."[31]

However, Goodall determined that, in general, "the social status of each individual was . . . fairly well defined."[32] In dyadic encounters— usually competition for bananas provided by the observers—which animals would prevail became highly predictable. Furthermore, some animals frequently vacated favored resting places when approached by certain others. In such interactions, all females were normally subordinate to all mature males.

The male dominance structure is somewhat similar to that of savanna baboons, although dominance-deference interactions appear to be less frequent among chimpanzees than among baboons. The basic common feature is the presence of co-operative, or "coalition"-type behavior within the dominance-competition context in both species. As with baboons, two chimpanzees may combine to express dominance over a single animal to which both "coalition" partners are individually subordinate. But at any time within a group, one male clearly occupies the "alpha" position; he most frequently threatens and sometimes attacks the other males but is almost never attacked and seldom threatened by any of them. Infrequently, certain young but mature males try to displace the current alpha male. Within the Gombe population, three successful attempts have been observed, and in two cases the challenger was supported closely in agonistic encounters by another mature male (known in one case to be the challenger's brother). Some males seem much more highly motivated to engage in dominance competition than do others, and intelligence seems to be more important than size and strength as a determinant of success in rising to the alpha position.[33]

Discerning the adaptive functions of dominance-deference behavior in chimpanzees is very difficult, and the leading observers of their behavior in the wild have largely refrained from speculating on this point. The recent events at Gombe suggest the possibility that the hierarchical order may serve, in most circumstances, to restrain overt expressions of the dangerous—even deadly—aggressiveness which these animals have now surprisingly manifested. But why they are that aggressive is another unsolved evolutionary puzzle; the aggressiveness might be, in part, a phylogenetic holdover from an earlier, savanna-dwelling phase of chimpanzee evolution.[34] But perhaps, ironically, comparisons with human behavior might prove to be the most promising route for arriving at some understanding of intraspecifically lethal, group-territorial aggressive behavior in chimpanzees.

PRIMATE-BASED STRATIFICATION CONCEPTS

A sociologist has recently argued that biologically based proclivities may well be a cause of dominance-deference behavior in various primate species, including man.[35] Mazur points out that status differentiation within established face-to-face groups exists in all known human cultures. Extracting from the sociological literature seven characteristics typical of such status orders, he seeks to compare the behavior of seven primate species—ranging from the most primitive in evolutionary terms, the tree shrew, to man's nearest relatives, chimpanzees and gorillas— with respect to these traits of human groups. On the basis of admittedly incomplete evidence, Mazur concludes that most of these status-relevant behaviors are manifested in subhuman primate species and that a trend seems to exist for more of these traits to appear in species which are closer to than those which are more distant from man on the evolutionary time- scale. He concludes that status differentiation *as such* (i.e., the underly- ing pattern of motivation for the great variety of particular forms this phenomenon assumes among different groups in diverse cultures) very probably has a "noncultural" (phylogenetic) basis. Indeed, he tentatively advances an even broader suggestion: "Perhaps sociologists whose inter- ests are limited to humans should accept cross-species behaviors as 'given' and requiring no further explanation, as most of us accept hunger and the sex drive as given."[36]

The relevance of primate behavior studies to the understanding of political stratification in human societies may be clarified somewhat through consideration of two theoretical conceptions that have been advanced by primatologists. One of these is an essentially functional concept: Bernstein notes that in numerous species of Old and New World monkeys and apes (including the species reviewed above, except perhaps for the chimpanzee), a "control role," "defending group or troop mem- bers against internal and external sources of disturbance, has been recog- nized. . . . " This social role has been noted in nearly all species which manifest strong intragroup dominance relationships and also in some species in which rank order is either difficult to discern or very poorly developed.[37]

Recently Bernstein has suggested that an established rank order within a primate group contributes to the regularity and predictability of indi- viduals' responses and thus to the ordered distribution of roles—essen- tially to the maintenance of order—within the group. He even concludes that intragroup aggression seems "to be motivated *primarily* by efforts to preserve established social position and to enforce expected patterns of social behavior, rather than resulting from active competition leading to conflict."[38] In sum, social order itself—at least among a number of primate species—may be mainly a consequence of individuals' moti- vations to establish and maintain places for themselves in a dominance- deference rank order.

A somewhat more highly developed conception—a kind of "proto- theory"—has been formulated by Michael Chance and elaborated by him in collaboration with Clifford Jolly.[39] Chance is leery of functional generalizations, given the fragmentary state of current data on primate behavior. He considers a structural conception to be much more tenable and thus advances the idea of "attention structure" as the behavioral common denominator in most, if not all, rank-oriented primate groups. Instead of differential access to incentives,

> A more rewarding way of defining the dominance status of a supremely domi- nant individual is that he or she is the *focus of attention* of those holding subordinate status within the same group. . . . A redefinition of dominance is now proposed on the assumption that the attention-binding effect of an animal in a group is essentially the quality which puts it in a behaviourally focal position, and which also tends to place it near the group's spatial centre. The dominant animal therefore may be said to dominate the attention of others at most, if not all, times, and usually without specific actions to do so.[40]

In this perspective, the focus is on the behavior of subordinates as much as if not more than on that of dominant animals, and the differen- tial distribution of group members' attention does appear to hold consis- tently across group structures in many more primate species than is the case with aggressive dominance or linear rank order. Among savanna baboons and macaques the central hierarchy males are very much the predominant focus of attention, both of females, who remain relatively near them, and of peripheral males, who most often remain a certain distance away from the spatial center of the troop. Members of a gorilla group seem to take nearly all their behavioral cues from the dominant silver-backed male, while other mature males remain in locations peripheral to the core of the group. Processes of group movement and of inter-male agonistic competition in chimpanzees indicate that some of these animals tend to exert an attention-binding effect on the others.[41] The "attention structure" concept also seems to account for rank order behavior among species not specifically discussed above, such as Japanese and bonnet macaques and hamadryas baboons.[42]

Of critical importance for Chance's proto-theory is the "concept of attention structure as a *cause* as well as an effect" of dominance.[43] For it is on this hypothesis that Chance and Jolly base their interpretation of charismatic leadership (in Weber's sense) in human societies. Rather than being attended to because of his position in the official dominance hierarchy, the charismatic individual attains some kind and degree of dominance by means of his capacity to attract the attention of individuals who then become his adherents. In times of severe social crisis, confused and frightened people are more likely to attend to individuals who promise them personal or political salvation solely on the authority of that individual's distinctive personhood or the doctrine which he seems to embody. Because such individuals tend to receive attention far out of proportion to their objective ability to remedy the perceived crisis, "in attempting to explain charismatic movements we should look for the operation of an ethologically based attention-binding mechanism." Further evidence for such a "mechanism" is that not infrequently political leaders "capture the primitive allegiance of groups of men without necessarily having displayed a policy at that stage."[44]

Several anthropologists have attempted thus far to apply Chance's "attention structure" concept to the analysis of human political and social status hierarchies.[45]

I shall single out for brief discussion Larsen's formulations, since he seeks to integrate Bernstein's "control role" into the "attention structure" framework. Specifically, Larsen speculates that the control role—"defending group or troop members against internal and external sources of disturbance"—is the primary *function* of the centripetal hierarchical attention *structure*.[46]

From this perspective, Larsen seeks to reinterpret Weber's typology of traditional, legal, and charismatic authority. It seems more parsimonious to propose that there may be only one basic *type* of authority—a centripetal attention structure—and that Weber's "types" represent various stages or manifestations of this pattern. "Charismatic leadership" would thus "be viewed as a raw expression of attention structuring and the process of recreating centripetal hierarchy." This "primitive adaptive process" meets the urgent needs of followers in crisis circumstances, for it "facilitates group cohesion, integration, and stress reduction." Traditional and legal authority can be seen, then, as resulting from the routinization and institutionalization of centripetal attention structures (Weber's "routinization of charisma"), and "successful routinization involves providing the same satisfactions as the primitive pattern does."[47]

EVOLUTION AND DOMINANCE

This argument that propensities to learn and persist in some form of dominance-deference behavior may well inhere in the human genotype requires some support from the highly controversial sphere of speculations about man's evolutionary history. The hominid fossil record is extremely fragmentary, certainly does not speak for itself, and obviously includes no fossilized behavior (though much can be discerned about diet from teeth, posture and gait from leg bones, manual dexterity from hand bones, and culture from artifacts associated with bones). Nevertheless, holding that we have inherited behavioral proclivities requires some kind of attempt to reconstruct how and why certain behaviors may have evolved—that is, what their adaptive value could have been for our evolutionary ancestors.

Because this topic is very broad and complex, and to do it justice would require extended separate treatment, I shall focus on only one speculative reconstruction[48]—Robert Bigelow's "The Evolution of Cooperation, Aggression, and Self-Control."[49] This account very ably integrates paleontological, anatomical, genetic, ecological, psychological, historical, anthropological, and ethological data (including a significant emphasis on primate behavior) into an explanatory theory of human evolution in which dominance-deference behavior plays an essential part. (The reader should keep very much in mind, however, that Bigelow's version of man's evolution is presented here only as an *example* of such a reconstruction; it is in no sense "proved" or "definitive" and on numerous points is open to honest disagreement and criticism.) Bigelow's central concern is to explain the evolutionary growth in size of the human brain. The fossil record seems to indicate that the brain in the hominid line has at least doubled and perhaps tripled in average size during the past three million years, and that this trend was apparently an accelerating process, with the bulk of the increase occurring during the past million years or less. Within the perspective of evolutionary time, this is an extremely brief period for a structure as incredibly complex as the brain of *Homo sapiens* to develop. (An individual's brain size *per se* does not necessarily signify a particular level of intelligence, but in comparisons between species, size correlates very highly with complexity of organization, hence with species-typical intelligence.) Thus some distinctive selective pressures must have been working upon the hominid line; Bigelow's controversial hypothesis is that the most influential of these forces (in conjunction with generally accepted ones such as tool-making and tool-use) was intergroup competition among hominids—not limited to but definitely including aggressive violence.[50]

According to Bigelow, it seems possible, even likely, that this is how we evolved: Early hominids, as primates, lived in social groups; intra-group communication and co-ordination were necessary to protect these ground-dwellers against predators such as lions and leopards.[51] Hominids would have needed a capacity to respond aggressively against attacks, coupled with an ability to control potentially disruptive aggression during intragroup encounters. Groups competed occasionally with others for food and mates, though natural selection would have minimized such competition when hominids were seriously vulnerable to predators and thus needed to attend primarily to their defenses against other species. When such intergroup contests did occur, however, their outcome normally was determined by capacities for aggressive and intelligent group response (which neccessitates intragroup cooperation). [52]

As brains and, consequently, social capacities, evolved, abilities to deal more effectively with predators increased so that hominid intergroup competition could, and presumably did, intensify (largely for the territories most capable of supporting a hunting-gathering way of life). On the average the most co-operative, intelligently self-controlled groups would have succeeded in driving competing groups into less desirable peripheral areas. Successful human groups were the selective force which pushed less intelligently co-operative groups into relatively inhospitable habitats, severely lessening their chances of contributing to the genetic future of the species. As intelligence increased, some individuals would have become capable of perceiving the advantages of co-operation with groups other than their own; this would have required not only intelligence but self-control in the form of inhibitions against attacking former enemies. A primary motive of intergroup co-operation, presumably, was to compete more effectively with still other human groups, and the selective premium on an optimal combination of intragroup (or intra-coalition) co-operation and intelligent self-control for the sake of effective intergroup competition would have increased. Success stemming from these traits, in a positive feedback process, would have selected for increased size and complexity of the brain. [53]

At some unknown point in hominid evolution, linguistic communication emerged (presumably as a result of selective pressures for more effective communication, building upon a foundation made up of relatively high intelligence in combination with a typical primate capacity for vocalization of signals). [54] This made possible even more highly co-ordinated intragroup activity and may well have intensified group integration. But language differences made communication even more difficult with members of other groups and would have acted as an additional impetus to intergroup misunderstanding and hostility. Thus, "conceptual and emotional differences between 'us' and 'them' would have been accentuated." [55]

Within this scenario for man's evolution, self-control is critical:

Capacities for self-control are provided by the actual physical structure of the brain, particularly the cerebral cortex. The result of human evolution was not an array of bodiless "instincts,"but a network of physical nerves and endocrine organs. As this physical organization became more complex and efficient it provided greater capacities for learning from experience, for the repression of emotional drives, and hence for more intelligent self-control. Human capacities for learning, communications, government, science, and art are products of biological evolution, just as running, or any other manifestation of animal behavior, is an expression of the biological potential of interacting muscles, bones, and nerves. [56]

"Self-control" (or apparent inhibition of basic drives) is evidenced in many primates—for example, in thirsty baboons waiting till their group as a unit moves to a water source, in an adult male hamadryas baboon's refraining from copulating with members of a neighbor's "harem," and in a central heirarchy savanna baboon's learning not to respond aggressively and competitively to the initiatives of his "coalition partners." In this context, the dominance hierarchy within a primate group can be seen as an evolved control system at a supra-individual level which tends to reinforce the self-control systems built into the nervous systems of individual group members. [57]

Man, Bigelow believes, is a typical primate in these respects. Without using the precise terms, he emphasizes the "control" function of dominance (and of the rules, laws, and customs enforced by dominant authorities) and, implicitly, the significance of a "centripetal attention structure" for coordinating vital intragroup co-operative efforts during the course of hominid evolution. We have inherited this readiness to learn dominance-deference behavior, and, Bigelow asserts, we still cannot do without effective dominance heirarchies. Like our ancestors, we combine capacities for violence and for self-control, but the latter is not automatically sufficient to control the former. We have learned to extend our co-operative self-control from the small scope of prehistoric clans and tribes to that of groups comprising hundreds of millions, but "We are still learning, and until we have learned to live in peace with one another on a global scale we will have to be restrained—by force, if necessary." [58]

LEADERS AND FOLLOWERS

From a perspective which seeks to encompass studies and theories of primate behavior and scientific speculations, such as Bigelow's, about the course and behavioral effects of man's evolution, it may prove useful to attempt to reinterpret in a summary way of some social-psychological materials on leader-follower behavior. Fiedler's attempts to describe the nature of leadership in face-to-face groups appear to fit readily within the dominance-deference conception analyzed above: "The leader is one who succeeds in getting others to follow him"[59] (focal point of an "attention structure"). "Leadership, essentially, means power over other people . . . .we shall here define the leader as the individual in the group who has the task of directing and coordinating task-relevant group activities"[60] (the "control role").

Fiedler strongly emphasizes the interactional, contextual character of leadership: "there are no leaders where there are no followers. Above all, leadership is a relationship."[61] This accords well, I believe, with ethological-evolutionary perspectives. But before trying to clarify that point, it is necessary to discuss briefly the biological conception that (in its vulgar form) some individuals are "born leaders" (or possess "innate dominance"). [62] This idea should not be dismissed out of hand, even though it is obviously very much subject to abuse. Fiedler cites a study which found significant correlations between leadership and certain personality traits—e.g., intelligence, alertness, verbal facility, dependability, aggressiveness, sociability, cooperation, adaptability.[63] It is reasonable to assume that genetic capacities for developing these characteristics (given, of course, a supportive environment) vary widely among individuals. More specifically, Bigelow speculates that individual differences in "social intelligence"—the ability to predict the likely responses of others and to control one's emotional reactions under pressure—may rest, in part, upon a phylogenetic basis.[64]

In addition to abilities conducive to effective leadership, motivation to acquire high rank may also involve an innate component:

> . . . There are chiefs because there are, in any human group, men who, unlike most of their companions, enjoy prestige for its own sake, feel a strong appeal to responsibility, and to whom the burden of public affairs brings its own reward. These individual differences are certainly emphasized and "played up" by the different cultures, and to unequal degrees, but their clear-cut existence in a society as little competitive as the Nambikuara [the Amazon Indian tribe described in the article] strongly suggests to my mind that their origin itself is not cultural. They are rather part of those psychological raw materials out of which any given culture is made. Men are not all alike; and, in primitive societies . . . these individual differences are as keenly perceived and worked out as in our so-called "individualistic" civilization.[65]

However, no case has yet been made that there are any specific genes for generalized dominance or group leadership. It seems more likely that innate individual differences do exist in the capacity for developing certain personality traits which may enable an individual to become a leader in some circumstances but not in others. This hypothesis is compatible with the conclusion that "a person does not become a leader by virtue of his possession of any one particular pattern of personality traits, but the pattern of personal characteristics of the leader must bear relevant relationship to the present characteristics, activities, and goals of the group of which he is leader. [66]

This returns our attention to the subordinate-follower aspect of dominance-leadership, specifically to the "notion of submissiveness as a basic need in those who follow." [67] Much to this point, I believe, are Stanley Milgram's famous (even notorious) social-psychological "obedience" experiments. [68] They involved placing naive subjects in what they were told was a setting designed to test the effects of punishment on auditory memory. The subject would be seated at a genuine-looking (though phony) "shock generator" and instructed to give word tests to the experimenter's confederate, whom the subject believed to be a volunteer participant like himself. Each time the confederate made an error, the experimenter would order the subject to administer an electric shock to the "learner" by closing a switch. The switches were labeled at 15-volt intervals, from 15 through 450 volts. The experiment was actually intended, of course to determine how many subjects would obey the "scientific authority's" commands to inflict punishment (supposedly) on a person who had done them no harm.

The experiment was run in many versions and the principal result was quite astounding. Although both students of psychology and psychiatrists had predicted prior to the experiments that fewer than one-half of one percent of the subject would go all the way to 450 volts on the "shock panel," the actual range in most of the experimental variations was from 30 to 65 percent "fully obedient." Even when the confederate, in an adjoining room, banged on the wall and screamed about his weak heart, begging the subject to stop, 60 percent of the subjects were completely obedient to the experimenter. [69]

In Milgram's interpretation, this extremely surprising outcome resulted from many of the subjects forsaking their own autonomous judgment or "conscience" within the experimental context and entering into an "agentic state." That is, the compliant subjects ceased to evaluate or feel responsible for their own actions and came to consider themselves solely as obedient tools of the scientifically authoritative experimenter (all subjects were told that the experimenter would assume full responsibility for any harm suffered by the "shock victim"). Milgram believes that the rate at which the subjects assumed the "agentic" role indicates that the experiments must have tapped motivational sources too profound to be accounted for wholly in terms of the idiosyncracies of individuals' social conditioning. He turns, therefore, to evolutionary, biobehavioral theorizing as a mode of explaining his experimental results.

Essentially, he stresses the existence and importance of dominance structures within many animal societies and the probable survival values of hierarchy—including efficient division of labor, firmness of social organization, and maintenance of internal group order. He believes that natural selection has also built into the human species a propensity to create and maintain hierarchical social relationships, which entails a propensity to learn readily deference to authority: ". . . we are born with a potential for obedience, which then interacts with the influence of society to produce the obedient man." When such a person finds himself in the presence of a perceived authority-figure, his propensity to enter the "agentic state" is "exceedingly strong, and the shift is not freely reversible."[70]

The evolutionary theorizing of the late C. H. Waddington may help clarify further both the phylogenesis and ontogenesis of Milgram's "potential for obedience." Waddington stressed the protracted character of infant and childhood dependence (a trend that becomes progressively marked in primate species the nearer their evolutionary relationship to man). This dependence is both made possible and required by the human species' very great reliance upon learning as the individual's primary means of developing adaptive behavior. One ability which must be learned is what Bigelow called "self-control." It seems that the mechanism which we have inherited for controlling our own behavior normally involves accepting completely the authority of those on whom we are dependent when very young. The enormous dependence of our species upon cultural life, including moral norms, has resulted in the evolution of a tendency to "overlearn" and overgeneralize submissiveness to authority-figures and the norms which they supposedly represent.[71]

The evidence and ideas herein discussed that bear upon the dynamics and possible evolved mechanisms of "followership" or submissive behavior appear to provide strong support for Chance's and Larsen's stress upon the importance of the active role of subordinates in the "centripetal attention structure" of a dominance hierarchy. It seems quite likely, then, that phylogenetically determined propensities are profoundly influential on both sides of the leader-follower relationship. That hypothesis is strongly supported by a leading theorist of behavioral evolution: "Social individuals must actually inherit a kind of switch mechanism, which allows them to assume either the dominant or the subordinate role according to circumstances."[72]

To this point in my argument I have attempted, by discussing behavior, analogies, and theories concerning primate behavior, scientific speculation about man's evolution, and some social psychological evidence and concepts, to indicate why it is at least probable that "it is in the nature of human beings as members of a species to create hierarchical orders, some members of which necessarily constitute an elite."[73]

Because that hypothesis is very likely to be misunderstood, I should like—before attempting to explore some of its implications for normative political theory—to state as clearly as possible what my artgument does *not* include or imply. I am not asserting that political hierarchies are or ever have been founded exclusively on our genetic proclivities; these can only be expressed through particular, distinctive, and varying cultural patterns and circumstances. I do not argue that economic, educational, and family differences among people do not critically affect individuals' placement within political hierarchies. I am not arguing that any single *type* of dominance hierarchy is the only "natural" pattern; nor do I mean that dominance must necessarily be harsh and repressive and involve extremes of stratification. Finally, I am not asserting, nor do I believe, that deliberate attempts to construct or reconstruct orders of political stratification are necessarily futile, in any sense "unnatural," or doomed to failure; I very definitely do not mean to imply that whatever is, is inevitable. The last thing I desire is to revivify the justly discredited ideas of "Social Darwinism."

The circumstances within which human behavioral capabilities evolved make it quite unlikely that the normal dominance hierarchy within hominid groups constituted a harsh and repressive tyranny. Our ancestors lived by means of hunting and gathering their food until the development of settled agricultural patterns about 8-10,000 years ago. Our phylogenetically conditioned behavioral propensities were shaped largely by the exigencies of leading a successful predatory existence.[74] Among the requirements of such a life are co-operation and integration of all mature males in the hunting group. In those circumstances, it seems more than likely that "dominance must tend toward the mild 'leadership' type. . . . "[75]

Further, as Tiger and Fox point out, humans must have developed a profound need for significant participation in face-to-face groups. Thus, they aver, we are so often frustrated by the remoteness and impersonality of bureaucracy because it is premised on a denial of our cravng for a "primate politics" which involves dealing with a few well-known persons face-to-face. Yet bureaucracy—made possible by the symbolizing abilities of the cerebral cortex, the most recently evolved part of the human brain—persists. It does so not only because of its functional indispensability in complex industrialized societies but because its structure builds upon other motivations which were essential for a successful hunting life—loyalty and orderliness, a sense of belonging to an ingroup and hostility to outgroups, hierarchy and competition.[76]

POSSIBLE NORMATIVE IMPLICATIONS

But however mild or harsh particular dominance structures may be or need to be, some kind of dominance will exist in any human society, along with deferential and obedient patterns of behavior. The evolutionary, primate behavior-based argument for this conclusion is clearly summarized by Jerome H. Barkow:

> How do we know . . . that human prestige-striving and nonhuman primate social dominance really share a common origin, that is, are homologous? Since our ancestors were nonhuman primates and primates exhibit social ranking, our ancestors presumably were socially ranked. We evolved from these ancestors while organized in cooperative bands of hunters and gatherers . . . . , and organization implies social ranking. It would seem that at no point during our phylogenesis did we lack social hierarchy. If human and nonhuman social dominance have apparently been continuous, they must necessarily be homologous. Cultural systems of social rank are based on, not opposed to, our primate heritage.[77]

It thus seems probable that Thomas Aquinas's Aristotelian view is correct: " . . . it is natural for man, more than for any other animal, to be a social and political animal, to live in a group. . . . If, then, it is natural for man to live in the society of many, it is necessary that there exist among men some means by which the group may be governed."[78]

I would suggest that this conclusion provides us with a reasonably secure hypothetical basis for theorizing about political obligation and about the problems of shaping political institutions to be optimally responsive to human needs and demands. In the remainder of this discussion, I shall focus primarily on political obligation.

The great progenitors of modern political thought—Hobbes, Locke, and Rousseau—share a critical premise: the radically artificial, contrived, contingent character of any and all political authority. Despite the very important differences among them, all three theorists deny that structures of dominance and deference inhere in human nature and concur on the fundamental significance of the question, what can possibly justify the existence of any kind of political authority and obligation? The answer common to all three: only the consent of individuals.

Hobbes and Locke severely qualified this principle for the sake of political order and stability (Hobbes in fact almost, but not quite, qualified it out of existence.) Rousseau, however, attempted in an absolutely serious and literal way to make of it the sole foundation of the polity. Man was originally free—independent, individually isolated except for brief encounters; by virtue of haphazard circumstances developed small-scale societies of mutual accord; but then fell into the chains of extreme dependence and servitude because of the effects of covetousness as manifested in private property.[79] We now know, of course, as Rousseau could not, that every primate species lives within some kind of ordered social group, and that man was never absolutely "free" in the sense of complete isolation and independence.[80] Further, we have seen that dominance hierarchies exist because they have been adaptive in primate evolution—and in species in which, even by analogy, we cannot say that there is "private property."

Nevertheless, Rousseau was led to set impossible conditions for the legitimacy of authority (though he considered it wise ordinarily to obey all *de facto* authority[81]). From premises like Rousseau's it was logical to conclude, as nineteenth-century anarchists and many socialists did, that putting an end to economic inequality and proletarian servitude would eventually bring the "withering away" of political authority. The government of men will be replaced by the administration of things, as "The society that will organize production on the basis of a free and equal association of the producers will put the whole machinery of state where it will then belong: into the museum of antiquities, by the side of the spinning wheel and the bronze ax."[82]

In no way do I underestimate or denigrate the great contributions of political theorists from Hobbes to Marx toward discrediting and undermining the authority of anachronistic, oppressive, and dysfunctional hierarchies. But a generalized and possibly justified suspicion of all political authorities is not really adequate reason for remaining attached to beliefs which seem to bear little or no relationship to empirical reality.

For a specific recent example of such a viewpoint, consider Robert Paul Wolff's ideas on political obligation.[83] He assumes that all men have free will and reason, are thereby responsible for their choices, and hence have a *right* to wholly autonomous individual self-governance. Even more relentlessly consistent than Rousseau, Wolff concludes that "all authority is equally illegitimate, although of course not therefore equally worthy or unworthy of support. . . . There would appear to be no state whose subjects have a moral obligation to obey its commands."[84]

Presumably Wolff does not mean his theory of political obligation to be counterempirical and thus, I believe, an irrelevant fantasy, for elsewhere he reveals a peculiar conception of man's relationship to nature: ". . . . while the natural world really does exist independently of man's beliefs or desires, and therefore exercises a constraint on his will which can at best be mitigated or combatted, the social world is nothing in itself, and consists merely of the totality of the habits, expectations, beliefs, and behavior patterns of all the individuals who live in it."[85] But it is the fundamental premise of evolutionary biology that man's social behavior is totally a part of the "natural world." If one does not assume the "social world" to be supernatural, it can *only* be "natural." And, given man's primate social nature, there seems to be no more reason to base a normative theory on the assumption that political stratification and authority are contingent and ultimately dispensable than to spend one's life pondering the consequencs for society of a dramatic mutation which would suddenly permit every human being to fly without mechanical assistance. Neither project is likely to get off the ground.

The realistic starting point for thinking about political obligation would appear to be not the question, what can justify authority *per se*, but a question something like this: What *kind(s)* of authority structure can be justified under what types of political and social circumstances? In itself, political authority is neither legitimate nor illegitimate; it simply *is*.[86]

In a sense, I am implying the need for an Aristotelian approach to political theory. I do not at all mean that one could or should accept Aristotle's metaphysical premises, ethical system, or political conclusions—but rather that one might set out from the now well-grounded premise that man is *by nature* a political animal and concentrate one's efforts upon trying to discern the empirical and normative relationships between particular kinds of societies and differing *types* of political authority structures.

Finally, this quasi-Aristotelian biobehavioral perspective on authority and political stratification seems likely to inspire concern about discovering and preserving effective restraints upon the wielders of political authority. If one believes that hierarchical authority is a historically bounded phenomenon that will disappear in the socially transformed future, one will oppose overweening and arbitrary authority *only* until one's own movement or party gains absolute power (Leninism is the overwhelmingly relevant example). But if one believes to the contrary that political authority structures are very likely to exist, no matter what movement or party rules or what kinds of socioeconomic transformations occur, then one will consider the structure and operations of the authority system to be a problem of both pressing and permanent significance— especially for the great majority of people who are not members of a "central hierarchy."

Referring again to subhuman primate behavior, one should note in this context the intricately adaptive nature of dominance in species such as the savanna baboons. The central hierarchy males keep order within the troop, protect females and their offspring from predators, lead troop movement, and apparently do most of the breeding—passing on the genetic components of their greater than average capacities for co-operation, intelligent leadership, and aggressive defense. Thus males who achieve dominance invariably behave so as to protect the best interests of the troop as a whole.

It is more than evident that in groups and societies of our species this kind of automatic fit between success in dominance competition and effective substantive leadership no longer exists. Presumably a baboon-like congruence between them was present during the hundreds of thousands of millennia when our ancestors lived in small groups which could not survive without effective leadership and co-ordination of efforts in hunting, food-sharing, and group protection. But in populous, complex societies, political authorities are usually removed from the immediate contexts in which their decisions are implemented. They do not therefore get immediate or necessarily reliable feedback on their wisdom or effectiveness—something which no prehistoric hunter chief could avoid when he and his group either fed well or went hungry.

The transferring of authority structures from the context of face-to-face interaction to that of an ultra-symbolic remoteness also makes it much more difficult for the governed to determine how their own condition is actually affected by the decisions of political authorities.[87] And, of course, historical experience indicates that individuals who achieve high political rank may be too ignorant, arrogant, insensitive, or incompetent to cope satisfactorily with important social problems.

Yet dominance structures there will be in social groupings of the human species, and therefore discovering methods to make and keep them responsive to the substantive needs and desires of the society as a whole is a perennial dilemma. Although our complex societies have lost the automatic fit between dominance and adaptiveness typical of primate groups in their normal habitats, there has been in man an enormous development of a relevant generalized trait characteristic of nearly all primate species—the ability to learn how to adapt to varied circumstances.[88] Using that ability and building, no doubt, on our evolved capacity for self-control, men long ago learned and taught the desirability of subjecting the dominant as well as the subordinate to the restraint of custom and then to the more rationalized "rule of law": "Man, when perfected, is the best of animals; but if he be isolated from law and justice he is the worst of all."[89] And, from an evolutionary perspective:

> Laws and social customs are not unnatural impositions from a source somewhere outside biology. They arise from interactions between the cerebral cortex and other parts of a single body, and from interactions between the brains and eyes and ears and vocal cords of different bodies. They are biological results of biological behavior.[90]

To be precise, the problem is how to prevent political dominance from becoming political domination. A continuing concern with what Madison called the "auxiliary precautions" of constitutionalism[91] will not appear to be the trivial and irrelevant diversion of a decadent bourgeois liberalism if one assumes that we can, within indeterminate limits, choose the *kind* of authority structure by which we will be governed but that if we do not concern ourselves with that choice, it will inexorably be made for us.

NOTES

I am greatly indebted to Duane M. Rumbaugh, Georgia State University, for inspiring me to plunge into the primate literature, and to R. R. Larsen, Dalhousie University, and Roger D. Masters, Dartmouth College, for reading an earlier draft of this paper. Their criticisms were invaluable, but, of course, I alone should be held responsible for this final version.

1. E.g., zoologists: Konrad Lorenz, *Studies in Animal and Human Behaviour*, vol. II,

trans. Robert Martin (Cambridge: Harvard University Press, 1971); N. Tinbergen, "On War and Peace in Animals and Man," *Science* 160 (June 28, 1968): 1411–18; Robert Bigelow, "The Evolution of Cooperation, Aggression, and Self-Control," in *Nebraska Symposium on Motivation, 1972*, ed. James K. Cole and Donald D. Jenson (Lincoln: University of Nebraska Press, 1972), pp. 1–57; psychologists: John Nash, *Developmental Psychology: A Psychobiological Approach* (Englewood Cliffs, New Jersey: Prentice-Hall, 1970); Donald O. Hebb, *Textbook of Psychology*, 3rd ed. (Philadelphia: W. B. Saunders Co., 1972), esp. chap. 11, "Emotion and Motivation: The Social Context"; anthropologists: J. N. Spuhler, "Sociocultural and Biological Inheritance in Man," in *Genetics*, ed. David C. Glass (New York: Rockefeller University Press, 1968), pp. 102–10; V. Reynolds, "Open Groups in Hominid Evolution," *Man* 1 (December 1966): 441–52; Lionel Tiger and Robin Fox, *The Imperial Animal* (New York: Holt, Rinehart and Winston, 1971); sociologists: Bruce Eckland, "Genetics and Sociology: A Reconsideration," *American Sociological Review* 32 (April 1967): 173–94; Allan Mazur and Leon S. Robertson, *Biology and Social Behavior* (New York: Free Press, 1972).

2. E.g., Peter A. Corning, "The Biological Bases of Behavior and Some Implications for Political Science," *World Politics* 23 (April 1971): 321–70; Roger D. Masters, "Genes, Language, and Evolution," *Semiotica* 2, 4 (1970): 295–320; Fred H. Willhoite, Jr., "Ethology and the Tradition of Political Thought," *Journal of Politics* 33 (August 1971): 615–41. For a cataloguing of political science articles influenced in a variety of ways by biological considerations, see Albert Somit, "Review Article: Biopolitics," *British Journal of Political Science* 2 (April 1972): 209–38.

3. I would especially recommend to the curious reader, however, two of the most clearly written introductions to biobehavioral thinking: Robin Fox, "The Cultural Animal," in *Man and Beast: Comparative Social Behavior*, ed. J. F. Eisenberg and Wilton S. Dillon (Washington: Smithsonian Institution Press, 1971), pp. 273–96; Bigelow, "The Evolution of Co-operation, Aggression, and Self Control." A work that may become a basic point of reference for all biobehavioral thinking is Edward O. Wilson, *Sociobiology: The New Synthesis* (Cambridge: Belknap Press of Harvard University Press, 1975).

4. For lucid explanations of this theory, see Theodosius Dobzhansky, *Mankind Evolving* (New Haven: Yale University Press, 1962); George Gaylord Simpson, *The Meaning of Evolution*, rev. ed. (New Haven: Yale University Press, 1967), esp. chap. 14, "Forces of Evolution and Their Integration."

5. For a review and explanation of some of the experimental evidence and basic theory on this point, see Gerald E. McClearn, "Behavioral Genetics: An Overview," *Merrill-Palmer Quarterly of Behavior and Development* 14 (January 1968): 9–24.

6. Nash, *Developmental Psychology*, pp. 59, 115, 158, 233; David A. Hamburg, "Emotions in the Perspective of Human Evolution," in *Expression of the Emotions in Man*, ed. Peter H. Knapp (New York: International Universities Press, 1963), pp. 300–17; Sherwood L. Washburn and David A. Hamburg, "The Study of Primate Behavior," in *Primate Behavior: Field Studies of Monkeys and Apes*, ed. Irven DeVore (New York: Holt, Rinehart and Winston, 1965), pp. 5–6.

7. The computer "programming" analogy is developed in effective heuristic fashion in Tiger and Fox, *The Imperial Animal*, chap. 1, "Beginning Biogrammar." For a wealth of clearly explicated experimental evidence for the biobehavioral perspective, see *Biological Boundaries of Learning*, ed. Martin E. P. Seligman and Joanne L. Hager (New York: Appleton-Century-Crofts, 1972).

8. For a helpful attempt to specify the levels of comparison between human behavior and that of other species, see Roger D. Masters, "Functional Approaches to Analogical Comparison Between Species," paper presented at Conference on the Logic of Inference from Animal to Human Behavior, sponsored by the International Council on the Social Sciences, 1973. Masters distinguishes between a biological "analogy," which refers to common functions served by similar behaviors, and "homology," in which similarities between species stem from a common evolutionary ancestry. (Thus "those characteristics which are more or less common to all primates" might well constitute homologies, [Masters, personal communication.])

9. Michael R. A. Chance and Clifford J. Jolly, *Social Groups of Monkeys, Apes and Men* (New York: E. P. Dutton & Co., 1970), p. 209. The following are examples of anthropologists' attempts to reconstruct the origins of man and of his species-typical behavioral propensities, largely on the basis of primate studies: Reynolds, "Open Groups in Hominid Evolution"; Robin Fox, "In the Beginning: Aspects of Hominid Behavioural Evolution," *Man* 2 (September 1967):415–33; C. J. Jolly, "The Seed-Eaters: A New Model of Hominid Differentiation Based on a Baboon Analogy," *Man* 5 (March 1970): 5–26.

10. John Napier, *The Roots of Mankind* (Washington: Smithsonian Institution Press, 1970), p. 219. An important animal behavior approach that supplements significantly the primatologists' efforts to understand human behavior is the study of predators. Since man evolved as a hunter-gatherer, "human social systems are the product of the selective forces operating on man the primate and man the carnivore . . ." (George B. Schaller and Gordon R. Lowther, "The Relevance of Carnivore Behavior to the Study of Early Hominids," *Southwestern Journal of Anthropology* 25 [Winter 1969]: 336). Study of hunting species may reveal types of selective forces and convergent patterns of adaptation intrinsic to this way of life—despite the enormous phylogenetic distance between predators and man. Evidence thus far is somewhat equivocal, but there appear to be intraspecies competition and some forms—widely varying—of dominance-submission behavior in lions, hyenas, wild dogs, and wolves. The analogies between wolf pack structure and behavior and human social groups are especially striking. On lions, see George B. Schaller, *The Serengeti Lion: A Study of Predator-Prey Relations* (Chicago: University of Chicago Press, 1972), esp. chap. 5; on hyenas, Hans Kruuk, *The Spotted Hyena: A Study of Predation and Social Behavior* (Chicago: University of Chicago Press, 1972), esp. chap. 6; on wild dogs, Hugo and Jane van Lawick-Goodall, *Innocent Killers* (Boston: Houghton Mifflin, 1971), pp. 49–101; on wolves, Jerome H. Woolpy, "The Social Organization of Wolves," *Natural History* 77 (May 1968): 46–55, and L. David Mech, *The Wolf: The Ecology and Behavior of an Endangered Species* (Garden City, New York: Natural History Press, 1970), esp. chap. 3. For a preliminary attempt to compare the behavior of primates and carnivores to presumed behavior patterns of man's ancestors, see Schaller and Lowther, "The Relevance of Carnivore Behavior to the Study of Early Hominids,"

11. Roger D. Masters, "On Comparing Humans—and Human Politics—with Animal Behavior," paper presented to 1973 International Political Science Association Congress, p. 10.

12. Irwin S. Bernstein, "Primate Status Hierarchies," in *Primate Behavior: Developments in Field and Laboratory Research*, vol. I, ed. Leonard A. Rosenblum (New York and London: Academic Press, 1970), pp. 71–109.

13. Hans Kummer, *Primate Societies: Group Techniques of Ecological Adaptation* (Chicago: Aldine-Atherton, 1971), pp. 58–61. The tentativeness of all generalizations must be persistently kept in mind in considering observational data from such a recently developed and rapidly changing field as primate behavior study.

14. For such assertions about baboons and macaques, see Napier, p. 219; about chimpanzees, see Alison Jolly, *The Evolution of Primate Behavior* (New York: Macmillan, 1972), p. 132.

15. For a study of species in one of its native habitats, see Charles H. Southwick, Mirza Azhar Beg, and M. Rafig Siddiqi, "Rhesus Monkeys in North India," in *Primate Behavior*, ed. DeVore, pp. 111–59. Most of the description and analysis of rhesus behavior in the text is drawn from one of the Cayo Santiago studies: John H. Kaufmann, "Social Relations of Adult Males in a Free-ranging Band of Rhesus Monkeys," in *Social Communication Among Primates*, ed. Stuart A. Altmann (Chicago: University of Chicago Press, 1967), pp. 73–98.

16. Southwick et. al., pp. 144–51.

17. Kaufmann, passim.

18. This account is based on K. R. L. Hall and Irven DeVore, "Baboon Social Behavior," in *Primate Behavior*, ed. DeVore, pp. 53–110; and on I. DeVore, "Male Dominance and Mating Behavior in Baboons," in *Sex and Behavior*, ed. Frank A. Beach (New York: John Wiley and Sons, Inc., 1965), pp. 266–89.

19. Such a structure was reported in five troops by Hall and DeVore, p. 54.

20. DeVore, "Male Dominance and Mating Behavior in Baboons, p. 269.

21. DeVore, p. 280.

22. Ibid., pp. 274, 281.

23. Hall and DeVore, p. 71.

24. For a lucid explanation of the evidence for this evolutionary relationship, see S. L. Washburn and Ruth Moore, *Ape Into Man: A Study of Human Evolution* (Boston: Little, Brown, 1974), pp. 11–29.

25. This description is based primarily on George B. Schaller, "The Behavior of the Mountain Gorilla," in *Primate Behavior*, ed. DeVore, pp. 324–67. For a much more elaborate account of the same study, see George B. Schaller, *The Mountain Gorilla: Ecology and Behavior* (Chicago: University of Chicago Press, 1963).

26. Much more aggresiveness and activity than Schaller noted has been observed by Dian Fossey, who is currently engaged in a much longer-term study of mountain gorillas than was Schaller's. E.g., she observed some skirmishes between gorilla groups and, in three cases, saw lone males enter a group and engage in fights in which infants were killed (Jane Goodall, "Intra-specific Aggression," lecture delivered to Human Biology Core Course, Stanford University, October 17, 1975).

27. Most of our information on chimpanzee behavior comes from studies done by or under the direction of Jane Goodall, whose observations in the field began in 1960 and are still continuing. To date (January, 1976) her most comprehensive scientific report is Jane van Lawick-Goodall, "The Behaviour of Free-Living Chimpanzees in the Gombe Stream Reserve," *Animal Behaviour Monographs* 1, part 3, (1968): 165-311. See also Jane Goodall, "Chimpanzees of the Gombe Stream Reserve," in *Primate Behavior*, ed. DeVore, pp. 425–73 (Jane Goodall and Jane van Lawick-Goodall are the same person); also Vernon Reynolds and Frances Reynolds, "Chimpanzees of the Budongo Forest," in the same volume, pp. 368–424.

28. Van Lawick-Goodall, p. 167. In their study, the Reynoldses concurred (pp. 393–96).

29. Goodall, "Intra-specific Aggression"; see also Michael T. Malloy, "Man See, Man Do," *National Observer* (December 6, 1975), 1, 18.

30. Those of Goodall and the Reynoldses in *Primate Behavior*.

31. Jane Goodall, "Social Hierarchy and Dominance," lecture delivered to Human Biology Core Course, Stanford University, October 13, 1975.

32. Van Lawick-Goodall, p. 212.

33. Van Lawick-Goodall, p. 212; Goodall, "Social Hierarchy and Dominance."

34. According to Robin Fox, recent Japanese work indicates that the chimpanzee once had a wider distribution and lived in open territory. When faced with open country, chimpanzee groups became tightly organized in apparent expectation of predatory attacks; for example, such groups exclude young, subadult males. (Robin Fox, "Alliance and Constraint: Sexual Selection in the Evolution of Human Kinship Systems, in *Sexual Selection and the Descent of Man 1871–1971*, ed. Bernard Campbell [Chicago: Aldine, 1972], p. 295.

35. Allan Mazur, "A Cross-Species Comparison of Status in Small Established Groups," *American Sociological Review* 38 (October 1973): 513–30.

36. Ibid., pp. 513–14, 517–25, 526. Mazur's argument strikes me as consistent with the primate data and as logically persuasive. I believe that he is unnecessarily restrictive, however, in asserting that "there is no biological justification" for concluding that "large-scale social stratification must also be a noncultural characteristic" (p. 527). While it is certainly correct that macro-stratification has not been observed in nonhuman primates, that is fundamentally because of man's most important species distinction—an enormously developed symbolizing capacity, manifested primarily through language. In a book which Mazur cites because of his apparent disagreement with its authors on this point, Tiger and Fox argue cogently that the macrostructures of human societies exist only because of man's symbolic-cultural capacities but that symbolism mainly and fundamentally expresses variations on a finite number of behavioral themes which may be discerned by means of thorough and careful cross-species comparisons. (*The Imperial Animal*, pp. 10–20, 34–35, 217–18.)

37. Bernstein, "Primate Status Hierarchies," p. 74.

38. Irwin S. Bernstein and Thomas P. Gordon, "The Function of Aggression in Primate Societies," *American Scientist* 62 (May-June 1974): 308.

39. The initial formulation occurs in M. R. A. Chance, "Attention Structure as the Basis of Primate Rank Orders," *Man* 2 (December 1967): 503–18; see also Chance and Jolly, *Social Groups of Monkeys, Apes, and Men*, pp. 173–75.

40. Chance, p. 509. Emphasis in the original.

41. A particularly dramatic instance of rank-order change—one male's displacing another in the alpha position—can be readily interpreted as demonstrating the importance of attention structure among chimpanzees. This transformation was caused by an adult male's discovering some empty kerosene cans, seizing them, and using them to make an unusually horrendous noise during a ritualistic "charging run," one of the principal forms of dominance competition among adult males of this species. The attention that he thereby drew to himself persisted, and—after several nonviolent agonistic contests—he was deferred to by all other group members, including the previous alpha male. See Jane van Lawick-Goodall, "Some Aspects of Aggressive Behaviour in a Group

of Free-living Chimpanzees," *International Social Science Journal* 23, 1 (1971): 93–95; also van Lawick-Goodall, *In the Sahdow of Man* (Boston: Houghton Mifflin, 1971), pp. 112–17.

42. Chance and Jolly, p. 174. Some criticisms of the "attention structure" conception are mentioned briefly in Alison Jolly, *The Evolution of Primate Behavior*, pp. 192–93.

43. Chance, p. 511. My emphasis.

44. Chance and Jolly, pp. 208–09.

45. See, e.g., Lionel Tiger, "Dominance in Human Societies," *Annual Review of Ecology and Systematics* 1 (1970): 298–301; Tiger and Fox, *The Imperial Animal*, pp. 39–51; R. R. Larsen, "Leaders and Non-Leaders: Speculation on Charisma," paper presented to 1873 Southern Political Science Association Meeting.

46. Larsen, p. 3.

47. Ibid., pp. 7–8.

48. For some other representative viewpoints, see n. 9.

49. See n. 1.

50. Bigelow, pp. 1–3. That there was an important degree of prehistoric intergroup violence is perhaps Bigelow's most controversial—and controverted—point. This is a fairly typical critique of it by an anthropologist: " . . . the evidence for intergroup violent competition is exceedingly weak when we look at modern hunter-gatherer groups, the pre-historic tool assemblages, and fossil remains. I do agree, however, that there probably was competition between groups and that it was most likely linked to relative efficiency of resource exploitation and rate of population growth rather than aggressive interaction." (R. R. Larsen, personal communication.) Goodall's recent observations, discussed above, of group-territorial aggression in chimpanzees may provide some support for Bigelow's speculations.

51. Note the stress on the evolutionary importance of predation pressures on savanna baboons, in Irven DeVore and K. R. L. Hall, "Baboon Ecology," in *Primate Behavior*, ed. DeVore, p. 49.

52. Bigelow, pp. 3–4.

53. Ibid., pp. 4–5.

54. For relevant speculations, see Charles F. Hockett and Robert Ascher, "The Human Revolution," *Current Anthropology* 5 (June 1964): 135–47.

55. Bigelow, pp. 42–43.

56. Ibid., p. 6.

57. Ibid., pp. 27, 29, 31.

58. Ibid., p. 52.

59. W. H. Cowley, "Three Distinctions in the Study of Leaders." *Journal of Abnormal and Social Psychology* 23 (July-September 1928): 144, quoted in Fred E. Fiedler, "Leadership" (Morristown, New Jersey: General Learning Press, 1971), p. 2.

60. Fiedler, pp. 1, 2.

61. Ibid., p. 2.

62. A popularized but stimulating discussion of this idea is presented in Robert Ardrey, *The Social Contract* (New York: Atheneum, 1970), pp. 102–36.

63. Fiedler, p. 4.

64. Bigelow, pp. 48–51.

65. Claude Lévi-Strauss, "The Social and Psychological Aspects of Chieftainship in a Primitive Tribe; The Nambikuara of Northwestern Mato Grosso," in *Comparative Politi-*

cal Systems: Studies in the Politics of Pre-Industrial Societies, ed. Ronald Cohen and John Middleton (Garden City, New York: Natural History Press, 1967), pp. 61–62.

66. Cecil A. Gibb, "Leadership," in *The Handbook of Social Psychology*, vol. IV, ed. Gardner Lindzey and Elliot Aronson, 2d ed. (Reading, Massachusetts: Addison-Wesley Publishing Co., 1969), p. 226.

67. Ibid., p. 252.

68. First reported in Stanley Milgram, "Behavioral Study of Obedience," *Journal of Abnormal and Social Psychology* 67 (October 1963): 371–78; reviewed, analyzed, and interpreted in Stanley Milgram, *Obedience to Authority* (New York: Harper & Row, 1974).

69. Milgram, *Obedience to Authority*, pp. 30–35.

70. Milgram, pp. 123–25, 134. The possibility that Milgram had instead tapped a hidden wellspring of sadistic aggression is belied by the outcome of one version of his experiment. Subjects were allowed to choose the shock level they would use to punish the "learner." Only one of forty moved all the way up the panel to the "450" switch (ibid., pp. 70–72).

71. C. H. Waddington, *The Ethical Animal* (London: George Allen & Unwin Ltd., 1960), pp. 155–74. Submissive obedience can be, of course, horrendously destructive. E.g., note Hannah Arendt's observation that the vaunted aggressive toughness of Nazi SS men was actually, with few exceptions, "nothing but a myth of self-deception, concealing a ruthless desire for conformity at any price . . ." (Hannah Arendt, *Eichmann in Jerusalem: A Report onf the Banality of Evil* [New York: Viking Press, 1963], p. 157).

72. V. C. Wynne-Edwards, "Population Control and Social Selection in Animals," in *Genetics*, ed. David C. Glass, p. 162.

73. Tiger, "Dominance in Human Societies," p. 295.

74. One of the best brief discussions of the impact of hunting on the evolution of human behavior is Sherwood L. Washburn and C. S. Lancaster, "The Evolution of Hunting," in *Man the Hunter*, ed. Richard B. Lee and Irven DeVore (Chicago: Aldine, 1968), pp. 293–303. See also n. 10, above.

75. William Etkin, *Social Behavior from Fish to Man* (Chicago: University of Chicago Press, Phoenix Books, 1967), p. 140.

76. Tiger and Fox, *The Imperial Animal*, pp. 48–51. Therefore it seems likely that, in evolutionary terms, "consent" is as old as, in fact coterminous with, "command" in human authority structures. This may be viewed as some degree of validation of Hannah Arendt's insight into the "elementary dynamics" of political life—namely, her recurrent emphasis upon the spontaneity of small-scale participatory political groups during most modern revolutionary upheavals and her insistence upon popular consent as the basis of effective political power. See Hannah Arendt, *On Revolution* (New York: Viking Press, 1963), esp. pp. 259–85; Arendt, "Reflections on Violence," *Journal of International Affairs* 23, 1 (1969): 14–15.

77. Jerome H. Barkow, "Prestige and Culture: A Biosocial Interpretation," *Current Anthropology* 16 (December 1975): 554.

78. St. Thomas Aquinas, *On Kingship*, in *The Political Ideas of St. Thomas Aquinas*, ed. Dino Bigongiari (New York: Hafner, 1953), pp. 175, 176.

79. Jean-Jacques Rousseau, *Discourse on the Origin and Foundation of Inequality Among Mankind* (1755).

80. Sherwood L. Washburn and David A. Hamburg, "The Implications of Primate Research," in *Primate Behavior*, ed. DeVore, p. 612.

81. Jean-Jacques Rousseau, *Emile, or Education*, trans. Barbara Foxley (New York: E. P. Dutton, Everyman's Library, 1911, reprinted 1963), p. 274.

82. Friedrich Engels, *The Origin of the Family, Private Property and the State*, in *Marx and Engels: Basic Writings on Politics and Philosophy*, ed. Lewis S. Feuer (Garden City, New York: Doubleday Anchor Books, 1959), p. 394. It should be noted that Engels did not believe that all hierarchical authority would disappear under communism. In an essay on authority, he asserted that authority in the factory was a functional requirement of industrial production and thus unavoidable. In the same essay, however, Engels reiterated: "All socialists are agreed that the political state, and with it political authority will disappear as a result of the coming social revolution, that is, that public functions will lose their political character and be transformed into the simple administrative functions of watching over the true interests of society." ("On Authority," in *Basic Writings*, ed. Feuer. p. 485.)

83. Robert Paul Wolff, *In Defense of Anarchism* (New York: Harper Torchbooks, 1970).

84. Ibid., p. 19.

85. Ibid., p. 76.

86. Cf. Mazur, p. 526.

87. See Murray Edelman, *The Symbolic Uses of Politics* (Urbana: University of Illinois Press, 1964).

88. E.g., female savanna baboons were placed within a group of hamadryas baboons; within an hour each female had learned to remain near and follow the male which had threatened or attacked her. This is normal behavior for a hamadryas female but precisely opposite the usual behavior of a female savanna baboon among males of her own species. Conversely, hamadryas females placed among savanna baboons soon learned not to follow individual males as these females had always done among their own kind. (Kummer, *Primate Societies*, pp. 99–100.) The example cited above (n. 41) of a rank order change in a chimpanzee group can be viewed as an individual's learning to use a newly available resource—noisemaking tin cans—as a device to inhibit the dominance behavior of the alpha male, making it possible for the innovator to rise quickly to the top of the group hierarchy.

89. Aristotle, *Politics*, 1253a, trans. Ernest Barker (New York: Oxford University Press, 1946), p. 7.

90. Bigelow, p. 24.

91. *The Federalist*, No. 51.

16

SIGMUND FREUD

The Leader as Group Ideal

THE GROUP AND THE PRIMAL HORDE

IN 1912 I took up a conjecture of Darwin's to the effect that the primitive form of human society was that of a horde ruled over despotically by a powerful male. I attempted to show that the fortunes of this horde have left indestructible traces upon the history of human descent; and, especially, that the development of totemism, which comprises in itself the beginnings of religion, morality, and social organization, is connected with the killing of the chief by violence and the transformation of the paternal horde into a community of brothers.[1] To be sure, this is only a hypothesis, like so many others with which archaeologists endeavour to lighten the darkness of prehistoric times—a "Just-So Story," as it was amusingly called by a not unkind English critic;[2] but I think it is creditable to such a hypothesis if it proves able to bring coherence and understanding into more and more new regions.

Human groups exhibit once again the familiar picture of an individual of superior strength among a troop of equal companions, a picture which is also contained in our idea of the primal horde. The psychology of such a group, as we know it from the descriptions to which we have so often referred—the dwindling of the conscious individual personality,

From Sigmund Freud, *Group Psychology and the Analysis of the Ego*, trans. James Strachey (New York: Norton, 1954), chap. 10, "The Group and the Primal Horde," pp. 54–60. Reprinted by permission of W. W. Norton & Company, Inc., and The Hogarth Press. Copyright © 1959 by Sigmund Freud Copyrights, Ltd. Copyright © 1959 by James Strachey. Translation and editorial matter copyright © 1959, 1922 by the Institute of Psycho-Analysis and Angela Richards. First published in 1921.

the focusing of thoughts and feelings into a common direction, the predominance of the affective side of the mind and of unconscious psychical life, the tendency to the immediate carrying out of intentions as they emerge—all this corresponds to a state of regression to a primitive mental activity, of just such a sort as we should be inclined to ascribe to the primal horde.[3]

Thus the group appears to us as a revival of the primal horde. Just as primitive man survives potentially in every individual, so the primal horde may arise once more out of any random collection; in so far as men are habitually under the sway of group formation we recognize in it the survival of the primal horde. We must conclude that the psychology of groups is the oldest human psychology; what we have isolated as individual psychology, by neglecting all traces of the group, has only since come into prominence out of the old group psychology, by a gradual process which may still, perhaps, be described as incomplete. We shall later venture upon an attempt at specifying the point of departure of this development. . . .

Further reflection will show us in what respect this statement requires correction. Individual psychology must, on the contrary, be just as old as group psychology, for from the first there were two kinds of psychologies, that of the individual members of the group and that of the father, chief, or leader. The members of the group were subject to ties just as we see them to-day, but the father of the primal horde was free. His intellectual acts were strong and independent even in isolation, and his will needed no reinforcement from others. Consistency leads us to assume that his ego had few libidinal ties; he loved no one but himself, or other people only in so far as they served his needs. To objects his ego gave away no more than was barely necessary.

He, at the very beginning of the history of mankind, was the "superman" whom Nietzsche only expected from the future. Even to-day the members of a group stand in need of the illusion that they are equally and justly loved by their leader; but the leader himself need love no one else, he may be of a masterful nature, absolutely narcissistic, self-confident and independent. We know that love puts a check upon narcissism, and it would be possible to show how, by operating in this way, it became a factor of civilization.

The primal father of the horde was not yet immortal, as he later became by deification. If he died, he had to be replaced; his place was probably taken by a youngest son, who had up to then been a member of

the group like any other. There must therefore be a possibility of transforming group psychology into individual psychology; a condition must
be discovered under which such a transformation is easily accomplished,
just as it is possible for bees in case of necessity to turn a larva into a queen
instead of into a worker. One can imagine only one possibility: the primal
father had prevented his sons from satisfying their directly sexual impulsions; he forced them into abstinence and consequently into the emotional ties with him and with one another which could arise out of those
of their impulsions that were inhibited in their sexual aim. He forced
them, so to speak, into group psychology. His sexual jealousy and intolerance became in the last resort the causes of group psychology.[4]

Whoever became his successor was also given the possibility of sexual
satisfaction, and was by that means offered a way out of the conditions of
group psychology. The fixation of the libido to woman and the possibility
of satisfaction without any need for delay or accumulation made an end
of the importance of those of his sexual impulsions that were inhibited in
their aim, and allowed his narcissism always to rise to its full height. . . .

We may further emphasize, as being specially instructive, the relation
that holds between the contrivance by means of which an artificial group
is held together and the constitution of the primal horde. We have seen
that with an army and a Church this contrivance is the illusion that the
leader loves all of the individuals equally and justly. But this is simply an
idealistic remodelling of the state of affairs in the primal horde, where all
of the sons knew that they were equally *persecuted* by the primal father,
and *feared* him equally. This same recasting upon which all social duties
are built up is already presupposed by the next form of human society, the
totemic clan. The indestructible strength of the family as a natural group
formation rests upon the fact that this necessary presupposition of the
father's equal love can have a real application in the family.

But we expect even more of this derivation of the group from the
primal horde. It ought also to help us to understand what is still
incomprehensible and mysterious in group formations—all that lies hidden behind the enigmatic words "hypnosis" and "suggestion." And I think
it can succeed in this too. Let us recall that hypnosis has something
positively uncanny about it; but the characteristic of uncanniness suggests
something old and familiar that has undergone repression.[5] Let us consider how hypnosis is induced. The hypnotist asserts that he is in possession of a mysterious power that robs the subject of his own will; or, which
is the same thing, the subject believes it of him. This mysterious power
(which is even now often described popularly as "animal magnetism")

must be the same power that is looked upon by primitive people as the source of taboo, the same that emanates from kings and chieftains and makes it dangerous to approach them *(mana)*. The hypnotist, then, is supposed to be in possession of this power; and how does he manifest it? By telling the subject to look him in the eyes; his most typical method of hypnotizing is by his look. But it is precisely the *sight* of the chieftain that is dangerous and unbearable for primitive people, just as later that of the Godhead is for mortals. Even Moses had to act as an intermediary between his people and Jehovah, since the people could not support the sight of God; and when he returned from the presence of God his face shone—some of the *mana* had been transferred on to him, just as happens with the intermediary among primitive people.[6]

It is true that hypnosis can also be evoked in other ways, for instance by fixing the eyes upon a bright object or by listening to a monotonous sound. This is misleading and has given occasion to inadequate physiological theories. In point of fact these procedures merely serve to divert conscious attention and to hold it riveted. The situation is the same as if the hypnotist had said to the subject: "Now concern yourself exclusively with my person; the rest of the world is quite uninteresting." It would of course be technically inexpedient for a hypnotist to make such a speech; it would tear the subject away from his unconscious attitude and stimulate him to conscious opposition. The hypnotist avoids directing the subject's conscious thoughts towards his own intentions, and makes the person upon whom he is experimenting sink into an activity in which the world is bound to seem uninteresting to him; but at the same time the subject is in reality unconsciously concentrating his whole attention upon the hypnotist, and is getting into an attitude of *rapport*, of transference on to him. Thus the indirect methods of hypnotizing, like many of the technical procedures used in making jokes,[7] have the effect of checking certain distributions of mental energy which would interfere with the course of events in the unconscious, and they lead eventually to the same result as the direct methods of influence by means of staring or stroking.[8]

Ferenczi [1909] has made the true discovery that when a hypnotist gives the command to sleep, which is often done at the beginning of hypnosis, he is putting himself in the place of the subject's parents. He thinks that two sorts of hypnotism are to be distinguished: one coaxing and soothing, which he considers is modelled on the mother, and another threatening, which is derived from the father. Now the command to sleep in hypnosis means nothing more nor less than an order to withdraw all interest from the world and to concentrate it on the person of

the hypnotist. And it is so understood by the subject; for in this withdrawal of interest from the external world lies the psychological characteristic of sleep, and the kinship between sleep and the state of hypnosis is
based on it.

By the measures that he takes, then, the hypnotist awakens in the
subject a portion of his archaic heritage which had also made him compliant towards his parents and which had experienced an individual re-
animation in his relation to his father; what is thus awakened is the idea of
a paramount and dangerous personality, towards whom only a passive-
masochistic attitude is possible, to whom one's will has to be surrendered, —while to be alone with him, "to look him in the face," appears a
hazardous enterprise. It is only in some such way as this that we can
picture the relation of the individual member of the primal horde to the
primal father. As we know from other reactions, individuals have preserved a variable degree of personal aptitude for reviving old situations of
this kind. Some knowledge that in spite of everything hypnosis is only a
game, a deceptive renewal of these old impressions, may, however,
remain behind and take care that there is a resistance against any too
serious consequences of the suspension of the will in hypnosis.

The uncanny and coercive characteristics of group formations, which
are shown in the phenomena of suggestion that accompany them, may
therefore with justice be traced back to the fact of their origin from the
primal horde. The leader of the group is still the dreaded primal father;
the group still wishes to be governed by unrestricted force; it has an
extreme passion for authority; in Le Bon's phrase, it has a thirst for
obedience. The primal father is the group ideal, which governs the ego in
the place of the ego ideal. Hypnosis has a good claim to being described
as a group of two. There remains as a definition for suggestion: a conviction which is not based upon perception and reasoning but upon an
erotic tie.[9]

NOTES

The notes in brackets are those of James Strachey, Freud's translator. [BK]

1. *Totem and Taboo* (1912–13). [Essay IV. Freud uses the term 'horde' to signify a
relatively small collection of people.]
2. [In the 1st edition only, the name "Kroeger" appeared here. This was evidently a
misprint for "Kroeber"—incidentally the name of the well-known *American* anthro-

pologist. Kroeber's original review of *Totem and Taboo*, published in *Amer. Anthropol.*, New Series 22 (1920); 48, contained no reference to a "just-so story." This was pointed out by Kroeber himself in a second review, published nearly twenty years later in *Amer. J. Sociol.* 45 (1939): 446. The comparison with a "just-so story" was actually made in a review of *Totem and Taboo* by the English anthropologist R. R. Marett in *The Athenaeum*, Feb. 13, 1920, p. 206.]

3. What we have just described in our general characterization of mankind must apply especially to the primal horde. The will of the individual was too weak; he did not venture upon action. No impulses whatever came into existence except collective ones; there was only a common will, there were no single ones. An idea did not dare to turn itself into an act of will unless it felt itself reinforced by a perception of its general diffusion. This weakness of the idea is to be explained by the strength of the emotional tie which is shared by all the members of the horde; but the similarity in the circumstances of their life and the absence of any private property assist in determining the uniformity of their individual mental acts. As we may observe with children and soldiers, common activity is not excluded even in the excretory functions. The one great exception is provided by the sexual act, in which a third person is at best superfluous and in the extreme case is condemned to a state of painful expectancy.

4. It may perhaps also be assumed that the sons, when they were driven out and separated from their father, advanced from identification with one another to homosexual object-love, and in this way won freedom to kill their father. [See *Totem and Taboo*, *Standard Ed.*, 13, 144.]

5. Cf. 'The "Uncanny"' (1919h) [*Standard Ed.*, 17, 245].

6. See *Totem and Taboo* [second essay] and the sources there quoted.

7. [The distracting of attention as part of the technique of joking is discussed at some length in the latter half of Chapter V of Freud's book on jokes (1905c). For the possibility of this mechanism playing a part in "thought-transference" see "Psycho-Analysis and Telepathy," 1941d, *Standard Ed.*, 18, 184. See also the final chapter in *Studies on Hysteria* (Breuer and Freud, 1895). Towards the beginning of the second section of that chapter Freud brings forward this same mechanism as a possible part explanation of the efficacy of his "pressure" procedure. *Standard Ed.*, 2, 271. See too Part 1, Section 19, of the *Project* (*S.E.*, 1, 337).]

8. This situation, in which the subject's attitude is unconsciously directed towards the hypnotist, while he is consciously occupied with monotonous and uninteresting perceptions, finds a parallel among the events of psycho-analytic treatment, which deserves to be mentioned here. At least once in the course of every analysis a moment comes when the patient obstinately maintains that just now positively nothing whatever occurs to his mind. His free associations come to a stop and the usual incentives for putting them in motion fail in their effect. If the analyst insists, the patient is at last induced to admit that he is thinking of the view from the consulting-room window, of the wall-paper that he sees before him, or of the gas-lamp hanging from the ceiling. Then one knows at once that he has gone off into the transference and that he is engaged upon what are still unconscious thoughts relating to the physician; and one sees the stoppage in the patient's associations disappear, as soon as he has been given this explanation.

9. It seems to me worth emphasizing the fact that the discussions in this section have induced us to give up Bernheim's conception of hypnosis and go back to the *naïf* earlier

one. According to Bernheim all hypnotic phenomena are to be traced to the factor of suggestion, which is not itself capable of further explanation. We have come to the conclusion that suggestion is a partial manifestation of the state of hypnosis, and that hypnosis is solidly founded upon a predisposition which has survived in the unconscious from the early history of the human family. [Freud had already expressed his scepticism about Bernheim's views on suggestion in the preface to his translation of Bernheim's book on the subject (1888–9), *Standard Ed.*, 1, 78 ff. . . .]

17

ROBERT MICHELS

The Impossibility of Direct Government

IT was a Rhenish democrat, Moritz Rittinghausen, who first made a
brilliant attempt to give a real basis for direct legislation by the people.[1]
   According to this system the entire population was to be divided into
sections, each containing a thousand inhabitants, as was done temporarily for some days in Prussia during the elections of the years 1848
and 1849. The members of each section were to assemble in some pre-
arranged place—a school, townhall, or other public building—and to
elect a president. Every citizen was to have the right of speech. In this
way the intelligence of every individual would be placed at the service of
the fatherland. When the discussion was finished, each one would record
his vote. The president would transmit the result to the burgomaster, who
would notify the higher authorities. The will of the majority would be
decisive.
   No legislative proposal was to come from above. The government
should have no further initiative than to determine that on a given day all
the sections should discuss a given argument. Whenever a certain
number of the citizens demanded a new law of any kind, or the reform of
an existing law, the ministry concerned must invite the people to exercise
its sovereignty within a stated time, and to pass for itself the law in
question.[2] The law takes organic form from the discussion itself. First of
all, the president opens the debate upon the principal question. Subsequently subordinate points are discussed. Then comes the vote. That
proposition which has received the majority of votes is adopted. As soon

From Robert Michels, *Political Parties*, trans. Eden and Cedar Paul (New York: The Free Press,
1962), chap. 2, "Mechanical and Technical Impossibility of Direct Government by the Masses," pp.
63–77. Reprinted with permission of The Free Press, a division of Macmillan, Inc. Copyright ©
1962 by the Crowell-Collier Publishing Company. First published in 1911.

as all the returns of the voting have been sent to the ministry, a special commission must edit a clear and simple text of the law, formulating it in a manner which is not open to different interpretations, as is the case with most of the laws presented to modern parliaments, for these, as Rittinghausen sarcastically adds, would seem to incorporate a deliberate intention to favor the tendency of lawyers to ambiguity and hair-splitting.

The system here sketched is clear and concise, and it might seem at the first glance that its practical application would involve no serious difficulties. But if put to the test it would fail to fulfil the expectations of its creator.

The practical ideal of democracy consists in the self-government of the masses in conformity with the decisions of popular assemblies. But while this system limits the extension of the principle of delegation, it fails to provide any guarantee against the formation of an oligarchical camerilla. Undoubtedly it deprives the natural leaders of their quality as functionaries, for this quality is transferred to the people themselves. The crowd, however, is always subject to suggestion, being readily influenced by the eloquence of great popular orators; moreover, direct government by the people, admitting of no serious discussions or thoughtful deliberations, greatly facilitates *coups de main* of all kinds by men who are exceptionally bold, energetic, and adroit.

It is easier to dominate a large crowd than a small audience. The adhesion of the crowd is tumultuous, summary, and unconditional. Once the suggestions have taken effect, the crowd does not readily tolerate contradiction from a small minority, and still less from isolated individuals. A great multitude assembled within a small area is unquestionably more accessible to panic alarms, to unreflective enthusiasm, and the like, than is a small meeting, whose members can quietly discuss matters among themselves (Roscher).[3]

It is a fact of everyday experience that enormous public meetings commonly carry resolutions by acclamation or by general assent, whilst these same assemblies, if divided into small sections, say of fifty persons each, would be much more guarded in their assent. Great party congresses, in which are present the *élite* of the membership, usually act in this way. Words and actions are far less deliberately weighed by the crowd than by the individuals or the little groups of which this crowd is composed. The fact is incontestable—a manifestation of the pathology of the crowd. The individual disappears in the multitude, and therewith disappears also personality and sense of responsibility.

The most formidable argument against the sovereignty of the masses is, however, derived from the mechanical and technical impossibility of its realization.

The sovereign masses are altogether incapable of undertaking the most necessary resolutions. The impotence of direct democracy, like the power of indirect democracy, is a direct outcome of the influence of number. In a polemic against Proudhon (1849), Louis Blanc asks whether it is possible for thirty-four millions of human beings (the population of France at that time) to carry on their affairs without accepting what the pettiest man of business finds necessary, the intermediation of representatives. He answers his own question by saying that one who declares direct action on this scale to be possible is a fool, and that one who denies its possibility need not be an absolute opponent of the idea of the state.[4] The same question and the same answer could be repeated today in respect of party organization. Above all in the great industrial centers, where the labor party sometimes numbers its adherents by tens of thousands, it is impossible to carry on the affairs of this gigantic body without a system of representation. The great socialist organization of Berlin, which embraces the six constituencies of the city, as well as the two outlying areas of Niederbarnim and Teltow-Beeskow-Charlottenburg, has a member-roll of more than ninety thousand.

It is obvious that such a gigantic number of persons belonging to a unitary organization cannot do any practical work upon a system of direct discussion. The regular holding of deliberative assemblies of a thousand members encounters the gravest difficulties in respect of room and distance; while from the topographical point of view such an assembly would become altogether impossible if the members numbered ten thousand. Even if we imagined the means of communication to become much better than those which now exist, how would it be possible to assemble such a multitude in a given place, at a stated time, and with the frequency demanded by the exigencies of party life? In addition must be considered the physiological impossibility even for the most powerful orator of making himself heard by a crowd of ten thousand persons.[5] There are, however, other persons of a technical and administrative character which render impossible the direct self-government of large groups. If Peter wrongs Paul, it is out of the question that all the other citizens should hasten to the spot to undertake a personal examination of the matter in dispute, and to take the part of Paul against Peter.[6] By parity of reasoning, in the modern democratic party, it is impossible for the collectivity to undertake the direct settlement of all the controversies that may arise.

Hence the need for delegation, for the system in which delegates represent the mass and carry out its will. Even in groups sincerely animated with the democratic spirit, current business, the preparation and the carrying out of the most important actions, is necessarily left in the hands of individuals. It is well known that the impossibility for the people to exercise a legislative power directly in popular assemblies led the democratic idealists of Spain to demand, as the least of evils, a system of popular representation and a parliamentary state.[7]

Originally the chief is merely the servant of the mass. The organization is based upon the absolute equality of all its members. Equality is here understood in its most general sense, as equality of like men. In many countries, as in idealist Italy (and in certain regions in Germany where the socialist movement is still in its infancy), this equality is manifested, among other ways, by the mutual use of the familiar "thou," which is employed by the most poorly paid wage-laborer in addressing the most distinguished intellectual. This generic conception of equality is, however, gradually replaced by the idea of equality among comrades belonging to the same organization, all of whose members enjoy the same rights. The democratic principle aims at guaranteeing to all an equal influence and an equal participation in the regulation of the common interests. All are electors, and all are eligible for office. The fundamental postulate of the *Déclaration des Droits de l'Homme* finds here its theoretical application. All the offices are filled by election. The officials, executive organs of the general will, play a merely subordinate part, are always dependent upon the collectivity, and can be deprived of their office at any moment. The mass of the party is omnipotent.

At the outset, the attempt is made to depart as little as possible from pure democracy by subordinating the delegates altogether to the will of the mass, by tieing them hand and foot. In the early days of the movement of the Italian agricultural workers, the chief of the league required a majority of four-fifths of the votes to secure election. When disputes arose with the employers about wages, the representative of the organization, before undertaking any negotiations, had to be furnished with a written authority, authorized by the signature of every member of the corporation. All the accounts of the body were open to the examination of the members, at any time. There were two reasons for this. First of all, the desire was to avoid the spread of mistrust through the mass, "this poison which gradually destroys even the strongest organism." In the second place, this usage allowed each one of the members to learn bookkeeping, and to acquire such a general knowledge of the working of the corporation as to enable him at any time to take over its leadership.[8] It is obvious that democracy in this sense is applicable only on a very small scale. In the infancy of the English labor movement, in many of the trade unions, the delegates were either appointed in rotation from among all the members, or were chosen by lot.[9] Gradually, however, the delegates' duties became more complicated; some individual ability becomes essential, a certain oratorical gift, and a considerable amount of objective knowledge. It thus becomes impossible to trust to blind chance, to the fortune of alphabetic succession, or to the order of priority, in the choice of a delegation whose members must possess certain peculiar personal aptitudes if they are to discharge their mission to the general advantage.

Such were the methods which prevailed in the early days of the labor movement to enable the masses to participate in party and trade-union administration. Today they are falling into disuse, and in the development of the modern political aggregate there is a tendency to shorten and stereotype the process which transforms the led into a leader—a process which has hitherto developed by the natural course of events. Here and there voices make themselves heard demanding a sort of official consecration for the leaders, insisting that it is necessary to constitute a class of professional politicians, of approved and registered experts in political life. Ferdinand Tönnies advocates that the party should institute regular examinations for the nomination of socialist parliamentary candidates, and for the appointment of party secretaries.[10] Heinrich Herkner goes even farther. He contends that the great trade unions cannot long maintain their existence if they persist in entrusting the management of their affairs to persons drawn from the rank and file, who have risen to command stage by stage solely in consequence of practical aptitudes acquired in the service of the organization. He refers, in this connection, to the unions that are controlled by the employers, whose officials are for the most part university men. He foresees that in the near future all the labor organizations will be forced to abandon proletarian exclusiveness, and in the choice of their officials to give the preference to persons of an education that is superior alike in economic, legal, technical, and commercial respects.[11]

Even today, the candidates for the secretaryship of a trade union are subject to examination as to their knowledge of legal matters and their capacity as letter-writers. The socialist organizations engaged in political action also directly undertake the training of their own officials. Everywhere there are coming into existence "nurseries" for the rapid supply of officials possessing a certain amount of "scientific culture." Since 1906 there has existed in Berlin a Party-School in which courses of instruction are given for the training of those who wish to take office in the socialist party or in trade unions. The instructors are paid out of the funds of the socialist party, which was directly responsible for the foundation of the school. The other expenses of the undertaking, including the maintenance of the pupils, are furnished from a common fund supplied by the party and the various trade unions interested. In addition, the families of the pupils, in so far as the attendance of these at the school deprives the families of their breadwinners, receive an allowance from the provincial branch of the party or from the local branch of the union to which each pupil belongs. The third course of this school, from October 1, 1908, to April 3, 1909, was attended by twenty-six pupils, while the first year there had been thirty-one and the second year thirty-three. As pupils, preference is given to comrades who already hold office in the party or in one of the labor unions.[12] Those who do not already belong to the labor bureaucracy make it their aim to enter that body, and cherish the secret hope that attendance at the school will smooth their path. Those who fail to attain this end are apt to exhibit a certain discontent with the party which, after having encouraged their studies, has sent them back to manual labor. Among the 141 students of the year 1910–11, three classes were to be distinguished: one of these consisted of old and tried employees in the different branches of the labor movement (fifty-two persons); a second consisted of those who obtained employment in the party or the trade unions directly the course was finished (forty-nine persons); the third consisted of those who had to return to manual labor (forty persons).[13]

In Italy, *L'Umanitaria*, a philanthropic organization run by the socialists, founded at Milan in 1905 a "Practical School of Social Legislation," whose aim it is to give to a certain number of workers an education which will fit them for becoming factory inspectors, or for taking official positions in the various labor organizations, in the friendly societies, or in the labor exchanges.[14] The course of instruction lasts for two years, and at its close the pupils receive, after examination, a diploma which entitles them to the title of "Labor Expert." In 1908 there were two hundred and two pupils, thirty-seven of whom were employees of trade unions or of cooperative societies, four were secretaries of labor exchanges, forty-five employees in or members of the liberal professions, and a hundred and twelve working men.[15] At the outset most of the pupils came to the school as a matter of personal taste, or with the aim of obtaining the diploma in order to secure some comparatively lucrative private employment. But quite recently the governing body has determined to suppress the diploma, and to institute a supplementary course open to those only who are already employed by some labor organization or who definitely intend to enter such employment. For those engaged upon this special course of study there will be provided scholarships of £2 a week, the funds for this purpose being supplied in part by *L'Umanitaria* and in part by the labor organizations which wish to send their employees to the school.[16] In the year 1909, under the auspices of the *Bourse du Travail*, there was founded at Turin a similar school *(Scuola Pratica di Cultura e Legislazione Sociale)*, which, however, soon succumbed.

In England the trade unions and cooperative societies make use of Ruskin College, Oxford, sending thither those of their members who aspire to office in the labor organizations, and who have displayed special aptitudes for this career. In Austria it is proposed to found a party school upon the German model.

It is undeniable that all these educational institutions for the officials of the party and of the labor organizations tend, above all, towards the artificial creation of an *élite* of the working class, of a caste of cadets composed of persons who aspire to the command of the proletarian rank and file. Without wishing it, there is thus effected a continuous enlargement of the gulf which divides the leaders from the masses.

The technical specialization that inevitably results from all extensive organization renders necessary what is called expert leadership. Consequently the power of determination comes to be considered one of the specific attributes of leadership, and is gradually withdrawn from the masses to be concentrated in the hands of the leaders alone. Thus the leaders, who were at first no more than the executive organs of the collective will, soon emancipate themselves from the mass and become independent of its control.

Organization implies the tendency to oligarchy. In every organization, whether it be a political party, a professional union, or any other association of the kind, the aristocratic tendency manifests itself very clearly. The mechanism of the organization, while conferring a solidity of structure, induces serious changes in the organized mass, completely inverting the respective position of the leaders and the led. As a result of organization, every party or professional union becomes divided into a minority of directors and a majority of directed.

It has been remarked that in the lower stages of civilization tyranny is dominant. Democracy cannot come into existence until there is attained a subsequent and more highly developed stage of social life. Freedoms and privileges, and among these latter the privilege of taking part in the direction of public affairs, are at first restricted to the few. Recent times have been characterized by the gradual extension of these privileges to a widening circle. This is what we know as the era of democracy. But if we pass from the sphere of the state to the sphere of party, we may observe that as democracy continues to develop, a backwash sets in. With the advance of organization, democracy tends to decline. Democratic evolution has a parabolic course. At the present time, at any rate as far as party life is concerned, democracy is in the descending phase. It may be enunciated as a general rule that the increase in the power of the leaders is directly proportional with the extension of the organization. In the various parties and labor organizations of different countries the influence of the leaders is mainly determined (apart from racial and individual grounds) by the varying development of organization. Where organization is stronger, we find that there is a lesser degree of applied democracy.

Every solidly constructed organization, whether it be a democratic state, a political party, or a league of proletarians for the resistance of economic oppression, presents a soil eminently favorable for the differentiation of organs and of functions. The more extended and the more ramified the official apparatus of the organization, the greater the number of its members, the fuller its treasury, and the more widely circulated its press, the less efficient becomes the direct control exercised by the rank and file, and the more is this control replaced by the increasing power of committees. Into all parties there insinuates itself that indirect electoral system which in public life the democratic parties fight against with all possible vigor. Yet in party life the influence of this system must be more disastrous than in the far more extensive life of the state. Even in the party congresses, which represent the party-life seven times sifted, we find that it becomes more and more general to refer all important questions to committees which debate *in camera*.

As organization develops, not only do the tasks of the administration become more difficult and more complicated, but, further, its duties become enlarged and specialized to such a degree that it is no longer possible to take them all in at a single glance. In a rapidly progressive movement, it is not only the growth in the number of duties, but also the higher quality of these, which imposes a more extensive differentiation of function. Nominally, and according to the letter of the rules, all the acts of the leaders are subject to the ever vigilant criticism of the rank and file. In theory the leader is merely an employee bound by the instruction he receives. He has to carry out the orders of the mass, of which he is no more than the executive organ. But in actual fact, as the organization increases in size, this control becomes purely fictitious. The members have to give up the idea of themselves conducting or even supervising the whole administration, and are compelled to hand these tasks over to trustworthy persons specially nominated for the purpose, to salaried officials. The rank and file must content themselves with summary reports, and with the appointment of occasional special committees of inquiry. Yet this does not derive from any special change in the rules of the organization. It is by very necessity that a simple employee gradually becomes a "leader," acquiring a freedom of action which he ought not to possess. The chief then becomes accustomed to dispatch important business on his own responsibility, and to decide various questions relating to the life of the party without any attempt to consult the rank and file. It is obvious that democratic control thus undergoes a progressive diminution, and is ultimately reduced to an infinitesimal minimum. In all the socialist parties there is a continual increase in the number of functions withdrawn from the electoral assemblies and transferred to the executive committees. In this way there is constructed a powerful and complicated edifice. The principle of division of labor coming more and more into operation, executive authority undergoes division and subdivision. There is thus constituted a rigorously defined and hierarchical bureaucracy. In the catechism of party duties, the strict observance of hierarchical rules becomes the first article. The hierarchy comes into existence as the outcome of technical conditions, and its constitution is an essential postulate of the regular functioning of the party machine.

It is indisputable that the oligarchical and bureaucratic tendency of party organization is a matter of technical and practical necessity. It is the inevitable product of the very principle of organization. Not even the most radical wing of the various socialist parties raises any objection to this retrogressive evolution, the contention being that democracy is only a form of organization and that where it ceases to be possible to harmonize democracy with organization, it is better to abandon the former than the latter. Organization, since it is the only means of attaining the ends of socialism, is considered to comprise within itself the revolutionary content of the party, and this essential content must never be sacrificed for the sake of form.

In all times, in all phases of development, in all branches of human activity, there have been leaders. It is true that certain socialists, above all the orthodox Marxists of Germany, seek to convince us that socialism knows nothing of "leaders," that the party has "employees" merely, being a democratic party, and the existence of leaders being incompatible with democracy. But a false assertion such as this cannot override a sociological law. Its only result is, in fact, to strengthen the rule of the leaders, for it serves to conceal from the mass a danger which really threatens democracy.

For technical and administrative reasons, no less than for tactical reasons, a strong organization needs an equally strong leadership. As long as an organization is loosely constructed and vague in its outlines, no professional leadership can arise. The anarchists, who have a horror of all fixed organization, have no regular leaders. In the early days of German socialism, the *Vertrauensmann* (homme de confiance) continued to exercise his ordinary occupation. If he received any pay for his work for the party, the remuneration was on an extremely modest scale, and was no more than a temporary grant. His function could never be regarded by him as a regular source of income. The employee of the organization was still a simple workmate, sharing the mode of life and the social condition of his fellows. Today he has been replaced for the most part by the professional politician, *Berzirksleiter* (U.S. ward-boss), etc. The more solid the structure of an organization becomes in the course of the evolution of the modern political party, the more marked becomes the tendency to replace the emergency leader by the professional leader. Every party organization which has attained to a considerable degree of complication demands that there should be a certain number of persons who devote all their activities to the work of the party. The mass provides these by delegations, and the delegates, regularly appointed, become permanent representatives of the mass for the direction of its affairs.

For democracy, however, the first appearance of professional leadership marks the beginning of the end, and this, above all, on account of the logical impossibility of the "representative" system, whether in parliamentary life or in party delegation. Jean Jacques Rousseau may be considered as the founder of this aspect of the criticism of democracy. He defines popular government as "the exercise of the general will" and draws from this the logical inference that "it can never be alienated from itself, and the sovereign—who is nothing but a collective concept—can only be represented by himself. Consequently the instant a people gives itself to representatives, it is no longer free."[17] A mass which delegates its sovereignty, that is to say transfers its sovereignty to the hands of a few individuals, abdicates its sovereign functions. For the will of the people is not transferable, nor even the will of the single individual. However much in practice, during the confused years of the Terror, the doctrine was abandoned by the disciples of the philosopher of Geneva, it was at this time in theory universally admitted as incontrovertible. Robespierre himself accepted it, making a subtle distinction between the "representative of the people" who has no right to exist "because will cannot be represented" and "the agent to whom the people have given primary power."

The experience of attentive observers of the working of the first attempts at a representative system contributed to establish more firmly the theory of the limits of democracy. Towards the middle of the nineteenth century this theory, the outcome of an empirical psychology, was notably enlarged, its claim to general validity was sustained, and it was formulated as the basis of definite rules and precepts. Carlo Pisacane, the theorist, too soon forgotten, of the national and social revolution in Italy, expounds in his *Saggio sulla Rivoluzione* how the men in whose hands supreme political power is placed must, from their very nature as human beings, be subject to passions and to the physical and mental imperfections therefrom resulting. For this reason the tendency and the acts of their rule are in direct contrast with the tendency and the acts of the mass, "for the latter represent the mean of all individual judgments and determinations, and are therefore free from the operation of such influences." To maintain of a government that it represents public opinion and the will of the nation is simply to mistake a part for the whole.[18] He thus considers delegation to be an absurdity. Victor Considérant, a contemporary of Pisacane and the representative of a similiar tendency, also followed in the tracks of Rousseau: "If the people delegate their sovereignty, they resign it. The people no longer govern themselves; they are governed. . . . Then, People, delegate your sovereignty! I guarantee you a fate the opposite of Saturn's: your sovereignty will be devoured by your daughter, the Delegation."[19] The theorists of democracy are never tired of asserting that, when voting, the people is at one and the same time exercising its sovereignty and renouncing it. The great democrat Ledru-Rollin, the father of universal and equal suffrage in France, goes so far as to demand the suppression of president and parliament, and the recognition of the general assembly of the people as the sole legislative organ. If people, he continues, find it possible in the course of the year to waste so much time upon public entertainments, holidays, and loafing, they could surely make a better use of their time by devoting it "to strengthening their independence, their greatness and their prosperity."[20]

Victor Considérant fiercely opposed the theory that popular sov-

ereignty is guaranteed by the representative system. Even if we make the
theoretical admission that *in abstracto* parliamentary government does
indeed embody government by the masses, in practical life it is nothing
but a continuous fraud on the part of the dominant class. Under representative government the difference between democracy and monarchy,
which are both rooted in the representative system, is altogether insignificant—a difference not in substance but in form. The sovereign people
elects, in place of a king, a number of kinglets. Not possessing sufficient
freedom and independence to direct the life of the state, it tamely allows
itself to be despoiled of its fundamental right. The one right which the
people reserves is the "ridiculous privilege" of choosing from time to time
a new set of masters.[21] To this criticism of the representative system may
be appended the remark of Proudhon, to the effect that the representatives of the people have no sooner been raised to power than they set to
work to consolidate and reinforce their influence. They continue
unceasingly to surround their positions by new lines of defense, until they
have succeeded in emancipating themselves completely from popular
control. All power thus proceeds in a natural cycle: issuing from the
people, it ends by raising itself above the people.[22] In the forties of the last
century these ideas were widely diffused and their truth was almost universally admitted, and in France more particularly by students of social
science and by democratic statesmen. Even the clericals mingled their
voices with those which condemned the representative system. Louis
Veuillot, the Catholic, said: "When I voted, my equality tumbled into
the box with my ballot; they disappeared together."[23] Today this theory is
the central feature of the political criticism of the various schools of
anarchists, who often expound it eloquently and acutely.[24] Finally Marx
and his followers, who in theory regard parliamentary action as but one
weapon among many, but who in practice employ this weapon alone, do
not fail to recognize incidentally the perils of the representative system,
even when based upon universal suffrage. But the Marxists hasten to add
that the socialist party is quite free from these dangers.[25]

Popular sovereignty has recently been subjected to a profound criticism by a group of Italian writers conservative in their tendency. Gaetano
Mosca speaks of "the falsity of the parliamentary legend." He says that the
idea of popular representation as a free and spontaneous transference of
the sovereignty of the electors (collectivity) to a certain number of elected
persons (minority) is based upon the absurd premise that the minority can
be bound to the collective will by unbreakable bonds.[26] In actual fact,

directly the election is finished, the power of the mass of electors over the delegate comes to an end. The deputy regards himself as authorized arbiter of the situation, and really is such. If among the electors any are to be found who possess some influence over the representative of the people, their number is very small; they are the big guns of the constituency or of the local branch of the party. In other words, they are persons who, whilst belonging by social position to the class of the ruled, have in fact come to form part of the ruling oligarchy.[27]

This criticism of the representative system is applicable above all in our own days, in which political life continually assumes more complex forms. As this complexity increases, it becomes more and more absurd to attempt to "represent" a heterogeneous mass in all the innumerable problems which arise out of the increasing differentiation of our political and economic life. To represent, in this sense, comes to mean that the purely individual desire masquerades and is accepted as the will of the mass.[28] In certain isolated cases, where the questions involved are extremely simple, and where the delegated authority is of brief duration, representation is possible. But permanent representation will always be tantamount to the exercise of dominion by the representatives over the represented.

NOTES

1. Moritz Rittinghausen, *Über die Organisation der direkten Gesetzgebung durch das Volk*, Social. Demokrat. Schriften, no. 4, Cöln, 1870, p. 10. The merit of having for the first time ventured to put forward practical proposals of this nature for the solution of the social problem unquestionably belongs to Rittinghausen. Victor Considérant, who subsequently resumed the attempt to establish direct popular government upon a wider basis and with a more far-reaching propagandist effect, expressly recognized Rittinghausen as his precursor (Victor Considérant, *La Solution ou Le Gouvernement Direct du Peuple*. Librairie Phalanstérienne, Paris, 1850, p. 61).

2. In the American constitution those states only are termed *federalist* (the name being here used to imply a democratic character) in which the people assemble for such a legislative purpose, whilst the states with representative popular government are called *republics*.

3. Wilhelm Roscher, *Politik, Geschichtliche Naturlehre der Monarchie, Aristokratie und Demokratie*, 3d ed. (Stuttgart-Berlin: Cotta, 1908), p. 35f.

4. Louis Blanc, "L'état dans une démocratie," *Questions d'aujourd'hui et de demain*, Dentu, Paris, 1880, vol. iii, p. 150.

5. Roscher, op. cit., p. 351.

6. Louis Blanc, op. cit., p. 144.

7. Cf. the letter of Antonio Quiroga to King Ferdinand VII, dated January 7, 1820 (Don Juan van Halen, *Mémoires*, Renouard, Paris, 1827, Part II, p. 382).

8. Egidio Bernaroli, *Manuale per la constituzione e il funzionamento delle leghe dei contadini*. Libreria Soc. Ital., Rome, 1902, pp. 20, 26, 27, 52.

9. Sidney and Beatrice Webb, *Industrial Democracy* (German edition), Stuttgart, 1898, vol. i, p. 6.

10. Ferdinant Tönnies, *Politik und Moral*, Neuer Frankf. Verl., Frankfort, 1901, p. 46.

11. Heinrich Herkner, *Die Arbeiterfrage*, Guttentag, Berlin, 1908, 5th ed., pp. 116, 117.

12. *Protokoll des Parteitags zu Leipzig*, 1909, "Vorwärts," Berlin, 1909, p. 48.

13. Heinrich Schulz, *Fünf Jahre Parteischule*, "Neue Zeit," anno xxix, vol. ii, fasc. 49, p. 807.

14. *Scuola Prat. di Legislaz. Sociale* (Programma e Norme), anno iii, Soc. Umanitaria, Milan, 1908.

15. Ibid., anno iv, Milan, 1909, p. 5.

16. Rinaldo Rigola, *I funzionari delle organizzazioni*, "Avanti," anno xiv, no. 341.

17. Jean Jacques Rousseau, *Le Contrat social*, 6th ed. (Paris: Bibliothèque Nationale, 1871), pp. 40 et seq.

18. Carlo Pisacane, *Saggio sulla Rivoluzione*, with a preface by Napoleone Colajanni, Lib. Treves di Pietro Virano, Bologna, 1894, pp. 121-5.

19. Trans. from Victor Considérant, op. cit., pp. 13–15.

20. A. A. Ledru-Rollin, *Plus de Président, plus de Représentants*, ed. de "La Voix du Proscrit," Paris, 1851, 2nd ed., p. 7.

21. Victor Considérant, op. cit., pp. 11–12.

22. Cf. P. J. Proudhon, *Les Confessions d'un Révolutionnaire. Pour servir à la Révolution de Février*, Verboeckhoven, Paris, 1868, new ed., p. 286.

23. Trans. from Louis Veuillot, *Ça et là*, Caume Frères et Duprey, Paris, 1860, 2nd ed., vol. i, p. 368.

24. Cf., for example, Enrico Malatesta in two pamphlets: *L'anarchia* (Casa ed. Pensiero, Rome, 6th ed., 1907), and *La Politica parlamentare del Partito socialista* (ediz. dell' "Allarme," Turin, 1903). Cf. also Ferdinand Domela Nieuwenhuis, *Het Parlamentarisme in zijn Wezen en Toepassing*, W. Sligting, Amsterdam, 1906, pp. 149 et seq.

25. Cf. Karl Kautsky, Rosa Luxemburg, and others. In the works of Karl Marx we find traces here and there of a theoretical mistrust of the representative system; see especially this writer's *Revolution u. Kontre-Revolution in Deutschland*, Dietz, Stuttgart, 1896, p. 107.

26. Cf. Gaetano Mosca, *Questioni pratiche di Diritto constituzionale*, Fratelli Bocca, Turin, 1898, pp. 81 et seq. Also *Sulla Teorica del Governi e sul Governo parlamentare*, Loescher, Rome, 1884, pp. 120 et seq.

27. "An electional system simply places power in the hands of the most skillful electioneers" (H. G. Wells, *Anticipations of the Reaction of Mechanical and Scientific Progress upon Human Life and Thought*, Chapman and Hall, London, 1904, p. 58). Of course, this applies only to countries with a republican-democratic constitution.

28. Fouillée writes aptly in this connection: "If I make personal use of my right to go and come from Paris to Marseille, I do not prevent you from going from Paris to Marseille; the exercise of my civil right does not remove yours. But when I send a deputy

to the Chamber who will work at your expense for measures you have always protested, this manner of governing myself implies a manner of governing you which distresses you and which could be unjust. Civil right is personal freedom; political right is a right over others as well as oneself." (Trans. from Alfred Fouillée, *Erreurs sociologiques et morales de la Sociologie,* "Revue des deux Mondes," liv. p. 330.)

PART IV

WHAT ARE THE TYPES OF LEADERS?

THIS section takes a functional approach to leadership. The premise is that anyone able to get others to follow where he or she leads, by whatever method, can properly be labeled a leader.

We are interested here in exploring different *types* of leaders. There is some confusion, however, about what exactly typologies of leaders are. Some are based on differences intrinsic to the leadership process; others on differences in the outcomes of that process; and still others on differences in sources of power. The following selections include all of these. Those that address democratic and totalitarian types are concerned primarily with process. Those that explore revolutionary and entrepreneurial leaders focus on what happens as a result of the leaders' initiatives. And some of the other essays—on charismatic leaders, for example—base their analyses on sources of power.

The first three selections are about democratic leaders. Harold Lasswell's brief statement outlines what a genuinely democratic leader looks like. He suggests a relationship between the capacity to employ democratic methods and the "personality formation" of the leader.

The essay by Alexander Hamilton reflects his search for the delicate balance between an emasculated leader and a despotic one. Significantly, it was Hamilton, well known as a defender of a strong unified executive, who wrote this piece from *The Federalist Papers* on the need for executive restraint. Cagily, he justified his call for a strong executive by arguing that it was just this sort of arrangement that lent itself best to careful monitoring: "It is far more safe there should be a single object for the jealousy and watchfulness of the people; and, in a word, that all multiplication of the executive is rather dangerous than friendly to liberty."

The excerpt from Joseph Schumpeter's classic *Capitalism, Socialism and Democracy* defends the proposition that democratic leadership implies no more than the competition for power. Thus the democratic leader simply "commands more support than do any of the competing individuals or teams."

Hannah Arendt's inquiry into the nature of totalitarianism—which focuses on Hitler's Germany and Stalin's Russia—explores the role of "the Leader" in the system. It is structure rather than personality which interests Arendt. "At the center of the movement," she writes, "as the motor that swings it into motion, sits the Leader." She explains the phenomenon of the totalitarian leader on the basis of strong organization, arguing that what binds people to him, people who believe neither in ideological clichés nor in the infallability of the leader, is their conviction that superior organization is the lynchpin of effective political action. Thus, according to Arendt, the totalitarian leader's greatest resources are first his personal capacities, and second his position at the summit of the powerful organization that is his own creation.

Among present-day social scientists, no type of leadership has generated as much attention as revolutionary leadership. Within the last years alone, several books on the subject have been published, including E. Victor Wolfenstein's *The Revolutionary Personality: Lenin, Trotsky, Gandhi*, Bruce Mazlish's *The Revolutionary Ascetic: Evolution of a Political Type*, and Mostafa Rejai and Kay Phillip's *Leaders of Revolution* and *World Revolutionary Leaders*. Nevertheless, it is Crane Brinton's 1938 classic *The Anatomy of Revolution* that still contains some of the best writing on revolutionary leadership. Brinton teaches about revolutionary leaders by describing how the "extremists" are organized and the organizational tasks met during each stage of the revolutionary process. Brinton draws his material from the English, American, French, and Russian revolutions. Among his most salient points is that all revolutionary leaders have one thing in common: "They combine, in varying degrees, very high ideals and a complete contempt for the inhibitions and principles which serve most other men as ideals. . . . They are not philosopher-kings but philosopher-killers."

Max Weber's essay on "The Type of Authority and Imperative Co-ordination," in which he posits three pure leader types, is the single most influential piece in the modern literature on leadership. Students of leadership have found Weber's formulations on rational and charismatic authority to be especially useful. His postulation that rational authority underlies the order of all modern organizations still dominates organization theory, and the notion of charismatic authority has actually become part of our modern sensibility. The selection on charisma from Ann Ruth Willner's *The Spellbinders* expands on Weber's original concept. By elaborating on the characteristics of charismatic leadership, Willner further explains how these leaders are able to arouse such impassioned support.

The idea that there are entrepreneurial leaders in politics as well as in business was put forth recently by Eugene Lewis in his book *Public Entreprenuership*. Lewis defines a public entrepreneur as a person who "creates or profoundly elaborates a public organization so as to alter greatly the existing pattern of allocation of scarce public resources." Hyman Rickover, J. Edgar Hoover, and Robert Moses are used as examples. Who were the followers of these leaders? In the main, they were the men and women who worked under them. They shared their leader's particular vision, his cause as it were, and, in the main, gladly did as he asked.

Finally, we consider the distinction between the constituted leader who occupies an official position in a political order and the nonconstituted leader who holds informal power, usually by successfully capitalizing on a strong public sentiment. Robert C. Tucker's small book, *Politics as Leadership*, explores this difference in some detail. Here I have included only a short discussion on the nonconstituted leader. Tucker has performed a service by drawing our attention to nonconstituted leaders for, as he correctly points out, conventional political science has generally neglected those who do not occupy formal political roles.[1] The time has come to change all that, for clearly the nonconstituted leader deserves further study.

NOTE

1. Actually, Tucker's word is "power." That is, he writes that nonconstituted leaders "lack power." I would argue that by his definition they do not, in fact, lack power. What they lack is formal, i.e., legal, authority.

18

HAROLD D. LASSWELL

Democratic Leadership

W E come, finally, to the specific needs of democracy. In a democratic commonwealth, power is not only shared but subordinated to respect for the dignity of human personality. In common with every form of political society, democracy depends upon rearing, choosing and supporting leaders who can protect and perfect its values and institutions. The principal expectation contained in democratic ideology is that it is possible to attain universal democracy by bringing into existence on a global scale the equilibrium that has repeatedly been achieved in more parochial communities. The democrat identifies himself with mankind as a whole and with all subordinate groups whose demands are in harmony with the larger loyalty. The technique appropriate to democracy comprises all the skills of thinking, observing and management that contribute to the survival of the commonwealth, and all the methods by which a social equilibrium in support of democracy can be achieved and maintained.

Unless leaders with the personality formation appropriate to democracy are supported by the community, it is obvious that the equilibrium essential to sustain the democratic commonwealth cannot be maintained. Hence, on analysis, the problem of democratic leadership to which we are addressing ourselves becomes nothing less than the task of dealing with society as a whole. To meet our definition of democracy, leaders must be drawn from the community at large, rather than from a

From Harold D. Lasswell, *Power and Personality* (New York: Norton, 1948), chap 6, "Democratic Leadership and the Policy Sciences," pp. 108–10. Reprinted by permission of W. W. Norton & Company, Inc. Copyright 1948 by W. W. Norton & Company, Inc. Copyright renewed 1976 by Harold D. Lasswell.

few social strata. The term "elite" is used in descriptive political science to designate the social formation from which leaders are recruited. In non-democracies the elite is limited. It is composed, perhaps, of a few land-holding families, or the families of the main merchants, manufacturers and bankers. The elite may be restricted to the families of the chief party officials, or government officials, or officers in the armed services (including the political police). Democratic leadership is selected from a broad base and remains dependent upon the active support of the entire community. With few exceptions every adult is eligible to have as much of a hand in the decision-making process as he wants and for which he is successful in winning the assent of his fellow citizens. There is no monopoly of power in a ruling caste when such conditions prevail, and the whole community is a seedbed from which rulers and governors come. The elite of democracy ("the ruling class") is society-wide.

The distinction between leaders and the elite enables us to avoid the confusion that often arises when someone points out that government is always government by the few, whether carried on in the name of the *few* or the *one* or the *many*. James Bryce made the point in these words:

> In all assemblies and groups and organized bodies of men, from a nation down to a committee of a club, direction and decisions rest in the hands of a small percentage, less and less in proportion to the larger size of the body, till in a great population it becomes an infinitesimally small proportion of the whole number. This is and always has been true of all forms of government, though in different degrees.[1]

The proposition is true when it is understood to mean that "government is always government by a few *leaders*." It is false if it is construed to mean that "government is always government by a highly restricted *elite*," and that democracy is by definition impossible. In a modern large-scale society the leaders do exert an enormous impact on war and peace and on major questions of domestic policy. But democracy is not extinguished unless a community-wide basis of selection and responsibility is done away with.

It should not be denied that the long-run aim of societies aspiring toward human freedom is to get rid of power and to bring into existence a free man's commonwealth in which coercion is neither threatened, applied nor desired. This is the thread of anarchist idealism that appears in all uncompromising applications of the key conception of human dignity. When Engels wrote of the eventual "withering away of the state" he was voicing the hope, though not necessarily the certainty, of the radical democrat. In our day, however, the probability that we can reduce power to the vanishing point seems very remote indeed. The urgent task is to chasten and subordinate power to the service of respect.

NOTE

1. James Bryce, *Modern Democracies* (New York: Macmillan, 1921), chap. 75.

19

JOSEPH A. SCHUMPETER

Democracy as Competition for Leadership

I think that most students of politics have by now come to accept the criticisms leveled at the classical doctrine of democracy in the preceding chapter. I also think that most of them agree, or will agree before long, in accepting another theory which is much truer to life and at the same time salvages much of what sponsors of the democratic method really mean by this term. Like the classical theory, it may be put into the nutshell of a definition.

It will be remembered that our chief troubles about the classical theory centered in the proposition that "the people" hold a definite and rational opinion about every individual question and that they give effect to this opinion—in a democracy—by choosing "representatives" who will see to it that opinion is carried out. Thus the selection of the representatives is made secondary to the primary purpose of the democratic arrangement which is to vest the power of deciding political issues in the electorate. Suppose we reverse the roles of these two elements and make the deciding of issues by the electorate secondary to the election of the men who are to do the deciding. To put it differently, we now take the view that the role of the people is to produce a government, or else an intermediate body which in turn will produce a national executive[1] or government. And we define: the democratic method is that institutional arrangement for arriving at political decisions in which individuals acquire the power to decide by means of a competitive struggle for the people's vote.

From Joseph A. Schumpeter, *Capitalism, Socialism and Democracy* (New York: Harper, 1942), chap. 22, "Another Theory of Democracy," pp. 269–73. Copyright by Joseph A. Schumpeter. Reprinted by permission of Harper & Row, Publishers, Inc., and George Allen & Unwin, Ltd.

Defense and explanation of this idea will speedily show that, as to both plausibility of assumptions and tenability of propositions, it greatly improves the theory of the democratic process.

First of all, we are provided with a reasonably efficient criterion by which to distinguish democratic governments from others. We have seen that the classical theory meets with difficulties on that score because both the will and the good of the people may be, and in many historical instances have been, served just as well or better by governments that cannot be described as democratic according to any accepted usage of the term. Now we are in a somewhat better position partly because we are resolved to stress a *modus procedendi* the presence or absence of which it is in most cases easy to verify.[2]

For instance, a parliamentary monarchy like the English one fulfills the requirements of the democratic method because the monarch is practically constrained to appoint to cabinet office the same people as parliament would elect. A "constitutional" monarchy does not qualify to be called democratic because electorates and parliaments, while having all the other rights that electorates and parliaments have in parliamentary monarchies, lack the power to impose their choice as to the governing committee: the cabinet ministers are in this case servants of the monarch, in substance as well as in name, and can in principle be dismissed as well as appointed by him. Such an arrangement may satisfy the people. The electorate may reaffirm this fact by voting against any proposal for change. The monarch may be so popular as to be able to defeat any competition for the supreme office. But since no machinery is provided for making this competition effective the case does not come within our definition.

Second, the theory embodied in this definition leaves all the room we may wish to have for a proper recognition of the vital fact of leadership. The classical theory did not do this but, as we have seen, attributed to the electorate an altogether unrealistic degree of initiative which practically amounted to ignoring leadership. But collectives act almost exclusively by accepting leadership—this is the dominant mechanism of practically any collective action which is more than a reflex. Propositions about the working and the results of the democratic method that take account of this are bound to be infinitely more realistic than propositions which do not. They will not stop at the execution of a *volonté générale* but will go some way toward showing how it emerges or how it is substituted or faked. What we have termed Manufactured Will is no longer outside the theory, an aberration for the absence of which we piously pray; it enters on the ground floor as it should.

Third, however, so far as there are genuine group-wise volitions at all—for instance the will of the unemployed to receive unemployment benefit or the will of other groups to help—our theory does not neglect them. On the contrary we are now able to insert them in exactly the role they actually play. Such volitions do not as a rule assert themselves directly. Even if strong and definite they remain latent, often for decades, until they are called to life by some political leader who turns them into political factors. This he does, or else his agents do it for him, by organizing these volitions, by working them up and by including eventually appropriate items in his competitive offering. The interaction between sectional interests and public opinion and the way in which they produce the pattern we call the political situation appear from this angle in a new and much clearer light.

Fourth, our theory is of course no more definite than is the concept of competition for leadership. This concept presents similar difficulties as the concept of competition in the economic sphere, with which it may be usefully compared. In economic life competition is never completely lacking, but hardly ever is it perfect. Similarly, in political life there is always some competition, though perhaps only a potential one, for the allegiance of the people. To simplify matters we have restricted the kind of competition for leadership which is to define democracy, to free competition for a free vote. The justification for this is that democracy seems to imply a recognized method by which to conduct the competitive struggle, and that the electoral method is practically the only one available for communities of any size. But though this excludes many ways of securing leadership which should be excluded,[3] such as competition by military insurrection, it does not exclude the cases that are strikingly analogous to the economic phenomena we label "unfair" or "fraudulent" competition or restraint of competition. And we cannot exclude them because if we did we should be left with a completely unrealistic ideal.[4] Between this ideal case which does not exist and the cases in which all competition with the established leader is prevented by force, there is a continuous range of variation within which the democratic method of government shades off into the autocratic one by imperceptible steps. But if we wish to understand and not to philosophize, this is as it should be. The value of our criterion is not seriously impaired thereby.

Fifth, our theory seems to clarify the relation that subsists between democracy and individual freedom. If by the latter we mean the existence of a sphere of individual self-government the boundaries of which are historically variable—*no* society tolerates absolute freedom even of conscience and of speech, *no* society reduces that sphere to zero—the question clearly becomes a matter of degree. We have seen that the democratic method does not necessarily guarantee a greater amount of individual freedom than another political method would permit in similar circumstances. It may well be the other way round. But there is still a relation between the two. If, on principle at least, everyone is free to compete for political leadership[5] by presenting himself to the electorate, this will in most cases though not in all mean a considerable amount of freedom of discussion *for all*. In particular it will normally mean a considerable amount of freedom of the press. This relation between democracy and freedom is not absolutely stringent and can be tampered with. But, from the standpoint of the intellectual, it is nevertheless very important. At the same time, it is all there is to that relation.

Sixth, it should be observed that in making the primary function of the electorate to produce a government (directly or through an intermediate body) I intended to include in this phrase also the function of evicting it. The one means simply the acceptance of the leader or a group of leaders, the other means simply the withdrawal of this acceptance. This takes care of an element the reader may have missed. He may have thought that the electorate controls as well as installs. But since electorates normally do not control their political leaders in any way except by refusing to reelect them or the parliamentary majorities that support them, it seems well to reduce our ideas about this control in the way indicated by our definition. Occasionally, spontaneous revulsions occur which upset a government or an individual minister directly or else enforce a certain course of action. But they are not only exceptional, they are, as we shall see, contrary to the spirit of the democratic method.

Seventh, our theory shed much-needed light on an old controversy. Whoever accepts the classical doctrine of democracy and in consequence believes that the democratic method is to guarantee that issues be decided and policies framed according to the will of the people must be struck by the fact that, even if that will were undeniably real and definite, decision by simple majorities would in many cases distort it rather than give effort to it. Evidently the will of the majority is the will of the majority and not the will of "the people." The latter is a mosaic that the former completely fails to "represent." To equate both by definition is not to solve the problem. Attempts at real solutions have however been made by the authors of the various plans for Proportional Representation.

These plans have met with adverse criticism on practical grounds. It is in fact obvious not only that proportional representation will offer opportunities for all sorts of idiosyncrasies to assert themselves but also that it may prevent democracy from producing efficient governments and thus prove a danger in times of stress.[6] But before concluding that democracy becomes unworkable if its principle is carried out consistently, it is just as well to ask ourselves whether this principle really implies proportional representation. As a matter of fact it does not. If acceptance of leadership is the true function of the electorate's vote, the case for proportional representation collapses because its premises are no longer binding. The principle of democracy then merely means that the reins of government should be handed to those who command more support than do any of the competing individuals or teams. And this in turn seems to assure the standing of the majority system within the logic of the democratic method, although we might still condemn it on grounds that lie outside of that logic.

NOTES

1. The insincere word "executive" really points in the wrong direction. It ceases however to do so if we use it in the sense in which we speak of the "executives" of a business corporation who also do a great deal more than "execute" the will of stockholders.

2. See however the fourth point below.

3. It also excludes methods which should not be excluded, for instance, the acquisition of political leadership by the people's tacit acceptance of it or by election *quasi per inspirationem*. The latter differs from election by voting only by a technicality. But the former is not quite without importance even in modern politics; the sway held by a party boss *within his party* is often based on nothing but tacit acceptance of his leadership. Comparatively speaking however these are details which may, I think, be neglected in a sketch like this.

4. As in the economic field, *some* restrictions are implicit in the legal and moral principles of the community.

5. Free, that is, in the same sense in which everyone is free to start another textile mill.

6. The argument against proportional representation has been ably stated by Professor F. A. Hermens in "The Trojan Horse of Democracy," *Social Research*, November 1938.

20

ALEXANDER HAMILTON

Federalist Paper No. 69

I proceed now to trace the real characters of the proposed executive, as they are marked out in the plan of the convention. This will serve to place in a strong light the unfairness of the representations which have been made in regard to it.

The first thing which strikes our attention is that the executive authority, with few exceptions, is to be vested in a single magistrate. This will scarcely, however, be considered as a point upon which any comparison can be grounded; for if, in this particular, there be a resemblance to the king of Great Britain, there is not less a resemblance to the Grand Seignior, to the khan of Tartary, to the Man of the Seven Mountains, or to the governor of New York.

That magistrate is to be elected for *four* years; and is to be re-eligible as often as the people of the United States shall think him worthy of their confidence. In these circumstances there is a total dissimilitude between *him* and a king of Great Britain, who is an *hereditary* monarch, possessing the crown as a patrimony descendible to his heirs forever; but there is a close analogy between *him* and a governor of New York, who is elected for *three* years, and is re-eligible without limitation or intermission. If we consider how much less time would be requisite for establishing a dangerous influence in a single State than for establishing a like influence throughout the United States, we must conclude that a duration of *four* years for the Chief Magistrate of the Union is a degree of permanency far less to be dreaded in that office, than a duration of *three* years for a corresponding office in a single State.

From *The Federalist Papers* (New York: New American Library, 1961), pp. 415–23. First published in 1787.

The President of the United States would be liable to be impeached, tried, and, upon conviction of treason, bribery, or other high crimes or misdemeanors, removed from office; and would afterwards be liable to prosecution and punishment in the ordinary course of law. The person of the King of Great Britain is sacred and inviolable; there is no constitutional tribunal to which he is amenable; no punishment to which he can be subjected without involving the crisis of a national revolution. In this delicate and important circumstance of personal responsibility, the President of Confederated America would stand upon no better ground than a governor of New York, and upon worse ground than the governors of Virginia and Delaware.

The President of the United States is to have power to return a bill, which shall have passed the two branches of the legislature, for reconsideration; but the bill so returned is not to become a law unless, upon that reconsideration, it be approved by two thirds of both houses. The king of Great Britain, on his part, has an absolute negative upon the acts of the two houses of Parliament. The disuse of that power for a considerable time past does not affect the reality of its existence and is to be ascribed wholly to the crown's having found the means of substituting influence to authority, or the art of gaining a majority in one or the other of the two houses, to the necessity of exerting a prerogative which could seldom be exerted without hazarding some degree of national agitation. The qualified negative of the President differs widely from this absolute negative of the British sovereign and tallies exactly with the revisionary authority of the council of revision of this State, of which the governor is a constituent part. In this respect the power of the President would exceed that of the governor of New York, because the former would possess, singly, what the latter shares with the chancellor and judges; but it would be precisely the same with that of the governor of Massachusetts, whose constitution, as to this article, seems to have been the original from which the convention have copied.

The President is to be the "commander-in-chief of the army and navy of the United States, and of the militia of the several States, when called into the actual service of the United States. He is to have power to grant reprieves and pardons for offenses against the United States, *except in cases of impeachment*; to recommend to the consideration of Congress such measures as he shall judge necessary and expedient; to convene, on extraordinary occasions, both houses of the legislature, or either of them, and, in case of disagreement between them *with respect to the time of adjournment*, to adjourn them to such time as he shall think proper; to take care that the laws be faithfully executed; and to commission all officers of the United States." In most of these particulars, the power of the President will resemble equally that of the king of Great Britain and of the governor of New York. The most material points of difference are these:—*First.* The President will have only the occasional command of such part of the militia of the nation as by legislative provision may be called into the actual service of the Union. The king of Great Britain and the governor of New York have at all times the entire command of all the militia within their several jurisdictions. In this article, therefore, the power of the President would be inferior to that of either the monarch or the governor. *Second.* The President is to be commander-in-chief of the army and navy of the United States. In this respect his authority would be nominally the same with that of the king of Great Britain, but in substance much inferior to it. It would amount to nothing more than the supreme command and direction of the military and naval forces, as first general and admiral of the Confederacy; while that of the British king extends to the *declaring* of war and to the *raising* and *regulating* of fleets and armies—all which, by the Constitution under consideration, would appertain to the legislature.[1] The governor of New York, on the other hand, is by the constitution of the State vested only with the command of its militia and navy. But the constitutions of several of the States expressly declare their governors to be commanders-in-chief, as well of the army as navy; and it may well be a question whether those of New Hampshire and Massachusetts, in particular, do not, in this instance, confer larger powers upon their respective governors than could be claimed by a President of the United States. *Third.* The power of the President, in respect to pardons, would extend to all cases, *except those of impeachment.* The governor of New York may pardon in all cases, even in those of impeachment, except for treason and murder. Is not the power of the governor, in this article, on a calculation of political consequences, greater than that of the President? All conspiracies and plots against the government which have not been matured into actual treason may be screened from punishment of every kind by the interposition of the prerogative of pardoning. If a governor of New York, therefore, should be at the head of any such conspiracy, until the design had been ripened into actual hostility he could insure his accomplices and adherents an entire impunity. A President of the Union, on the other hand, though he may even pardon treason, when prosecuted in the ordinary course of law, could shelter no offender, in any degree, from the effects of impeachment and conviction. Would not the prospect of a total indemnity for all the preliminary steps be a greater temptation to undertake and persevere in an enterprise against the public liberty, than the mere prospect of an exemption from death and confiscation, if the final execution of the design, upon an actual appeal to arms, should miscarry? Would this last expectation have any influence at all, when the probability was computed that the person who was to afford that exemption might himself be involved in the consequences of the measure, and might be incapacitated by his agency in it from affording the desired impunity? The better to judge of this matter, it will be necessary to recollect that, by the proposed Constitution, the offense of treason is limited "to levying war upon the United States, and adhering to their enemies, giving them aid and comfort"; and that by the laws of New York it is confined within similiar bounds. *Fourth.* The President can only adjourn the national legislature in the single case of disagreement about the time of adjournment. The British monarch may prorogue or even dissolve the Parliament. The governor of New York may also prorogue the legislature of this State for a limited time; a power which, in certain situations, may be employed to very important purposes.

The President is to have power, with the advice and consent of the Senate, to make treaties, provided two thirds of the senators present concur. The king of Great Britain is the sole and absolute representative of the nation in all foreign transactions. He can of his own accord make treaties of peace, commerce, alliance, and of every other description. It has been insinuated that his authority in this respect is not conclusive, and that his conventions with foreign powers are subject to the revision, and stand in need of the ratification, of Parliament. But I believe this doctrine was never heard of until it was broached upon the present occasion. Every jurist[2] of that kingdom, and every other man acquainted with its Constitution knows, as an established fact, that the prerogative of making treaties exists in the crown in its utmost plenitude; and that the compacts entered into by the royal authority have the most complete legal validity and perfection, independent of any other sanction. The Parliament, it is true, is sometimes seen employing itself in altering the existing laws to conform them to the stipulations in a new treaty; and this may have possibly given birth to the imagination that its co-operation was necessary to the obligatory efficacy of the treaty. But this parliamentary interposition proceeds from a different cause: from the necessity of adjusting a most artificial and intricate system of revenue and commercial laws, to the changes made in them by the operation of the treaty; and of adapting new provisions and precautions to the new state of things, to keep the machine from running into disorder. In this respect, therefore, there is no comparison between the intended power of the President and the actual power of the British sovereign. The one can perform alone what the other can only do with the concurrence of a branch of the legislature. It must be admitted that in this instance the power of the federal executive would exceed that of any State executive. But this arises naturally from the exclusive possession by the Union of that part of the sovereign power which relates to treaties. If the Confederacy were to be dissolved, it would become a question whether the executives of the several States were not solely invested with that delicate and important prerogative.

The President is also to be authorized to receive ambassadors and other public ministers. This, though it has been a rich theme of declamation, is more a matter of dignity than of authority. It is a circumstance which will be without consequence in the administration of the government; and it was far more convenient that it should be arranged in this manner than that there should be a necessity of convening the legislature, or one of its branches, upon every arrival of a foreign minister, though it were merely to take the place of a departed predecessor.

The President is to nominate, and, *with the advice and consent of the Senate,* to appoint ambassadors and other public ministers, judges of the Supreme Court, and in general all officers of the United States established by law, and whose appointments are not otherwise provided for by the Constitution. The king of Great Britain is emphatically and truly styled the fountain of honor. He not only appoints to all offices, but can create offices. He can confer titles of nobility at pleasure, and has the disposal of an immense number of church preferments. There is evidently a great inferiority in the power of the President, in this particular, to that of the British king; nor is it equal to that of the governor of New York, if we are to interpret the meaning of the constitution of the State by the practice which has obtained under it. The power of appointment is with us lodged in a council, composed of the governor and four members of the Senate, chosen by the Assembly. The governor *claims*, and has frequently *exercised*, the right of nomination, and is *entitled* to a casting vote in the appointment. If he really has the right of nominating, his authority is in this respect equal to that of the President, and exceeds it in the article of the casting vote. In the national government, if the Senate should be divided, no appointment could be made; in the government of New York, if the council should be divided, the governor can turn the scale and confirm his own nomination.[3] If we compare the publicity which must necessarily attend the mode of appointment by the President and an entire branch of the national legislature, with the privacy in the mode of appointment by the governor of New York, closeted in a secret apartment with at most four, and frequently with only two persons; and if we at the same time consider how much more easy it must be to influence the small number of which a council of appointment consists than the considerable number of which the national Senate would consist, we cannot hesitate to pronounce that the power of the chief magistrate of this State, in the disposition of offices, must, in practice, be greatly superior to that of the Chief Magistrate of the Union.

Hence it appears that, except as to the concurrent authority of the President in the article of treaties, it would be difficult to determine whether that magistrate would, in the aggregate, possess more or less power than the governor of New York. And it appears yet more unequivocally that there is no pretense for the parallel which has been attempted between him and the king of Great Britain. But to render the contrast in this respect still more striking, it may be of use to throw the principal circumstances of dissimilitude into a closer group.

The President of the United States would be an officer elected by the people for *four* years; the king of Great Britain is a perpetual and *hereditary* prince. The one would be amenable to personal punishment and disgrace; the person of the other is sacred and inviolable. The one would have a *qualified* negative upon the acts of the legislative body; the other has an *absolute* negative. The one would have a right to command the military and naval forces of the nation; the other, in addition to this right, possesses that of *declaring* war, and of *raising* and *regulating* fleets and armies by his own authority. The one would have a concurrent power with a branch of the legislature in the formation of treaties; the other is the *sole possessor* of the power of making treaties. The one would have a like concurrent authority in appointing to offices; the other is the sole author of all appointments. The one can confer no privileges whatever; the other can make denizens of aliens, noblemen of commoners; can erect corporations with all the rights incident to corporate bodies. The one can prescribe no rules concerning the commerce or currency of the nation; the other is in several respects the arbiter of commerce, and in this capacity can establish markets and fairs, can regulate weights and measures, can lay embargoes for a limited time, can coin money, can authorize or prohibit the circulation of foreign coin. The one has no particle of spiritual jurisdiction; the other is the supreme head and governor of the national church! What answer shall we give to those who would persuade us that things so unlike resemble each other? The same that ought to be given to those who tell us that a government, the whole power of which would be in the hands of the elective and periodical servants of the people, is an aristocracy, a monarchy, and a despotism.

NOTES

1. A writer in a Pennsylvania paper, under the signature of TAMONY, has asserted that the king of Great Britain owes his prerogative as commander-in-chief to an annual mutiny bill. The truth is, on the contrary, that his prerogative in this respect is immemorial, and was only disputed "contrary to all reason and precedent," as Blackstone, vol. i, page 262, expresses it, by the Long Parliament of Charles I; but by the statute the 13th of Charles II, chap. 6, it was declared to be in the king alone, for that the sole supreme government and command of the militia within his Majesty's realms and dominions, and of all forces by sea and land, and of all forts and places of strength, EVER WAS AND IS the undoubted right of his Majesty and his royal predecessors, kings and queens of England, and that both or either house of Parliament cannot nor ought to pretend to the same.

2. *Vide* Blackstone's *Commentaries*, vol. I, p. 257.

3. Candor, however, demands an acknowledgment that I do not think the claim of the governor to a right of nomination well founded. Yet it is always justifiable to reason from the practice of a government till its propriety has been constitutionally questioned. And independent of this claim, when we take into view the other considerations and pursue them through all their consequences, we shall be inclined to draw much the same conclusion.

21

HANNAH ARENDT

The Totalitarian Leader

In the center of the movement, as the motor that swings it into motion, sits the Leader. He is separated from the elite formation by an inner circle of the initiated who spread around him an aura of impenetrable mystery which corresponds to his "intangible preponderence."[1] His position within this intimate circle depends upon his ability to spin intrigues among its members and upon his skill in constantly changing its personnel. He owes his rise to leadership to an extreme ability to handle inner-party struggles for power rather than to demagogic or bureaucratic-organizational qualities. He is distinguished from earlier types of dictators in that he hardly wins through simple violence. Hitler needed neither the SA nor the SS to secure his position as leader of the Nazi movement; on the contrary, Röhm, the chief of the SA and able to count upon its loyalty to his own person was one of Hitler's inner-party enemies. Stalin won against Trotsky, who not only had a far greater mass appeal but, as chief of the Red Army, held in his hands the greatest power potential in Soviet Russia at the time.[2] Not Stalin, but Trotsky, moreover, was the greatest organizational talent, the ablest bureaucrat of the Russian Revolution.[3] On the other hand, both Hitler and Stalin were masters of detail and devoted themselves in the early stages of their careers almost entirely to questions of personnel, so that after a few years hardly any man of importance remained who did not owe his position to them.[4]

Such personal abilities, however, though an absolute prerequisite for the first stages of such a career and even later far from insignificant, are no longer decisive when a totalitarian movement has been built up, has established the principle that "the will of the Fuehrer is the Party's law," and when its whole hierarchy has been efficiently trained for a single purpose—swiftly to communicate the will of the Leader to all ranks. When this has been achieved, the Leader is irreplaceable because the whole complicated structure of the movement would lose its *raison d'être* without his commands. Now, despite eternal cabals in the inner clique and unending shifts of personnel, with their tremendous accumulation of hatred, bitterness, and personal resentment, the Leader's position can remain secure against chaotic palace revolutions not because of his superior gifts, about which the men in his intimate surroundings frequently have no great illusions, but because of these men's sincere and sensible conviction that without him everything would be immediately lost.

The supreme task of the Leader is to impersonate the double function characteristic of each layer of the movement—to act as the magic defense of the movement against the outside world; and at the same time, to be the direct bridge by which the movement is connected with it. The Leader represents the movement in a way totally different from all ordinary party leaders; he claims personal responsibility for every action, deed, or misdeed, committed by any member of functionary in his official capacity. This total responsibility is the most important organizational aspect of the so-called Leader principle, according to which every functionary is not only appointed by the Leader but is his walking embodiment, and every order is supposed to emanate from this one ever-present source. This thorough identification of the Leader with every appointed subleader and this monopoly of responsibility for everything which is being done are also the most conspicuous signs of the decisive difference between a totalitarian leader and an ordinary dictator or despot. A tyrant would never identify himself with his subordinates, let alone with every one of their acts;[5] he might use them as scapegoats and gladly have them criticized in order to save himself from the wrath of the people, but he would always maintain an absolute distance from all his subordinates and all his subjects. The Leader, on the contrary, cannot tolerate criticism of his subordinates, since they act always in his name; if he wants to correct his own errors, he must liquidate those who carried them out; if he wants to blame his mistakes on others, he must kill them.[6] For within this organizational framework a mistake can only be a fraud: the impersonation of the Leader by an imposter.

This total responsibility for everything done by the movement and this total identification with every one of its functionaries have the very practical consequence that nobody ever experiences a situation in which he has to be responsible for his own actions or can explain the reasons for them. Since the Leader has monopolized the right and possibility of explanation, he appears to the outside world as the only person who knows what he is doing, i.e., the only representative of the movement with whom one may still talk in nontotalitarian terms and who, if reproached or opposed, cannot say: Don't ask me, ask the Leader. Being in the center of the movement; the Leader can act as though he were above it. It is therefore perfectly understandable (and perfectly futile) for outsiders to set their hopes time and again on a personal talk with the Leader himself when they have to deal with totalitarian movements or governments. The real mystery of the totalitarian Leader resides in an organization which makes it possible for him to assume the total responsibility for all crimes committed by the elite formations of the movement *and* to claim at the same time, the honest, innocent respectability of its most näıve fellow-traveler.[7] . . .

The machine that generates, organizes, and spreads the monstrous falsehoods of totalitarian movements depends again upon the position of the Leader. To the propaganda assertion that all happenings are scientifically predictable according to the laws of nature or economics, totalitarian organization adds the position of one man who has monopolized this knowledge and whose principal quality is that he "was always right and will always be right."[8] To a member of a totalitarian movement this knowledge has nothing to do with truth and this being right nothing to do with the objective truthfulness of the Leader's statements which cannot be disproved by facts, but only by future success or failure. The Leader is always right in his actions and since these are planned for centuries to come, the ultimate test of what he does has been removed beyond the experience of his contemporaries.[9]

The only group supposed to believe loyally and textually in the Leader's words are the sympathizers whose confidence surrounds the movement with an atmosphere of honesty and simple-mindedness, and helps the Leader to fulfill half his task, that is, to inspire confidence in the movement. The party members never believe public statements and are not supposed to, but are complimented by totalitarian propaganda on that superior intelligence which supposedly distinguishes them from the nontotalitarian outside world, which, in turn, they know only from the abnormal gullibility of sympathizers. Only Nazi sympathizers believed Hitler when he swore his famous legality oath before the supreme court of the Weimar Republic; members of the movement knew very well that he lied, and trusted him more than ever because he apparently was able to fool public opinion and the authorities. When in later years Hitler repeated the performance for the whole world, when he swore to his good intentions and at the same time most openly prepared his crimes, the admiration of the Nazi membership naturally was boundless. Similarly, only Bolshevik fellow-travelers believed in the dissolution of the Comintern, and only the nonorganized masses of the Russian people and the fellow-travelers abroad were meant to take at face value Stalin's pro-democratic statements during the war. Bolshevik party members were explicitly warned not to be fooled by tactical maneuvers and were asked to admire their Leader's shrewdness in betraying his allies.[10]

Without the organizational division of the movement into elite for-mations, membership, and sympathizers, the lies of the Leader would not work. The graduation of cynicism expressed in a hierarchy of con-tempt is at least as necessary in the face of constant refutation as plain gullibility. The point is that the sympathizers in front organizations despise their fellow-citizens' complete lack of initiation, the party mem-bers despise the fellow-travelers' gullibility and lack of radicalism, the elite formations despise for similar reasons the party membership, and within the elite formations a similar hierarchy of contempt accompanies every new foundation and development.[11] The result of this system is that the gullibility of sympathizers makes lies credible to the outside world, while at the same time the graduated cynicism of membership and elite formations eliminates the danger that the Leader will ever be forced by the weight of his own propaganda to make good his own statements and feigned respectability. It has been one of the chief handicaps of the outside world in dealing with totalitarian systems that it ignored this system and therefore trusted that, on one hand, the very enormity of totalitarian lies would be their undoing and that, on the other, it would be possible to take the Leader at his word and force him, regardless of his original intentions, to make it good. The totalitarian system, unfortu-nately, is foolproof against such normal consequences; its ingeniousness rests precisely on the elimination of that reality which either unmasks the liar or forces him to live up to his pretense.

While the membership does not believe statements made for public consumption, it believes all the more fervently the standard clichés of ideological explanation, the keys to past and future history which totalitarian movements took from nineteenth-century ideologies, and transformed, through organization, into a working reality. These ideological elements in which the masses had come to believe anyhow, albeit rather vaguely and abstractly, were turned into factual lies of an all-comprehensive nature (the domination of the world by the Jews instead of a general theory about races, the conspiracy of Wall Street instead of a general theory about classes) and integrated into a general scheme of action in which only the "dying"—the dying classes of capitalist countries or the decadent nations—are supposed to stand in the way of movement. In contrast to the movements' tactical lies which change literally from day to day, these ideological lies are supposed to be believed like sacred untouchable truths. They are surrounded by a carefully elaborated system of "scientific" proofs which do not have to be convincing for the completely "uninitiated," but still appeal to some vulgarized thirst for knowledge by "demonstrating" the inferiority of the Jews or the misery of people living under a capitalist system.

The elite formations are distinguished from the ordinary party membership in that they do not need such demonstrations and are not even supposed to believe in the literal truth of ideological clichés. These are fabricated to answer a quest for truth among the masses which in its insistence on explanation and demonstration still has much in common with the normal world. The elite is not composed of ideologists; its members' whole education is aimed at abolishing their capacity for distinguishing between truth and falsehood, between reality and fiction. Their superiority consists in their ability immediately to dissolve every statement of fact into a declaration of purpose. In distinction to the mass membership which, for instance, needs some demonstration of the inferiority of the Jewish race before it can safely be asked to kill Jews, the elite formations understand that the statement, all Jews are inferior, means, all Jews should be killed; they know that when they are told that only Moscow has a subway, the real meaning of the statement is that all subways should be destroyed, and are not unduly surprised when they discover the subway in Paris. The tremendous shock of disillusion which the Red Army suffered on its conquering trip to Europe could be cured only by concentration camps and forced exile for a large part of the occupation troops; but the police formations which accompanied the Army were prepared for the shock, not by different and more correct information—there is no secret training school in Soviet Russia which gives out authentic facts about life abroad—but simply by a general training in supreme contempt for all facts and all reality.

This mentality of the elite is no mere mass phenomenon, no mere consequence of social rootlessness, economic disaster, and political anar-

chy; it needs careful preparation and cultivation and forms a more important, though less easily recognizable, part of the curriculum of totalitarian
leadership schools, the Nazi *Ordensburgen* for the SS troops, and the
Bolshevik training centers for Comintern agents, than race indoctrination
or the techniques of civil war. Without the elite and its artifically induced
inability to understand facts as facts, to distinguish between truth and
falsehood, the movement could never move in the direction of realizing
its fiction. The outstanding negative quality of the totalitarian elite is that
it never stops to think about the world as it really is and never compares
the lies with reality. Its most cherished virtue, correspondingly, is loyalty
to the Leader, who, like a talisman, assures the ultimate victory of lie and
fiction over truth and reality.

The topmost layer in the organization of totalitarian movements is the
intimate circle around the Leader, which can be a formal institution, like
the Bolshevik Politburo, or a changing clique of men who do not necessarily hold office, like the entourage of Hitler. To them ideological
clichés are mere devices to organize the masses, and they feel no com-
punction about changing them according to the needs of circumstances if
only the organizing principle is kept intact. In this connection, the chief
merit of Himmler's reorganization of the SS was that he found a very
simple method for "solving the problem of blood by action," that is, for
selecting the members of the elite according to "good blood" and preparing them to "carry on a racial struggle without mercy" against everyone
who could not trace his "Aryan" ancestry back to 1750, or was less than 5
feet 8 inches tall ("I know that people who have reached a certain height
must possess the desired blood to some degree") or did not have blue eyes
and blond hair.[12] The importance of this racism in action was that the
organization became independent of almost all concrete teachings of no
matter what racial "science," independent also of antisemitism insofar as
it was a specific doctrine concerning the nature and role of the Jews,
whose usefulness would have ended with their extermination.[13] Racism
was safe and independent of the scientificality of propaganda once an elite
had been selected by a "race commission" and placed under the authority
of special "marriage laws,"[14] while at the opposite end and under the
jurisdiction of this "racial elite," concentration camps existed for the sake
of "better demonstration of the laws of inheritance and race."[15] On the
strength of this "living organization," the Nazis could dispense with dogmatism and offer friendship to Semitic peoples, like the Arabs, or enter
into alliances with the very representatives of the Yellow Peril, the Japanese. The reality of a race society, the formation of an elite selected from

an allegedly racial viewpoint, would indeed have been a better safeguard for the doctrine of racism than the finest scientific or pseudo-scientific proof.

The policy-makers of Bolshevism show the same superiority to their own avowed dogmas. They are quite capable of interrupting every existing class struggle with a sudden alliance with capitalism without undermining the reliability of their cadres or committing treason against their belief in class struggle. The dichotomous principle of class struggle having become an organizational device, having, as it were, petrified into uncompromising hostility against the whole world through the secret police cadres in Russia and the Comintern agents abroad, Bolshevik policy has become remarkably free of "prejudices."

It is this freedom from the content of their own ideologies which characterizes the highest rank of the totalitarian hierarchy. These men consider everything and everybody in terms of organization, and this includes the Leader who to them is neither an inspired talisman nor the one who is infallibly right, but the simple consequence of this type of organization; he is needed, not as a person, but as a function, and as such he is indispensable to the movement. In contrast, however, to other despotic forms of government, where frequently clique rules and the despot plays only the representative role of a puppet ruler, totalitarian leaders are actually free to do whatever they please and can count on the loyalty of their entourage even if they choose to murder them.

The more technical reason for this suicidal loyalty is that succession to the supreme office is not regulated by any inheritance or other laws. A successful palace revolt would have as disastrous results for the movement as a whole as a military defeat. It is in the nature of the movement that once the Leader has assumed his office, the whole organization is so absolutely identified with him that any admission of a mistake or removal from office would break the spell of infallibility which surrounds the office of the Leader and spell doom to all those connected with the movement. It is not the truthfulness of the Leader's words but the infallibility of his actions which is the basis for the structure. Without it and in the heat of a discussion which presumes fallibility, the whole fictitious world of totalitarianism goes to pieces, overwhelmed at once by the factuality of the real world which only the movement steered in an infallibly right direction by the Leader was able to ward off.

However, the loyalty of those who believe neither in ideological clichés nor in the infallibility of the Leader also has deeper, nontechnical reasons. What binds these men together is a firm and sincere belief in human omnipotence. Their moral cynicism, their belief that everything is permitted, rests on the solid conviction that everything is possible. It is true that these men, few in number, are not easily caught in their own specific lies and that they do not necessarily believe in racism or economics, in the conspiracy of the Jews or of Wall Street. Yet they too are deceived, deceived by their impudent conceited idea that everything can be done and their contemptuous conviction that everything that exists is merely a temporary obstacle that superior organization will certainly destroy. Confident that power of organization can destroy power of substance, as the violence of a well-organized gang might rob a rich man of ill-guarded wealth, they constantly underestimate the substantial power of stable communities and overestimate the driving force of a movement. Since, moreover, they do not actually believe in the factual existence of a world conspiracy against them, but use it only as an organizational device, they fail to understand that their own conspiracy may eventually provoke the whole world into uniting against them.

Yet no matter how the delusion of human omnipotence through organization is ultimately defeated, within the movement its practical consequence is that the entourage of the Leader, in case of disagreement with him, will never be very sure of their own opinions, since they believe sincerely that their disagreements do not really matter, that even the maddest device has a fair chance of success if properly organized. The point of their loyalty is not that they believe the Leader is infallible, but that they are convinced that everybody who commands the instruments of violence with the superior methods of totalitarian organization can become infallible. This delusion is greatly strengthened when totalitarian regimes hold the power to demonstrate the relativity of success and failure, and to show how a loss in substance can become a gain in organization. (The fantastic mismanagement of industrial enterprise in Soviet Russia led to the atomization of the working class, and the terrifying mistreatment of civilian prisoners in Eastern territories under Nazi occupation, though it caused a "deplorable loss of labor," "thinking in terms of generations, [was] not to be regretted."[16] Moreover, the decision regarding success and failure under totalitarian circumstances is very largely a matter of organized and terrorized public opinion. In a totally fictitious world, failures need not be recorded, admitted, and remembered. Factuality itself depends for its continued existence upon the existence of the nontotalitarian world.

NOTES

1. Boris Souvarine, *Stalin: A Critical Survey of Bolshevism* (New York, 1939), p. 648. The way the totalitarian movements have kept the private lives of their leaders (Hitler and Stalin) absolutely secret contrasts with the publicity value which all democracies find in parading the private lives of Presidents, Kings, Prime Ministers, etc., in public. Totalitarian methods do not allow for identification based on the conviction: Even the highest of us is only human.

Souvarine, *op. cit.*, p. xiii, quotes the most frequently used tags to describe Stalin: "Stalin, the mysterious host of the Kremlin"; "Stalin, impenetrable personality"; "Stalin, the Communist Sphinx"; "Stalin, the Enigma," the "insoluable mystery," etc.

2. If [Trotsky] had chosen to stage a military *coup d'état* he might perhaps have defeated the triumvirs. But he left office without the slightest attempt at rallying in his defence the army he had created and led for seven years" (Isaac Deutscher, *Stalin: A Political Biography* (New York, 1949), p. 297.

3. The Commissariat for War under Trotsky "was a model institution" and Trotsky was called in all cases of disorder in other departments. Souvarine, op. cit., p. 288.

4. The circumstances surrounding Stalin's death seem to contradict the infallibility of these methods. There is the possibility that Stalin, who, before he died, undoubtedly planned still another general purge, was killed by someone in his environment because no one felt safe any longer, but despite a great deal of circumstantial evidence this cannot be proved.

5. Thus Hitler personally cabled his responsibility for the Potempa murder to the SA assassins in 1932, although presumably he had nothing whatever to do with it. What mattered here was establishing a principle of identification, or, in the language of the Nazis, "the mutual loyalty of the Leader and the people" on which "the Reich rest" (Hans Frank, *Recht und Verwattung* [Munich, 1939]).

6. "One of Stalin's distinctive characteristics . . . is systematically to throw his own misdeeds and crimes, as well as his political errors . . . on the shoulders of those whose discredit and ruin he is plotting" (Souvarine, op. cit., p. 655). It is obvious that a totalitarian leader can choose freely whom he wants to impersonate his own errors since all acts committed by subleaders are supposed to be inspired by him, so that anybody can be forced into the role of an impostor.

7. That it was Hitler himself—and not Himmler, or Bormann, or Goebbels—who always initiated the actually "radical" measures; that they were always more radical than the proposals made by his immediate environment; that even Himmler was appalled when he was entrusted with the "final solution" of the Jewish question—all this has now been proved by innumerable documents. And the fairy tale that Stalin was more moderate than the leftist factions of the Bolshevist Party is no longer believed, either. It is all the more important to remember that totalitarian leaders invariably try to appear more moderate to the outside world and that their real role—namely, to drive the movement forward at any price and if anything to step up its speed—remains carefully concealed. See, for instance, Admiral Erich Raeder's memo on "My Relationship to Adolf Hitler and to the Party" in *Nazi Conspiracy and Aggression* (Washington, D.C.: Office of the U.S. Chief of Counsel for the Prosecution of Axis Criminality, 1946), VIII, 707 ff. "When information

of rumours arose about radical measures of the Party and the Gestapo, one could come to the conclusion by the conduct of the Fuehrer that such measures were not ordered by the Fuehrer himself. . . . In the course of future years, I gradually came to the conclusion that the Fuehrer himself always leaned toward the more radical solution without letting on outwardly."

8. Rudolf Hess in a broadcast in 1934. *Nazi Conspiracy*, I, 193.

9. Werner Best explained: "Whether the will of the government lays down the 'right' rules . . . is no longer a question of law, but a question of fate. For actual misuses . . . will be punished more surely before history by fate itself with misfortune and overthrow and ruin, because of the violation of the 'laws of life,' than by a State Court of Justice." Translation quoted from *Nazi Conspiracy*, IV, 490.

10. See Victor Kravchenko, *I Chose Freedom: The Personal and Political Life of a Soviet Official* (New York, 1946), p. 422. "No properly indoctrinated Communist felt that the Party was 'lying' in professing one set of policies in public and its very opposite in private."

11. The National Socialist despises his fellow German, the SA man the other National Socialists, the SS man the SA man" (Konrad Heiden, *Der Führer: Hitler's Rise to Power* [Boston, 1944], p. 308.

12. Himmler originally selected the candidates of the SS from photographs. Later a Race Commission, before which the applicant had to appear in person, approved or disapproved of his racial appearance. See Himmler on "Organization and Obligation of the SS and the Police," *Nazi Conspiracy*, IV, 616 ff.

13. Himmler was well aware of the fact that it was one of his "most important and lasting accomplishments" to have transformed the racial question from "a negative concept based on matter-of-course antisemitism" into "an organizational task for building up the SS" (*Der Reichsführer SS und Chef der deutschen Polizei*, "exclusively for use within the police"; undated). Thus, "for the first time, the racial question had been placed into, or, better still, had become the focal point, going far beyond the negative concept underlying the natural hatred of Jews. The revolutionary idea of the Fuehrer had been infused with warm lifeblood" (*Der Weg der SS. Der Reichsfürer SS*. SS-Hauptamt-Schulungsamt. Dust jacket: "Not for publication," undated, p. 25.

14. As soon as he was appointed chief of the SS in 1929, Himmler introduced the principle of racial selection and marriage laws and added: "The SS knows very well that this order is of great significance. Taunts, sneers or misunderstanding don't touch us; the future is ours." Quoted from D'Alquen, op. cit., And again, fourteen years later, in his speech at Kharkov (*Nazi Conspiracy*, IV, 572 ff.), Himmler reminds his SS leaders that "we were the first really to solve the problem of blood by action . . . and by problem of blood, we of course do not mean antisemitism. Antisemitism is exactly the same as delousing. Getting rid of lice is not a question of ideology. It is a matter of cleanliness. . . . But for us the question of blood was a reminder of our own worth, a reminder of what is actually the basis holding this German people together."

15. Himmler, op. cit., *Nazi Conspiracy*, IV, 616 ff.

16. Himmler in his speech at Posen, *Nazi Conspiracy*, IV, 558.

22

CRANE BRINTON

The Accession of the Extremists

THE COUP D'ÉTAT

T HE struggle between the moderates and the extremists, which begins almost as soon as the dramatic overthrow of the old regime is effected, is marked by a series of exciting episodes: here street fighting, there a forced seizure of property, almost everywhere heated debates, attempted repressions, a steady stream of violent propaganda. Tempers are strained to the breaking point over matters that in a stable society are capable of an almost automatic solution. There is an almost universal state of tension. The fever is working its way to a crisis. As with many fevers, its progress is in detail jerky, with now an apparent improvement and then a sudden jump ahead. But the cumulative effect is unmistakable. With the final overthrow of the moderates the revolution may be said to have entered its crisis stage.

Before we attempt to describe the behavior of men in societies in such a crisis, we shall have to go a bit further into the process by which the extremists acceded to power. In a sense, such an analysis will be but pointing out in reverse what we have already said of the moderates: the reason why the extremists succeeded are but the other side of the reasons why the moderates failed. Where the moderates were weak, the extremists were strong. The actual steps by which the extremists rise to power are, however, too important to be left with this general statement. We must parallel our analysis of moderate weakness with an analysis of extremist strengths.

The extremists win out because they secure control of the illegal

From Crane Brinton, *The Anatomy of Revolution* (Englewood Cliff, N.J.: Prentice-Hall, 1938), pp. 148–60. Copyright © 1938, 1952, 1965 by Prentice-Hall, Inc., renewed 1980 by Cecilia Bogner.

221

government and turn it in a decisive *coup d'état* against the legal government. The problem of the dual sovereignty is solved by the revolutionary
acts in which the Independents, the Jacobins, and the Bolsheviks seized
power. But the moderates had once shared with them the control of the
organizations which they had turned against the government. The key to
the success of the extremists lies in their monopoly of control over these
organizations—New Model Army and Independent churches, Jacobin
clubs, and soviets.

They obtain this monopoly by ousting, usually in a series of conflicts,
any and all *active and effective* opponents from these organizations. The
discipline, single mindedness, and centralization of authority which
mark the rule of the triumphant extremists are first developed and
brought to perfection in the revolutionary groups of the illegal government. The characteristics which were formed in the growth of the illegal
government remain those of the radicals after the illegal government
becomes the legal. Indeed, many of these useful characteristics were first
molded even further back in the days of the old regime, when the extremist were very small concentrated groups subject to the full "tyranny" of the
government.

The Independents gained discipline and devotion from a long series
of persecutions which began under Elizabeth, whose famed love of tolerance was not extended to Catholics or Brownists. The French radicals
were not so badly treated under the old regime as their descendants and
historians like to think, but the censorship, the Bastille, and the *lettres de
cachet* were real enough, even if they rarely fell to the lot of the rank and
file of the enlightened. As for Russia, its extremists were molded in the
most melodramatic traditions of oppression, were backed by almost a
century of secret organization, plotting, oaths, and martyrdom. We shall
see later that the great Russian Revolution is indeed over; but many of the
authoritarian features of the extremist period have clearly survived in
Russia of today. One of the reasons for that survival is the very great
strength of the Communist authoritarian discipline, forged by years of
underground conspiracy and control from above and within.

ORGANIZATION OF THE EXTREMISTS

The first thing likely to strike an observer of the successful extremists in
the English, French, and Russian revolutions, and indeed, the not quite
so radical patriots who put through the American Revolution, is their
fewness in numbers. The membership of the formal organizations which

did the work of beating the moderates was never more than a small minority of the total population. Their active membership was of course always smaller than the membership on the books. It is not easy to get exact figures, either for membership or for populations, but the following figures are not erroneous enough to be misleading. The New Model Army was created at a membership of 22,000, and was not more than 40,000 in its most obstreperous days. The population of England was somewhere between three and five million. The Jacobins at the most generous estimate numbered in their struggle with the moderates about 500,000. The population of France was probably over rather than under twenty million. The Communist party in Russia has always prided itself on its numerical smallness; this is no bloated bourgeois party, full of indifferent members who cast a lazy vote, or don't even vote at all. Figures again are uncertain, but it seems likely that at no time during the active revolution—say up to Stalin's final acquisition of power by the expulsion of the "Rightist opposition" in 1929—did the Communist party number even 1 per cent of a population of well over one hundred million. In America the difficulty of even approximate figures is greater, since the patriots were not organized into a single body. It is clearly not fair to take the relatively small continental armies as exactly measuring the strength of the patriot—or Whig—group. Nevertheless, the best authorities are agreed that if you count out avowed Loyalists and the very numerous indifferent or neutral, cultivating their own gardens throughout the war, the group which actively engineered, supported, and fought the American Revolution is a minority, probably not more than 10 per cent of the population.

It is easy to remark that though the facts clearly show that these revolutionary groups are very small minorities indeed, all politically active groups are minorities, and that in these revolutions the radicals in some way "represented" or "carried out" what the soul, will, genius, of their nations demanded. This may well be so in terms familiar to the metaphysician, but the relation involved is one which at present we cannot pretend to be able to study by the methods we have laid down in this book. Perhaps the Jacobins were the agents of the general will of the French people; but the general will is a metaphysical concept the relation of which with tangible Jacobins we cannot possibly measure here.

Trotsky in one of his less realistic moods had a fine time reconciling the fewness of the Bolsheviks in 1917 with the largeness of Russia, and with the various groups clearly hostile to the Bolsheviks. "The Bolsheviks," he wrote, in a fine anticipation of George Orwell's *1984*, "took the people as preceding history had created them, and as they were called to achieve the Revolution. The Bolsheviks saw it as their mission to stand at the head of this people. *Those against the insurrection were 'everybody'—except the Bolsheviks. But the Bolsheviks were the people."* Trotsky wasn't quite metaphysician—or psychologist—enough to insist that the Bolsheviks were forcing the Russian people to be free.

In fact, neither revolutionists of the Right nor of the Left have in the twentieth century quite dared to take a consistently Nietzschean position in this matter of the relation between their own elect few and their own masses; that is, they have not dared to say that the elect should be masters in the full connotation of that term and the rest should be slaves in the full connotation of that term. Lenin seems often on the edge of this Nietzschean position, and Hitler in *Mein Kampf* falls over into it not infrequently. But the official position of the Communist, Nazi, and Fascist parties was that the party, the elect, the minority in power, is really a trustee, a shepherd of the people, ruling to improve the people's lot; and Communism to this day holds out the promise that eventually—in a long "eventually," after world capitalism is beaten—the distinction between leaders and led, between party and people, between brain workers and manual workers, will vanish in the classless society.

In all our societies these radicals were very conscious and usually very proud, of their small numbers. They felt definitely set off from their countrymen, consecrated to a cause which their countrymen were certainly not consciously and actively equal to. Some of the radicals may have satisfied themselves that they really represented the better selves of their fellow countrymen, that they were the reality of which the others were the potentiality. But here and now they were very sure that they were superior to the inert and flabby many. The English saints of the seventeenth century, the elect of a God more exclusive than any poor worldly king, made no attempt to conceal their contempt for the damned masses—and dukes and earls were of course masses for these determined Puritans. The Jacobins inherited from the Enlightenment a belief in the natural goodness or the natural reasonableness of the common man, and this belief put a limit to their expressed scorn for their fellows. But the scorn is there, and the Jacobin was almost as loftily consecrated as was the Independent. The Bolsheviks were brought up to believe that dialectical materialism works through an elite of the laboring classes aided by intellectuals, and that the peasants in particular were incapable of working out their own salvation. The Bolsheviks therefore took their fewness naturally enough, and their superiority as well.

There is also a good deal of evidence that as the revolutions go on, a very large number of people just drop out of active politics, make no attempt to register their votes. Now it may be that most of these people again are at heart in sympathy with the active radicals; but on the whole it looks as if most of them were cowed conservatives or moderates, men and women not anxious for martyrdom, but quite incapable of the mental and moral as well as physical strain of being a devoted extremist in the crisis of a revolution. We have very clear evidence of this dropping out of the ordinary man in *two* of our revolutions, and we may reasonably assume that it is one of the uniformities we are seeking.

In Russia, the February Revolution brought in universal suffrage as a matter of course. Russia had at last caught up with the West. At the first elections almost everybody, men and women alike, took the opportunity to vote in various local elections. But very shortly there set in a noticeable decline in the total number of votes cast. In the June, 1917, elections for the Moscow district dumas the Social-Revolutionary groups received 58 per cent of the votes; in the September elections the Bolsheviks received 52 per cent. A clear gain for the Bolsheviks by democratic methods? Not at all. In June the Social-Revolutionaries got 375,000 votes out of 647,000 cast; in September the Bolsheviks got 198,000 out of 381,000 cast. In three months half the electorate dropped out. Trotsky himself has a simple explanation for this: "many small-town people who, in the vapor of the first illusions, had joined the Compromisers fell back soon after into political non-existence." The same story is graphically recorded in French municipal and national elections between the rosy days of 1789, days of almost universal suffrage in practice, and 1793, when in some cases less than a tenth of the qualified voters actually voted. The "people" did not vote for Bolsheviks or Jacobins, and it seems more than likely that if most Englishmen could have voted at all in 1648, they would not have voted for Independents, Levellers, Diggers, Fifth Monarchy Men, or Millenarians. It seems likely also that a full referendum or plebiscite on the American Declaration of Independence in 1776 would have been pretty close. The great numbers of qualified voters just don't vote; in Trotsky's compact phrase, they are politically nonexistent.

Their political nonexistence is not achieved without a good deal of help from the extremists. The elections are supposedly free and open, but the extremists are not hindered by any beliefs in freedom they may have expressed on other days. They soon take steps familiar in this country through the history of groups like the Ku Klux Klan and Tammany Hall. They beat up well-known aristocrats and suchlike class enemies, they start riots at polling places or electoral assemblies, they break windows and start street fights, they howl down moderate candidates, they bring to bear good journalists, skilled at libel and innuendo, and in a hundred ways which any realistic student of politics can uncover with a little study, they make it very difficult for ordinary, peaceful, humdrum men and women to go to the polls and cast their votes for the moderates to whom ordinary, peaceful, humdrum men and women seem attracted. Not that terrorism alone scares off the ordinary man. Mere laziness, an inability to give to political affairs the ceaseless attention revolutions demand, is also instrumental in keeping the man in the street from expressing himself. He gets fed up with the constant meetings, the deputations, the papers, the elections of dogcatchers, general inspectors, presidents, the committees, the rituals, the ceaseless moil and toil of self-government on a more than Athenian basis. At any rate he quits, and the extremists have the field to themselves.

Their fewness is indeed one of the great sources of the extremists' strength. Great numbers are almost as unwieldy in politics as on the battlefield. In the politics of revolutions what counts is the ability to move swiftly, to make clear and final decisions, to push through to a goal without regard for injured human dispositions. For such a purpose the active political group must be small. You cannot otherwise obtain the single-mindedness and devotion, the energy and the discipline, necessary to defeat the moderates. You cannot maintain the fever of fanaticism in large numbers of people long enough to secure the ultimate victory. The masses do not make revolutions. They may be enlisted for some impressive pageantry once the active few have won the revolution. Our twentieth-century revolutions, both of the Right and the Left, have achieved apparent miracles of mass participation. But the impressive demonstrations the camera has recorded in Germany, Italy, Russia and China ought not to deceive the careful student of politics. Neither Communist, Nazi, nor Fascist victory over the moderates was achieved by the participation of the many; all were achieved by small, disciplined, principled, fanatical bodies.

Nor at this stage of revolution do the victorious radicals dare make use of the plebiscite. They cannot risk anything like a free election. Only later, when the crisis is followed by a convalescence, by a return to normal ways, does the plebiscite stage arrive, if it ever does. This interval may not be a very long one, and in the case of Rightist revolutions may be very brief, since the full fury of the Ideal rarely inspires the men of the Right. But certainly for the revolutions we are here studying, the generalization holds: the honest plebiscite is absent from the struggle between extremists and moderates, and is not used by the extremists even after their accession to power. This still holds true in Russia and in her satellites.

The extremists are not only few: they are fanatically devoted to their cause. Their awareness of being few seems correlated with the intensity of their fanaticism. One feeds upon and strengthens the other. With their objects, with the content of their dreams of a better world, we shall concern ourselves later. For those who think that only in the service of a personal God can feelings properly defined as "fanatical" be aroused, our application of the word to Jacobins and Bolsheviks may seem illegitimate. But this is surely an undue narrowing of a clear and useful word. Bolsheviks and Jacobins were as convinced as any Calvinist that they alone were right, that what they proposed was the only possible course. All of our revolutionary radicals displayed a willingness to work hard, to sacrifice their peace and security, to submit to discipline, to submerge their personalities in the group. They were all aware of the spiritual difficulties of keeping "always at the height of revolutionary circumstances," as the Jacobins used to put it; but to a surprising extent they overcame these difficulties and maintained on this earth an *esprit de corps*, an active moral union, that is far beyond the powers of ordinary men in ordinary circumstances to attain and to maintain.

And they are disciplined. Partly, as we have explained, this is an inheritance from their oppressed past. It correlates with their fewness and with their fanatical strength. The New Model Army is an excellent example. It defeated the haphazard aggregations which the ordinary recruiting methods of the Royalists opposed to it; it defeated the cream of the opposing forces, the cavalry recruited from faithful country gentlemen and their dependents. The New Model was recruited from ardent Puritans, vouched for by men who knew them; and it was submitted to a brief but effective course of training incomparably more severe than any that had yet been used in English military history. The result was a fine army—and a compact body of hard revolutionists who could cut through the best intentions and the best rhetoric of the moderates. The discipline of the Jacobins was not military, but it was very rigorous, and indeed resembled the kind of discipline which a militant religious body imposes on its members. The Jacobins were always scrutinizing their own membership, submitting to the ordeal of an *épuration*, literally a "purification," better, a "purge." The slightest deviation from the established order of the day might bring a warning and possible expulsion. With the Spartan ways of the Russian Communist party in the early days of the Soviet state most of us are familiar; it is a point on which all reporters, kindly and unkindly, are agreed.

The extremists put their disciplined skill into the realization of the Revolutionary ends. There has been worked out in the last few hundred years an elaborate technique of revolutionary action, of which the Russian, Chinese, and Cuban Communists were the latest heirs. A good deal has been written about this technique, which is in part simply the technique of any successful pressure group: propaganda, electioneering, lobbying, parading, street fighting, guerrilla warfare, Gandhian non-violent violence, delegation making, direct pressure on magistrates, sporadic terrorism of the tar-and-feather or castor-oil variety and other techniques in various combinations. Jacobins, Communists, and Sons of Liberty did a notably good job at this sort of thing. But it is rather surprising to note how many of these techniques can be found in England, and especially in London, as early as the seventeenth century. In this respect, as in many others, the English Revolution is clearly of modern type. Here is a bit that might have come from the French Revolution: during the debate on the Militia Order, a crowd of apprentices "came into the House of Commons and kept the door open, and their hats on . . . and called out as they stood, 'Vote, vote,' and in this arrogant posture stood until the votes passed." One suspects that these apprentices did not march in spontaneously. This is the kind of thing that takes organization.

Finally, the extremists follow their leaders with a devotion and a unanimity not to be found among the moderates. Theories of democratic equality, which crop up at the start of all our revolutions, prove no obstacle to the development among the extremists of something very like the "Führer" principle we associate with Fascist movements. Here it is the moderates who live up to their theories, and in the early stages of the revolutions it is not uncommon to find complaints that So-and-so is arrogating to himself powers, a personal leadership, no good man would want to possess. Mirabeau and Kerensky, to take neat examples, were accused by moderates and extremists alike of aiming at personal dictatorship. Yet Robespierre and Lenin followed in their footsteps almost literally and for them only the cheering could be heard—at least in the homeland. This magnifying of the principle of leadership runs right through the organization, from the subalterns up to the great national heroes—Cromwell, Robespierre, Lenin.

On the whole, this leadership is effective, and especially so at the very top. Now if they are seen as full and rounded human beings, there are unquestionably differences among the men who make up the general staffs of the extremists. The psychologist and the novelist, indeed the historian as well, could not lump them all together. Yet they have in common one aspect which is of great importance to the sociologist; they combine, in varying degrees, very high ideals and a complete contempt for the inhibitions and principles which serve most other men as ideals. They present a strange variant of Plato's pleasant scheme: they are not philosopher-kings but philosopher-killers. They have the realistic, the practical touch very few of the moderate leaders had, and yet they have also enough of the prophet's fire to hold followers who expect the New Jerusalem around the next corner. They are practical men unfettered by common sense, Machiavellians in the service of the Beautiful and the Good.

A bit from Lenin's life will make the point clear. At a secret meeting of the Central Committee of the Bolshevik party just before the October Revolution, Lenin was urging insurrection on the more tender-minded of his colleagues, who thought that the Bolsheviks ought to respect the will of the majority of Russians, which was clearly against them. "We are inclined to consider the systematic preparation of an uprising as something in the nature of a political sin," said he. "To wait for the Constituent Assembly, which will clearly not be with us, is senseless." There is the practical Lenin, unworried by a democratic dogma that stands in his way. After the October Revolution he wrote in *Pravda* of "the crisis which has arisen as a result of the lack of correspondence between the elections to the Constitution Assembly and the will of the people and the interest of the toiling and exploited classes." Here the will of the people is somehow at bottom the will of the minority party of Bolsheviks. We are back again in the midst of democratic dogma. Parallel cases could readily be drawn from Robespierre, Cromwell, and even, one fears, from Jefferson.

Hypocrisy? To those of little imagination or experience of the world, such acts must always seem hypocritical. But, on a less heroic scale, they are far too much a part of normal human action to deserve so opprobrious a label. The Robespierre who, as an enlightened young man, had held capital punishment wrong did not hypocritically send his enemies to the guillotine. He had convinced himself that his enemies were scarcely men at all; they were sinners, corrupt souls, agents of a worse-than-Satan, and their removal from this earth wasn't really capital punishment in the conventional sense at all. You could still treat ordinary criminals in full accord with the most humanitarian principles of jurisprudence. Most of us make this sort of compromise with ourselves often enough in daily life.

But with us comfort, convenience, habit, even common sense, determine the limits of compromise. For the revolutionary extremist such limits are off; in the delirium, in the crisis, there is an extraordinary reversal of the roles played in normal times by the real and the ideal. Here briefly and at last the blind—or the seer—is king; plain earthly seeing, the kind that concerns the oculist, is for once of very little use. The seers have just enough of it to keep their positions of leadership. Cromwell, indeed, had a good deal of what seems an English sense of the contingent, and Lenin was certainly no academic idealist. Robespierre is in some ways the most unadulterated seer of the lot.

Yet all of them, including even Robespierre, were what the world calls men of action. They could and did get things done, were administrators and executives, ran organizations for which tradition and routine had not yet been able to build up much that worked automatically. If they have left behind them a reputation for unusual ruthlessness, this may be in part a reflection of the ill repute terrorism has for most of us. And the ruthlessness, in the proper service of the ideal, went while they were alive into the making of their leadership. Cromwell gained credit among the Saints for his Irish massacres. The guillotine in France was for a few months the "holy guillotine." Trotsky, early in his famous rallying of the Bolshevik troops in the Civil War, ordered shot the commander, commissar, and one soldier out of ten in a Petrograd workers' regiment that had fled the enemy, and to the dismay of the gentler colleagues showed no hesitation about continuing the policy of discipline through bloodshed. Trotsky became briefly a savior and a hero. We are a long way from Order Number One!

For most men, there is a gap between their deeds and their professions, between what they are and what they would like to be, between what they are and what they think they are. Normally, however, they manage to keep the gap small enough, or turn their attention away from one side of it or the other, so that they are not unduly troubled by it. For the leaders of the extremists in times of revolution the gap looks to an outside observer enormous, bigger than it ever is in normal times. A few men, like Fouché, seem to have been terrorists to save their own skins. But, in general, only a sincere extremist in a revolution can kill men because he loves man, attain peace through violence, and free men by enslaving them. Such contrasts in action would paralyze a conventionally practical leader, but the extremist seems quite undisturbed by it. Where the ordinary man would be troubled by something like a split personality, where his conscience or his sense of reality, or both, would be haunted, the extremist goes boldly ahead. Wide though the gap between the real and the ideal is in the crisis period, he can cross it at his own convenience. He has, for the moment, the best of both worlds. He can manipulate with equal skill the concrete and complex human beings on committees, deputations, bureaus, ministries, all the unsettling problems of administration, and yet use gracefully and convincingly the abstract, indispensable, haunting words which have in revolutions such magic power over large groups of men.

It is this last gift that seems to lie all but wholly beyond the capacity of the most ambitious hypocrite. The great leaders of the Terrors are fitted for their task by a genuine vocation, a vocation which in ordinary times would exclude them from political power. Their belief in the Absolute is not assumed, and is as real as their ability to handle the contingent. And for once the Absolute is practical politics. F. W. Maitland has a passage, suggested by Coleridge, which puts the point neatly:

Coleridge has remarked how, in times of great political excitement, the terms in which political theories are expressed become, not more and more practical, but more and more abstract and impractical. It is in such times that men clothe their theories in universal terms. . . . The absolute spirit is abroad. Relative or partial goods seems a poor ideal. It is not of these, or those men that speak, of this nation or that age, but of Man.

23

MAX WEBER

Types of Authority

THE BASIS OF LEGITIMACY

2: The Three Pure Types of Legitimate Authority

There are three pure types of legitimate authority. The validity of their claims to legitimacy may be based on:

1. Rational grounds—resting on a belief in the "legality" of patterns of normative rules and the right of those elevated to authority under such rules to issue commands (legal authority).

2. Traditional grounds—resting on an established belief in the sanctity of immemorial traditions and the legitimacy of the status of those exercising authority under them (traditional authority); or finally,

3. Charismatic grounds—resting on devotion to the specific and exceptional sanctity, heroism or exemplary character of an individual person, and of the normative patterns or order revealed or ordained by him (charismatic authority).

In the case of legal authority, obedience is owed to the legally established impersonal order. It extends to the persons exercising the authority of office under it only by virtue of the formal legality of their commands and only within the scope of authority of the office. In the case of traditional authority, obedience is owed to the *person* of the chief who

From Max Weber, *The Theory of Social and Economic Organization*, trans. A. M. Henderson and Talcott Parsons, ed. Talcott Parsons (New York: The Free Press, 1947), chap. 3, "The Types of Authority and Imperative Co-ordination," pp. 328–34, 341–42, 359–63. Reprinted with permission of The Free Press, a division of Macmillan, Inc. Copyright 1947, renewed 1975 by Talcott Parsons. First published as *Wirtschaft und Gesellschaft*, 1921.

occupies the traditionally sanctioned position of authority and who is (within its sphere) bound by tradition. But here the obligation of obedience is not based on the impersonal order, but is a matter of personal loyalty within the area of accustomed obligations. In the case of charismatic authority, it is the charismatically qualified leader as such who is obeyed by virtue of personal trust in him and his revelation, his heroism or his exemplary qualities so far as they fall within the scope of the individual's belief in his charisma.

1. The usefulness of the above classification can only be judged by its results in promoting systematic analysis. The concept of "charisma" ("the gift of grace") is taken from the vocabulary of early Christianity. For the Christian religious organization Rudolf Sohm, in his *Kirchenrecht*, was the first to clarify the substance of the concept, even though he did not use the same terminology. Others (for instance, Hollin, *Enthusiasmus und Bussgewalt*) have clarified certain important consequences of it. It is thus nothing new.

2. The fact that none of these three ideal types, the elucidation of which will occupy the following pages, is usually to be found in historical cases in "pure" form, is naturally not a valid objection to attempting their conceptual formulation in the sharpest possible form. In this respect the present case is no different from many others. Later on (§ 11 ff.) the transformation of pure charisma by the process of routinization will be discussed and thereby the relevance of the concept to the understanding of empirical systems of authority considerably increased. But even so it may be said of every empirically historical phenomenon of authority that it is not likely to be "as an open book." Analysis in terms of sociological types has, after all, as compared with purely empirical historical investigation, certain advantages which should not be minimized. That is, it can in the particular case of a concrete form of authority determine what conforms to or approximates such types of "charisma," "hereditary charisma" (§ 10, 11), "the charisma of office," "patriarchy" (§ 7), "bureaucracy" (§ 4), the authority of status groups,[1] and in doing so it can work with relatively unambiguous concepts. But the idea that the whole of concrete historical reality can be exhausted in the conceptual scheme about to be developed is as far from the author's thoughts as anything could be.

LEGAL AUTHORITY WITH A BUREAUCRATIC ADMINISTRATIVE STAFF[2]

3: *Legal Authority: The Pure Type with Employment of a Bureaucratic Administrative Staff*

The effectiveness of legal authority rests on the acceptance of the validity of the following mutually inter-dependent ideas.

1. That any given legal norm may be established by agreement or by imposition, on grounds of expediency or rational values or both, with a claim to obedience at least on the part of the members of the corporate group. This is, however, usually extended to include all persons within the sphere of authority or of power in question—which in the case of territorial bodies is the territorial area—who stand in certain social relationships or carry out forms of social action which in the order governing the corporate group have been declared to be relevant.

2. That every body of law consists essentially in a consistent system of abstract rules which have normally been intentionally established. Furthermore, administration of law is held to consist in the application of these rules to particular cases; the administrative process in the rational pursuit of the interests which are specified in the order governing the corporate group within the limits laid down by legal precepts and following principles which are capable of generalized formulation and are approved in the order governing the group, or at least not disapproved in it.

3. That thus the typical person in authority occupies an "office." In the action associated with his status, including the commands he issues to others, he is subject to an impersonal order to which his actions are oriented. This is true not only for persons exercising legal authority who are in the usual sense "officials," but, for instance, for the elected president of a state.

4. That the person who obeys authority does so, as it is usually stated, only in his capacity as a "member" of the corporate group and what he obeys is only "the law." He may in this connexion be the member of an association, of a territorial commune, of a church, or a citizen of a state.

5. In conformity with point 3, it is held that the members of the corporate group, in so far as they obey a person in authority, do not owe this obedience to him as an individual, but to the impersonal order. Hence, it follows that there is an obligation to obedience only within the sphere of the rationally delimited authority which, in terms of the order, has been conferred upon him.

The following may thus be said to be the fundamental categories of rational legal authority:—

(1) A continuous organization of official functions bound by rules.

(2) A specified sphere of competence. This involves (a) a sphere of obligations to perform functions which has been marked off as part of a systematic division of labour. (b) The provision of the incumbent with the necessary authority to carry out these functions. (c) That the necessary means of compulsion are clearly defined and their use is subject to definite conditions. A unit exercising authority which is organized in this way will be called an "administrative organ."[3]

There are administrative organs in this sense in large-scale private organizations, in parties and armies, as well as in the state and the church. An elected president, a cabinet of ministers, or a body of elected representatives also in this sense constitute administrative organs. This is not, however, the place to discuss these concepts. Not every administrative organ is provided with compulsory powers. But this distinction is not important for present purposes.

(3) The organization of offices follows the principle of hierarchy; that is, each lower office is under the control and supervision of a higher one. There is a right of appeal and of statement of grievances from the lower to the higher. Hierarchies differ in respect to whether and in what cases complaints can lead to a ruling from an authority at various points higher in the scale, and as to whether changes are imposed from higher up or the responsibility for such changes is left to the lower office, the conduct of which was the subject of complaint.

(4) The rules which regulate the conduct of an office may be technical rules or norms.[4] In both cases, if their application is to be fully rational, specialized training is necessary. It is thus normally true that only a person who has demonstrated an adequate technical training is qualified to be a member of the administrative staff of such an organized group, and hence only such persons are eligible for appointment to official positions. The administrative staff of a rational corporate group thus typically consists of "officials," whether the organization be devoted to political, religious, economic—in particular, capitalistic—or other ends.

(5) In the rational type it is a matter of principle that the members of the administrative staff should be completely separated from ownership of the means of production or administration. Officials, employees, and workers attached to the administrative staff do not themselves own the non-human means of production and administration. These are rather

provided for their use in kind or in money, and the official is obligated to render an accounting of their use. There exists, furthermore, in principle complete separation of the property belonging to the organization, which is controlled within the sphere of office, and the personal property of the official, which is available for his own private uses. There is a corresponding separation of the place in which official functions are carried out, the "office" in the sense of premises, from living quarters.

(6) In the rational type case, there is also a complete absence of appropriation of his official position by the incumbent. When "rights" to an office exist, as in the case of judges, and recently of an increasing proportion of officials and even of workers, they do not normally serve the purpose of appropriation by the official, but of securing the purely objective and independent character of the conduct of the office so that it is oriented only to the relevant norms.

(7) Administrative acts, decisions, and rules are formulated and recorded in writing, even in cases where oral discussion is the rule or is even mandatory. This applies at least to preliminary dicussions and proposals, to final decisions, and to all sorts of orders and rules. The combination of written documents and a continuous organization of official functions constitutes the "office" [5] which is the central focus of all types of modern corporate action.

(8) Legal authority can be exercised in a wide variety of different forms which will be distinguished and discussed later. The following analysis will be deliberately confined for the most part to the aspect of imperative co-ordination in the structure of the administrative staff. It will consist in an analysis in terms of ideal types of officialdom or "bureaucracy."

In the above outline no mention has been made of the kind of supreme head appropriate to a system of legal authority. This is a consequence of certain considerations which can only be made entirely understandable at a later stage in the analysis. There are very important types of rational imperative co-ordination which, with respect to the ultimate source of authority, belong to other categories. This is true of the hereditary charismatic type, as illustrated by hereditary monarchy and of the pure charismatic type of a president chosen by plebiscite. Other cases involve rational elements at important points, but are made up of a combination of bureaucratic and charismatic components, as is true of the cabinet form of government. Still others are subject to the authority of the chief of other corporate groups, whether their character be charismatic or bureaucratic; thus the formal head of a government department under a parliamentary regime may be a minister who occupies his position because of his authority in a party. The type of rational, legal administrative staff is capable of application in all kinds of situations and contexts. It is the most important mechanism for the administration of everyday profane affairs. For in that sphere, the exercise of authority and, more broadly, imperative co-ordination, consists precisely in administration.

4: Legal Authority: The Pure Type with Employment of a Bureaucratic Administrative Staff—(Continued)

The purest type of exercise of legal authority is that which employs a bureaucratic administrative staff. Only the supreme chief of the organization occupies his position of authority by virtue of appropriation, of election, or of having been designated for the succession. But even *his* authority consists in a sphere of legal "competence." The whole administrative staff under the supreme authority then consists, in the purest type, of individual officials who are appointed and function according to the following criteria:[6]

(1) They are personally free and subject to authority only with respect to their impersonal official obligations.

(2) They are organized in a clearly defined hierarchy of offices.

(3) Each office has a clearly defined sphere of competence in the legal sense.

(4) The office is filled by a free contractual relationship. Thus, in principle, there is free selection.

(5) Candidates are selected on the basis of technical qualifications. In the most rational case, this is tested by examination or guaranteed by diplomas certifying technical training, or both. They are *appointed*, not elected.

(6) They are remunerated by fixed salaries in money, for the most part with a right to pensions. Only under certain circumstances does the employing authority, especially in private organizations, have a right to terminate the appointment, but the official is always free to resign. The salary scale is primarily graded according to rank in the hierarchy; but in addition to this criterion, the responsibility of the position and the requirements of the incumbent's social status may be taken into account.

(7) The office is treated as the sole, or at least the primary, occupation of the incumbent.

(8) It constitutes a career. There is a system of "promotion" according to seniority or to achievement, or both. Promotion is dependent on the judgment of superiors.

(9) The official works entirely separated from ownership of the means of administration and without appropriation of his position.

(10) He is subject to strict and systematic discipline and control in the conduct of the office. . . .

TRADITIONAL AUTHORITY

6: *Traditional Authority*

A system of imperative co-ordination will be called "traditional" if legitimacy is claimed for it and believed in on the basis of the sanctity of the order and the attendant powers of control as they have been handed down from the past, "have always existed." The person or persons exercising authority are designated according to traditionally transmitted rules. The object of obedience is the personal authority of the individual which he enjoys by virtue of his traditional status. The organized group exercising authority is, in the simplest case, primarily based on relations of personal loyalty, cultivated through a common process of education. The person exercising authority is not a "superior," but a personal "chief."[7]

His administrative staff does not consist primarily of officials, but of personal retainers.[8] Those subject to authority are not "members" of an association, but are either his traditional "comrades" or his "subjects." What determines the relations of the administrative staff to the chief is not the impersonal obligation of office, but personal loyalty to the chief.

Obedience is not owed to enacted rules, but to the person who occupies a position of authority by tradition or who has been chosen for such a position on a traditional basis. His commands are legitimized in one of two ways: (a) partly in terms of traditions which themselves directly determine the content of the command and the objects and extent of authority. In so far as this is true, to overstep the traditional limitations would endanger his traditional status by undermining acceptance of his legitimacy. (b) In part, it is a matter of the chief's free personal decision, in that tradition leaves a certain sphere open for this. This sphere of traditional prerogative rests primarily on the fact that the obligations of obedience on the basis of personal loyalty are essentially unlimited.[9] There is thus a double sphere: on the one hand, of action which is bound to specific tradition; on the other hand, of that which is free of any specific rules.

In the latter sphere, the chief is free to confer "grace" on the basis of his personal pleasure or displeasure, his personal likes and dislikes, quite arbitrarily, particularly in return for gifts which often become a source of regular income. So far as his action follows principles at all, these are principles of substantive ethical common sense, of justice, or of utilitarian expediency. They are not, however, as in the case of legal authority, formal principles. The exercise of authority is normally oriented to the question of what the chief and his administrative staff will normally permit, in view of the traditional obedience of the subjects and what will or will not arouse their resistance. When resistance occurs, it is directed against the person of the chief or of a member of his staff. The accusation is that he has failed to observe the traditional limits of his authority. Opposition is not directed against the system as such.

It is impossible in the pure type of traditional authority for law or administrative rules to be deliberately created by legislation. What is actually new is thus claimed to have always been in force but only recently to have become known through the wisdom of the promulgator. The only documents which can play a part in the orientation of legal administration are the documents of tradition; namely, precedents. . . .

CHARISMATIC AUTHORITY

10: *The Principal Characteristics of Charismatic Authority and Its Relation to Forms of Communal Organization*

The term "charisma" will be applied to a certain quality of an individual personality by virtue of which he is set apart from ordinary men and treated as endowed with supernatural, superhuman, or at least specifically exceptional powers or qualities. These are such as are not accessible to the ordinary person, but are regarded as of divine origin or as exemplary, and on the basis of them the individual concerned is treated as a leader. In primitive circumstances this peculiar kind of deference is paid to prophets, to people with a reputation for therapeutic or legal wisdom, to leaders in the hunt, and heroes in war. It is very often thought of as resting on magical powers. How the quality in question would be ultimately judged from any ethical, aesthetic, or other such point of view is naturally entirely indifferent for purposes of definition. What is alone important is how the individual is actually regarded by those subject to charismatic authority, by his "followers" or "disciples."

For present purposes it will be necessary to treat a variety of different types as being endowed with charisma in this sense. It includes the state of a "berserker" whose spells of maniac passion have, apparently wrongly, sometimes been attributed to the use of drugs. In Medieval Byzantium a group of people endowed with this type of charismatic war-like passion were maintained as a kind of weapon. It includes the "shaman," the kind of magician who in the pure type is subject to epileptoid seizures as a means of falling into trances. Another type is that of Joseph Smith, the founder of Mormonism, who, however, cannot be classified in this way with absolute certainty since there is a possibility that he was a very sophisticated type of deliberate swindler. Finally it includes the type of intellectual, such as Kurt Eisner,[10] who is carried away with his own demagogic success. Sociological analysis, which must abstain from value judgments, will treat all these on the same level as the men who, according to conventional judgments, are the 'greatest' heroes, prophets, and saviours.

1. It is recognition on the part of those subject to authority which is decisive for the validity of charisma. This is freely given and guaranteed by what is held to be a "sign" or proof,[11] originally always a miracle, and consists in devotion to the corresponding revelation, hero worship, or absolute trust in the leader. But where charisma is genuine, it is not this which is the basis of the claim to legitimacy. This basis lies rather in the conception that it is the *duty* of those who have been called to a charismatic mission to recognize its quality and to act accordingly. Psychologically this "recognition" is a matter of complete personal devotion to the possessor of the quality, arising out of enthusiasm, or of despair and hope.

No prophet has ever regarded his quality as dependent on the attitudes of the masses toward him. No elective king or military leader has ever treated those who have resisted him or tried to ignore him otherwise than as delinquent in duty. Failure to take part in a military expedition under such leader, even though recruitment is formally voluntary, has universally been met with disdain.

2. If proof of his charismatic qualification fails him for long, the leader endowed with charisma tends to think his god or his magical or heroic powers have deserted him. If he is for long unsuccessful, above all if his leadership fails to benefit his followers, it is likely that his charismatic authority will disappear. This is the genuine charismatic meaning of the "gift of grace."[12]

Even the old Germanic kings were sometimes rejected with scorn. Similar phenomena are very common among so-called "primitive" peoples. In China the charismatic quality of the monarch, which was transmitted unchanged by heredity, was upheld so rigidly that any misfortune whatever, not only defeats in war, but drought, floods, or astronomical phenomena which were considered unlucky, forced him to do public penance and might even force his abdication. If such things occurred, it was a sign that he did not possess the requisite charismatic virtue, he was thus not a legitimate "Son of Heaven."

3. The corporate group which is subject to charismatic authority is based on an emotional form of communal relationship.[13] The administrative staff of a charismatic leader does not consist of "officials"; at least its members are not technically trained. It is not chosen on the basis of social privilege nor from the point of view of domestic or personal dependency. It is rather chosen in terms of the charismatic qualities of its members. The prophet has his disciples; the war lord his selected henchmen; the leader, generally, his followers. There is no such thing as "appointment" or "dismissal," no career, no promotion. There is only a "call" at the instance of the leader on the basis of the charismatic qualification of those he summons. There is no hierarchy; the leader merely intervenes in general or in individual cases when he considers the members of his staff inadequate to a task with which they have been entrusted. There is no such thing as a definite sphere of authority and of competence, and no appropriation of official powers on the basis of social privileges. There may, however, be territorial or functional limits to charismatic powers and to the individual's "mission." There is no such thing as a salary or a benefice. Disciples or followers tend to live primarily in a communistic relationship with their leader on means which have been provided by voluntary gift. There are no established administrative organs. In their place are agents who have been provided with charismatic authority by their chief or who possess charisma of their own. There is no system of formal rules, of abstract legal principles, and hence no process of judicial decision oriented to them. But equally there is no legal wisdom oriented to judicial precedent. Formally concrete judgments are newly created from case to case and are originally regarded as divine judgments and revelations. From a substantive point of view, every charismatic authority would have to subscribe to the proposition, "It is written . . . , but I say unto you . . ."[14] The genuine prophet, like the genuine military leader and every true leader in this sense, preaches, creates, or demands *new* obligations. In the pure type of charisma, these are imposed on the authority of revolution by oracles, or of the leader's own will, and are recognized by the members of the religious, military, or party group, because they come from such a source. Recognition is a duty. When such an authority comes into conflict with the competing authority of another who also claims charismatic sanction, the only recourse is to some kind of a contest, by magical means or even an actual physical battle

of the leaders. In principle, only one side can be in the right in such a conflict; the other must be guilty of a wrong which has to be expiated.

Charismatic authority is thus specifically outside the realm of everyday routine and the profane sphere.[15] In this respect, it is sharply opposed both to rational, and particularly bureaucratic, authority, and to traditional authority, whether in its patriarchal, patrimonial, or any other form. Both rational and traditional authority are specifically forms of everyday routine control of action; while the charismatic type is the direct antithesis of this. Bureaucratic authority is specifically rational in the sense of being bound to intellectually analysable rules; while charismatic authority is specifically irrational in the sense of being foreign to all rules. Traditional authority is bound to the precedents handed down from the past and to this extent is also oriented to rules. Within the sphere of its claims, charismatic authority repudiates the past, and is in this sense a specifically revolutionary force. It recognizes no appropriation of positions of power by virtue of the possession of property, either on the part of a chief or of socially privileged groups. The only basis of legitimacy for it is personal charisma, so long as it is proved; that is, as long as it receives recognition and is able to satisfy the followers or disciples. But this lasts only so long as the belief in its charismatic inspiration remains.

The above is scarcely in need of further discussion. What has been said applies to the position of authority of such elected monarchs as Napoleon, with his use of the plebiscite. It applies to the "rule of genius," which has elevated people of humble origin to thrones and high military commands, just as much as it applies to religious prophets or war heroes.

4. Pure charisma is specifically foreign to economic considerations. Whenever it appears, it constitutes a "call" in the most emphatic sense of the word, a "mission" or a "spiritual duty." In the pure type, it disdains and repudiates economic exploitation of the gifts of grace as a source of income, though, to be sure, this often remains more an ideal than a fact. It is not that charisma always means the renunciation of property or even of acquisition, as under certain circumstances prophets and their disciples do. The heroic warrior and his followers actively seek "booty"; the elective ruler or the charismatic party leader requires the material means of power. The former in addition requires a brilliant display of his authority to bolster his prestige. What is despised, so long as the genuinely charismatic type is adhered to, is traditional or rational everyday economizing, the attainment of a regular income by continuous economic activity devoted to this end. Support by gifts, sometimes on a grand scale involv-

ing foundations, even by bribery and grand-scale honoraria, or by begging, constitute the strictly voluntary type of support. On the other hand, "booty," or coercion, whether by force or by other means, is the other typical form of charismatic provision for needs. From the point of view of rational economic activity, charisma is a typical anti-economic force. It repudiates any sort of involvement in the everyday routine world. It can only tolerate, with an attitude of complete emotional indifference, irregular, unsystematic, acquisitive acts. In that it relieves the recipient of economic concerns, dependence on property income can be the economic basis of a charismatic mode of life for some groups; but that is not usually acceptable for the normal charismatic "revolutionary."

The fact that incumbency of church office has been forbidden to the Jesuits is a rationalized application of this principle of discipleship. The fact that all the "virtuosi" of asceticism, the mendicant orders, and fighters for a faith belong in this category, is quite clear. Almost all prophets have been supported by voluntary gifts. The well-known saying of St. Paul, "If a man does not work, neither shall he eat," was directed against the swarm of charismatic missionaries. It obviously has nothing to do with a positive valuation of economic activity for its own sake, but only lays it down as a duty of each individual somehow to provide for his own support. This because he realized that the purely charismatic parable of the lilies of the field was not capable of literal application, but at best "taking no thought for the morrow" could be hoped for. On the other hand, in such a case as primarily an artistic type of charismatic discipleship, it is conceivable that insulation from economic struggle should mean limitation of those who were really eligible to the "economically independent"; that is, to persons living on income from property. This has been true of the circle of Stefan George, at least in its primary intentions.

5. In traditionally stereotyped periods, charisma is the greatest revolutionary force. The equally revolutionary force of "reason" works from without by altering the situations of action, and hence its problems finally in this way changing men's attitudes toward them; or it intellectualizes the individual. Charisma, on the other hand, may involve a subjective or internal reorientation born out of suffering, conflicts, or enthusiasm. It may then result in a radical alteration of the central system of attitudes and directions of action with a completely new orientation of all attitudes toward the different problems and structures of the "world."[16] In prerationalistic periods, tradition and charisma between them have almost exhausted the whole of the orientation of action.

NOTES

1. *Ständische.* There is no really acceptable English rendering of this term. —ED.

2. The specifically modern type of administration has intentionally been taken as a point of departure in order to make it possible later to contrast the others with it.

3. *Behörde.*

4. Weber does not explain this distinction. By a "technical rule" he probably means a prescribed course of action which is dictated primarily on grounds touching efficiency of the performance of the immediate functions, while by "norms" he probably means rules which limit conduct on grounds other than those of efficiency. Of course, in one sense all rules are norms in that they are prescriptions for conduct, conformity with which is problematical. —ED.

5. *Bureau.* It has seemed necessary to use the English word "office" in three different meanings, which are distinguished in Weber's discussion by at least two terms. The first is *Amt*, which means "office" in the sense of the institutionally defined status of a person. The second is the "work premises" as in the expression "he spent the afternoon in his office." For this Weber uses *Bureau* as also for the third meaning which he has just defined, the "organized work process of a group." In this last sense an office is a particular type of "organization," or *Betrieb* in Weber's sense. This use is established in English in such expressions as "the District Attorney's Office has such and such functions." Which of the three meanings is involved in a given case will generally be clear from the context. — ED.

6. This characterization applies to the "monocratic" as opposed to the "collegial" type, which will be discussed below.

7. *Herr.*

8. *Diener.*

9. This does not seem to be a very happy formulation of the essential point. It is not necessary that the authority of a person in such a position, such as the head of a household, should be unlimited. It is rather that its extent is unspecified. It is generally limited by higher obligations, but the burden of proof rests upon the person on whom an obligation is laid that there is such a conflicting higher obligation. —ED.

10. The leader of the communistic experiment in Bavaria in 1919. —ED.

11. *Bewährung.*

12. *Gottesgnadentum.*

13. Weber uses the term *Gemeinde*, which is not directly translatable. —ED.

14. Something contrary to what was written, as Jesus said in opposition to the Scribes and Pharisees. —ED.

15. Weber used the antithesis of *Charisma* and *Alltag* in two senses. On the one hand, of the extraordinary and temporary as opposed to the everyday and routine; on the other hand, the sacred as opposed to the profane. See the editor's *Structure of Social Action*, ch. xvii. —ED.

16. Weber uses *Welt* in quotation marks, indicating that it refers to its meaning in what is primarily a religious context. It is the sphere of "worldly" things and interests as distinguished from transcendental religious interests. —ED.

24

ANN RUTH WILLNER

Charismatic Leadership

W_E owe the notion of political charisma to the fertile mind of Max Weber, the outstanding German social scientist of the early twentieth century. Weber introduced the concept of the charismatic leader in the context of his now classic classification of authority or legitimate domination into three ideal types: legal or rational, traditional, and charismatic.[1] The basis of his classification is the content of the prevailing beliefs in a society that govern is dominant pattern of command and compliance.

By what right, asked Weber, do some individuals in social systems claim to exercise command over others and gain acceptance of their claims and obedience to their directives from those others as their right?

In the legal-rational and traditional types of authority, Weber stated, rights to the exercise of authority are recognized as legitimate because of beliefs in offices or statuses that have become institutionalized in societies over time. Thus, legal-rational authority is based upon a belief in the legality of rules and in the right of those who occupy offices by virtue of these rules to give commands. The belief in the rules of a constitution, for example, confers authority upon a duly selected prime minister or president.

Traditional authority is derived from "an established belief in the sanctity of immemorial traditions"[2] and thus in statuses traditionally recognized. The status of monarch or chieftain, for example, has been achieved in different societies in different ways, such as through lineage and inheritance or ordeal and combat. But the individual who gains that

From Ann Ruth Willner, *The Spellbinders* (New Haven: Yale University Press, 1984), pp. 3–8.

status by whatever means tradition has decreed has legitimacy by virtue of belief in that tradition.

In both these types, therefore, the claim of an individual to the exercise of authority or legitimate command is recognized largely because of his/her occupancy of an office or status.

Charismatic authority by contrast is distinctly personal. It rests on "devotion to the specific sanctity, heroism, or exemplary character of an individual person, and the normative patterns or order revealed or ordained by him"[3] Charismatic authority, therefore, is lodged neither in office nor in status but derives from the capacity of a particular person to arouse and maintain belief in himself or herself as the source of legitimacy.[4]

This specifically personal character of charismatic authority has understandably but mistakenly led to its being treated as interchangeable with charismatic leadership. As the final section of this chapter explains, charismatic leadership is not identical to charisma as the basis for authority in a social system, although they may overlap.[5] Nor is charisma an aspect of leadership in general, as some scholars have asserted.[6]

Charismatic leadership is a very special subtype of leadership with unusual qualities not found in leadership in general. Leadership, in the general sense of the term in common usage,[7] denotes a relatively sustained and asymmetric exercise of influence by one individual, the leader, over others, the followers. It is a patterned relationship of influence between one member of a group and its other members. Those who receive and respond to the influence, the followers, are crucial to the relationship, for a potential or an aspirant leader's claim to mold the views or direct the actions of others is not realized until the potential followers recognize and act upon that claim.[8]

The difference between charismatic leadership and this general leadership relationship can be seen by examining four dimensions that characterize follower recognition of and response to the leader. These are: (1) the leader-image dimension, (2) the idea-acceptance dimension, (3) the compliance dimension, and (4) the emotional dimension.

The leader-image dimension refers to beliefs that followers hold about the person of their leader. Leaders frequently are believed by their followers to have skills or qualities necessary to accomplish tasks or to further goals important to them. Leaders are often perceived by their followers to possess qualities regarded as admirable in their particular cultures, such as wisdom, foresight, firmness, benevolence, guile, strength of character, or subtlety.

In the charismatic relationship, followers believe their leader to have superhuman qualities or to possess to an extraordinary degree the qualities highly esteemed in their culture. They attribute to their leader qualities commonly associated in their culture with the realm of the divine or the supernatural, with gods, demigods, or outstanding heroes.[9]

The second dimension relates to follower receptivity to a leader's statements and ideas. This idea-acceptance dimension refers to the basis on which and the extent to which followers believe and internalize a leader's definitions and ideas. There are normally many bases upon which followers can accept what a leader tells them—because it sounds reasonable, because it conforms with knowledge obtained from other sources, because it accords with their own experience, because of the leader's status or prestige, to mention only a few.

In the charismatic relationship, however, these other bases for belief either do not exist or do not count. Followers believe statements made and ideas advanced by their leader simply because it is *he* who has made the statement or advanced the idea. It is not necessary for them to weigh or test the truth of the statement or the plausibility of the idea. For *he* knows and it is therefore enough for them that *he* has said it. If he has said it, it is unquestionably true, and it must be right.[10]

The compliance dimension refers to follower obedience to a leader's directives. There are many bases upon which followers comply with commands of leaders—because they seem reasonable or lawful, because it is to their advantage to obey, because of fear of losses or penalties if they fail to comply, because of the means of coercion the leader can use, because of the leader's persuasiveness, or because of other motives.

For followers in the charismatic relationship, however, such motives are minor or irrelevant. They comply because for them it is sufficient that their leader has given the command. If *he* has ordered, it is their duty to obey.

Noncharismatic leadership generally includes an intervening phase, however brief, between the communication of a leader's message or directive to his followers and their acceptance of or obedience to it. This phase involves followers in processes of calculation and evaluation. For even highly respected leaders cannot count on their followers to surrender to them regularly and without question the mandate to choose and judge.

This surrender, however, is typical of the charismatic leadership relationship. The followers abdicate choice and judgment to the leader. Belief and obedience are almost automatic. Followers accept and believe that the past was as the leader portrays it, that the present is as he depicts it, and that the future will be as he predicts it. And they follow without hesitation his prescriptions for action.

The emotional dimension relates to the type and intensity of emotional commitment of followers to a leader. Leadership often involves an emotional response on the part of the followers toward a leader and, at times, a fairly strong emotional attachment. Highly popular leaders can elicit such emotions as affection, admiration, trust, and even love.

In the charismatic relationship, however, the emotions aroused are not only more intense in degree, but they are also of a somewhat different order. Followers respond to their leader with devotion, awe, reverence, and blind faith, in short, with emotions close to religious worship.[11]

It is worth noting that charismatic leaders have rarely provoked indifference, neutrality, or mild reactions. Treated as godlike by their followers, they have often been regarded as diabolic by many of those not susceptible to their appeal. Whatever underlay the kinds of intensity of emotion they have generated, even their opponents have recognized and feared them as far beyond the ordinary and even beyond the unusual in human experience.

Charismatic leadership can therefore be defined briefly as a relationship between a leader and a group of followers that has the following properties:

1. The leader is perceived by the followers as somehow superhuman.

2. The followers blindly believe the leader's statements.

3. The followers unconditionally comply with the leader's directives for action.

4. The followers give the leader unqualified emotional commitment.

Charismatic political leadership denotes a relationship between a political leader and a segment of his following that has these properties.

NOTES

1. Max Weber, *Economy and Society*, ed. Guenther Roth and Claus Wittich, 3 vols. (New York: Bedminster Press, 1968), 1, pp. 212–301, and 3, pp. 941–1211. For summaries and interpretations of Weber's concept of authority, see especially: Reinhard Bendix, *Max Weber: An Intellectual Portrait* (Garden City, N.Y.: Doubleday, 1960), pp. 298–99, 301–10; Joseph Bensman and Michael Givant, "Charisma and Modernity: The Use and Abuse of a Concept," *Social Research* 69 (Winter 1975): 571–80; Julian Freund, *The Sociology of Max Weber* (New York: Pantheon, 1968), pp. 232–34; W. G. Runciman,

"Charismatic Legitimacy and One-Party Rule in Ghana," *Archives Européenes de Sociologie* 4, no. 1 (1963): 148–63; Dankwart A. Rustow, *A World of Nations: Problems of Political Modernization* (Washington, D.C.: Brookings Institution, 1967), pp. 149–53. For the origins of the concept and its entry into contemporary usage, see Daniel Bell, "Sociodicy: A Guide to Modern Usage," *American Scholar* 35 (Autumn 1966): 702–05.

2. Weber, *Economy*, 1, p. 213.

3. Ibid.

4. For the sake of convenience, masculine pronouns are used subsequently and are to be understood as referring to persons within the category irrespective of gender.

5. Bendix, in *Max Weber*, pp. 301–04, is one of the few scholars who has recognized the need to distinguish "domination as a result of charismatic leadership . . . from domination as a result of charismatic authority."

6. See, for example, Renzo Sereno, *The Rulers* (New York, Evanston, and London: Harper & Row, 1968), p. 120, and Alfred de Grazia, *Political Behavior* (New York: Free Press, 1962), p. 90. For Edward Shils, charisma extends far beyond leadership and authority to cover a host of other phenomena ("Charisma, Order and Status," *American Sociological Review* 30, 2 [Apr. 1965]: 199–213).

7. For approaches to and definitions of leaderhip influenced by social psychology and stressing interpersonal influence and interaction within groups, see Ralph M. Stogdill, ed., *Handbook of Leadership: A Survey of Theory and Research* (New York: Free Press, 1974). For a survey of studies on political leadership, see Glenn D. Paige, *The Scientific Study of Political Leadership* (New York: Free Press, 1977), pp. 1–96.

8. See the distinction between "attempted leadership" and "successful leadership" in John K. Hemphill, "Why People Attempt to lead," *Leadership and Interpersonal Behavior*, ed. Luigi Petrullo and Bernard M. Bass (New York: Holt, Rinehart & Winston, 1961), pp. 201–02.

9. It should be noted that what some religions have polarized as the divine and the demonic have been seen in others as different manifestations of the same presence, for example, Shiva as both Creator and Destroyer.

10. As succinctly stated by Marion Levy, Jr., in *Modernization and the Structure of Societies*, 2 vols. (Princeton: Princeton University Press, 1966), p. 350: "In the eyes of a true follower of a charismatic leader . . . the fact that the leader says a given thing is right makes it right.

11. "In its pure form," according to Bendix, *Max Weber*, p. 300, "charismatic leadership involves a degree of commitment on the part of the disciples that has no parallel in other types of domination."

25

EUGENE LEWIS

The Political Leader as Entrepreneur

THE CONCEPT OF THE PUBLIC ENTREPRENEUR

A public entrepreneur may be defined as a person who creates or profoundly elaborates a public organization so as to alter greatly the existing pattern of allocation of scarce public resources. Such persons arise and succeed in organizational and political milieus which contain contradictory mixes of values received from the past. Public entrepreneurs characteristically exploit such contradictions.

Entrepreneurs of the public variety engage in characteristic strategies of organizational design that simultaneously grant them high degrees of autonomy and flexibility, minimize external interference with core technologies, and which appear to be isomorphic with the most inclusive needs, wants, values and goals of crucial aspects of the task environment.[1]

Hyman Rickover, J. Edgar Hoover and Robert Moses serve as prime illustrations of this minimal definition. Each either began or greatly elaborated one or more powerful public organizations. Each exploited contradictions with great facility. Rickover saw the basic ambiguity of the role of the military in the Atomic Energy Act of 1946 as an exploitable resource which could be used to obtain unheard of amounts of autonomy from his Navy superiors and from the Atomic Energy Commission itself. Hoover went to his grave denouncing anything like a national police force: of course, Hoover *created a national police force* during the long career he spent damning the very thing he was, in fact, building. Moses was a public entrepreneur who not only thrived on contradiction in

From Eugene Lewis, *Public Entrepreneurship* (Bloomington: Indiana University Press, 1980), pp. 9–11, 14–25. Reprinted by permission.

received value mixes but who created whole new organizations which fit nicely into the crevices of contradictions in the New York State political system. Later we shall see him employing the same strategy with parks, highways and other public artifacts.

All three public entrepreneurs managed to follow strategies leading to undisputed domination over their respective organizations. They each achieved, moreover, degrees of autonomy and flexibility which are popularly believed to be impossible in government bureaucracies. Rickover thoroughly dominated nuclear development in the Navy and, for a brief period, in civilian reactor development, too, in order to "buffer his core technology." This phrase, supplied by James D. Thompson, is used to indicate the extent to which the basic action of the organization is protected from disruption by outside sources of contingency.[2] Thus, if an organization is in the business of designing, developing, and building the first nuclear power reactor for a submarine, it must protect these processes by "buffering." Buffering might take the form of "infiltrating" private companies, so as to reduce the probability of dependence on some organization beyond Rickover's control. Such dependence might have had a threatening effect on the efficiency and quality of the core technology of the Nuclear Power Branch of the Bureau of Ships. Hoover controlled a crucial source of contingency by creating his own internal personnel system, thoroughly independent of the U.S. Civil Service Commission. This creation permitted him to pay his agents more than comparable federal agents received and to have an amount of control over their actions virtually unavailable to any other nonelected administrative official in America. Moses's multiple buffering strategies included the creation of public authorities which were effectively placed outside of the jurisdiction of state and local government.

One of the interesting things about these characteristic buffering and autonomy-seeking strategies is that public entrepreneurs also manage to make buffering behavior appear reasonable, sensible and even occasionally patriotic. Thus, Hoover successfully managed to create the impression that his personnel system *had* to be separate from the rest of the government because his agents *had* to be thoroughly responsible to him and to him alone if corruption, bribery, or the slightest misconduct were to be prevented. Control over core technologies in the FBI had to be total for reasons of national security as well. Different reasons and needs were given by Moses (who also operated several organizationally separate civil service systems) and by Rickover for a variety of buffering activities.

There are, of course, other public entrepreneurs, some of whom are but briefly mentioned in the text. Among those who might have been included here to illustrate the general point about the roles that such people play in policy making are James Webb during his NASA days, David Lilienthal as TVA entrepreneur, Admiral William Raborn of *Polaris* fame, and William Ronan, presently head of the Port of New York Authority. One suspects that General Leslie Groves, creator of the Manhattan District, who is mentioned in the chapters on Rickover, would also qualify. The numbers and varieties of public entrepreneurs are, however, largely undiscussed in the text which follows. A detailed analysis of such people requires a book of greater length and much more research. . . .

If we continue to employ the brief stipulation given above for the public entrepreneur (that he be a person who creates or profoundly elaborates a public organization so as to greatly alter the existing pattern of allocation of scarce resources), then further discussion is necessary. Such discussion must focus on (a) the structural conditions conducive to public entrepreneurship and (b) the "natural history" of the public entrepreneur himself, as he is to be discovered in the pages that follow.

One starts with the premise that most such entrepreneurship begins in an organizational setting; that the entrepreneur has the minimal qualifications for membership (unless he creates the organization, as Robert Moses did in several cases); and finally, that sufficient time is available for the development of the specific issue or area upon which the budding entrepreneur wishes to work. One should also look to the availability of slack resources within or quite close to the organizational boundaries, to the existence of sufficient technical capacity to provide whatever expert knowledge or services are needed for the entrepreneurial act and, finally, to the ebb and flow of general historical conditions of a structural variety which are conducive to the entrepreneurship. . . .

THE NATURAL HISTORY OF THE PUBLIC ENTREPRENEUR

The natural history or progression of the entrepreneur involves three stages of increasing complexity and power. These are divided into eight aspects considered to be essential to the identification and analysis of the concept of public entrepreneurship and of the actual public entrepreneur.

Stage One involves two recognizably distinct aspects which characterize the entrepreneur in his earliest days. The first has to do with his *recruitment and imperfect socialization to organizational life*. Typically, the young entrepreneur-to-be enters the organization imbued with a zeal seldom equaled by many of his peers. He fully and unquestioningly accepts the major goals for which the organization putatively stands. Rickover, Hoover, and the young Moses of reform days entered their respective organizations with a certainty of purpose found only in the most enthusiastic recruits. Problems for each arose in the extent to which they were unwilling or unable to internalize the organizational norms that were supposed to lead toward meeting the major social goals. Thus for the Navy, the defense of the nation; for the FBI, the pursuit of criminals and information; and for the early Moses, the reform and reorganization of the city and state of New York were the ends in view that presumably mattered. Each man was confronted in his organization by traditions, values, norms, and procedures that were either inefficient, useless, irrelevant, or downright counterproductive. Each public entrepreneur was recruited under one general, idealized set of goals, only to rapidly discover that a more proximate set of norms stood directly in the way of his accomplishing the goals that had brought him into the organization.

Rickover faced social convention based on rank and technological fuddy-duddyism almost as soon as he entered the Naval Academy. As nearly as can be told, he continues to this day to damn the Navy for everything from excessive uniform wearing and ward-room socializing to inept technical education. In short, he remains utterly unhappy with most of the formal and informal rules of Navy life. Hoover entered the Justice Department as a fledgling lawyer and soon found himself surrounded by crooks, corrupt politicians, and incompetents. No matter one's construction of justice, Hoover's did not include the organizational values of the Justice Department under the Harding administration [e.g., bribery, patronage appointments, collusion, malfeasance]. His intolerance of those informal but potent values turned out to be his chief asset when the new broom came to sweep the stables. Moses was repeatedly faced with demands for compromise, bargaining and negotiation as proximate acts necessary for achieving ultimate goals. Quite simply, the newly recruited Robert Moses believed that to compromise thus would be to sacrifice major social goals, which to him meant the sacrifice of principles.

So, at the very beginnings of their careers, these men experienced dissonance between what they believed they were recruited for and what, in fact, they actually encountered. Certainly their experiences were not unique. On the contrary, the pattern is a familiar one; and the newly recruited acolyte to a public organization is usually taken aside and told the facts of life by an elder, who explains that idealism must be tempered with understanding and adherence to organizational values, not all of which promote the ends of the organization's owners—the citizenry of the United States. This is precisely the kind of counsel that public entrepreneurs typically fail to take. They tend not to give into the "go along to get along" values and the clubbiness of fraternal association. Instead, they studiously insist on serving the goals for which they entered the organization, and they do so as thoroughly as possible.

Most people faced with an acute variety of this dilemma decide to quit the organization rather than compromise. The public entrepreneur typically does not. Rather, he is incorporated by a second aspect, which shall be called *mentorship and the internalization of appropriate organizational goals.* If the budding entrepreneur is to survive the strain of imperfect socialization and to avoid being summarily cast aside by his more powerful superiors, he must come under the wing of a mentor, one who shares his values but not his impatience. Rickover was "saved" by several mentors, including a captain whose intervention got him into submarine school after he had been rejected. His most important mentor was Admiral Mills, about whom we shall hear further. Mills commanded the Bureau of Ships during a crucial period of Rickover's entrepreneurship. He fought for Rickover, protected him from many enemies and eventually created, as much as one person can, the opportunity for the entrepreneurial leap into nuclear propulsion that Rickover led.

Moses simply could not have thrived without the help of Mrs. Belle Moskowitz and Governor Alfred E. Smith. Both took the young Moses in tow and managed to temper his ego-centered zeal, while teaching him how to get the results he wanted without a crusade. Hoover, of course, had several mentors, including Harding's nefarious Attorney General Daugherty. But the person who really made J. Edgar Hoover the entrepreneur he became was Harlan F. Stone. Stone became Coolidge's Attorney General and moved to clean up the Justice Department left over from the Harding administration. Stone appointed Hoover to be Acting Director of the Bureau of Investigation and removed the "Acting" shortly thereafter. But Stone did more than hire Hoover. He counseled Hoover on the ways of Washington and the politics of law enforcement, bringing to bear wisdom and insight that stood Hoover in good stead for years to come. When Stone became Chief Justice he still consulted with and advised Hoover. He was probably the only soul in the universe who did so by then, but the point is that even J. Edgar Hoover had a mentor.

The mentorship which would-be entrepreneurs seem to need provides more than a protective wing under which the newly recruited may shelter themselves. Mentorship also involves the transfer of recognizable and discrete skills and lore appropriate to the organization. Typically, one would expect a mentor to coopt and mollify as he socialized. This is their effect for most of us, but less so for the budding entrepreneur, who comes to the organization with a sense of innocence and often with the brains of genius. Part of the organizational lore conveyed by the mentor tells the neophyte *how one really gets things done* in the natural system, the organization as normally experienced. The new person must then adjust his typically lofty vision of the organization's purposes to suit the facts of life and the personal needs of himself and others, needs which often conflict with those purposes. Typically, the entrepreneur enters the organization with little interest in personal success other than the extent to which his goals overlap with those of the organization. None of the three entrepreneurs began organizational life as a dedicated careerist might: paying careful attention to those who might help his climb to the upper reaches of the organization. On the contrary, Rickover and Moses, at least, were almost self-destructive in their narrow, near-literal devotion to public and major organizational purposes and goals. They both internalized such goals but consciously rejected many of the day-to-day rules for getting along in the organization. Hoover's beginnings are more difficult to characterize, as there simply is not enough known about his earliest days in the Justice Department; and what is known is less than trustworthy, since Hoover was a champion maker of myths about himself.

In any event, the mentor and his lessons permit the would-be entrepreneur to survive, if not flourish, during his early years in the organization. Moses, unlike the other two, managed to find himself in and out of several organizations before he had the opportunity to create one for himself. But the years of recruitment and imperfect socialization are not spent simply waiting. Future entrepreneurs commonly are brilliant students of the organizations and politics which they hope to master. Moses entered public service in 1913 and did not begin Stage Two until 1924. Hoover spent a similar amount of time, and Rickover had well over twenty years of service before his entrepreneurial leaps began. But all three spent their time to advantage.

Stage Two involves at least three recognizable aspects. The first is the *entrepreneurial leap*, which consists of an act that either creates or elaborates an organization in unforeseen ways such that major existing allocation patterns of scarce public resources are ultimately altered. A concomitant second aspect concerns the *creation of an apolitical shield* to protect or buffer the entrepreneurial leap. This practice by public entrepreneurs is vital to their continuing mission, because it serves to obscure what otherwise might be widely understood as political acts. If the entrepreneur is to succeed, he must make and sustain a public image of his actions and his organization that appears to be free of partisanship, greed, self-interest and personal self-aggrandizement. Such a posture eventually becomes mythic and is essential to beating back questions and competition from those who are publicly understood to be politicians. It is one of the ironies of American politics that politicians are suspect at almost all times because they have always to worry about the next election, while bureaucratic servants of the state can often wrap themselves in the cloak of neutrality and dispassionate concern for the public interest. The ability to capitalize on this contradiction is central for the public entrepreneur precisely because he seeks resources competitively in ways somewhat similar to, but much more effective than, those of electoral politicians.

Aspect three concerns the *struggle for autonomy*. Once the entrepreneurial leap is made by the introduction of a new organizational mission or the creation of a new organization, there remains the problem that public organizations are subject to supervision, inspection and competition. No entrepreneurial leap is by itself automatically sustaining. Rather, the entrepreneur must bargain, threaten and seduce others into allowing him autonomy over his mission and over the organization(s) which he must command to achieve that mission.

For Rickover the entrepreneurial leap occurred when he was finally able to dominate a sufficient number of organizational structures to control the complete development of nuclear propulsion for the Navy and the Atomic Energy Commission simultaneously. Hoover's leap was made in the first days of the Roosevelt administration when he began his famous campaign against the gangsters. This campaign catapulted the FBI into the national spotlight and paved the way for unprecedented mandates, resulting in the establishment of a national police force and secret police. Moses's leap is readily identified. He created a new aspect to public intervention, one which he continued to elaborate for nearly two generations, the day he took the helm of the Long Island Park Commission, which he had created.

Each entrepreneur added to these initial leaps, of course; but the point about the initial leap is that the move to create and dominate successfully is the first clear sign which separates the public entrepreneur from the bureaucrat or the politician. The public entrepreneur distinguishes himself from others in that he uses organizations and their resources to achieve great aims, with minimal direction from other elements in the political system.

Another distinguishing feature of the public entrepreneur is his capacity to recognize and employ the apolitical shield. The disdain in which politicians are periodically held has its counterpoint in the general approbation accorded to "hard working professionals trying to do their duty." The extent to which Rickover created and secured this potent screen from interference is amply documented in the pages which follow. Nuclear propulsion for naval vessels was a nonpolitical question for Rickover and his allies; no Republican or Democratic element was obviously connected. Yet, to describe Rickover's manipulation of congress, the Navy and the AEC as "nonpolitical" is worse than believing in the tooth fairy. The latter, after all, never cost the nation billions of dollars and never dominated the path of nuclear development in the entire society for decades.

Hoover achieved virtual autonomy by directly facing the issue of the apolitical shield in such a way as to add luster and depth to that creation. He did this by resolutely denying the requests of congressmen and party people who wanted favors from the Bureau of Investigation during his early years as Director. He gathered ever greater and more inclusive mandates while denying (and even fighting) the development of a national police force. Of course, the more blatant political acts of later years need no discussion. J. Edgar Hoover's FBI did more to choke and destroy legitimate political dissent than any public organization in American history. Not only did the FBI destroy organizations and people who were radical or left-wing, it also managed to intimidate uncounted numbers who feared to speak up, sign petitions, and the like, lest they receive notice in the notorious files of the Bureau, thus potentially ruining career or occupational possibilities.

Moses was constantly at war with legislatures, governors, mayors and city councils. He carefully orchestrated public opinion by fooling the press into viewing him and his many operations as being in opposition to elected politicians. The myth which he sold (and which nearly everybody bought) was that Robert Moses and his loyal troops wanted to build public facilities without political patronage and without gain of any sort. What that meant, in fact, was that Moses could employ the public's concern and the politicians' fear of that concern in order to reap enormous mandates, material rewards and patronage exceeding any held by machine politicians of the late nineteenth century.

The third and final aspect in this artificial construct, *the struggle for autonomy*, does not require extensive example. Each entrepreneur achieved a remarkable degree of autonomy over the allocation of resources for his continuing operations. Hoover never had a budget request denied during his seemingly endless tenure as FBI Director. Rickover anomalously commanded financial and human resources far beyond those of his putative superiors. As we shall see, he even managed to become autonomous enough to reverse Navy personnel practices regarding the promotion to admiral, a feat unknown since the procedures became law in 1916. Moses retired from an empire more tightly controlled by its leader than any other organization one can find in the public realm. Moses managed to have little or no responsibility to report to anyone about any of his decisions once he had achieved mature entrepreneurship. This freedom from accountability is yet another defining characteristic of the public entrepreneur.

The third and final Stage is one of mature entrepreneurship. This stage contains three aspects or elements which are: *the reduction of uncertainty in task environments, the spanning of boundaries for purposes of domain expansion,* and finally, *institutionalization and the problems of ultra-stability.*

Once the first entrepreneurial leap has been made and then consolidated into the newly emerging organizational structure, the public entrepreneur must attend to uncertainty reduction in his task environment. The term *task environment* is here employed as formulated by James D. Thompson. Organizations and groups upon which the entrepreneur's organization is highly dependent for sources of input or for absorption of output must be made as secure as possible if the entrepreneur is to consolidate his leap into an ongoing program. Thus Rickover literally structured and *(de facto)* absorbed an entire division of Westinghouse in order to reduce uncertainty in the delivery of drawings, supplies, machines and technologies vital to the nuclear submarine program. He even managed to coopt the Navy personnel system as it concerned the operation and maintenance of nuclear subs: Rickover got to personally select and train officers for command—a practice virtually unheard of in the Navy.

Hoover and Moses reduced uncertainty in many ways. Hoover managed the nation's most prestigious police training academy and secured a monopoly over the generation and supply of information vital to the ongoing needs of state and local police forces. The FBI became a crucial element in the task environments of the states and localities, while employing them to fill its own needs for data collection and control. . . .

Moses reduced uncertainty in his task environment through a whole range of strategies, the most potent of which was probably his innovation in the legal status of a public authority. Briefly, what he did was to write legislation such that the financial operations of public authorities were accomplished under a contractual agreement between the authority and its bondholders. This single action removed nearly every supervisory control one would normally expect to find in the presence of governors and legislatures—a wholly remarkable feat. At the same time Moses reduced his need for government funds by floating issues which depended strictly on the more or less guaranteed flow of nickles and dimes into his bridge coffers. Investment bankers considered such bonds gilt-edged. And Moses didn't have to worry about the possibility of a "raid" or even about loud questioning concerning how much money he controlled and how he spent it. . . .

Reduction of uncertainty in the task environment requires the most immediate kinds of buffering and cooptive actions in order to insure the continuing flow of resources crucial to the operation of the entrepreneur's program. Boundary spanning for purposes of expanding the entrepreneurial domain involves a somewhat different kind of act. The domain of the organization includes all competitor and cooperative organizations that have concerns in common with the organization. Rickover, for example, operated within the domain of the defense establishment, which includes the other military services, congressional committees, civilian leaders and outside contractors.

When Rickover had the atomic submarine project moving along steadily, he began to sniff the political winds for the chance of expanding from nuclear submarines to a nuclear fleet. Moreover, he was concerned about specific items of funding and about his role and that of his organization within the general framework of the Navy. In order to deal with these kinds of questions, Rickover became a friend and confidant of congressmen who could do him some good. He also employed public relations techniques very well, creating an ever-growing public awareness of his organization's successes. His inroads into the various branches of the Navy and into the civilian secretariat were also substantial, and they enabled him to expand his domain in directions he thought best.

Hoover's domain expansion is, of course, legendary by now. He dealt directly with Congress, Presidents and the public as though he were an autonomous prince in a medieval city-state, rather than a bureaucrat running a Justice Department bureau. He was able to do this partially as a result of an incredibly effective public and congressional relations effort which allowed him to pick and choose the mandates and resources he needed. Hoover's ability to establish ever more inclusive boundaries eventually resulted in his acquiring a large national public following and an unprecedented direct influence over state and local police forces. The various devices Hoover employed to achieve this eminence were innovative and complex. . . .

Moses, too, became a public figure through astute boundary spanning. Of equal significance was his ability to define or create new institutional relationships. The line separating federal functions from state and local responsibilities faded in a number of areas with which Moses was concerned. The construction of large public facilities like roads and bridges had, until the time of Moses, been thought of as strictly a state or local responsibility, with certain exceptions. Moses, as much as any person, guided, stimulated and helped to expand the federal role in these areas, as well as in housing and urban renewal. He was also among the first to move toward obliterating the boundary between levels of government. Of the multiple boundaries he spanned and of the new domains he conquered, more will be said. The point here is that entrepreneurs of the public type tend to span ever more inclusive boundaries in a variety of ways, in order to expand their domains.

The third and final aspect in Stage Three is *institutionalization and the problems of ultra-stability*. While it is true that a successful entrepreneurship tends to beget even more entrepreneurial leaps, stasis and routinization must be reached for the public entrepreneur and for the organization he has created or vastly elaborated. It is in the nature of the task and of the aging of man that there comes a time when the organization and its leader must spend more time on boundary maintenance than on boundary spanning for domain expansion. Entrepreneurial leaps become fewer and smaller, in part because they entail costs to the organization and to its leader which simply did not pertain in earlier stages. Any upheaval in the by now middle-aged or elderly organization will imply internal restructuring and altered resource allocation; and these are likely to threaten the maintenance of existing programs that had once been the dreamed-of goals of the public entrepreneur.

Thus, when Rickover had gone as far as he could to convince Congress, Presidents, and the public that the Navy should have only nuclear powered fleets, and by the time he had secured vast control and influence over nearly every aspect of nuclear propulsion, the kinds of problems he had to deal with were generally of the system maintenance variety. His programs successful, his point of view and personnel practices carried on by trusted and competent subordinates, his avenues of further expansion blocked, Rickover faced a familiar problem in very new form: what does one do with an organization which has become so successful that it appears to be ultra-stable and machinelike in its day-to-day servicing of what had been a major innovation?

Hoover faced a very different set of circumstances; for, unlike Rickover's, the entrepreneurship of the Director was not particularly bound up in technological or physical systems. What Hoover had done was to create an organization in his own image, one which he constantly had policed to insure that its personnel and its actions conformed to his standards. But this is system maintenance and even worse, stasis. Hoover was an entrepreneur who understood that his interests were not best served simply by obtaining mandates which expanded domain and resources. It was better to get mandates that he thought he could handle in terms of what he wanted the FBI to be. His conception of what the FBI should be became a limitation on his entrepreneurship. Thus, Hoover avoided the issues of organized crime, civil rights and drug trafficking because they were potentially threatening to the integrity of his FBI. He did not see these as fertile areas for domain expansion. He also feared that the FBI's ignorance about these matters might involve a loss of public face, something the Director believed to be potentially catastrophic. From building an FBI and spanning boundaries so inclusive as to make the agency part of popular culture, Hoover moved to preserving an institutionalized FBI, one characterized by stasis and boundary mainte-nance, a move which led eventually to painful decline.

Moses, as in most things, was another case entirely. For him, organi-zations and people were tools to get things done. When the tools proved ineffective or inefficient, he tended to ignore them. Slowly at first, then with increasing velocity, his world became crowded with major com-petitors, men who repeatedly insisted that Moses's goals and methods were outdated, if not dangerous. He clung to power as fiercely as Hoover did, but age and Nelson Rockefeller did him in, as did the growing public awareness that urban highways, public housing, and other of Moses's contributions were perhaps mixed blessings. He could have fought on, given the enormous powers he had carefully written into law, and given the very potent coalition of organized interests he held in his sway. But time and powerful (and untruthful) political actors showed him that the hour for his passing had come.

With each of the entrepreneurs discussed here . . . , there is a vaguely familiar pattern. One of Weber's definitions of bureaucracy is that it is "the routinization of charisma." In ideal-typical terms he explains that charismatic authority arises when a great, perhaps eventually deified, leader controls the tribe in such a way that his acts are seen as inspired by God, if not directed by Him. The leader's command is absolute and uniformly accepted. Historical and religious figures like Moses and Jesus and Mohammed fit the pattern of Weber's use of the term "charisma." Unfortunately, the modern world has seen fit to use the term more loosely. Today we have charismatic T.V. stars, politicians and movie actors. But if we go back to Weber's meaning, for the moment, we can see that a great problem faces the tribe or true believers with the passing of the great leader. How are they to govern themselves in his absence? None of them is divine or even divinely inspired. They have not the authority or legitimacy that such an association with God implies. Weber sees the solution in the routinization of the great leader's charisma by his followers, apostles or priests. Christ founds a church upon the rock that is Peter. As *the Church* grows and elaborates over time and space, it becomes recognizably bureaucratic, with hierarchical ranks and functional specialization of tasks and people (priests, nuns, monks, bishops, cardinals, Jesuits, Franciscans, etc.). All rest on the crucial central claim that what each does ultimately flows from Him. Thus a capsule history of the oldest continuing bureaucratic organization on the face of the planet.[3]

No implication is being made here that public entrepreneurs are charismatic leaders in the sense that Weber described such people. Yet, they do bring out the zealousness in themselves and in their subordinates in some interesting ways. Each not only creates a coterie of loyal subordinates, like "Moses men" or the "Rickover Navy" or every other FBI agent over the age of forty-five; they also inspire organizational members and others to a belief that the task they serve has about it something much more vital than the humdrum, self-interested cynicism of everyday life. Hoover's FBI forty years ago was *the* place for upstanding, patriotic, honest and hard-working American boys to want to go. Today it sounds like cheap public fantasy, a caricature of misplaced devotion. Yet, was it not something like the charismatic attraction of the Weberian myth, modernized and trivialized in secular surroundings?

Rickover's devotees and fans were no less enamoured of their chief. From the early, small group of officers at Oak Ridge . . . to the thousands of men who served under him with a fear and awe remarkable for this day and age, Hyman Rickover had something of the magician about him. He knew everything, it seemed. He saw everything. And he feared absolutely nothing, including the entire Navy brass. The single man, after Jesus, most admired by President Carter is Hyman Rickover, and Carter never even worked directly for the pugnacious, self-denying Admiral. Rickover inspired loyalty so thoroughly and in so many men that it was not at all unusual for men deliberately to hurt or to destroy their careers so that they could continue to work for Rickover, who lived his life only to build the nuclear submarine.

Moses, as much as the other two, inspired feelings of awe, fear and incredulity in intelligent, sophisticated men twenty, thirty and forty years after they had left his service. Nobody this side of ancient Egypt or Central America ever built public artifacts as Robert Moses did. Few men in modern history were able to work eighteen-hour days for sixty years as he did, chewing up whole inventories of knowledge as he prowled the urban scenes and rural pastures in search of something to build or change according to his desire and his perception of what the public wanted (or should want, if it thought about it). As with the other entrepreneurs, Moses created networks of adherents, men whose talents he recognized and developed until they could leave the home fires for Washington or other centers of public power.

The point of talking about a third stage in the development of an entrepreneur is to raise the general problem of what happens to a successful entrepreneurial organization when it has no new domains to conquer. How does the force, vision and power of the public entrepreneur get transferred to successors, if indeed it does? The suggestion made here by implication is that organizations come to resemble other organizations, at least as far as their entrepreneurial face is concerned, when the great leader passes from the scene, either literally or figuratively.

NOTES

1. Many of the ideas for this concept are derived from the following: Henry Mintzberg, *The Nature of Managerial Work* (New York: Harper & Row, 1973); Chris Argyris, *Executive Leadership: Appraisal of a Manager in Action* (New York: Harper & Row, 1953);

Chester I. Barnard, *The Functions of the Executive* (Cambridge, Mass.: Harvard University Press, 1938); Dorwin Cartwright, "Influence, Leadership and Control," in *Handbook of Organizations*, ed. James G. March (Chicago: Rand McNally, 1965); Melville Dalton, *Men Who Manage* (New York: John Wiley & Sons, Inc., 1959); Bertram M. Gross, *The Managing of Organizations* (New York: The Free Press, 1964); George C. Homans, *The Human Group* (New York: Harcourt, Brace, Jovanovich, 1950); Joseph A. Schumpeter, *The Theory of Economic Development* (Cambridge, Mass.: Harvard University Press, 1961); Philip Selznick, *Leadership in Administration* (New York: Harper & Row, 1957).

2. James D. Thompson, *Organizations in Action* (New York: McGraw-Hill, 1967), pp. 20–24.

3. Max Weber, *The Theory of Social and Economic Organization*, trans. A. M. Henderson and Talcott Parsons, ed. Talcott Parsons (New York: The Free Press, 1964), pp. 324–86; and Hans H. Gerth and C. Wright Mills, eds., *From Max Weber* (New York: Oxford University Press, 1958), pp. 245–53.

26

ROBERT C. TUCKER

Nonconstituted Leaders

*F*ROM the leadership perspective on politics, a key criterion for evaluating political systems along the spectrum from democracy to authoritarianism is the relative scope of opportunity that a society affords for the activities of what I have called "nonconstituted" leaders.[1] This can best be shown by examples. A woman named Rachel Carson, who had a love of wildlife, much technical knowledge, and writing talent, published a book in 1962 called *Silent Spring*. The idea for the title came to her from a line by Keats about winter, when "The sedge is wither'd from the lake and no birds sing." Given her concerns as a lover of wildlife, especially of birds, certain circumstances took on ominous meaning in her mind. Between the 1940s and 1960s, she wrote, over two hundred basic chemicals were created in American laboratories for killing insects, weeds, rodents, and other so-called pests; they were (and are) called *pesticides* and applied in sprays, dusts, and aerosols to farms, gardens, forests, and homes. Her book's title conjured up the haunting image that conveyed her definition of the situation: a spring would come when no birds would sing. She wrote, "The pollution of our world is happening," and said that this pointed ultimately to "the pollution of the total environment of mankind." The policy prescription flowing from her definition of the situation was: Strictly control and drastically reduce, if not eliminate, the use of chemical pesticides.

She knew that her definition of the problem and proposed response were controversial. The prevailing practice in our society at that time was

From Robert C. Tucker, *Politics as Leadership* (Columbia: University of Missouri Press, 1982), pp. 71–75. Reprinted by permission of the University of Missouri Press. Copyright 1981 by the Curators of the University of Missouri Press.

nondefinition of the danger situation, largely because of ignorance of the facts in the public mind. Behind the nondefinition of the situation, powerful influences were at work. As she put it, "The control men in state and federal governments—and of course the chemical manufacturers—steadfastly deny the facts reported by the biologists and declare they see little evidence of harm to wildlife. Like the priest and the Levite in the biblical story, they choose to pass by on the other side and to see nothing."[2] So, Carson became a nonconstituted leader, a foremost figure in the environmental movement that grew up in America, partly in response to *Silent Spring*. A U.S. secretary of the interior, Stewart Udall, recognized her importance as a leader when he said of her, "A great woman has awakened the nation by her forceful account of the dangers around us. We owe much to Rachel Carson."

Lest this account convey the impression that all nonconstituted leaders are admirable, a case of different character merits mention. Like Rachel Carson, the British psychologist Cyril Burt had some deep-seated beliefs and values. He believed in the rightness and inevitability of a class system of society. In his long, distinguished career, during which he held the influential post of editor of the *British Journal of Statistical Psychology*, he published numerous research findings supporting the view that people in the upper class were hereditarily superior in intelligence. His reported findings were that separated identical twins, brought up in different environments, remained alike in I.Q. His definition of human intelligence as hereditarily determined underlay a prescription for educational policy that children, after being tested at age eleven, be separated into three groups: only those with higher intelligence should be trained in elite schools preparatory for higher education, and the (working-class) majority would be schooled as befitted their lower genetic potentials, This was adopted as British educational policy after the Second World War, and Burt was rewarded with a knighthood for his services to education. His claimed research findings concerning separated identical twins were, however, subsequently exposed as thoroughly fraudulent.[3] He had derived his policy prescription from a diagnosis of human intelligence founded on fabricated circumstances. Although an effective nonconstituted leader, considering the impact of his work on educational policy, he was not an admirable one.

Nonconstituted leaders flourish best in conditions of political freedom that afford them full opportunity to put forward their definitions of the situation and their policy prescriptions in public and to seek to mobilize followings. In authoritarian political settings, where citizens lack free access to the media of public communication, nonconstituted leadership faces great obstacles and has correspondingly limited prospects of success. Nevertheless, no few unusual individuals have surmounted all the obstacles. A well-known contemporary example is the Russian nuclear physicist, Academician Andrei Sakharov.

Having led the project to create a Soviet hydrogen bomb, Sakharov in the 1950s was a much-decorated foremost figure in the scientific establishment, so highly valued that a special railway car, reportedly, would be placed at his disposal when he needed to travel. He began his political activity by working within the system. In 1958 he sought out Khrushchev for an interview in which he unsuccessfully tried to persuade the premier to cancel a scheduled nuclear test. In memoirs dictated long afterward, in retirement, Khrushchev recalled:

> He was obviously guided by moral and humanistic considerations. . . . He was, as they say, a crystal of morality among our scientists. . . . He was devoted to the idea that science should bring peace and prosperity to the world, that it should help preserve and improve the conditions for human life. He hated the thought that science might be used to destroy life, to contaminate the atmosphere, to kill people slowly by radioactive poisoning. However, he went too far in thinking he had the right to decide whether the bomb he had developed could ever be used in the future.[4]

Later, Sakharov was instrumental in getting the Soviet government to agree to conclude the 1963 treaty with the Americans banning further aboveground nuclear tests by the two nations.

His decisive move toward becoming a nonconstituted leader was the writing of a memorandum, "Progress, Coexistence, and Intellectual Freedom," which circulated in typescript and made its way West, where its publication in 1968 brought world fame to the author. Although he lost his favored position, he went on speaking his mind to fellow Soviet citizens and foreign correspondents. Gradually he grew convinced that the key problem was the denial of human rights in the closed Soviet society, and he became an outstanding leader of the unofficial human-rights movement in the USSR. In an essay entitled "Alarm and Hope," written in 1977 for the Norwegian Nobel Committee, at its request, he wrote: "A deeply cynical caste society has come into being, one which I consider dangerous (to itself as well as to all mankind). . . . It is precisely the society's 'closed' nature which facilitates the nation's expansionist capabilities and simultaneously secures its anti-democratic stability despite failures, by Western standards, in satisfying social needs."[5] His outspoken condemnation of the Soviet military occupation of Afghanistan in 1980 was followed by his exile to house arrest in Gorky. A mighty government exposed its inner weakness by silencing the one leader of great moral stature produced by Russia in the later twentieth century.

There are many would-be nonconstituted leaders for every one who becomes a leader in fact. A person can act as a leader by advancing a definition of public situation and a prescription for collective action to deal with it. But not unless he or she succeeds in mobilizing a following for the position thus taken does that individual *become* a leader. Although comparatively few do, the results are meaningful. Conventional political science more or less neglects the phenomenon of nonconstituted leadership because it considers politics to be about power only, and nonconstituted leaders, by definition, lack power. When and if they acquire it, they have transformed themselves into constituted leaders. Yet nonconstituted leadership is something that political science overlooks at its intellectual peril, because very much that is politically significant in the world thus remains outside its purview.

NOTES

1. I.e., persons who are political leaders without possessing formal power or occupying high political office. [BK]

2. Rachel Carson, *Silent Spring* (New York: Fawcett, 1962), p. 84.

3. Leon J. Kamin, *The Science and Politics of I.Q.* (New York: Halsted Press, 1974), and L. S. Hearnshaw, *Cyril Burt Psychologist* (Ithaca, N.Y.: Cornell University Press, 1980).

4. *Khrushchev Remembers: The Last Testament*, trans, and ed. Strobe Talbott (New York: Little, Brown, 1974), p. 69. For Sakharov's path to dissent, see the autobiographical introduction to *Sakharov Speaks*, ed. Harrison E. Salisbury (New York: Vintage Books, 1974), pp. 29–54.

5. Andrei D. Sakharov, "A Sick Society," *The New York Times*, 23 January 1980.

PART V

HOW DO LEADERS AND FOLLOWERS RELATE?

LEADERSHIP used to be studied through the person of the leader: What was the leader like? How did the leader behave? Today it is apparent that leadership involves at least two people—one to act, and the other to react. Consequently, leaders and followers are now examined in tandem.

There are two basic methods for looking at the leader-follower dyad. The first is to focus the investigation on the participants themselves—a study of Nazi Germany, for example, that explores the nature of both Hitler and the German people. The second is to give both sides equal measure by investigating their interaction per se. This section emphasizes the second approach. (Of course, typologies also provide information on the leader-follower relationship. Thus there is some overlap between the issues addressed in this and the previous section.) We will explore such questions as: What is the genesis of leader-follower relationships and how do they develop over time? What is the impact of situation and structure on leader-follower relationships? And what are the sources of power and influence over others?

The first essay by the great German sociologist Georg Simmel, is a fraction of a long exploration of subordination of the many under one. How does the ruler affect the group as a whole? And does the ruler affect individuals who constitute the group? These questions grow out of Simmel's basic premise: "Every sociological consideration immediately shows the immeasurable advantage which one man rule has for the fusion and energy saving guidance of the group forces."

Bruce Mazlish, a historian heavily influenced by psychoanalytic theory, is one of the most thoughtful of modern students of leadership. Of special interest is his concept of a "psychic respository," which consists of recurrent community themes, ideals, values, fantasies, imagery, symbols, myths, and legends. Gaining access to the community in fact depends on the leader's ability to draw on this collective culture. Mazlish's attention to image as opposed to reality is also noteworthy. As he puts it, "it is [the leader's] image, not the squirmy 'inner man,' that leads his followers."

In James MacGregor Burns's book titled simply *Leadership*, he makes a distinction between "transactional" and "transforming" leadership. Transactional leadership takes place when "one person takes the initiative in making contact with others for the purpose of an exchange of valued things." Transforming leadership, in contrast, has a moral dimension. It may be said to have occurred "when one or more persons *engage* with others in such a way that leaders and followers raise one another to higher levels of motivation and activity." Burns, also distinguishes between leaders and "power wielders." Leaders, he argues, in some way satisfy the motives of their followers. Power wielders, on the other hand, are intent only on realizing their own purposes, whether or not these are shared by the people over whom they exert their power. According to these criteria, Hitler, for example, was not a leader, but rather a power wielder.

The influential article by social psychologists John R. P. French, Jr., and Bertram Raven titled "The Bases of Social Power," distinguishes among various types of power in order to account for the different effects found in studies of social influence. French and Raven generate several hypotheses on social influence and power that focus on the person on whom the power is exerted. Five different bases of power are postulated: reward power, coercive power, legitimate power, referent power, and expert power.

The short selection that follows is from Talcott Parsons's *Political and Social Structure*. Parsons's book contains lengthy discourses on political leadership, particularly in two chapters titled "On the Concept of Political Power" and "On the Concept of Influence." Here I have included only a few pages on the "types of influence." The intention is to present a comparison between French and Raven on the one hand and Parsons on the other, on the subject of interpersonal influence or "social power."

Irving Janis is one of the few present-day social psychologists to address himself specifically and at some length to political life. His political investigations have focused primarily on the small group process, in particular on a dynamic he calls "groupthink." Groupthink is defined as a psychological drive for consensus which suppresses disagreement and prevents the appraisal of alternatives in cohesive decision-making groups. In a book originally titled *Victims of Groupthink*, Janis presents a series of case studies including the attack on Pearl Harbor, the Korean War, the Cuban Missile Crisis, and the Vietnam War (Watergate is added in the second edition). He argues that in all these situations, groupthink impaired policy making, in large part because group members were more concerned about their status in the group than with generating alternative solutions to the problem at hand. The selection included here explores the groupthink syndrome with regard to the Bay of Pigs invasion. For students of political leadership, it is John Kennedy's unwitting contribution to groupthink that is of special interest.

Erik Erikson, of course, remains the premier psychobiographer. His groundbreaking books on Martin Luther and Mahatma Gandhi are still widely considered remarkably successful syntheses of history, biography, and psychoanalytic theory. The diagram that concludes this section is taken from his essay, "On the Nature of Psycho-Historical Evidence: In Search of Gandhi." It is a most economical indicator of the complicated ways in which leaders, great leaders in any case, and their followers will inevitably interact.

27

GEORG SIMMEL

Subordination Under an Individual

§2. KINDS OF SUBORDINATION UNDER AN INDIVIDUAL

*T*HE subordination of a group under a single person results, above all, in a very decisive unification of the group. This unification is almost equally evident in both of two characteristic forms of this subordination. First, the group forms an actual, inner unit together with its head; the ruler leads the groups forces in their own direction, promoting and fusing them; superordination, therefore, here really means only that the will of the group has found a unitary expression or body. Secondly, the group feels itself in opposition to its head and forms a party against him.

In regard to the first form, every sociological consideration immediately shows the immeasurable advantage which one-man rule has for the fusion and energy-saving guidance of the group forces. I will cite only two instances of common subordination to one element. These cases are very heterogeneous as far as their contents are concerned, but nevertheless show how irreplaceable this subordination is for the unity of the whole. The sociology of religion must make a basic distinction between two types of religious organization. There may be the unification of group members which lets the common god grow, as it were, out of this togetherness itself, as the symbol and the sanctification of their belonging together. This is true in many primitive religions. On the other hand, only the conception of the god itself may bring the members together into a

From Kurt H. Wolff, trans. and ed., *The Sociology of Georg Simmel)* Glencoe, Ill.: The Free Press, 1950), pp. 190–94. Reprinted with permission of The Free Press, a division of Macmillan, Inc. Copyright 1950, renewed 1978 by The Free Press. First published as *Grundfragen der Soziologie*, 1917.

unit—members who before had no, or only slight, relations with one another. How well Christianity exemplifies this second type need not be described, nor is it necessary to emphasize how particular Christian sects find their specific and especially strong cohesion in the absolutely subjective and mystical relation to the person of Jesus, a relation which each member possesses as an individual, and thus quite independently of every other member and of the total group. But even of the Jews it has been asserted that they feel the contractual relation to Jehovah which they hold in common, that is, which directly concerns every one of them, as a real power and significance of membership in the Jewish nation.

By contrast, in other religions which originated at the same time as Judaism, it was kinship that connected each member with every other, and only the later, all of them with the divine principle. On the basis of its widely ramified personal dependencies and "services," medieval feudalism had frequent occasion to exemplify this same formal structure. It is perhaps most characteristically shown in the associations of the "ministers" (unfree court servants and house servants) who stood in a close, purely personal relation to the prince. Their associations had no objective basis whatever, such as the village communities under bondage had by virtue of the nearby manor. The "ministers" were employed in highly varied services and had their residences in different localities, but nevertheless formed tightly closed associations which nobody could enter or leave without their authorization. They developed their own family and property laws; they had freedom of contract and of social intercourse among one another, and they imposed the expiation of breach of peace within their group. But they had no other basis for the close unit than the identity of the ruler whom they served, who represented them to the outside, and who was their legal agent in matters involving the law of the land. Here, as in the case of religion mentioned before, the subordination under an individual power is not the consequence or expression of an already existing organic or interest group (as it is in many, especially political, cases). On the contrary, the superordination of one ruler is the *cause* of a commonness which in the absence of it could not be attained and which is not predetermined by any other relation among its members.

It should be noted that not only the equal, but often precisely the unequal, relation of the subordinates to the dominating head gives solidity to the social form characterized by subordination under one individual. The varying distance or closeness to the leader creates a differentiation which is not less firm and articulate because the internal aspect of these relations to him often is jealousy, repulsion, or haughtiness. The social level of the individual Indian caste is determined by its relation to the Brahman. The decisive questions are: Would the Brahman accept a gift from one of their members? Would he accept a glass of water from his hand without reluctance? Or with difficulty? Or would he reject it with abhorrence? That the peculiar firmness of caste stratification depends on such questions is characteristic of the form under discussion for the reason that the mere fact of a highest point determines, as a purely ideal factor, the structural position of every element, and thus the structure of the whole. That this highest layer should be occupied by a great many individuals is quite irrelevant, since the sociological form of the effect is here exactly like that of an individual: the relation to the "Brahman" is decisive. In other words, the formal characteristic of subordination under an individual *may* prevail even where there is plurality of superordinate individuals. The *specific* sociological significance of such a plurality will be shown later, in connection with other phenomena.

§3. Unification of a Group in Opposition to the Ruler

The unificatory consequence of subordination under one ruling power operates even when the group is in opposition to this power. The political group, the factory, the school class, the church congregation—all indicate how the culmination of an organization in a head helps to effect the unity of the whole in the case of either harmony or discord. Discord, in fact, perhaps even more stringently than harmony, forces the group to "pull itself together." In general, common enmity is one of the most powerful means for motivating a number of individuals or groups to cling together. This common enmity is intensified if the common adversary is at the same time the common ruler. In a latent, certainly not in an overt and effective, form, this combination probably occurs everywhere: in some measure, in some respect, the ruler is almost always an adversary. Man has an intimate dual relation to the principle of subordination. On the one hand, he wants to be dominated. The majority of men not only *cannot* exist without leadership; they also *feel* that they cannot: they *seek* the higher power which relieves them of responsibility; they seek a restrictive, regulatory rigor which protects them not only against the outside world but also against themselves. But no less do they need opposition to the leading power, which only through this opposition, through move and countermove, as it were, attains the right place in the life pattern of those who obey it.

One might even say that obedience and opposition are merely two sides or links of one human attitude which fundamentally is quite consistent. They are two sides that are oriented in different directions and only *seem* to be autonomous impulses. The simplest illustration here is from the field of politics. No matter of how many divergent and conflicting parties a nation may be composed, it nevertheless has a common interest in keeping the powers of the crown within limits or in restricting them—in spite of all the practical irreplaceability of the crown and even in spite of all sentimental attachment to it. For hundreds of years following the Magna Charta, there was a lively awareness in England that certain fundamental rights had to be preserved and increased for *all* classes; that nobility could not maintain its freedoms without the freedoms of the weaker classes being maintained at the same time; and that only the law which applied to nobility, burgher, and peasant alike represented a limitation of the personal reign. It has often been remarked that as long as this ultimate goal of the struggle—the restrictions upon monarchy—is endangered, nobility always has people and clergy on its side. And even where one-man rule does not engender this sort of unification, at least it creates a common arena for the fight of its subordinates—between those who are *for* the ruler and those who are *against* him. There is hardly a sociological structure, subject to a supreme head, in which this pro and con does not occasion a vitality of interactions and ramifications among the elements that in terms of an eventual unification is greatly superior to many peaceful but indifferent aggregates—in spite of all repulsions, frictions, and costs of the fight.

28

BRUCE MAZLISH

Leader and Led

T HE first thing to be said is that the "leader" as such does not exist, that is, there is no "leader" for all peoples and all seasons.[1] A potential leader must find the right circumstances and the right group to lead. Without the French Revolution, a Robespierre would at best have been a minor footnote in a provincial history of Arras. Without the outbreak of the American Civil War, Ulysses Grant would have been a failed army officer, rusticating in his family's leather business. On a less dramatic level, Walter Lippmann illustrates the needed correspondence between the leader and circumstances when he remarks *a propos* of two possible relationships in the 1920 Presidential election that Frank Lowden could lead the Democratic Party as its candidate if the public continued its quiescent, anticharismatic feelings, and William McAdoo, if the public gave him the correct leads, which he could then seize upon and promote effectively.[2]

The next thing of note is that the leader does not exist, fully formed, before the encounter with the group he is to lead. He discovers himself, forms and takes on his identity as a particular kind of leader, in the course of interacting with his chosen group. He also finds a public style, which may be quite separate from his private style. It is a creative encounter. A perceptive journalist, Henry Fairlie, has grasped this point well. He tells us:

> No political journalist who has followed such opponents as Winston Churchill and Aneurin Bevan, Charles de Gaulle and Gaston Deferre, on the stump

From Bruce Mazlish, "Leader and Led, Individual and Group," *The Psychohistory Review* 9, no. 3 (Spring 1981): 218–28. Reprinted by permission of Human Sciences Press, Inc., 72 Fifth Ave., New York, N.Y. 10011.

in great campaigns, can doubt that the interaction between candidate and crowd is of supreme importance to the candidate. It is out of this communion between the candidate and the crowd that the national leader is born; and nothing will replace it.[3]

The ambition may already be there, but it is vague and undirected. It takes on specific shape in the encounter. Thus, speaking of American presidents, Fairlie makes the general point when he goes on:

> A great politician, when he seeks the highest political office, must fit his ambition to the hour. He must become necessary; known to himself, and seen by the people, to be so. It is not his personal identity which he must discover, but his political identity which he must establish.[4]

In discovering, or creating his own political identity, the great leader also creates a political identity for his followers, that is, he makes them into a group, however amorphous in actual structure. This explains why with great frequency, the leader-to-be appeals to previously unpolitical people, and brings them into the political arena. A Robespierre draws to him the sans-culottes, a Hitler, the non-voting, lower middle class German, a Mao Tse-tung, the Chinese peasants. Thus, leadership is a creative act, which, psychologically-grounded, brings forth a political identity for both the leader and the led.

Of course, the leader also has a personal identity. Up to now psychohistory, as we have noted, has concentrated on this aspect of the problem. It is in this vein that even Kohut, in his "Creativeness, Charisma, Group Psychology," initially looks at the matter. Speaking of the artist's creativeness, but having in mind the politician's as well, Kohut says:

> In other words, we are dealing either (a) with the wish of a self, which feels enfeebled during a period of creativity, to retain its cohesion by expanding temporarily into the psychic structure of others, by finding itself in others, or to be confirmed by the admiration of others (resembling one of the varieties of a mirror transference), or (b) with the need to obtain strength from an idealized object (resembling an idealizing transference). Thus relationships which are established during creative periods do not predominantly involve the revival of a figure from the (oedipal) past which derives its transference significance primarily from the fact that it is still the target of the love and hate of the great man's childhood.[5]

I will have more to say about Kohut's path-breaking work, but for present purposes I want simply to point out that the discussion at this point—Kohut himself will go beyond it—is still mainly in terms of personal identity. Kohut's insight here is that the leader may better be understood in terms of psychology of the self than of classical Freudian theory; but that self is still being viewed primarily from the "personal" side. The challenge now is to probe the "political identity" side more fully.

To do this, we must look more closely at the "led" or the "group." Unfortunately we do not have a satisfactory theory of group psychology. Small group theory, such as Bion's and others will not do; the historian is mainly interested in large-scale, relatively unstructured mass movements—generally political or religious—grasped or called into being by a leader in particular historic circumstances and in the creative act we have been outlining. We need, therefore, to construct a satisfactory group psychology for ourselves.

IV

Let us begin by postulating that there is a "psychic repository" or culture on which the potential leader can draw. We can conceive of this repository a embodying recurrent themes, ideals, values, fantasies, imagery, symbols, myths and legends. A fuller exposition would need to sort these out. Such materials tend to be timeless, though their relation to historic events is always changing.[6] They embody elements in tension with one another. These elements in tension can be conceived of as ambivalences, but it is perhaps more fruitful to think of them as positive and negative images, in the manner employed by Erikson as he explored the polarities in American life and culture.[7]

Now, the study of themes and myths is the stock in trade of intellectual and cultural historians. I am willing to settle for Smith's definition of what is involved here: "collective representations," i.e., not the work of a single mind; "images," expressing collective desires and imposing coherence on the varied data of experience, with the image itself using concept and emotion into one intellectual construction.[8]

Our task is not to discover all this work anew, but to use if for psychohistorical purposes. Freud appealed to myths and legends for inspiration and confirmation of his clinical insights; we must appeal to them as our primary data. We can do so by bringing them into relation with the leader, for it is he who helps activate this repository, who captures and uses the emotions within it. The leader, in short, serves as a catalyst to our further understanding.

The culture, with its polarities, embodies and expresses the "splits" of what may be called the national or religious psyche; or perhaps group self is better. Analysis of this culture, in static terms, is often called national character studies. Such a culture is subject to dialectical swings, which mirror the splits, only now revealed over time. This is the stuff of history, To take America as an example, Jefferson had spoken of the dialogue of mind and heart. Such a "split" between the rational and emotional from the beginning has been a major theme of history. Made dynamic, it takes on specific dimensions, for example, in the movement surrounding Emerson and the transcendentalists, as in the comment that "The American Romantic movement was . . . another of those periodic upsurges of feelings, of a yearning for emotional fulfillment that have regularly counted the periodic cultural control of the rationalistic and scientific mind."9

It is obvious that this same split, and others like it, can be found in many, if not all, other cultures. The point is that such "eternal" themes take on specific form in particular national cultures, with specific emphasis and ambiances, in terms of specific myths, valuations, fantasies, etc. Each group, then, has a repository, which, though it necessarily resembles all others—just as each individual's psyche embodies universal traits—is unique.

What will be activated in that repository is a result, to a large extent, of circumstances and of the leader who creates himself and the group. One leader, for example, can utilize free-floating discontent at the breakdown of values, or a narcissistic desire for enhanced self-worth and inclusion, in a movement aimed at venting itself at scapegoats. Another can do so in a movement of constructive social protest. Robert Tucker, writing about Stalin's use of the Russian past, actual and mythical, especially concerning Ivan the Terrible, remarked:

> Patterns out of a nation's distant past do not rise again simply because they were there. But they can do so if a leader with great power finds them instructive for present policy and acts upon them as precedent.10

We need to generalize this remark, and apply it to the psychic repository, which includes all the timeless elements of myth, legend, etc., as well as the historical deposits of a people's recent experiences.

Circumstances will conspire to make certain features of the repository readily available to the would-be leader. He will energize these features, sifting out of the population at large the specific group of people who will help him define his leadership, while themselves being defined as a group in the process. The elements used by the leader will be a selection from the polarities available in the repository.

Almost always, *his* leadership will be defined in opposition to that of the leadership offered before him, as well as playing on cultural themes from the repository, To take the American example, a John F. Kennedy will embody the image of a vigorous President, succeeding a desultory Eisenhower—both images, incidentially, are partly mythical—a Jimmy Carter will stress his ordinariness and truthfulness—call me "Jimmy" and "I will never lie to you"—in opposition to Nixon's imperial claims and prevarications.[11] In the largest sense, the leader sets himself, and his followers apart from a negative image, and creates a positive image partly by that very fact—that which he is contrary to—and by activating certain themes, images, and myths in the repository that have lain more or less dormant for a time before him.

V

So far, we have been talking in general terms about political identity, i.e., the creation of self, individual and group, that takes place in the interaction of leader and led. I wish now to talk briefly about image, in the sense not so much of the leader making use of available images in the repository, but of making and projecting one of himself. It is the matter of how a leader is perceived, rather than what he may actually be, though there is a relation between the two. Recall Peter Sellers in the movie *Being There*, for example. One need only mention Teddy Kennedy's disastrous interview with Roger Mudd to make fresh in the mind the power of image, leaving reality aside. In *The Revolutionary Ascetic*, I have argued that a revolutionary ascetic has a functional advantage because of his traits; also suggested is that even a reputation for such traits gives a revolutionary leader a functional advantage in many circumstances.[12] The image has an importance connected to, but separable from, identity, with *political* identity necessarily combining the two.

We know that images can be largely created and manipulated, as long as they don't too drastically affront reality. Later, I will refer to attitudinal polling. Here, I want to make two separate points. The first is that the image is not simply something external to the leader's true self. It is essential and intrinsic to his political identity. The leader, in addition to actually organizing a political or religious movement, i.e., his reality role, himself *becomes* an image, a symbol. As such, he symbolizes the aspirations of his followers, and symbolizes, too, a means of allaying and defending against their fears and despairs. As an image, or symbol, he brings to focus all of their feelings, "binding" them and these feelings to himself. If he disappears from the scene, these feelings are set loose again, available for other, competing leaders to try and refocus in a new combination.[13]

The second point is that image is the way in which a leader's contemporaries perceive him or her; it is a vital part of the relationship, and not a fraudulent or misleading picture. When psychohistorians go in search of the "inner man," as in most life histories, they run the risk of opening up a real gulf between our understanding of the person and how his contemporaries perceived him. As D. A. Hamer argues in his article, "Gladstone: The Making of a Political Myth":

> The work of discovering "the man himself" tends to diminish our ability to understand how and why he mattered, what it was about him that made him important, perhaps an object of veneration or of detestation, in the eyes of his contemporaries. We see him through a very different medium, and we may dismiss what they said he was or represented as myth, worthy only to be discarded once we, as historians, have discovered the "truth" about the man and his motivations and aims.[14]

Most critics of psychohistory focus on reductionism as the great danger. I am suggesting that an equally great danger may be misunderstanding the reality of the leader-led relation. The leader unavoidably takes on many of the aspects of a "cult" figure. It is his image, not the squirmy "inner man," that leads his followers. Moreover, as we have noted, the leader becomes, in part, the actuality of that image, i.e., he finds his self defined by what develops between him and the group. As Hamer suggests, a leader such as Gladstone has to make his conduct conform to his myth if he is to maintain the connection to his followers.[15] The public style encroaches more and more on the private self, until, given the dramatic, even histrionic, nature of political leaders such as Gladstone, the two begin to merge. Life history, if it emphasizes only the "secret," "real" person and ignores image, misses the central identity, which is both political and personal, and thus, misses reality itself.

VI

What role does ideology play in the leader-led relation? Let us conceive of ideology as an effort to tie together, in a putatively logical and rational manner, a bundle of emotions selected from the psychic repository. It is a secular version of a religious system; a contrived imitation of myths and legends. It can persist after the leader's death, e.g., Leninism. The ideology is presumed, often, to be impersonal; once in place, it may serve as an "operational code," a total system directing one's thoughts and actions.

In an article "Thoughts on a Theory of Collective Action: Language, Affect and Ideology in Revolution," Gerald Platt advances a number of interesting theses.[16] He attacks what he calls "Categorical Analysis," which assumes that "some *predispositional* category, i.e., a subjective psychological state or an objective social position somehow compels [revolutionary] participation." Instead, Platt, using the experience of the Nazi Revolution and the English Civil War, recalls our attention to the facts: there was neither homogeneity of motive nor class among the supporters, nor indeed, opponents in the two events. For example, both the English Royalists and Parliamentarians were dominated by aristocrats.[17] Platt also asserts that ideologies, and their language, "are not *causes* of action, but rather modes through which action is made subjectively meaningful." It is not clear to me why ideologies cannot also be thought of in causal terms, inspiring men to action; in fact, a little further on Platt explains that, for example, exploitation of labor, discrimination of persons, etc. are "so experienced because the interpretive rules embedded in ideology inform its adherents that participative activities in the world should be ascribed with such meanings." It would seem to follow that once meaning is given to some actions, it could then serve as motive to further actions. In any case, Platt adds that "ideology is the mechanism by which diverse populations are bound together."

Let me add to Platt's useful formulations the role of the leader. Ideology is imaged forth for the group in the shape of a particular leader. Most populations, in fact, have a hard time understanding and identifying with an ideology, which, as Napoleon well knew, was the construction of intellectuals. As John Kifner says, reporting on the Iranian Revolution:

> The tendency to embody political thought in a single personality rather than articulate its ideology is a strong Persian tradition. This charismatic style is apparent in the universal use of faces on posters and is a large part of Ayatollah Ruhollah Khomeini's political strength.[18]

Even Lenin knew to speak to the Russian peasants about "Bread, Land, and Peace," and not about Marxist-Leninist ideology, which he reserved for Bolshevik theologians. Like Khomeini, Lenin, by his image, his personal qualities, examplified the ideology, and thus bound together the diverse population of followers. As James Fallows comments about a lesser leader, Barry Goldwater, he is a man "who exemplifies a creed in the nature of his personality" rather than in his thought.[19]

Without underestimating, therefore, the role of ideology, we can stress the role of the leader as well. Writing about "why America Loved Theodore Roosevelt; Or Charisma Is in the Eyes of the Beholders,"[20] Kathleen Dalton notes that "America loved Theodore Roosevelt because he tapped an emotional wellspring in the culture. He reached the people on more than rational grounds." As a true leader, a hero, he defined "a culture's aspirations and hopes." I am suggesting that out of the repository of the culture, a leader, such as Lenin or Theodore Roosevelt, selects a number of elements, parts of the polarities, and images them forth, partly in the form of what may be called an ideology, but mainly in the shape of his own person.

VII

There is one other aspect of the leader-led relation that needs to be highlighted. It is the role of organization. Some leaders are rhetorical and ideological in their genius, and leave organizational skills to others; a surprising number of the great leaders—a Lenin, a Mao—combine all the abilities in themselves.

My concern, however, is not with particular leader's organizational skill, or lack of it, but with the psychological functions fulfilled for the led by the organizational structure. I take my example from the Methodist organization created by John Wesley, who exhibited a special talent in this area. Wesley appealed mainly to the lower middle class in Great Britian, at a time of acute disruption to society at the end of the 18th century, caused by the changes associated with the terms commercial and industrial revolution, and eventually, exacerbated by the democratic upheavals of the American and French revolutions. The unfeeling rigidity of the Established Church offered no religious solace for those cast afloat from old moorings of value, or institution.

Into this breach, Wesley stepped. He created not only a new religious "ideology," but a new organization, the Methodist "society," which provided an enormous psychological support for its members. As Robert L. Moore says,

In his movement he had created and formalized a hierarchy of status and prestige which provided opportunities for upward mobility for those without access to the accepted channels of traditional society. The lowliest member of the societies could, by membership alone, be a part of a religious elite.[21]

Erikson had spoken of the great leader solving other people's problems in solving his own. We see here the mechanism by which, in part, this solution takes place—though the articulation is very different from what Erikson had in mind. Speaking of Wesley, Moore goes on,

In making possible the realization of his own special destiny he had given birth to an institution through which many of the dispossessed were able to find an alternative which promised hope and a role which offered a chance for personal development.[22]

"Personal development" is the key concept. Eighteenth-century British "industrial" culture—part of the psychic repository—preached the virtues of success, social mobility, and self-help. Methodism instructed its adherents how to progress up the ladder of spiritual success, a disciplined progress which then assured commercial success, and, most importantly provided an organizational framework in which that mobility could be exercised and rewarded. A personal development, which would have been blocked by the religious and social elitism of the eestablished world, was now fostered in a new setting.[23] A leader, Wesley, creating a new organization, the Methodist Church, provided the led the inspiration and means to become new men. Together, leader and led formed out of an emergent group a movement, which then became organized and institutionalized.

Whether a Wesleyan class, society or conference, all then being grouped into the Methodist Church, or a Bolshevik cell, network, or movement, being gathered into a Communist Party, we are confronted with the same phenomenon: organizations which through the roles they provide, offer the possibility, operationally, of realizing ego ideals.[24] The organization, in short, provides an opportunity for personal development that is a critical part of the creative encounter of the leader and the led.

NOTES

1. In back of the psychohistorical inquiry must stand a classification into different types of leaders—political, religious, intellectual, artistic, etc.—as well as a sociological

analysis, such as offered by Max Weber, who identifies charismatic, rational-bureaucratic, and traditional types of leadership. I shall not enter further into this matter here, but simply post the alert that the psychohistorian, in practice, must make clear what kind of leader he is studying. For present purposes, I am generalizing primarily about political or religious leaders, at the head of relatively large-scale historical groups.

2. *Early Writings of Walter Lippmann*, with introduction by Arthur Schlesinger, Jr. (New York: Liveright, 1970), pp. 179 and 185.

3. Henry Fairlie, *The Kennedy Promise* (Garden City, N.Y.: Doubleday, 1973), p. 65.

4. Ibid., p. 78.

5. Heinz Kohut, "Creativeness, Charisma, Group Psychology: Reflections on the Self-Analysis of Freud," in *Freud: the Fusion of Science and Humanism*, ed. John E. Gedo and George H. Pollock *Psychological Issues*, Monograph 34/35) (New York: International Universities Press, 1976). The quotation that follows is on p. 404.

6. Cf. Henry Nash Smith, *Virgin Land* (Cambridge, Mass.: Harvard, 1976), p. viii.

7. Erik H. Erikson, "Reflections on the American Identity," in *Childhood and Society*, 2d ed. (New York: W. W. Norton, 1963), especially pp. 285ff.

8. Smith, *Virgin Land*, p. xi.

9. Cleanth Brooks, R.G.B. Lewis, Robert Penn Warren, *American Literature* (New York: St. Martin's Press, 1973), p. 670.

10. *The New York Times*, 21 December 1979.

11. In other cases the leader will seek to define himself as a "successor" to his great predecessor, as Stalin did for a while with Lenin. Great imitative successors to great leaders are rare, I believe, for reasons adumbrated in such a work as Robert Jay Lifton, *Revolutionary Immortality: Mao Tse-tung and the Chinese Cultural Revolution* (New York: Random House, 1968); but the problem requires separate treatment from what I am according it here.

12. Bruce Mazlish, *The Revolutionary Ascetic* (New York: Basic Books, 1976).

13. We can see what is involved if we think for a moment of what Robert Mugabe symbolizes in Zimbabwe. If he were eliminated tomorrow, it is doubtful anyone could take his place. His lieutenants would compete for his place, splitting their followers and the feelings tied together by Mugabe. They would almost certainly detach the white feelings that Mugabe has been able to bring to his side. It is Mugabe's image, far more than the day-to-day reality of his political functioning, though we must not underestimate this last, that is the indispensable reality. Mugabe, as leader, symbolizes Zimbabwe, as a nation. The latter would not be the same, might not even exist cohesively, i.e., as a unified group, if he were to disappear.

14. D. A. Hamer, "Gladstone: The Making of a Political Myth," *Victorian Studies* 22 (Autumn 1978): 29.

15. Ibid, p. 30.

16. I have quoted from the original ms.; the quotations that follow are on pp. 3, 17, 29 and 17. The article has now been published in *New Directions in Psychohistory*, ed. Mel Albin (Lexington, Mass.: Lexington Books, 1980).

17. Cf. for a similar argument the paper by Fred Weinstein, "The Sociological Implications of Charismatic Leadership," delivered June 7, 1980, at the Conference on Psychohistorical Meanings of Leadership, Michael Reese Hospital, Chicago, Ill., June 6–8, 1980.

18. *The New York Times*, 15 March 1980.

19. *The New York Times Book Review,* 4 November 1979, p. 22.

20. *The Psychohistory Review* 8 (Winter 1979): 16–26.

21. Robert L. Moore, *John Wesley and Authority: A Psychological Perspective* (Missoula, Montana: Scholars Press, 1979), p. 190.

22. Ibid.

23. For example, Robert Southey, the poet laureate, as Geoffrey Carnall puts it, viewed Methodism as preaching "a means by which the lowest sort of tradesmen — bakers, barbers, tailors, even servants and labourers — are promoted to social eminence. These people find themselves in positions of influence for which by 'birth, education, knowledge, and intellect' they are quite unfit" (Geoffrey Carnall, *Robert Southey and His Age* [Oxford: Clarendon Press, 1960], pp. 70–71). Southey went on to compare the Methodist societies to the radical Corresponding Societies at the time of the French Revolution because of a supposedly similar democratic character.

24. The North Koreans, for example, understood this matter well, and acted in a reverse manner toward their American prisoners of war: they deliberately removed the American leaders from any influence, thereby destroying the authority structure and the command organization, and thus the roles that gave a sense of meaning and identity to the ordinary soldier. Such individuals were then presumed ready for "brain washing," i.e., the creation of a new set of values and a new identity.

29

JAMES MACGREGOR BURNS

The Difference Between Power
Wielders and Leaders

THE TWO ESSENTIALS OF POWER

W E all have *power* to do acts we lack the *motive* to do—to buy a gun
and slaughter people, to crush the feelings of loved ones who cannot
defend themselves, to drive a car down a crowded city sidewalk, to torture
an animal.

We all have the *motives* to do things we do not have the resources to
do—to be President or senator, to buy a luxurious yacht, to give away
millions to charity, to travel for months on end, to right injustices, to tell
off the boss.

The two essentials of power are motive and resource. The two are
interrelated. Lacking motive, resource diminishes; lacking resource,
motive lies idle. Lacking either one, power collapses. Because both
resource and motive are needed, and because both may be in short
supply, power is an elusive and limited thing. Human beings, both the
agents and the victims of power, for two thousand years or more have
tried to penetrate its mysteries, but the nature of power remains elusive.
Certainly no one has mastered the secrets of personal power as physicists
have penetrated the atom. It is probably just as well.

To understand the nature of leadership requires understanding of the
essence of power, for leadership is a special form of power. Forty years
ago Bertrand Russell called power the fundamental concept in social
science, "in the same sense in which Energy is a fundamental concept in

From James MacGregor Burns, *Leadership* (New York: Harper & Row, 1978), pp. 12–22. Copyright
© 1978 by James MacGregor Burns. Reprinted by permission of Harper & Row, Publishers, Inc.

physics." This is a compelling metaphor; it suggests that the source of power may lie in immense reserves of the wants and needs of the wielders and objects of power, just as the winds and the tides, oil and coal, the atom and the sun have been harnessed to supply physical energy. But it is still only a metaphor.

What is power? The "power of A over B," we are told, "is equal to maximum force which A can induce on B minus the maximum resisting force which B can mobilize in the opposite direction." One wonders about the As and the Bs, the Xs and the Ys, in the equations of power. Are they mere croquet balls, knocking other balls and being knocked, in some game of the gods? Or do these As and Xs and the others have wants and needs, ambitions and aspirations, of their own? And what if a ball does not obey a god, just as the children's nurse stood in the autocrat's way. Surely this formula is more physics than power. But the formula offers one vital clue to power: power is a *relationship* among persons.

Power, says Max Weber—he uses the term *Macht*—"is the probability that one actor within a social relationship will be in a position to carry out his own will despite resistance, regardless of the basis on which this probability rests." This formula helps the search for power, since it reminds us that there is no certain relationship between what P (power holder) does and how R (power recipient) responds. Those who have pressed a button and found no light turned on, or who have admonished a child with no palpable effect, welcome the factor of probability, But what controls the *degree* of probability? Motive? Intention? Power resources? Skill? Is P acting on his own, or is he the agent of some other power holder? And what if P orders R to do something to someone else— who then is the *real* power recipient? To answer such questions, P and R and all the other croquet players, mallets, and balls must be put into a broader universe of power relationships—that is, viewed as a *collective* act. Power and leadership become part of a system of social causation.

Essential in a concept of power is the role of *purpose*. This absolutely central values has been inadequately recognized in most theories of power. Power has been defined as the production of intended effects, but the crux of the matter lies in the dimensions of "intent." What is the nature (intensity, persistence, scope) of purpose? How is P's purpose communicated to R—and to what degree is that intent perceived by R as it is by P? Assuming an intent of P, to what extent is there a power relation if P's intent is influenced by P's prior knowledge and anticipation of R's intent? To what extent is intent part of a wider interaction among wants, needs, and values of P and R, before any overt behavior takes place? Few persons have a single intent; if P has more than one, are these intentions deemed equal, hierarchial, or unrelated? These relationships also define the exercise of power as a collective act.

A *psychological* conception of power will help us cut through some of these complexities and provide a basis for understanding the relation of power to leadership. This approach carries on the assumptions above: that power is first of all a *relationship* and not merely an entity to be passed around like a baton or hand grenade; that it involves the *intention* or *purpose* of both power holder and power recipient; and hence that it is *collective*, not merely the behavior of one person. On these assumptions I view the power process as one *in which power holders (P), possessing certain motives and goals, have the capacity to secure changes in the behavior of a respondent (R), human or animal, and in the environment, by utilizing resources in their power base, including factors of skill, relative to the targets of their power-wielding and necessary to secure such changes.* This view of power deals with three elements in the process: the motives and resources of power holders; the motives and resources of power recipients; and the relationship among all these.

The power holder may be the person whose "private motives are displaced onto public objects and rationalized in terms of public interest," to quote Harold Lasswell's classic formula. So accustomed are we to observing persons with power drives or complexes; so sensitive to leaders with the "will to power," so exposed to studies finding the source of the power urge in early deprivation, that we tend to assume the power motive to be exclusively that of seeking to dominate the behavior of others. "But must *all* experiences of power have as their ultimate goal the exercise of power over others?" David McClelland demands. He and other psychologists find that persons with high need for power ("*n* Power") may derive that need for power not only from deprivation but from other experiences. One study indicated that young men watching a film of John F. Kennedy's Inaugural felt strengthened and inspirited by this exposure to an admired leader. Other persons may draw on internal resources as they grow older and learn to exert power against those who constrain them, like children who self-consciously recognize their exercise of power as they resist their mothers' directions. They find "sources of strength in the self to develop the self."

These and other findings remind us that the power holder has a variety of motives besides that of wielding power over others. They help us correct the traditional picture of single-minded power wielders bent on exerting control over respondents. (Their main motive may be to institute

power over *themselves.*) In fact power holders may have as varied motives—of wants, needs, expectations, etc.—as their targets. Some may
pursue not power but status, recognition, prestige, and glory, or they may
seek power as an intermediate value instrumental to realizing those loftier
goals. Some psychologists consider the need to achieve ("*n* Achievement") a powerful motive, especially in western cultures, and one whose
results may be prized more as an *attainment* than as a means of social
control. Some use power to collect possessions such as paintings, cars, or
jewelry; they may collect wives or mistresses less to dominate them than
to love or to display them. Others will use power to seek novelty and
excitement. still others may enjoy the exercise of power mainly because it
enables them to exhibit—if only to themselves—their skill and knowledge, their ability to stimulate their own capacities and to master their
environment. Those skilled in athletics may enjoy riding horseback or
skiing as solitary pastimes, with no one but themselves to admire their
skills. The motivational base of this kind of competence has been labeled
"effectance" by Robert White.

Still, there *are* the single-minded power wielders who fit the classical
images of Machiavelli or Hobbes or Nietzsche, or at least the portraits
of the modern power theorists. They consciously exploit the external
resources (economic, social, psychological, and institutional) and their
"effectance," their training, skill, and competence, to make persons
and things do what they want done. The key factor here is indeed
"what they want done." The motives of power wielders may or may
not coincide with what the respondent wants done; it is P's intention
that controls. Power wielders may or may not recognize respondents'
want and needs; if they do, they may recognize them only to the
degree necessary to achieve their goals; and if they must make a choice
between satisfying their own purposes and satisfying respondents' needs,
they will choose the former. Power wielders are not free agents. They
are subject—even slaves—to pressures working on them and in them.
But once their will and purpose is forged, it may be controlling. If P
wants circuses and R wants bread, the power wielder may manipulate
popular demand for bread only to the degree that it helps P achieve
circuses. At the "naked power" extremity on the continuum of types of
power holders are the practitioners of virtually unbridled power—
Hitler, Stalin, and the like—subject always, of course, to empowering
and constraining circumstances.

The foundation of this kind of control lies in P's "power base" *as it is
relevant to those at the receiving end of power.* The composition of the
power base will vary from culture to culture, from situation to situation.

Some power holders will have such pervasive control over factors influencing behavior that the imbalance between P's and R's power bases, and between the possibility of realizing P's and R's purposes, will be overwhelming. Nazi death camps and communist "re-education" camps are examples of such overwhelming imbalances. A dictator can put respondents physically in such isolation and under such constraint that they cannot even appeal to the dictator's conscience, if he has one, or to sympathetic opinion outside the camp or outside the country, if such exists. More typical, in most cultures, is the less asymmetric relationship in which P's power base supplies P with extensive control over R but leaves R with various resources for resisting. Prisons, armies, authoritarian families, concentration camps such as the United States relocation centers for Japanese-Americans during World War II, exemplify this kind of imbalance. There is a multitude of power balances in villages, tribes, schools, homes, collectives, business, trade unions, cities, in which most persons spend most of their lives.

To define power not as a property or entity or possession but as a *relationship* in which two or more persons tap motivational bases in one another and bring varying resources to bear in the process is to perceive power as drawing a vast range of human behavior into its orbit. The arena of power is no longer the exclusive preserve of a power elite or an establishment of persons clothed with ligitimacy. Power is ubiquitous; it permeats human relationships. It exists whether or not it is quested for. It is the glory and the burden of most of humanity. A common, highly asymmetric, and sometimes cruel power relation can exist, for example, when one person is in love with another but the other does not reciprocate. The wants and needs and expectations of the person in love are aroused and engaged by a partner whose resources of attractiveness or desirability are high and whose own cluster of motives is less vulnerable. The person possessed by love can maneuver and struggle but still is a slave to the one loved, as the plight of Philip in Somerset Maugham's marvelously titled *Of Human Bondage* illustrates.

Because power can take such multifarious, ubiquitous, and subtle forms, it is reflected in an infinite number of combinations and particularities in specific contexts. Even so, observers *in* those contexts may perceive their particular "power mix" as the basic and universal type, and they will base elaborate descriptions and theories of power on one model—their own. Even Machiavelli's celebrated portrait of the uses and abuses of power, while revelant to a few other cultures and eras, is essentially culture-bound and irrelevant to a host of other power situations and systems. Thus popular tracts on power—how to win power and influence people—typically are useful only for particular situations and may disable the student of power coping with quite different power constellations.

Still there are ways of breaking power down into certain attributes that allow for some generalization and even theory-building. Robert Dahl's breakdown of the reach and magnitude of power is useful and parsimonious. One dimension is *distribution*—the concentration and dispersion of power among persons of diverse influence in various political, social, and economic locations such as geographical areas, castes and classes, status positions, skill groups, communications centers, and the like. Another dimension is *scope*—the extent to which power is generalized over a wide range or is specialized. Persons who are relatively powerful in relation to one kind of activity, Dahl notes, may be relatively weak in other power relationships. Still another dimension is *domain*— the number and nature of power respondents influenced by power wielders compared to those who are not. These dimensions are not greatly different from Lasswell and Abraham Kaplan's conception of the weight, scope, and domain of power.

A more common way to organize the data of power is in terms of the *size* of the *arena* in which power is exercised. The relation of P and R is, in many studies, typically one of micropower, as Edward Lehman calls it. Most power relations embrace a multiplicity of power holders; the relation is one among many Ps and many Rs. As power holders and respondents multiply, the number of relationships increases geometrically. Macropower, as Lehman contends, has distinct attributes of its own; the complex relations involved in the aggregate are not simply those of micropower extended to a higher plane. Causal interrelations become vastly more complex as a greater number of power actors and power components comes into play. Paradoxically, we may, with modern techniques of fact-gathering and of empirical analysis, gain a better understanding of mass phenomena of power and leadership than of the more intricate and elusive interactions in micropower situations.

Whatever the dimensions or context, the fundamental process remains the same. *Power wielders draw from their power bases resources relevant to their own motives and the motives and resources of others upon whom they exercise power.* The power base may be narrow and weak, or it may consist of ample and multiple resources useful for vast and long-term exercises of power, but the process is the same. Dominated by personal motives, P draws on supporters, on funds, on ideology, on institutions, on old friendships, on political credits, on status, and on his own skills of calculation, judgment, communication, timing, to mobilize those elements that relate to the motives of the persons P wishes to control—even if in the end P overrides their values and goals—just as P mobilizes machines and fuel and manpower and engineering expertise relevant to the tasks of building dams or clearing forests.

Power shows many faces and takes many forms. It may be as visible as the policeman's badge or billy or as veiled as the politician's whisper in the back room. It may exist as an overwhelming presence or as a potential that can be drawn on at will. It may appear in the form of money, sex appeal, authority, administrative regulation, charisma, munitions, staff resources, instruments for torture. But all these resources must have this in common: *they must be relevant to the motivations of the power recipients.* Even the most fearsome of power devices, such as imprisonment or torture or denial of food or water, may not affect the behavior of a masochist or a martyr.

The exception to this qualification is the appalling power totally to dominate a power object physically or mentally through slavery, imprisonment, deportation, hypnotism. This kind of power has two significant implications. One is the expenditure of effort and resources by P to exercise this kind of control; unless power has been inherited, P has invested, over a period of time and through many power-related acts, in power resources that permit exertion of "total" power. The other is the constraint that may tighten when P exercises total psychological or physical control; P may gain power over a limited number of persons or goods at the expense of antagonizing other persons—perhaps millions of them—by threatening and attacking their values. Power can be fully analyzed and measured only by viewing it in the context of multiple human interaction and broad causal relationships.

LEADERSHIP AND FOLLOWERSHIP

Leadership is an aspect of power, but it is also a separate and vital process in itself.

Power over other persons, we have noted, is exercised when potential power wielders, motivated to achieve certain goals of their own, marshal in their power base resources (economic, military, institutional, or skill) that enable them to influence the behavior of respondents by activating motives of respondents relevant to those resources and to those goals. This is done in order to realize the purposes of the *power wielders, whether or not these are also the goals of the respondents.* Power wielders also exercise influence by mobilizing their own power base in such a way as to establish direct physical control over others behavior, as in a war of conquest or through measures of harsh deprivation, but these are highly restricted exercises of power, dependent on certain times, cultures, and personalities, and they are often self-destructive and transitory.

Leadership over human beings is exercised when persons with certain motives and purposes mobilize, in competition or conflict with others, institutional, political, psychological, and other resources so as to arouse, engage, and satisfy the motives of followers. This is done in order to realize goals mutually held by *both* leaders and followers, as in Lenin's calls for peace, bread, and land. In brief, leaders with motive and power bases tap followers' motives in order to realize the purposes of both leaders and followers. Not only must motivation be relevant, as in power generally, but its purposes must be realized and satisfied. Leadership is exercised in a condition of *conflict* or *competition* in which leaders contend in appealing to the motive bases of potential followers. Naked power, on the other hand, admits of no competition or conflict—there is no engagement.

Leaders are a particular kind of power holder. Like power, leadership is relational, collective, and purposeful. Leadership shares with power the central function of achieving purpose. But the reach and domain of leadership are, in the short range at least, more limited than those of power. Leaders do not obliterate followers' motives though they may arouse certain motives and ignore others. They lead other creatures, not things (and lead animals only to the degree that they recognize animal motives—i.e., leading cattle to shelter rather than to slaughter). To control *things*—tools, mineral resources, money, energy—is an act of power, not leadership, for things have no motives. Power wielders may treat people as things. Leaders may not.

All leaders are actual or potential power holders, but not all power holders are leaders.

These definitions of power and of leadership differ from those that others have offered. Lasswell and Kaplan hold that power must be relevant to people's valued things; I hold that it must be relevant to the *power wielder's* valued things and may be relevant to the *recipient's* needs or values only as necessary to exploit them. Kenneth Janda defines power as "the ability to cause other persons to adjust their behavior in conformance with communicated behavior patterns." I agree, assuming that those behavior patterns aid the purpose of the power wielder. According to Andrew McFarland, "If the leader causes changes that he intended, he has exercised power; if the leader causes changes that he did not intend or want, he has exercised influence, but not power. . . ." I dispense with the concept of influence as unnecessary and unparsimonious. For me the leader is a very special, very circumscribed, but potentially the most effective of power holders, judged by the degree of intended "real change" finally achieved. Roderick Bell et al. contend that power is a relationship rather than an entity—an entity being something that "could be smelled and touched, or stored in a keg"; while I agree that power is a relationship, I contend that the relationship is one in which some entity— part of the "power base"—plays an indispensable part, whether that keg is a keg of beer, of dynamite, or of ink.

The crucial variable, again, is *purpose*. Some define leadership as leaders making followers do what *followers* would not otherwise do, or as leaders making followers do what the *leaders* want them to do; I define leadership as leaders inducing followers to act for certain goals that represent the values and the motivations—the wants and needs, the aspirations and expectations—*of both leaders and followers*. And the genius of leadership lies in the manner in which leaders see and act on their own and their followers' values and motivations.

Leadership, unlike naked power-wielding, is thus inseparable from followers' needs and goals. The essence of the leader-follower relation is the interaction of persons with different levels of motivations and of power potential, including skill, in pursuit of a common or at least joint purpose. The interaction, however, takes two fundamentally different forms. The first I will call *transactional* leadership. . . . Such leadership occurs when one person takes the initiative in making contact with others for the purpose of an exchange of valued things. The exchange could be economic or political or psychological in nature: a swap of goods or of one good for money; a trading of votes between candidate and citizen or between legislators; hospitality to another person in exchange for willingness to listen to one's troubles. Each party to the bargain is conscious of the power resources and attitudes of the other. Each person recognizes the other as a *person*. Their purposes are related, at least to the extent that the purposes stand within the bargaining process and can be advanced by maintaining that process. But beyond this the relationship does not go. The bargainers have no enduring purpose that holds them together; hence they may go their separate ways. A leadership act took place, but it was not one that binds leader and follower together in a mutual and continuing pursuit of a higher purpose.

Contrast this with *transforming* leadership. Such leadership occurs when one or more persons *engage* with others in such a way that leaders and followers raise one another to higher levels of motivation and morality. . . . Their purposes, which might have started out as separate but related, as in the case of transactional leadership, became fused. Power bases are linked not as counterweights but as mutual support for common purpose. Various names are used for such leadership, some of them derisory; elevating, mobilizing, inspiring, exalting, uplifting, preaching, exhorting, evangelizing. The relationship can be moralistic, of course. But transforming leadership ultimately becomes *moral* in that it raises the level of human conduct and ethical aspiration of both leader and led, and thus it has a transforming effect on both. Perhaps the best modern example is Gandhi, who aroused and elevated the hopes and demands of millions of Indians and whose life and personality were enhanced in the process. Transcending leadership is dynamic leadership in the sense that the leaders throw themselves into a relationship with followers who will feel "elevated" by it and often become more active themselves, thereby creating new cadres of leaders. Transcending leadership is leadership *engagé*. Naked power-wielding can be neither transactional nor transforming; only leadership can be.

Leaders and followers may be inseparable in function, but they are not the same. The leader takes the initative in making the leader-led connection; it is the leader who creates the links that allow communication and exchange to take place. An office seeker does this in accosting a voter on the street, but if the voter espies and accosts the politician, the voter is assuming a leadership function, at least for that brief moment. The leader is more skillful in evaluating followers' motives, anticipating their responses to an initiative, and estimating their power bases, than the reverse. Leaders continue to take the major part in maintaining and effectuating the relationship with followers and will have the major role in ultimately carrying out the combined purpose of leaders and followers. Finally, and most important by far, leaders address themselves to followers wants, needs, and other motivations, as well as to their own, and thus they serve as an *independent force in changing the makeup of the followers' motive base through gratifying their motives.*

Certain forms of power and certain forms of leadership are near-extremes on the power continuum. One is the kind of absolute power that, Lord Acton felt, "corrupts absolutely." It also coerces absolutely. The essence of this kind of power is the capacity of power wielders, given the necessary motivation, to override the motive and power bases of their targets. Such power objectifies its victims; it literally turns them into objects, like the inadvertant weapon tester in Mtésa's court. Such power wielders, as well, are objectified and dehumanized. Hitler, according to Richard Hughes, saw the universe as containing no persons other than himself, only "things." The ordinary citizen in Russia, says a Soviet linguist and dissident, does not identify with his government. "With us, it is there, like the wind, like a wall, like the sky. It is something permanent, unchangable. So the individual acquiesces, does not dream of changing it—except a few, few people. . . ."

At the other extreme is leadership so sensitive to the motives of potential followers that the roles of leader and follower become virtually interdependent. Whether the leadership relationship is transactional or transforming, in it motives, values, and goals of leader and led merged. It may appear that at the other extreme from the raw power relationship, dramatized in works like Arthur's Koestler's *Darkness at Noon* and George Orwell's *1984*, is the extreme of leadership-led merger dramatized in novels about persons utterly dependent on parents, wives, or lovers. Analytically these extreme types of relationships are not very preplexing. To watch one person absolutely dominate another is horrifying; to watch one person disappear, his motives and values submerged into those of another to the point of loss of individuality, is saddening. But puzzling out the nature of these extreme relationships is not intellectually challenging because each in its own way lacks the qualities of complexity and conflict. Submersion of one personality in another is not genuine merger based on mutual respect. Such submersion is an example of brute power subtly applied, perhaps with the acquiescence of the victim.

More complex are relationships that lie between these poles of brute power and wholly reciprocal leadership-followership. Here empirical and theoretical questions still perplex both the analysts and the practitioners of power. One of these concerns the sheer measurement of power (or leadership). Traditionally we measure power resources by calculating each one and adding them up: constituency support plus access to leadership plus financial resources plus skill plus "popularity" plus access to information, etc., all in relation to the strength of opposing forces, similarly computed. But these calculations omit the vital factor of motivation and purpose and hence fall of their own weight. Another controversial measurement device is *reputation*. Researchers seek to learn from informed observers their estimates of the power or leadership role and resources of visible *community* leaders (projecting this into national arenas of power is a formidable task). Major questions arise as to the reliability of the estimates, the degree of agreement between interviewer and interviewee over their definition of power and leadership, the transferability of power from one area of decision-making to another. Another device for studying power and leadership is *linkage theory*, which requires elaborate mapping of communication and other interrelations among power holders in different spheres, such as the economic and the military. The difficulty here is that communication, which may expedite the processes of power and leadership, is not a substitute for them.

My own measurement of power and leadership is simpler in concept but no less demanding of analysis: *power and leadership are measured by the degree of production of intended effects.* This need not be a theoretical exercise. Indeed, in ordinary political life, the power resources and the motivations of presidents and prime ministers and political parties are measured by the extent to which presidential promises and party programs are carried out. Note that the variables are the double ones of *intent* (a function of motivation) and of *capacity* (a function of power base), but the test of the extent and quality of power and leadership is the degree of *actual accomplishment* of the promised change.

Other complexities in the study of power and leadership are equally serious. One is the extent to which power and leadership are exercised not by positive action but by *inaction* or *nondecision*. Another is that power and leadership are often exercised not directly on targets but indirectly, and perhaps through multiple channels, on multiple targets. We must ask not only whether P has the power to do X to R, but whether P can induce or force R to do Y to Z. The existence of power and leadership in the form of a stream of multiple direct and indirect forces operating over time must be seen as part of the broader sequences of historical causation. Finally, we must acknowledge the knotty problem of events of history that are beyond the control of identifiable persons capable of foreseeing developments and powerful enough to influence them and hence to be held accountable for them. We can only agree with C. Wright Mills that these are matters of fate rather than power or leadership.

We do well to approach these and other complexities of power or leadership with some humility as well as a measure of boldness. We can reject the "gee whiz" approach to power that often takes the form of the automatic presumption of "elite control" of communities, groups, institutions, entire nations. Certain concepts and techniques of the "elitist" school of power are indispensible in social and political analysis, but "elitism" is often useds as a concept that *presupposes* the existence of the very degree and kind of power that is to be estimated and analyzed. Such "elite theorists" commit the gross error of equating power and leadership with the assumed power bases of preconceived leaders and power holders, without considering the crucial role of *motivations* of leaders and followers. Every good detective knows that one must look for the motive as well as the weapon.

30

J. R. P. FRENCH, JR., and B. RAVEN

The Bases of Social Power

THE processes of power are pervasive, complex, and often disguised in our society. Accordingly one finds in political science, in sociology, and in social psychology a variety of distinctions among different types of social power or among qualitatively different processes of social influence (1, 7, 14, 20, 23, 29, 30, 38, 40). Our main purpose is to identify the major types of power and to define them systematically so that we may compare them according to the changes which they produce and the other effects which accompany the use of power. The phenomena of power and influence involve a dyadic relation between two agents which may be viewed from two points of view: (a) What determines the behavior of the agent who exerts power? (b) What determines the reactions of the recipient of this behavior? We take this second point of view and formulate our theory in terms of the life space of P, the person upon whom the power is exerted. In this way we hope to define basic concepts of power which will be adequate to explain many of the phenomena of social influence, including some which have been described in other less genotypic terms.

Recent empirical work, especially on small groups, has demonstrated the necessity of distinguishing different types of power in order to account for the different effects found in studies of social influence. Yet there is no doubt that more empirical knowledge will be needed to make final decisions concerning the necessary differentiations, but this knowledge will be obtained only by research based on some preliminary theoretical distinctions. We present such preliminary concepts and some of the hypotheses they suggest.

POWER, INFLUENCE AND CHANGE

Psychological Change

Since we shall define power in terms of influence, and influence in terms of psychological change, we begin with a discussion of change. We want to define change at a level of generality which includes changes in behavior, opinions, attitudes, goals, needs, values, and all other aspects of the person's psychological field. We shall use the word "system" to refer to any such part of the life space.[1] Following Lewin (26, p. 305) the state of a system at time 1 will be denoted $s_1(a)$.

Psychological change is defined as any alteration of the state of some system a over time. The amount of change is measured by the size of the difference between the states of the system a at time 1 and at time 2:

$$ch\ (a)\ =\ s_2\ (a)\ \text{-}\ s_1\ (a).$$

Change in any psychological system may be conceptualized in terms of psychological forces. But it is important to note that the change must be coordinated to the resultant force of all the forces operating at the moment. Change in an opinion, for example, may be determined jointly by a driving force induced by another person, a restraining force corresponding to anchorage in a group opinion, and an own force stemming from the person's needs.

Social Influence

Our theory of social influence and power is limited to influence on the person, P, produced by a social agent, O, where O can be either another person, a role, a norm, a group, or a part of a group. We do not consider social influence exerted on a group.

The influence of O on system a in the life space of P is defined as the resultant force on system a which has its source in an act of O. This resultant force induced by O consists of two components: a force to change the system in the direction induced by O and an opposing resistance set up by the same act of O.

By this definition the influence of O does not include P's own forces nor the forces induced by other social agents. Accordingly the "influence" of O must be clearly distinguished from O's "control" of P. O may be able to induce strong forces on P to carry out an activity (i.e., O exerts strong influence on P); but if the opposing forces induced by another person or by P's own needs are stronger, then P will locomote in an opposite direction (i.e., O does not have control over P). Thus psychological change in P can be taken as an operational definition of the social influence of O on P only when the effects of other forces have been eliminated.

It is assumed that any system is interdependent with other parts of the life space so that a change in one may produce changes in others. However, this theory focuses on the primary changes in a system which are produced directly by social influence; it is less concerned with secondary changes which are indirectly effected in the other systems or with primary changes produced by nonsocial influences.

Commonly social influence takes place through an intentional act on the part of O. However, we do not want to limit our definition of "act" to such conscious behavior. Indeed, influence might result from the passive presence of O, with no evidence of speech or overt movement. A policeman's standing on a corner may be considered an act of an agent for the speeding motorist. Such acts of the inducing agent will vary in strength, for O may not always utilize all of his power. The policeman, for example, may merely stand and watch or act more strongly by blowing his whistle at the motorist.

The influence exerted by an act need not be in the direction intended by O. The direction of the resultant force on P will depend on the relative magnitude of the induced force set up by the act of O and the resisting force in the same direction which is generated by that same act. In cases where O intends to influence P in a given direction, a resultant force in the same direction may be termed positive influence whereas a resultant force in the opposite direction may be termed negative influence.

If O produces the intended change, he has exerted positive control; but if he produces a change in the opposite direction, as for example in the negativism of young children or in the phenomena of negative reference groups, he has exerted negative control.

Social Power

The *strength of power* of O/P in some system *a* is defined as the maximum potential ability of O to influence P in *a*.

By this definition influence is kinetic power, just as power is potential influence. It is assumed that O is capable of various acts which, because of some more or less enduring relation to P, are able to exert influence on P.[2] O's power is measured by his maximum possible influence, though he may often choose to exert less than his full power.

An equivalent definition of power may be stated in terms of the resultant of two forces set up by the act of O: one in the direction of O's influence attempt and another resisting force in the opposite direction. Power is the maximum resultant of these two forces:

$$\text{power of O/P } (a) = (f_{a,x} - f_{\overline{ax}})^{\max}$$

where the source of both forces is an act of O.

Thus the power of O with respect to system a of P is equal to the maximum resultant force of two forces set up by any possible act of O: (a) the force which O can set up on the system a to change in the direction x, (b) the resisting force[3] in the opposite direction. Whenever the first component force is greater than the second, positive power exists; but if the second component force is greater than the first, then O has negative power over P.

It is necessary to define power with respect to a specified system because the power of O/P may vary greatly from one system to another. O may have great power to control the behavior of P but little power to control his opinions. Of course a high power of O/P does not imply a low power of P/O: the two variables are conceptually independent.

For certain purposes it is convenient to define the range of power as the set of all systems within which O has power of strength greater than zero. A husband may have a broad range of power over his wife but a narrow range of power over his employer. We shall use the term "magnitude of power" to denote the summation of O's power over P in all systems of his range.

The Dependence of S (a) ON O

Several investigators have been concerned with differences between superficial conformity and "deeper" changes produced by social influence (1, 5, 7, 11, 12, 20, 21, 22, 23, 26, 36, 37). The kinds of systems which are changed and the stability of these changes have been handled by distinctions such as "public versus private attitudes," "overt versus covert behavior," "compliance versus internalization," and "own versus induced forces." Though stated as dichotomies, all of these distinctions suggest an underlying dimension of the degree of dependence of the state of a system on O.

We assume that any change in the state of a system is produced by a change in some factor upon which it is functionally dependent. The state of an opinion, for example, may change because of a change either in some internal factor such as a need or in some external factor such as the arguments of O. Likewise the maintenance of the same state of a system is produced by the stability or lack of change in the internal and external factors, In general, then, psychological change and stability can be conceptualized in terms of dynamic dependence. Our interest is focused on the special case of dependence on an external agent, O (31).

In many cases the initial state of the system has the character of a quasi-stationary equilibrium with a central force field around s_1 (a) (26, 106). In such cases we may derive a tendency toward retrogression to the original state as soon as the force induced by O is removed.[4] Let us suppose that O exerts influence producing a new state of the system, s_2 (a). Is s_2 (a) now dependent on the continued presence of O? In principle we could answer this question by removing any traces of O from the life space of P and by observing the consequent state of the system at time 3. If s_3 (a) retrogresses completely back to s_1 (a), then we may conclude that maintenance of s_2 (a) was completely dependent on O: but if s_3 (a) equals s_2 (a), this lack of change shows that s_2 (a) has become completely independent of O. In general the degree of dependence of s_2 (a) on O, following O's influence, may be defined as equal to the amount of retrogression following the removal of O from the life space of P:

$$\text{degree of dependence of } s_2 \, (a) \text{ on}$$
$$O = s_2 \, (a) - s_3 \, (a)$$

A given degree of dependence at time 2 may later change, for example, through the gradual weakening of O's influence. At this later time, the degree of dependence of s_4 (a) on O would still be equal to the amount of retrogression toward the initial state of equilibrium s_1 (a). Operational measures of the degree of dependence on O will, of course, have to be taken under conditions where all other factors are held constant.

Consider the example of three separated employees who have been working at the same steady level of production despite normal, small fluctuations in the work environment. The supervisor orders each to increase his production, and the level of each goes up from 100 to 115 pieces per day. After a week of producing at the new rate of 115 pieces per day, the supervisor is removed for a week. The production of employee A immediately returns to 100 but B and C return to only 110 pieces per day. Other things being equal, we can infer that A's new rate was completely dependent on his supervisor whereas the new rate of B and C was dependent on the supervisor only to the extent of 5 pieces. Let us further assume that when the supervisor returned, the production of B and of C returned to 115 without further orders from the supervisor. Now another month goes by during which B and C maintain a steady 115 pieces per day. However, there is a difference between them: B's level of production still depends on O to the extent of 5 pieces whereas C has come to rely on his own sense of obligation to obey the order of his legitimate supervisor rather than on the supervisor's external pressure for the maintenance of his 115 pieces per day. Accordingly, the next time the supervisor departs, B's production again drops to 110 but C's remains at 115 pieces per day. In cases like employee B, the degree of dependence is contingent on the perceived probability that O will observe the state of the system and not P's conformity (5, 7, 11, 12, 23). The level of observability will in turn depend on both the nature of the system (e.g., the difference between a covert opinion and overt behavior) and on the environmental barriers to observation (e.g., O is too far away from P). In other cases, for example that of employee C, the new behavior pattern is highly dependent on his supervisor, but the degree of dependence of the new state will be related not to the level of observability but rather to factors inside P, in this case a sense of duty to perform an act legitimately prescribed by O. The internalization of social norms is a related process of decreasing degree of dependence of behavior on an external O and increasing dependence on an internal value; it is usually assumed that internalization is accompanied by a decrease in the effects of level of observability (37).

The concepts "dependence of a system on O" and "observability as a basis for dependence" will be useful in understanding the stability of conformity. In the next section we shall discuss various types of power and the types of conformity which they are likely to produce.

THE BASES OF POWER

By the basis of power we mean the relationship between O and P which is the source of that power. It is rare that we can say with certainty that a given empirical case of power is limited to one source. Normally, the relation between O and P will be characterized by several qualitatively different variables which are bases of power (30). Although there are undoubtedly many possible bases of power which may be distinguished, we shall here define five which seem especially common and important. These five bases of O's power are: (a) reward power, based on P's perception that O has the ability to mediate rewards for him; (b) coercive power, based on P's perception that O has the ability to mediate punishments for him; (c) legitimate power, based on the perception by P that O has a legitimate right to prescribe behavior for him; (d) referent power, based on P's identification with O; (e) expert power, based on the perception that O has some special knowledge or expertness.

Our first concern is to define the bases which give rise to a given type of power. Next, we describe each type of power according to its strength, range, and the degree of dependence of the new state of the system which is most likely to occur with each type of power. We shall also examine the other effects which the exercise of a given type of power may have upon P and his relatonship to O. Finally, we shall point out the interrelationships between different types of power, and the effects of use of one type of power by O upon other bases of power which he might have over P. Thus we shall both define a set of concepts and propose a series of hypotheses. Most of these hypotheses have not been systematically tested, although there is a good deal of evidence in favor of several. No attempt will be made to summarize that evidence here.

Reward Power

Reward power is defined as power whose basis is the ability to reward. The strength of the reward power of O/P increases with the magnitude of the rewards which P perceives that O can mediate for him. Reward power depends on O's ability to administer positive valences and to remove or decrease negative valences. The strength of reward power also depends upon the probability that O can mediate the reward, as perceived by P. A common example of reward power is the addition of a piece-work rate in the factory as an incentive to increase production.

The new state of the system induced by a promise of reward (for example, the factory worker's increased level of production) will be highly dependent on O. Since O mediates the reward, he controls the probability that P will receive it. Thus P's new rate of production will be dependent on his subjective probability that O will reward him for conformity minus his subjective probability that O will reward him even if he returns to his old level. Both probabilities will be greatly affected by the level of observability of P's behavior. Incidentally, a piece rate often seems to have more effect on production than a merit rating system because it yields a higher probability of reward for conformity and a much lower probability of reward for nonconformity.

The utilization of actual rewards (instead of promises) by O will tend over time to increase the attraction of P toward O and therefore the referent power of O over P. As we shall note later, such referent power will permit O to induce changes whch are relatively independent. Neither rewards nor promises will arouse resistance in P, provided P considers it legitimate for O to offer rewards.

The range of reward power is specific to those regions within which O can reward P for conforming. The use of rewards to change systems within the range of reward power tends to increase reward power by increasing the probability attached to future promises. However, unsuccessful attempts to exert reward power outside the range of power would tend to decrease the power; for example, if O offers to reward P for performing an impossible act, this will reduce for P the probability of receiving future rewards promised by O.

Coercive Power

Coercive power is similar to reward power in that it also involves O's ability to manipulate the attainment of valences. Coercive power of O/P stems from the expectation on the part of P that he will be punished by O if he fails to conform to the influence attempt. Thus negative valences will exist in given regions of P's life space, corresponding to the threatened punishment by O. The strength of coercive power depends on the magnitude of the negative valence of the threatened punishment multiplied by the perceived probability that P can avoid the punishment by conformity, i.e., the probability of punishment for nonconformity minus the probability of punishment for conformity (11). Just as an offer of a piece-rate bonus in a factory can serve as a basis for reward power, so the ability to fire a worker if he falls below a given level of production will result in coercive power.

Coercive power leads to dependent change also, and the degree of dependence varies with the level of observability of P's conformity. An excellent illustration of coercive power leading to dependent change is provided by a clothes presser in a factory observed by Coch and French (3). As her efficiency rating climbed above average for the group the other workers began to "scapegoat" her. That the resulting plateau in her production was not independent of the group was evident once she was removed from the presence of the other workers. Her production immediately climbed to new heights.[5]

At times, there is some difficulty in distinguishing between reward power and coercive power. Is the withholding of a reward really equivalent to a punishment? Is the withdrawal of punishment equivalent to a reward? The answer must be a psychological one—it depends upon the situation as it exists for P. But ordinarily we would answer these questions in the affirmative; for P, receiving a reward is a positive valence as is the relief of suffering. There is some evidence (5) that conformity to group norms in order to gain acceptance (reward power) should be distinguished from conformity as a means of forestalling rejection (coercive power).

The distinction between these two types of power is important because the dynamics are different. The concept of "sanctions" sometimes lumps the two together despite their opposite effects. While reward power may eventually result in an independent system, the effects of coercive power will continue to be dependent. Reward power will tend to increase the attraction of P toward O; coercive power will decrease this attraction (11, 12). The valence of the region of behavior will become more negative, acquiring some negative valence from the threatened punishment. The negative valence of punishment would also spread to other regions of the life space. Lewin (25) has pointed out this distinction between the effects of rewards and punishment. In the case of threatened punishment, there will be a resultant force on P to leave the field entirely. Thus, to achieve conformity, O must not only place a strong negative valence in certain regions through threat of punishment, but O must also introduce restraining forces, or other strong valences, so as to prevent P from withdrawing completely from O's range of coercive power. Otherwise the probability of receiving the punishment, if P does not conform, will be too low to be effective.

LEGITIMATE POWER

Legitimate power is probably the most complex of those treated here, embodying notions from the structural sociologist, the group-norm and role oriented social psychologist, and the clinical psychologist.

There has been considerable investigation and speculation about socially prescribed behavior, particularly that which is specific to a given role or position. Linton (29) distinguishes group norms according to whether they are universals for everyone in the culture, alternatives (the individual having a choice as to whether or not to accept them), or specialties (specific to given positions). Whether we speak of internalized norms, role prescriptions and expectations (34), or internalized pressures (15), the fact remains that each individual sees certain regions toward which he should locomote, some regions toward which he should not locomote, and some regions toward which he may locomote if they are generally attractive for him. This applies to specific behaviors in which he may, should, or should not engage; it applies to certain attitudes or beliefs which he may, should, or should not hold. The feeling of "oughtness" may be an internalization from his parents, from his teachers, from his religion, or may have been logically developed from some idiosyncratic system of ethics. He will speak of such behaviors with expressions like "should," "ought to," or "has a right to." In many cases, the original source of the requirement is not recalled.

Though we have oversimplified such evaluations of behavior with a positive-neutral-negative trichotomy, the evaluation of behaviors by the person is really more one of degree. This dimension of evaluation we shall call "legitimacy." Conceptually, we may think of legitimacy as a valence in a region which is induced by some internalized norm or value. This value has the same conceptual property as power, namely an ability to induce force fields (26, 40–41). It may or may not be correct that values (or the superego) are internalized parents, but at least they can set up force fields which have a phenomenal "oughtness" similar to a parent's prescription. Like a value, a need can also induce valences (i.e., force fields) in P's psychological environment, but these valences have more the phenomenal character of noxious or attractive properties of the object or activity. When a need induces a valence in P, for example, when a need makes an object attractive to P, this attraction applies to P but not to other persons. When a value induces a valence, on the other hand, it not only sets up forces on P to engage in the activity, but P may feel that all others ought to behave in the same way. Among other things, this evaluation applies to the legitimate right of some other individual or group to prescribe behavior or beliefs for a person even though the other cannot apply sanctions.

Legitimate power of O/P is here defined as the power which stems from internalized values in P which dictate that O has a legitimate right to influence P and that P has an obligation to accept this influence. We note that legitimate power is very similar to the notion of legitimacy of authority which has long been explored by sociologists, particularly by Weber (41), and more recently by Goldhammer and Shils (14). However, legitimate power is not always a role relation: P may accept an induction from O simply because he had previously promised to help O and he values his word too much to break the promise. In all cases, the notion of legitimacy involves some sort of code or standard, accepted by the individual, by virtue of which the external agent can assert his power. We shall attempt to describe a few of these values here.

Basis for Legitimate Power. Cultural values constitute one common basis for the legitimate power of one individual over another. O has characteristics which are specified by the culture as giving him the right to prescribe behavior for P, who may not have these characteristics. These bases, which Weber (41) has called the authority of the "eternal yesterday," include such things as age, intelligence, caste, and physical characteristics. In some cultures, the aged are granted the right to prescribe behavior for others in practically all behavior areas. In most cultures, there are certain areas of behavior in which a person of one sex is granted the right to prescribe behavior for the other sex.

Acceptance of the social structure is another basis for legitimate power. If P accepts as right the social structure of his group, organization or society, especially the social structure involving a hierarchy of authority, P will accept the legitimate authority of O, who occupies a superior office in the hierarchy. Thus legitimate power in a formal organization is largely a relationship between offices rather than between persons. And the acceptance of an office as *right* is a basis for legitimate power—a judge has a right to levy fines, a foreman should assign work, a priest is justified in prescribing religious beliefs, and it is the management's prerogative to make certain decisions (10). However, legitimate power also involves the perceived right of the person to hold the office.

Designation by a legitimizing agent is a third basis for legitimate power. An influencer O may be seen as legitimate in prescribing behavior for P because he has been granted such power by a legitimizing agent whom P accepts. Thus a department head may accept the authority of his vice-president in a certain area because that authority has been specifically delegated by the president. An election is perhaps the most common example of a group's serving to legitimize the authority of one individual or office for other individuals in the group. The success of such legitimizing depends upon the acceptance of the legitimizing agent and procedure. In this case it depends ultimately on certain democratic values concerning election procedures. The election process is one of legitimizing a person's right to an office which already has a legitimate range of power associated with it.

Range of Legitimate Power of O/P. The areas in which legitimate power may be exercised are generally specified along with the designation of that power. A job description, for example, usually specifies supervisory activities and also designates the person to whom the job-holder is responsible for the duties described. Some bases for legitimate authority carry with them a very broad range. Culturally derived bases for legitimate power are often especially broad. It is not uncommon to find cultures in which a member of a given caste can legitimately prescribe behavior for all members of lower castes in practically all regions. More common, however, are instances of legitimate power where the range is specifically and narrowly prescribed. A sergeant in the army is given a specific set of regions within which he can legitimately prescribe behavior for his men.

The attempted use of legitimate power which is outside of the range of legitimate power will decrease the legitimate power of the authority figure. Such use of power which is not legitimate will also decrease the attractiveness of O (11, 12, 36).

Legitimate Power and Influence. The new state of the system which results from legitimate power usually has high dependence on O though it may become independent. Here, however, the degree of dependence is not related to the level of observability. Since legitimate power is based on P's values, the source of the forces induced by O include both these internal values and O. O's induction serves to activate the values and to relate them to the system which is influenced, but thereafter the new state of the system may become directly dependent on the values with no mediation by O. Accordingly this new state will be relatively stable and consistent across varying environmental situations since P's values are more stable than his psychological environment.

We have used the term legitimate not only as a basis for the power of an agent, but also to describe the general behaviors of a person. Thus, the individual P may also consider the legitimacy of the attempts to use other types of power by O. In certain cases, P will consider that O has a legitimate right to threaten punishment for nonconformity; in other cases, such use of coercion would not be seen as legitimate. P might change in response to coercive power of O, but it will make a considerable difference in his attitude and conformity if O is not seen as having a legitimate right to use such coercion. In such cases, the attraction of P for O will be particularly diminished, and the influence attempt will arouse more resistance (11). Similarly the utilization of reward power may vary in legitimacy; the word "bribe," for example, denotes an illegitimate reward.

Referent Power

The referent power of O/P has its basis in the identification of P with O. By identification, we mean a feeling of oneness of P with O, or a desire for such an identity. If O is a person toward whom P is highly attracted, P will have a desire to become closely associated with O. If O is an attractive group, P will have a feeling of membership or a desire to join. If P is already closely associated with O he will want to maintain this relationship (40). P's identification with O can be established or maintained if P behaves, believes, and perceives as O does. Accordingly O has the ability to influence P, even though P may be unaware of this referent power. A verbalization of such power by P might be, "I am like O, and therefore I shall behave or believe as O does," or "I want to be like O, and I will be more like O if I behave or believe as O does." The stronger the identification of P with O the greater the referent power of O/P.

Similar types of power have already been investigated under a number of different formulations. Festinger (6) points out that in an ambiguous situation the individual seeks some sort of "social reality" and may adopt the cognitive structure of the individual or group with which he identifies. In such a case, the lack of clear structure may be threatening to the individual and the agreement of his beliefs with those of a reference group will both satisfy his need for structure and give him added security through increased identification with his group (16, 19).

We must try to distinguish between referent power and other types of power which might be operative at the same time. If a member is attracted to a group and he conforms to its norms only because he fears ridicule or expulsion from the group for nonconformity, we would call this coercive power. On the other hand if he conforms in order to obtain praise for conformity, it is a case of reward power. The basic criterion for distinguishing referent power from both coercive and reward power is the mediation of the punishment and the reward by O: to the extent that O mediates the sanctions (i.e., has means control over P) we are dealing with coercive and reward power; but to the extent that P avoids discomfort or gains satisfaction by conformity based on identification, regardless of O's responses, we are dealing with referent power. Conformity with majority opinion is sometimes based on a respect for the collective wisdom of the group, in which case it is expert power. It is important to distinguish these phenomena, all grouped together elsewhere as "pressures toward uniformity," since the type of change which occurs will be different for different bases of power.

The concepts of "reference group" (39) and "prestige suggestion" may be treated as instances of referent power. In this case, O, the prestigeful person or group, is valued by P; because P desires to be associated or identified with O, he will assume attitudes or beliefs held by O. Similarly a negative reference group which O dislikes and evaluates negatively may exert negative influence on P as a result of negative referent power.

It has been demonstrated that the power which we designate as referent power is especially great when P is attracted to O (2, 6, 8, 9, 13, 23, 30). In our terms, this would mean that the greater the attraction, the greater the identification, and consequently the greater the referent power. In some cases, attraction or prestige may have a specific basis, and the range of referent power will be limited accordingly: a group of campers may have great referent power over a member regarding campcraft, but considerably less effect on other regions (30). However, we hypothesize that the greater the attraction of P toward O, the broader the range of referent power of O/P.

The new state of a system produced by referent power may be dependent on or independent of O; but the degree of dependence is not affected by the level of observability to O (7, 23). In fact, P is often not consciously aware of the referent power which O exerts over him. There is probably a tendency for some of these dependent changes to become independent of O quite rapidly.

Expert Power

The strength of the expert power of O/P varies with the extent of the knowledge or perception which P attributes to O within a given area. Probably P evaluates O's expertness in relation to his own knowledge as well as against an absolute standard. In any case expert power results in primary social influence on P's cognitive structure and probably not on other types of systems. Of course changes in the cognitive structure can change the direction of forces and hence of locomotion, but such a change of behavior is secondary social influence. Expert power has been demonstrated experimentally (9, 33). Accepting an attorney's advice in legal matters is a common example of expert influence; but there are many instances based on much less knowledge, such as the acceptance by a stranger of directions given by a native villager.

Expert power, where O need not be a member of P's group, is called "informational power" by Deutsch and Gerard (4). This type of expert power must be distinguished from influence based on the content of communication as described by Hovland et al. (17, 18, 23, 24). The influence of the content of a communication upon an opinion is presumably a secondary influence produced after the *primary* influence (i.e., the acceptance of the information). Since power is here defined in terms of the primary changes, the influence of the content on a related opinion is not a case of expert power as we have defined it, but the initial acceptance of the validity of the content does seem to be based on expert power or referent power. In other cases, however, so-called facts may be accepted as self-evident because they fit into P's cognitive structure; if this impersonal acceptance of the truth of the fact is independent of the more-or-less enduring relationship between O and P, then P's acceptance of the fact is not an actualization of expert power. Thus we distinguish between expert power based on the credibility of O and informational influence which is based on characteristics of the stimulus such as the logic of the argument or the "self-evident facts."

Wherever expert influence occurs it seems to be necessary both for P to think that O knows and for P to trust that O is telling the truth (rather than trying to deceive him).

Expert power will produce a new cognitive structure which is initially relatively dependent on O, but informational influence will produce a more independent structure. The former is likely to become more independent with the passage of time. In both cases the degree of dependence on O is not affected by the level of observability.

The "sleeper effect" (18, 24) is an interesting case of change in the degree of dependence of an opinion on O. An unreliable O (who probably had negative referent power but some positive expert power) presented "facts" which were accepted by the subjects and which would normally produce secondary influence on their opinions and beliefs. However, the negative referent power aroused resistance and resulted in negative social influence on their beliefs (i.e., set up a force in the direction opposite to the influence attempt), so that there was little change in the subjects' opinions. With the passage of time, however, the subjects tended to forget the identity of the negative communicator faster than they forgot the contents of his communication, so there was a weakening of the negative referent influence and a consequent delayed positive change in the subjects' beliefs in the direction of the influence attempt ("sleeper effect"). Later, when the identity of the negative communicator was experimentally reinstated, these resisting forces were reinstated, and there was another negative change in belief in a direction opposite to the influence attempt (24).

The range of expert power, we assume, is more delimited than that of referent power. Not only is it restricted to cognitive systems but the expert is seen as having superior knowledge or ability in very specific areas, and his power will be limited to these areas, though some "halo effect" might occur. Recently, some of our renowned physical scientists have found quite painfully that their expert power in physical sciences does not extend to regions involving international politics. Indeed, there is some evidence that the attempted exertion of expert power outside of the range of expert power will reduce that expert power. An undermining of confidence seems to take place.

SUMMARY

We have distinguished five types of power: referent power, expert power, reward power, coercive power, and legitimate power. These distinctions led to the following hypotheses.

1. For all five types, the stronger the basis of power the greater the power.
2. For any type of power the size of the range may vary greatly, but in general referent power will have the broadest range.
3. Any attempt to utilize power outside the range of power will tend to reduce the power.
4. A new state of a system produced by reward power or coercive power will be highly dependent on O, and the more observable P's conformity the more dependent the state. For the other three types of power, the new state is usually dependent, at least in the beginning, but in any case the level of observability has no effect on the degree of dependence.
5. Coercion results in decreased attraction of P toward O and high resistance; reward power results in increased attraction and low resistance.
6. The more legitimate the coercion the less it will produce resistance and decreased attraction.

NOTES

1. The word "system" is here used to refer to a whole or to a part of the whole.

2. The concept of power has the conceptual property of *potentiality*, but it seems useful to restrict this potential influence to more or less enduring power relations between O and P by excluding from the definition of power those cases where the potential influence is so momentary or so changing that it cannot be predicted from the existing relationship. Power is a useful concept for describing social structure only if it has a certain stability over time; it is useless if every momentary social stimulus is viewed as actualizing social power.

3. We define resistance to an attempted induction as a force in the opposite direction which is set up by the same act of O. It must be distinguished from opposition which is

316   *J. R. P. French, Jr., and B. Raven*

defined as existing opposing forces which do not have their source in the same act of O. For example, a boy might resist his mother's order to eat spinach because of the manner of the induction attempt, and at the same time he might oppose it because he didn't like spinach.

4. Miller (32) assumes that all living systems have this character. However, it may be that some systems in the life space do not have this elasticity.

5. Though the primary influence of coercive power is dependent, it often produces secondary changes which are independent. Brainwashing, for example, utilizes coercive power to produce many primary changes in the life space of the prisoner, but these dependent changes can lead to identification with the aggressor and hence to secondary changes in ideology which are independent.

REFERENCES

1. Asch, S. E. *Social Psychology.* New York: Prentice-Hall, 1952.
2. Back, K. "Influence Through Social Communication. *Journal of Abnormal and Social Psychology* 46 (1951): 9–23.
3. Coch, L., and French, J. R. P., Jr. "Overcoming Resistance to Change." *Human Relations* 1 (1948): 512–32.
4. Deutsch, M., and Gerard, H. "A Study of Normative and Informational Influences upon Individual Judgment." *Journal of Abnormal and Social Psychology* 51 (1955): 629–36.
5. Dittes, J., and Kelley, H. "Effects of Different Conditions of Acceptance upon Conformity to Group Norms." *Journal of Abnormal and Social Psychology,* 53 (1956): 629–36.
6. Festinger, L. "Informal Social Communication." *Psychological Review* 57 (1950): 271–52.
7. Festinger, L. "An Analysis of Complaint Behavior." In M. Sherif and M. O. Wilson, eds., *Group Relations at the Crossroads.* New York: Harper, 1953, pp. 232–50.
8. Festinger, L., Schachter, S., and Back, K. *Social Pressures in Informal Groups.* New York: Harper, 1950, Chap. 5.
9. Festinger, L., et al. "The Influence Process in the Presence of Extreme Deviates." *Human Relations,* 5 (1952): 327–46.
10. French, J. R. P., Jr., Israel, J., and Ås, D. *Arbeidernes medvirkning i industribedriften: En eksperimentell undersøkelse.* Oslo, Norway: Institute for Social Research, 1957.
11. French, J. R. P., Jr., Morrison, H. W., and Levinger, G. "Coercive Power and Forces Affecting Conformity." *Journal of Abnormal and Social Psychology* 61 (1960): 93–101.
12. Raven, B., and French, J. R. P., Jr. "Legitimate Power, Coercive Power, and Observability in Social Influence. *Sociometry* 21 (1958): 83–97.
13. Gerard, H. "The Anchorage of Opinions in Face-to-face Groups. *Human Relations* 7 (1954): 313–25.
14. Goldhammer, H., and Shils, E. "Types of Power and Status." *American Journal of Sociology* 45 (1939): 171–78.

15. Herbst, P. "Analysis and Measurement of a Situation." *Human Relations* 2 (1953): 113–40.
16. Hochbaum, G. "Self-confidence and Reactions to Group Pressures." *American Sociological Review* 19 (1954): 678–87.
17. Hovland, G., Lumsdaine, A., and Sheffield, F. *Experiments on Mass Communication*. Princeton, N. J.: Princeton Univ. Press, 1949.
18. Hovland, C., and Weiss, W. "The Influence of Source Credibility on Communication Effectiveness." *Public Opinion Quarterly* 15 (1951): 635–50.
19. Jackson, J., and Saltzstein, H. "The Effective of Person-Group Relationships on Conformity Processes." *Journal of Abnormal and Social Psychology* 57 (1958): 17–24.
20. Jahoda, M. "Psychological Issues in Civil Liberties." *The American Psychologist* 11 (1956): 234–40.
21. Katz, D., and Schank, R. *Social Psychology*. New York: Wiley, 1938.
22. Kelly, H., and Volkart, E. "The Resistance to Change of Group-anchored Attitudes." *American Sociological Review* 17 (1952): 153–65.
23. Kelman, H. "Three Processes of Acceptance of Social Influence: Compliance, Identification, and Internalization." Paper read at the meetings of the American Psychological Association, August 1956.
24. Kelman, H., and Hovland, C. "Reinstatement of the Communicator in Delayed Measurement of Opinion Change." *Journal of Abnormal and Social Psychology* 48 (1953): 327–35.
25. Lewin, K. *Dynamic Theory of Personality*. New York: McGraw-Hill, 1935. Pp. 114–70.
26. Lewin, K. *Field Theory in Social Science*. New York: Harper, 1951.
27. Lewin, K., Lippitt, R., and White, R. K. "Patterns of Aggressive Behavior in Experimentally Created Social Climates." *Journal of Social Psychology* 10 (1939): 271–301.
28. Lasswell, H., and Kaplan, A., *Power and Society: A Framework for Political Inquiry*. New Haven, Conn.: Yale University Press, 1950.
29. Linton, R. *The Cultural Background of Personality*. New York: Appleton-Century-Crofts, 1945.
30. Lippitt, R. et al. "The Dynamics of Power." *Human Relations* 5 (1952): 37–64.
31. March, J. "An Introduction to the Theory of Measurement of Influence." *American Political Science Review* 49 (1955): 431–51.
32. Miller, J. "Toward a General Theory for the Behavioral Sciences." *The American Psychologist* 10 (1955): 513–31.
33. Moore, H. "The Comparative Influence of Majority and Expert Opinion." *American Journal of Psychology* 32 (1921): 16–20.
34. Newcomb, T. *Social Psychology*. New York: Dryden, 1950.
35. Raven, B. "Social Influence on Opinions and the Communication of Related Content." *Journal of Abnormal and Social Psychology* 58 (1959): 119–28.
36. Raven, B., and French, J. "Group Support, Legitimate Power, and Social Influence." *Journal of Personality*, 26 (1958): 400–09.
37. Rommetveit, R. *Social Norms and Roles*. Minneapolis: University of Minnesota Press, 1953.
38. Russell, B. *Power: A New Social Analysis*. New York: Norton, 1938.
39. Swanson, G., Newcomb, T., and Hartley, E. *Readings in Social Psychology*. New York: Holt, 1952.

40. Torrance, E., and Mason, R. "Instructor Effort to Influence: An Experimental Evaluation of Six Approaches." Paper presented at USAF-NRC Symposium on Personnel, Training, and Human Engineering, Washington, D.C., 1956.
41. Weber, M. *The Theory of Social and Economic Organization.* Oxford: Oxford University Press, 1947.

31

TALCOTT PARSONS

Types of Influence

W E may now approach the problem of classification of types or modes of influence. Here is it essential to bear in mind that the influence system is not a closed system. On the one hand, of course, it is used to get consent to particular attitudes and opinions that are to influence what particular commodities and services are to money. In this sense, we may think of influence as a "circulating" medium. To get consent, an "opinion leader" must expend some of his influence. He must therefore carefully husband it by choosing the occasions on which to intervene and the appropriate mode of intervention. The classic type of thriftless expenditure is illustrated by the nursery story about the repetition of the cry, "Wolf! Wolf!" so that when the wolf actually came, the warning was not believed. This is to say that by wasting his influence, the author of the cry had lost his influence, that is, his capacity to convince.

The circulating character of influence as a medium can be brought out more clearly if we break it down into types, since in each context it is easier to identify the nature of the flow in both ways than if it is treated on the more general level. I should like to suggest the following tentative classification: (1) "political" influence, (2) "fiduciary" influence, (3) influence through appeal to differential loyalties, and (4) influence oriented to the interpretation of norms. The fact that, in order to characterize the last two types, it is necessary to resort to cumbrous phrases rather than succinct single-word designations indicates clearly that the subject is rather underdeveloped and needs elucidation. An important guide line for inter-

From Talcott Parsons, *Politics and Social Structure* (New York: The Free Press, 1969), pp. 419–26. Reprinted with permission of The Free Press, a division of Macmillan, Inc. Copyright © 1969 by The Free Press.

preting the first three types lies in the convertibility of each with one of the other three types of generalized media we have discussed.

1. When speaking of political influence, I mean it in an analytical sense, but one in which there is a directly significant relation between influence and power. The prototypical structural context is that of the democratic association, whether it be in the field of government at any one of several levels, or of private associations. The democratic association is characterized by a structure of offices the incumbents of which are authorized to take certain decisions binding on the collectivity as a whole and, hence, on its members in their respective capacities.[1] Such authorization is for action defined within constitutional norms, and there are also constitutional procedures by which incumbents of office are chosen, summed up as election and appointment.

The making of decisions binding on a collectivity I interpret to be an exercise of power, which includes the exercise of the franchise in the electoral procedure, since it is the aggregate of votes which determines who is elected to office. But both in seeking election and in office, officers and candidates are continually using other ways of getting the results they want besides the use of power in a strict sense. They are, of course, giving information and announcing intentions, in the detailed sense. They may well be offering inducements, making coercive threats outside the context of the power of office, and activating their own and others' commitments. But they are, above all, operating with influence, in our technical sense.

There are, as I conceive it, two main contexts in which this is the case. Because associations are typically differentiated on the axis of leadership-followership, we may use this axis here. One focus of influence, then, is the establishment of leadership position or reputation, either as incumbent of office or as explicit or implicit candidate, so that, for the followership in question, there will be a basis of trust going beyond the direct exercise of power, the giving of specific information and the like, and also beyond the manipulation of inducements, informal threats, etc. A leader, I suggest, must try to establish a basis on which he is trusted by a "constituency," in the symbolic sense of this discussion, so that when he "takes a position," he can count on a following "going along with him" on it, or even actively working for its implementation according to their respective capacities and roles. We often put this by saying that a leader "takes responsibility" for such positions. In any case, I would treat the concept of leadership as focusing on the use of influence, and the concept of office, on the use of power.

The other context is the obverse, that of the processes by which units not in a leadership position in the relevant respects can have and use influence oriented to having an effect on leadership. This is by and large the well-known field of "interest groups," very broadly in the sense of parts of the constituencies of parties and officeholders. The influence may be used in electoral processes, trying to establish terms on which electoral support—a form of power—will be given. Or, it may play on incumbents of office by trying to influence their decisions of policy. In either case, it is the use of a basis of presumptive "trust" and, hence, "right to speak" to try to swing a balance in favor of what the influencer advocates—or opposes—relative to alternatives, whether these be candidates or policies.

Political influence, then, we would conceive as influence operating in the context of the goal-functioning of collectivities, as generalized persuasion without power—i.e., independent of the use of power or direct threat,[2]—used, on the one hand, by units either exercising or bidding for leadership position and, on the other, by nonleaders seeking to have an effect on the decisions and orientations of leaders. Though political influence is analytically independent of power, we conceive the two to be closely interconnected. Very generally, leaders expect a major share of their influence to be translated into binding support, particularly through the franchise, and constituents in turn expect an important part of theirs to be translated into binding decisions congenial to them. But the independence of influence from power means that the influence system is an open one. To tie it to power in direct, matching terms would be to reduce the power-influence relation to a barter basis, and thus destroy the element of symbolic generalization we have treated as essential.

2. The second type of influence suggested has been called "fiduciary." The relevant context here is not the effective determination of an attainment of collective goals, but the allocation of resources in a system where both collectives and their goals are plural and the justification of each among the plural goals is problematical. The interests in control of resources and in attainment of goals are the classical instances of the operation of "interests" in social systems. In a more or less pluralistic system, the allocation of resources must, however, be subject to normative control; distribution must be justified by reference to norms more general than the mere desirability to the unit in question of getting what it wants. Furthermore, resources constitute, from the point of view of goal attainment, the principal opportunity factor that conditionally controls prospects of success. Hence, influence bearing on the allocation of resources is a particularly important field of trust.

There is a relation to money in this case which is in certain respects parallel to that to power in the case of political influence. This derives from the fact that, in a society in which the economy is highly differentiated relative to other elements of the social structure, money becomes the most inportant allocative mechanism, not only over commodities, but over human services. Hence, the focus of the fiduciary function is in the allocation of funds, because the professor of funds is in turn in a position to claim, through market channels, control over the indicated share of "real" resources.

The interchanges we have in mind here do not constitute the use of money as a circulating medium, but rather as a measure of value. On the monetary side, an example is setting up a budget. The various interests that expect to share in a budget "assert their claims," and the budget-making agency reaches some kind of allocative ranking of these claims. This is the expression of need and of "right" in monetary terms. But both claims and accession of right in turn are subject to standards of justification, in our technical sense. These are never assertions of value as such, because the agency, dealing as it does with scarce and allocable resources, must always consider situational exigency and competing claims. It operates, that is, at the level of norms, not of values. Those who assert claims may concretely, of course, use power to gain them; they may use inducements—in the extreme case, bribery—or various other means. But a special role is played by influence. A good example would be, in budgetary negotiations, the assertion of a highly qualified and trustworthy technical expert that to fulfill expectations he must have a certain specific minimum of resources at his disposal—an assertion that a budgetary officer, not himself an expert in the field, will find it difficult to contest. On the other hand, decisions of allocation in turn must be justified by reference to agreed standards of proper priority in claims. Such standards, of course, are likely to be made most explicit where there is an unaccustomed stringency of resources and hence sacrifices must be justified. Just as the budgetary officer is often unable to judge the needs of the technical expert, so the latter, operating only in one specialized sector of the system, is not qualified to judge the urgency of the claims competing with his own. Hence the necessity for mutual influence to operate to cover this gap.

The case of a budget is the neatest case, because the relevant system is more or less closed by unitary organizational control of the resources and by power, in the strict sense, to make the allocative decisions binding. The same basic principles, however, apply in processes of allocation through free market channels. The economist's ideal of free competition is here the limiting case in which influence as an independent factor disappears. Here, then, it is in two areas that influence is most obviously operative. One is the establishment of norms by which the allocative process is regulated, as through tax legislation and the like; the other is through such modifications of "pure" market process as the involvement of voluntary contributions in allocations. The very term "fiduciary" is also most generally used for cases where certain "interested parties" cannot be expected to protect their interests without help, for example, administration of the property interests of minors by "trustees," i.e., people who can be trusted to apply acceptable standards even though their actions are not dictated by personal financial interest.

3. The third category has been called "influence through appeal to differential loyalties." Whereas in the political influence case the differentiation on the axis of leadership was the central structural focus, and in the fiduciary influence case it was the problem of allocation of scarce resources, in this case it is the pluralistic structure of memberships in society. This operates at the level both of individuals in roles and of collectives. The more highly differentiated the society is structurally, the more every concrete unit is a responsible member of a plurality of collectivities.[3] He is therefore in a position of having to balance the claims of these plural collectives on his loyalties, i.e., a class of his normative commitments.

For the individual, particularly the adult male, the most important case is normally the relation between kinship and occupation, since for most men it is essential to participate in both, and in modern societies they are structurally independent of each other. Generally, in a reasonably stable situation, the broad lines of allocation of obligation are institutionally settled, but there are always areas of indeterminacy and of shift in the light of changing circumstances. Moreover, our society is rapidly changing, and one of the principal aspects of such change is the rise of new collectives, and hence loyalties to them, and the decline of old ones. A large part of the population is thus faced with decisions about whether to take on new commitments or to sacrifice old ones, or both, or to shift balances among loyalties.

The commitments we have in mind are grounded in institutionalized values, which can, for purposes of analysis, be presumed to be shared by members of a society. But it is in the nature of a differentiated society that there is an important difference between asserting, however sincerely, the desirability of a value and, on the other hand, taking personal responsibility for its implementation, since the capacities and opportunities of units for effective contribution are inherently limited, and, moreover, such kinds of attempt would infringe the prerogatives of other units. It is with this problem that the present type of influence is concerned. It is a matter of the justification of assuming particular responsibilities in particular collectivity and subcollectivity contexts.

A person, then, will be faced by manifold demands for commitment through participation in collectivities, and will often be put in a position of having to justify the allocative decisions he makes. The normative structure (of "commitments") governing such processes then involves, on the one hand, appeals to common values and, on the other, assertion of norms governing the practical decisions of allocation of commitment among plural loyalties. The categories of influence, then, are, first, the plea that an actor ought, as a practical matter, to undertake such and such a collective responsibility (not merely that it is desirable that the function be effectively performed independently of *his* commitment; that is an assertion of its value), and second, the assertion of the norms it is held should govern such decisions, again at the level of practical allocation.

In one sense, this, like the last category of influence, concerns the allocation of "resources." But what I am here referring to as loyalties are not the same kind of resource as money and power, or the concrete utilities and modes of effectiveness controlled by them. From the point of view of the unit, the question is not with what means he will implement his commitments, but *whether he will undertake the commitment in the first place.* It is not, given that he "intends" to do something, a question of *how* he is to accomplish it, but rather whether he *ought*—in our sense of justification—to undertake it at all. Commitments in this sense surely constitute a societal resource, but, in the analysis of unit action, they concern the "orientational" side, not the situational side, of the action paradigm.[4]

As noted earlier in this paper, I consider generalized commitments to constitute a symbolic medium operating on the interaction process in the same basic sense that money, power, and influence do. Any promise by which the actor forecloses certain alternatives may be regarded as a *particular* commitment. By invoking a *generalized* commitment, however, the actor is enabled to command a series of more particular commitments, to be in a position to "activate" them in response to appropriate circumstances, as we have said above. A good example is securing the acceptance of a job offer. Commitment to the job by the prospective employee then entails a commitment to perform a complex series of more particular acts as occasion arises, including commitment to accept certain types of authority within the organization.

Being grounded in values, generalized commitments in some sense involve the "honor" of the actors concerned, the more so the more generalized they are. They therefore cannot in general be altered lightly. Nevertheless, in a pluralistic and changing society, complete rigidity of commitments would introduce an intolerable rigidity into this structure. Commitments must therefore involve priority scales of seriousness, i.e., be referred to general standards, and there must be norms defining the situations in which particular commitments may be changed, not only new ones assumed but also old ones abandoned, even where this means the breaking of promises made and accepted in good faith. A good example here is the general norm that even in occupations where rules of tenure bind the employing organization, incumbents of such positions are generally considered entitled to resign subject only to giving "reasonable" notice. The category of influence with which we are now concerned operates in this range of flexibility of commitments and concerns the relation between the justification for change and the more generalized loyalties to fulfillment of commitments made.

4. The three types of influence so far discussed deal with the relations of the normative or integrative system to the other primary functional subsystems of the society, namely, what I should call the "polity," the "economy," and the "pattern maintenance" (in a structural aspect, the value maintenance) systems respectively.[5] The fourth and final type, which was referred to as influence oriented to the interpretation of norms, is internal to the integrative system. Here the prototype is the process of interpretation of legal norms in the appellate phase of the judicial process.

Since norms mediate between value commitments and particular interests and situational exigencies, they are, in formulation, in need of continual adjustment to the variations at these levels. Furthermore, since their primary function in the social system is integrative, the problem of consistency is a particularly important one. Hence, in a complex system of normative regulation, the interpretive function is highly important. A category of influence is organized about it of which the best example is the influence involved in the reputations of judges and lawyers. As in so many other fields, substantive arguments, i.e., particular justifications, of course play a central part. But there is the same need for symbolic generalization here as in the other fields. Another type of example of interpretive influence would be in the field of exegesis of ethical norms, which plays such an important part in many religious traditions.

This has been an exceedingly sketchy and tentative attempt to review a typology of the different contexts of the operation of influence. All, I think, are fields in which the general themes of the above analysis can be illustrated in sufficiently well-known terms to carry conviction of the reality and importance of the phenomena here called "influence." Let me reiterate that the critical common fact is a mechanism of persuasion that is generalized beyond appeal to particular facts, particular intentions, particular obligations and commitments, particular normative rules. The general suggestion is that, in the absence of a ramified system of influence in this sense, there would either be a much more pervasive atmosphere of distrust than in fact obtains, or the level of trust could be raised only by introducing more rigid specification as to who could be trusted in what specific ways, which would greatly limit the ranges of flexibility so important to a complex society.

NOTES

1. Of course, for this analysis to be relevant, the association in question need not be "fully" democratic, but this problem of ranges in degrees of democracy need not concern the present very limited discussion.

2. Incumbents of office, though they have power, are often very careful when pleading for certain measures to make clear that they will directly bring their power to bear in the particular case. A good example is when officeholders who are adherents of a particular party lend their influence to strictly nonpartisan causes. Thus a state governor who is a good Republic may plead for *all* the people, regardless of party, to contribute generously to the Red Cross campaign.

3. For the collectivity as unit the relevant membership is that in more inclusive collectivities; e.g., a department is a subcollectivity in a university faculty.

4. Cf. Talcott Parsons, "Pattern Variables Revisited," *American Sociological Review* 25 (1960): 467–83, and *Sociological Theory and Modern Society* (New York: Free Press, 1967), chapter 7, for an elucidation of this essential distinction.

5. This refers to a generalized paradigm of analysis in terms of four functional categories, elaborated more fully, for example, in the General Introduction to *Theories of Society* (Glencoe, Ill.: Free Press, 1961) and in "Pattern Variables Revisited," as cited.

32

IRVING L. JANIS

Groupthink

ACCORDING to the groupthink hypothesis, members of any small cohesive group tend to maintain esprit de corps by unconsciously developing a number of shared illusions and related norms that interfere with critical thinking and reality testing. If the available accounts describe the deliberations accurately, typical illusions can be discerned among the members of the Kennedy team during the period when they were deciding whether to approve the CIA's [plan to invade Cuba].

THE ILLUSION OF INVULNERABILITY

An important symptom of groupthink is the illusion of being invulnerable to the main dangers that might arise from a risky action in which the group is strongly tempted to engage. Essentially, the notion is that "If our leader and everyone else in our group decides that it is okay, the plan is bound to succeed. Even if it is quite risky, luck will be on our side." A sense of "unlimited confidence" was widespread among the "New Frontiersmen" as soon as they took over their high government posts, according to a Justice Department confidant, with whom Robert Kennedy discussed the secret CIA plan on the day it was launched:

> It seemed that, with John Kennedy leading us and with all the talent he had assembled, *nothing could stop us.* We believed that if we faced up to the nation's problems and applied bold, new ideas with common sense and hard work, we would overcome whatever challenged us.

From Irving L. Janis, *Groupthink* (Boston: Houghton Mifflin, 1982), pp. 35–47, 281–83. Reprinted by permission of Houghton Mifflin Company. Copyright 1982.

That this attitude was shared by the members of the President's inner circle is indicated by Schlesinger's statement that the men around Kennedy had enormous confidence in his ability and luck: "Everything had broken right for him since 1956. He had won the nomination and the election against all the odds in the book. Everyone around him thought he had the Midas touch and could not lose." Kennedy and his principal advisers were sophisticated and skeptical men, but they were, nevertheless, "affected by the euphoria of the new day." During the first three months after he took office—despite growing concerns created by the emerging crisis in Southeast Asia, the gold drain, and the Cuban exiles who were awaiting the go-ahead signal to invade Cuba—the dominant mood in the White House, according to Schlesinger, was "buoyant optimism." It was centered on the "promise of hope" held out by the President: *"Euphoria reigned; we thought for a moment that the world was plastic and the future unlimited."*

All the characteristic manifestations of group euphoria—the buoyant optimism, the leader's great promise of hope, and the shared belief that the group's accomplishments could make "the future unlimited"—are strongly reminiscent of the thoughts and feelings that arise among members of many different types of groups during the phase when the members become cohesive. At such a time, the members become somewhat euphoric about their newly acquired "we-feeling"; they share a sense of belonging to a powerful, protective group that in some vague way opens up new potentials for each of them. Often there is boundless admiration of the group leader.

Once this euphoric phase takes hold, decision-making for everyday activities, as well as long-range planning, is likely to be seriously impaired. The members of a cohesive group become very reluctant to carry out the unpleasant task of critically assessing the limits of their power and the real losses that could arise if their luck does not hold. They tend to examine each risk in black and white terms. If it does not seem overwhelmingly dangerous, they are inclined simply to forget about it, instead of developing contingency plans in case it materializes. The group members know that no one among them is a superman, but they feel that somehow the group is a supergroup, capable of surmounting all risks that stand in the way of carrying out any desired course of action: "Nothing can stop us!" Athletic teams and military combat units may often benefit from members' enthusiastic confidence in the power and luck of their group. But policy-making committees usually do not.

We would not expect sober government officials to experience such exuberant esprit de corps, but a subdued form of the same tendency may have been operating—inclining the President's advisers to become reluctant about examining the drawbacks of the invasion plan. In group meetings, this groupthink tendency can operate like a low-level noise that prevents warning signals from being heeded. Everyone becomes somewhat biased in the direction of selectively attending to the messages that feed into the members' shared feelings of confidence and optimism, disregarding those that do not.

When a cohesive group of executives is planning a campaign directed against a rival or enemy group, their discussions are likely to contain two themes, which embody the groupthink tendency to regard the group as invulnerable: (1) "We are a strong group of good guys who will win in the end." (2) "Our opponents are stupid, weak, bad guys." It is impressive to see how closely the six false assumptions fit these two themes.[1] The notion running through the assumptions is the overoptimistic expectation that "we can pull off this invasion, even though it is a long-shot gamble." The policy advisers were probably unaware of how much they were relying on shared rationalizations in order to appraise the highly risky venture as a safe one. Their overoptimistic outlook would have been rudely shaken if they had allowed their deliberations to focus on the potentially devastating consequences of the obvious drawbacks of the plan, such as the disparity in size between Castro's military forces of two hundred thousand and the small brigade of fourteen hundred exiles. In a sense, this difference made the odds against their long-shot gamble 200,000 to 1,400 (over 140 to 1).

When discussing the misconceptions that led to the decision to approve the CIA's plan, Schlesinger emphasizes the gross underestimation of the enemy. Castro was regarded as a weak "hysteric" leader whose army was ready to defect; he was considered so stupid that "although warned by air strikes, he would do nothing to neutralize the Cuban underground." This is a stunning example of the classical stereotype of the enemy as weak and ineffectual.

In a concurrence-seeking group, there is relatively little healthy skepticism of the glib ideological formulas on which rational policy-makers, like many other people who share their nationalistic goals, generally rely in order to maintain self-confidence and cognitive mastery over the complexities of international politics. One of the symptoms of groupthink is the members' persistence in conveying to each other the cliché and oversimplified images of political enemies embodied in long-standing ideological stereotypes. Throughout their deliberations they use the same old stereotypes, instead of developing differentiated concepts derived from an open-minded inquiry enabling them to discern which of their original ideological ssumptions, if any, apply to the foreign policy issue at hand. Except in unusual circumstances of crisis, the members of a concurrence-seeking group tend to view any antagonistic out-group against whom they are plotting not only as immoral but also as weak and stupid. These wishful beliefs continue to dominate their thinking until an unequivocal defeat proves otherwise, whereupon—like Kennedy and his advisers—they are shocked at the discrepancy between their stereotyped conceptions and actuality.

A subsidiary theme, which also involved a strong dose of wishful thinking, was contained in the Kennedy group's notion that "we can get away with our clever cover story." When the daily newspapers were already demonstrating that this certainly was not so, the undaunted members of the group evidently replaced the original assumption with the equally overoptimistic expectation that "anyhow, the non-Communist nations of the world will side with us. After all, we *are* the good guys."

Overoptimistic expectations about the power of their side and the weakness of the opponents probably enable members of a group to enjoy a sense of low vulnerability to the effects of any decision that entails risky action against an enemy. In order to maintain this complacent outlook, each member must think that everyone else in the group agrees that the risks can be safely ignored.[2]

THE ILLUSION OF UNANIMITY

When a group of people who respect each other's opinions arrive at a unanimous view, each member is likely to feel that the belief must be true. This reliance on consensual validation tends to replace individual critical thinking and reality-testing, unless there are clear-cut disagreements among the members. The members of a face-to-face group often become inclined, without quite realizing it, to prevent latent disagreements from surfacing when they are about to initiate a risky course of action. The group leader and the members support each other, playing up the areas of convergence in their thinking, at the expense of fully exploring divergences that might disrupt the apparent unity of the group. Better to share a pleasant, balmy group atmosphere than to be battered in a storm.

This brings us to the second outstanding symptom of groupthink manifested by the Kennedy team—a shared illusion of unanimity. In the formal sessions dealing with the Cuban invasion plan, the group's consensus that the basic features of the CIA plan should be adopted was relatively free of disagreement.

According to Sorensen, "No strong voice of opposition was raised in any of the key meetings, and no realistic alternatives were presented." According to Schlesinger, "the massed and caparisoned authority of his senior officials in the realm of foreign policy and defense was unanimous for going ahead. . . . Had one senior advisor opposed the adventure, I believe that Kennedy would have canceled it. No one spoke against it."

Perhaps the most crucial of Schlesinger's observations is, "Our meetings took place in a *curious atmosphere of assumed consensus.*" His additional comments clearly show that the assumed consensus was an illusion that could be maintained only because the major participants did not reveal their own reasoning or discuss their idiosyncratic assumptions and vague reservations. President Kennedy thought that prime consideration was being given to his prohibition of direct military intervention by the United States. He assumed that the operation had been pared down to a kind of unobtrusive infiltration that, if reported in the newspapers, would be buried in the inside pages. Rusk was certainly not on the same wavelength as the President, for at one point he suggested that it might be better to have the invaders fan out from the United States naval base at Guantánamo, rather than land at the Bay of Pigs, so that they could readily retreat to the base if necessary. Implicit in his suggestion was a lack of concern about revealing United States military support as well as implicit distrust in the assumption made by the others about the ease of escaping from the Bay of Pigs. But discussion of Rusk's strange proposal was evidently dropped long before he was induced to reveal whatever vague misgivings he may have had about the Bay of Pigs plan. At meetings in the State Department, according to Roger Hilsman, who worked closely with him, "Rusk asked penetrating questions that frequently caused us to reexamine our position." But at the White House meetings Rusk said little except to offer gentle warnings about avoiding excesses.

As usually happens in cohesive groups, the members assumed that "silence gives consent." Kennedy and the others supposed that Rusk was in substantial agreement with what the CIA representatives were saying about the soundness of the invasion plan. But about one week before the invasion was scheduled, when Schlesinger told Rusk in private about his objections to the plan, Rusk, surprisingly, offered no arguments against Schlesinger's objections. He said that he had been wanting for some time to draw up a balance sheet of the pros and cons and that he was annoyed at the Joint Chiefs because "they are perfectly willing to put the President's head on the block, but they recoil at doing anything which might risk Guantánamo." At that late date, he evidently still preferred his suggestion to launch the invasion from the United States naval base in Cuba, even though doing so would violate President Kennedy's stricture against involving America's armed forces.

McNamara's assumptions about the invasion were quite different from both Rusk's and Kennedy's. McNamara thought that the main objective was to touch off a revolt of the Cuban people to overthrow Castro. The members of the group who knew something about Cuban politics and Castro's popular support must have had strong doubts about this assumption. Why did they fail to convey their misgivings at any of the meetings?

SUPPRESSION OF PERSONAL DOUBTS

The sense of group unity concerning the advisability of going ahead with the CIA's invasion plan appears to have been based on superficial appearances of complete concurrence, achieved at the cost of self-censorship of misgivings by several of the members. From post-mortem discussions with participants, Sorensen concluded that among the men in the State Department, as well as those on the White House staff, "doubts were entertained but never pressed, partly out of a fear of being labelled 'soft' or undaring in the eyes of their colleagues." Schlesinger was not at all hesitant about presenting his strong objections in a memorandum he gave to the President and the Secretary of State. But he became keenly aware of his tendency to suppress objections when he attended the White House meetings of the Kennedy team, with their atmosphere of assumed consensus:

> In the months after the Bay of Pigs I bitterly reproached myself for having kept so silent during those crucial discussions in the Cabinet Room, though my feelings of guilt were tempered by the knowledge that a course of objection would have accomplished little save to *gain me a name as a nuisance*. I can only explain my failure to do more than raise a few timid questions by reporting that one's impulse to blow the whistle on this nonsense was simply undone by the *circumstances of the discussion*.

Whether or not his retrospective explanation includes all his real reasons for having remained silent, Schlesinger appears to have been quite aware of the need to refrain from saying anything that would create a nuisance by breaking down the assumed consensus.[3]

Participants in the White House meetings, like members of many other discussion groups, evidently felt reluctant to raise questions that might cast doubt on a plan that they thought was accepted by the consensus of the group, for fear of evoking disapproval from their associates. This type of fear is probably not the same as fear of losing one's effectiveness or damaging one's career. Many forthright men who are quite willing to speak their piece despite risks to their career become silent when faced with the possibility of losing the approval of fellow members of their primary work group. The discrepancy between Schlesinger's critical memoranda and his silent acquiescence during the meetings might be an example of this.

Schlesinger says that when the Cuban invasion plan was being presented to the group, "virile poses" were conveyed in the rhetoric used by the representatives of the CIA and Joint Chiefs of Staff. He thought the State Department representatives and others responded by becoming anxious to show that they were not softheaded idealists but really were just as tough as the military men. Schlesinger's references to the "virile" stance of the militant advocates of the invasion plan suggest that the members of Kennedy's in-group may have been concerned about protecting the leader from being embarrassed by their voicing "unvirile" concerns about the high risks of the venture.

At the meetings, the members of Kennedy's inner circle who wondered whether the military venture might prove to be a failure or whether the political consequences might be damaging to the United States must have had only mild misgivings, not strong enough to overcome the social obstacles that would make arguing openly against the plan slightly uncomfortable. By and large, each of them must have felt reasonably sure that the plan was a safe one, that at worst the United States would not lose anything from trying it. They contributed, by their silence, to the lack of critical thinking in the group's deliberations.

SELF-APPOINTED MINDGUARDS

Among the well-known phenomena of group dynamics is the alacrity with which members of a cohesive in-group suppress deviational points of view by putting social pressure on any member who begins to express a view that deviates from the dominant beliefs of the group, to make sure that he will not disrupt the consensus of the group as a whole. This pressure often takes the form of urging the dissident member to remain silent if he cannot match up his own beliefs with those of the rest of the group. At least one dramatic instance of this type of pressure occurred a few days after President Kennedy had said, "we seem now destined to go ahead on a quasi-minimum basis." This was still several days before the final decision was made.

At a large birthday party for his wife, Robert Kennedy, who had been constantly informed about the Cuban invasion plan, took Schlesinger aside and asked him why he was opposed. The President's brother listened coldly and then said, "You may be right or you may be wrong, but the President has made his mind up. Don't push it any further. Now is the time for everyone to help him all they can." Here is another symptom of groupthink, displayed by a highly intelligent man whose ethical code committed him to freedom of dissent. What he was saying, in effect, was, "You may well be right about the dangerous risks, but I don't give a damn about that; all of us should help our leader right now by not sounding any discordant notes that would interfere with the harmonious support he should have."

When Robert Kennedy told Schlesinger to lay off, he was functioning in a self-appointed role that I call being a "mindguard." Just as a bodyguard protects the President and other high officials from injurious physical assaults, a mindguard protects them from thoughts that might damage their confidence in the soundness of the policies to which they are committed or to which they are about to commit themselves.

At least one member of the Kennedy team, Secretary of State Rusk, also effectively functioned as a mindguard, protecting the leader and the members from unwelcome ideas that might set them to thinking about unfavorable consequences of their preferred course of action and that might lead to dissension instead of a comfortable consensus. Undersecretary of State Chester Bowles, who had attended a White House meeting at which he was given no opportunity to express his dissenting views, decided not to continue to remain silent about such a vital matter. He prepared a strong memorandum for Secretary Rusk opposing the CIA plan and, keeping well within the prescribed bureaucratic channels, requested Rusk's permission to present his case to the President. Rusk told Bowles that there was no need for any concern, that the invasion plan would be dropped in favor of a quiet little guerrilla infiltration. Rusk may have believed this at the time, but at subsequent White House meetings he must soon have learned otherwise. Had Rusk transmitted the undersecretary's memorandum, the urgent warnings it contained might have reinforced Schlesinger's memorandum and jolted some of Kennedy's in-group, if not Kennedy himself, to reconsider the decision. But Rusk kept Bowles' memorandum firmly buried in the State Department files.

Rusk may also have played a similar role in preventing Kennedy and the others from learning about the strong objections raised by Edward R. Murrow, whom the President had just appointed director of the United States Information Agency. In yet another instance, Rusk appears to have functioned as a dogged mindguard, protecting the group from the oppos-ing ideas of a government official with access to information that could have enabled him to assess the political consequences of the Cuban invasion better than anyone present at the White House meetings could. As director of intelligence and research in the State Department, Roger Hilsman got wind of the invasion plan from his colleague Allen Dulles and strongly warned Secretary Rusk of the dangers. He asked Rusk for permission to allow the Cuban experts in his department to scrutinize thoroughly the assumptions relevant to their expertise. "I'm sorry," Rusk told him, "but I can't let you. This is being too tightly held." Rusk's reaction struck Hilsman as strange because all the relevant men in his department already had top security clearance. Hilsman assumed that Rusk turned down his urgent request because of pressure from Dulles and Bissell to adhere to the CIA's special security restrictions. But if so, why, when so much was at stake, did the Secre-tary of State fail to communicate to the President or to anyone else in the core group that his most trusted intelligence expert had grave doubts about the invasion plan and felt that it should be appraised by the Cuban specialists? As a result of Rusk's handling of Hilsman's request, the President and his advisers remained in the curious posi-tion, as Hilsman put it, of making an important political judgment without the benefit of advice from the government's most relevant intelligence experts.

Taking account of the mindguard functions performed by the Attorney General and the Secretary of State, together with the President's failure to allow time for discussion of the few oppositional viewpoints that occasionally did filter into the meetings, we surmise that some form of collusion was going on. That is to say, it seems plausible to infer that the leading civilian members of the Kennedy team colluded—perhaps unwittingly—to protect the proposed plan from critical scrutiny by them-selves and by any of the government's experts.

DOCILITY FOSTERED BY SUAVE LEADERSHIP

The group pressures that help to maintain a group's illusions are some-times fostered by various leadership practices, some of which involve subtle ways of making it difficult for those who question the initial con-sensus to suggest alternatives and to raise critical issues. The group's agenda can readily be manipulated by a suave leader, often with the tacit approval of the members, so that there is simply no opportunity to discuss the drawbacks of a seemingly satisfactory plan of action. This is one of the conditions that fosters groupthink.

President Kennedy, as leader at the meetings in the White House, was probably more active than anyone else in raising skeptical questions; yet he seems to have encouraged the group's docility and uncritical acceptance of the defective arguments in favor of the CIA's plan. At each meeting, instead of opening up the agenda to permit a full airing of the opposing considerations, he allowed the CIA representatives to dominate the entire discussion. The President permitted them to refute immedi-ately each tentative doubt that one of the others might express, instead of asking whether anyone else had the same doubt or wanted to pursue the implications of the new worrisome issue that had been raised.

Moreover, although the President went out of his way to bring to a crucial meeting an outsider who was an eloquent opponent of the inva-sion plan, his style of conducting the meeting presented no opportunity for discussion of the controversial issues that were raised. The visitor was Senator J. William Fulbright. The occasion was the climactic meeting of April 4, 1961, held at the State Department, at which the apparent consensus that had emerged in earlier meetings was seemingly confirmed by an open straw vote. The President invited Senator Fulbright after the Senator had made known his concern about newspaper stories forecasting a United States invasion of Cuba. At the meeting, Fulbright was given an opportunity to present his opposing views. In a "sensible and strong" speech Fulbright correctly predicted many of the damaging effects the invasion would have on United States foreign relations. The President did not open the floor to discussion of the questions raised in Fulbright's rousing speech. Instead, he returned to the procedure he had initiated earlier in the meeting; he had asked each person around the table to state his final judgment and after Fulbright had taken his turn, he continued the straw vote around the table. McNamara said he approved the plan. Berle was also for it; his advice was to "let her rip." Mann, who had been on the fence, also spoke in favor of it.

Picking up a point mentioned by Berle, who had said he approved but did not insist on "a major production," President Kennedy changed the agenda by asking what could be done to make the infiltration more quiet. Following discussion of this question—quite remote from the fundamental moral and political issues raised by Senator Fulbright—the meeting ended. Schlesinger mentions that the meeting broke up before completion of the intended straw vote around the table. Thus, wittingly or unwittingly, the President conducted the meeting in such a way that not only was there no time to discuss the potential dangers to United States foreign relations raised by Senator Fulbright, but there was also no time to call upon Schlesinger, the one man present who the President knew strongly shared Senator Fulbright's misgivings.

Of course, one or more members of the group could have prevented this by-passing by suggesting that the group discuss Senator Fulbright's arguments and requesting that Schlesinger and the others who had not been called upon be given the opportunity to state their views. But no one made such a request.

The President's demand that each person, in turn, state his overall judgment, especially after having just heard an outsider oppose the group consensus, must have put the members on their mettle. These are exactly the conditions that most strongly foster docile conformity to a group's norms. After listening to an opinion leader (McNamara, for example) express his unequivocal acceptance, it becomes more difficult than ever for other members to state a different view. Open straw votes generally put pressure on each individual to agree with the apparent group consensus, as has been shown by well-known social psychological experiments.

A few days before the crucial meeting of April 4, another outsider who might have challenged some of the group's illusions attended one of the meetings but was never given the opportunity to speak his piece. At the earlier meeting, the outsider was the acting Secretary of State, Chester Bowles, attending in place of Secretary Rusk, who was abroad at a SEATO conference. Like Senator Fulbright, Bowles was incredulous and at times even "horrified" at the group's complacent acceptance of the CIA's invasion plans. However, President Kennedy had no idea what Bowles was thinking about the plan, and he probably felt that Bowles was there more in the role of a reporter to keep Rusk up to date on the deliberations than as a participant in the discussion. In any case, the President neglected to give the group the opportunity to hear the reactions of a fresh mind; he did not call upon Bowles at any time. Bowles sat through the meeting in complete silence. He felt he could not break with formal bureaucratic protocol, which prevents an undersecretary from volunteering his opinion unless directed to do so by his chief or by the President. Bowles behaved in the prescribed way and confined his protestations to a State Department memorandum addressed to Rusk, which, as we have seen, was not communicated to the President.

An additional bit of information about Bowles' subsequent career seems to fit in with all of this, from the standpoint of group psychology. During the bitter weeks following the Bay of Pigs fiasco, Chester Bowles was the first man in the new administration to be fired by President Kennedy. Some of Bowles' friends had told the press that he had opposed the Cuban venture and had been right in his forecasts about the outcome. Evidently this news annoyed the President greatly. Bowles' opponents in the administration pointed out that even if Bowles had not leaked the story to the press, he had discussed the matter with his friends at a time when it would embarrass the White House. This may have contributed to the President's solution to the problem of what to do about the inept leadership of the inefficient State Department bureaucracy. He decided to shift Bowles out of his position as second-in-command, instead of replacing Rusk, whom he liked personally and wanted to keep as a central member of his team. "I can't do that to Rusk," Kennedy later said when someone suggested shifting Rusk to the United Nations. "He is such a *nice* man."

During the Bay of Pigs planning sessions, President Kennedy, probably unwittingly, allowed the one-sided CIA memoranda to monopolize the attention of the group by failing to circulate opposing statements that might have stimulated an intensive discussion of the drawbacks and might therefore have revealed the illusory nature of the group's consensus. Although the President read and privately discussed the strongly opposing memoranda prepared by Schlesinger and Senator Fulbright, he never distributed them to the policy-makers whose critical judgment he was seeking. Kennedy also knew that Joseph Newman, a foreign correspondent who had just visited Cuba, had written a series of incisive articles that disagreed with forecasts concerning the ease of generating a revolt against Castro. But, although he invited Newman to the White House for a chat, he did not distribute Newman's impressive writings to the advisory group.

The members themselves, however, were partially responsible for the President's biased way of handling the meetings. They need not have been so acquiescent about it. Had anyone suggested to the President that it might be a good idea for the group to gain more perspective by studying statements of opposing points of view, Kennedy probably would have welcomed the suggestion and taken steps to correct his own-sided way of running the meetings.

THE TABOO AGAINST ANTAGONIZING VALUABLE NEW MEMBERS

It seems likely that one of the reasons the members of the core group accepted the President's restricted agenda and his extaordinarily indulgent treatment of the CIA representatives was that a kind of informal group norm had developed, producing a desire to avoid saying anything that could be construed as an attack on the CIA's plan. The group apparently accepted a kind of taboo against voicing damaging criticisms. This may have been another important factor contributing to the group's tendency to indulge in groupthink.

How could such a norm come into being? Why would President Kennedy give preferential treatment to the two CIA representatives? Why would Bundy, McNamara, Rusk, and the others on his team fail to challenge this preferential treatment and accept a taboo against voicing critical opposition? A few clues permit some conjectures to be made, although we have much less evidence to go on than for delineating the pattern of preferential treatment itself.

It seems that Allen Dulles and Richard Bissell, despite being hold-overs from the Eisenhower administration, were not considered outsiders by the inner core of the Kennedy team. President Kennedy and his closest associates did not place these two men in the same category as the Joint Chiefs of Staff, who were seen as members of an outside military clique established during the earlier administration, men whose primary loyalties belonged elsewhere and whose presence at the White House meetings was tolerated as a necessary requirement of governmental protocol. (Witness Secretary Rusk's unfriendly comments about the Joint Chiefs being more loyal to their military group in the Pentagon than to the President, when he was conversing privately with fellow in-group member Schlesinger.) President Kennedy and those in his inner circle admired Dulles and Bissell, regarded them as valuable new members of the Kennedy team, and were pleased to have them on board. Everyone in the group was keenly aware of the fact that Bissell had been devoting his talents with great intensity for over a year to developing the Cuban invasion project and that Dulles was also deeply committed to it. Whenever Bissell presented his arguments, "we all listened transfixed," Schlesinger informs us, "fascinated by the workings of this superbly clear, organized and articulate intelligence." Schlesinger reports that Bissell was regarded by the group as "a man of high character and remarkable intellectual gifts." In short, he was accepted as a highly prized member.

The sense of power of the core group was probably enhanced by the realization that the two potent bureaucrats who were in control of America's extensive intelligence network were affiliated with the Kennedy team. The core members of the team would certainly want to avoid antagonizing or alienating them. They would be inclined, therefore, to soft-pedal their criticisms of the CIA plan and perhaps even to suspend their critical judgment in evaluating it.

The way Dulles and Bissell were treated by President Kennedy and his associates after their plan had failed strongly suggests that both men continued to be fully accepted as members of the Kennedy team during the period of crisis generated by their unfortunate errors. According to Sorensen, Kennedy's regard for Richard Bissell did not change after the Bay of Pigs disaster, and he regretted having to accept Bissell's resignation. When Dulles submitted his resignation, President Kennedy urged him to postpone it and asked him to join a special commission to investigate the causes of the fiasco. During the days following the defeat, Kennedy refrained from openly criticizing either Bissell or Dulles (this must have required considerable restraint). On one occasion when a mutual friend of Dulles and Kennedy told the President self-righteously that he was deliberately going to avoid seeing the CIA director, Kennedy went out of his way to support Dulles by inviting him for a drink and ostentatiously putting his [arm] around him in the presence of the would-be ostracizer. This is a typical way for a leader of a cohesive group to treat one of the members who is temporarily "in the dog house."

The picture we get, therefore, is that the two CIA representatives, both highly esteemed men who had recently joined the Kennedy team, were presenting their "baby" to the rest of the team. As protagonists, they had a big head start toward eliciting a favorable consensus. New in-group members would be listened to much more sympathetically and much less critically than outsiders representing an agency that might be trying to sell one of its own pet projects to the new President.

Hilsman, who also respected the two men, says that Dulles and Bissell "had become emotionally involved . . . so deeply involved in the development of the Cuban invasion plans that they were no longer able to see clearly or to judge soundly." He adds, "There was so deep a commitment, indeed, that there was an unconscious effort to confine consideration of the proposed operation to as small a number of people as possible, so as to avoid too harsh or thorough a scrutiny of the plans." If Hilsman is correct, it is reasonable to assume that the two men managed to convey to the other members of the Kennedy team their strong desire "to avoid too harsh or thorough a scrutiny."[4]

Whatever may have been the political or psychological reasons that motivated President Kennedy to give preferential treatment to the two CIA chiefs, he evidently succeeded in conveying to the other members of the core group, perhaps without realizing it, that the CIA's "baby" should not be treated harshly. His way of handling the meetings, particularly his adherence to the extraordinary procedure of allowing every critical comment to be immediately refuted by Dulles or Bissell without allowing the group a chance to mull over the potential objections, probably set the norm of going easy on the plan, which the two new members of the group obviously wanted the new administration to accept. Evidently the members of the group adopted this norm and sought concurrence by continually patching the original CIA plan, trying to find a better version, without looking too closely into the basic arguments for such a plan and without debating the questionable estimates sufficiently to discover that the whole idea ought to be thrown out.

CONCLUSION

Although the available evidence consists of fragmentary and somewhat biased accounts of the deliberations of the White House group, it nevertheless reveals gross miscalculations and converges on the symptoms of groupthink. My tentative conclusion is that President Kennedy and the policy advisers who decided to accept the CIA's plan were victims of groupthink. If the facts I have culled from the accounts given by Schlesinger, Sorensen, and other observers are essentially accurate, the groupthink hypothesis makes more understandable the deficiencies in the government's decision-making that led to the enormous gap between conception and actuality.

The failure of Kennedy's inner circle to detect any of the false assumptions behind the Bay of Pigs invasion plan can be at least partially accounted for by the group's tendency to seek concurrence at the expense of seeking information, critical appraisal, and debate. The concurrence-seeking tendency was manifested by shared illusions and other symptoms, which helped the members to maintain a sense of group solidarity. Most crucial were the symptoms that contributed to complacent overconfidence in the face of vague uncertainties and explicit warnings that should have alerted the members to the risks of the clandestine military operation—an operation so ill conceived that among literate people all over the world the name of the invasion site has become the very symbol of perfect failure.

NOTES

1. These false assumptions are: 1) no one will know that the United States was responsible for the invasion of Cuba; 2) the Cuban Air Force is so ineffective that it can be knocked out completely just before the invasion begins; 3) the men in the brigade of Cuban exiles are willing to carry out the invasion without any support from the United States ground troops; 4) Castro's army is so weak that the Cuban brigade will be able to establish a well-protected beachhead; 5) the invasion will probably lead to the toppling of the Castro regime; and 6) the Cuban brigade can in any case retreat to the mountains and reinforce guerrilla units holding out against the Castro regime. [BK]

2. Peter Wyden, *Bay of Pigs: The Untold Story* (New York: Simon & Schuster, 1979), suggests the possibility that President Kennedy may have made his decision to approve the CIA's invasion plan independently of his advisers' influence. He says that the decision was "not made in a group," and that in mid-April 1961, Kennedy gave the final "go" order over the telephone to Bissell "after extensive lonely soul-searching" (p. 316). But it seems to me that the available evidence consistently indicates that Kennedy worked on and arrived at the decision in group settings, including informal as well as formal meetings with his advisers. Robert Kennedy and Schlesinger, from their own direct personal observations, have reported that the President was very strongly influenced by a consensus of his key advisers. McGeorge Bundy's memorandum, prepared right after the group meeting on March 11, 1961, implies that Kennedy was highly responsive to his advisers' acceptance of the invasion plan, even though he asked the CIA to modify the plan so as to reduce apparent U.S. involvement: "The President expects to authorize U.S. support for an appropriate number of patriotic Cubans to return to their homeland" (quoted by Wyden, p. 101). At the formal meeting on April 4, 1961, after allowing Senator Fulbright to state his objections, the President cut off any discussion of the questions raised by requiring his advisers to vote yes or no on the CIA invasion plan. Secretary of State Dean Rusk was not the only one there who felt that the President wanted to "close ranks" in the face of Fulbright's opposition; Paul Nitze and William Bundy told Wyden that they had much the same impression (see Wyden, pp. 148–49). Bissell left the meeting with "a sense of finality," believing that the chances were now very high that he would get presidential approval of his plan, especially since the President had required his advisers to vote, which put them on record as wanting to go ahead (Wyden, 1979, p. 150). During the next week, in informal talks with Robert Kennedy and other members of his in-group, the President continued to convey his positive responsiveness to the advice he was receiving.

Drawing on Sorensen's account, Wyden succinctly summarizes President Kennedy's appraisal of the CIA plan: Although he had had "grave doubts" about the Cuban operation, he felt it should not be "scrapped" for a number of reasons.

To the President, the plan seemed to entail no actual aggression by the U.S., no evident risk of U.S. involvement, *little risk of failure. . . .*

When he did give the "go" order, "I really thought they had a good chance," he told Sorensen. Besides, it looked like a *no-lose solution.* If a group of Castro's own countrymen could, without overt U.S. help, establish a new government, rally the people and oust Castro, all Latin America would be safer. If the exiles were forced into the mountains as guerrillas, the operation was still a *net gain.* (Wyden, p. 308, italics added)

Note that Kennedy's appraisal, as summarized by Wyden, is the same as that of the key members of his team who advised him to accept the plan. . . . He shared with them the overoptimistic expectation that the risks of failure and of embarrassment to the United States government were so slight that they need not be a deterrent to approving the clandestine operation. Wyden also acknowledges that during this early period of his administration, Kennedy shared with the members of his team the buoyant sense of optimism that characterized "the flowering of Camelot" (p. 316). Wyden quotes Schlesinger's analysis ("Everyone around him thought he had the Midas touch and could not lose") and adds, "His confidence in his own luck was unbounded" (p. 316).

But what about Kennedy's "grave doubts," which would seem to contradict the conclusion that he shared in his team's optimism about the chances of success? Careful examination of the doubts and skeptical comments Kennedy made at meetings with his advisers reveals that those seemingly critical comments were limited to specific details of the overall CIA plan which he wanted to improve. He did *not* raise skeptical questions about the basic plan itself or ask for independent appraisals of any of its main assumptions. If he had, he and his advisers would have had the benefit of candid evaluations of the military prospects from the Joint Chiefs of Staff and candid evaluations of the key assumptions from the Cuban specialists in the CIA (who were never consulted) and in the State Department (who were also excluded).

What Kennedy was primarily concerned about in asking for specific changes was the visibility of United States involvement and the unfavorable political damage that could result from adverse publicity, especially if the United States were branded as an aggressor. Almost all of his skeptical and critical comments were in this category. Here are the five main instances of Kennedy's critical stance: (1) in early March 1961, he told the planners that the landing site they had selected (Trinidad) would make the operation "too spectacular" (Wyden, p. 100); (2) a few days later when the CIA planners changed the landing site to the Bay of Pigs, he wanted them to "reduce the noise level" by unloading the ships at night rather than in daylight (Wyden, p. 102); (3) on March 29 at another meeting, Kennedy was still troubled by the "noise level" and asked if the large-scale air strikes were really essential (Wyden, p. 139); (4) during the meeting on April 4 at which he asked his advisers to vote and was given a go-ahead consensus, his skeptical questioning of the military planners was confined to expressing "concern that the operation would look too much like a World War II invasion, "and this prompted an answer that the assaults would be relatively small, spread over four separate beaches, and carried out at night, which "seemed to make the President feel easier" (Wyden, p. 150); and (5) at a meeting on April 12, he wondered if the planned air strikes, "even as modified, were still too noisy" (Wyden, p. 163).

This limited type of doubting, which led to cosmetic changes of the basic CIA invasion plan, is not inconsistent with Wyden's summary of Kennedy's overall view that the plan entailed "little risk of failure." As a matter of fact, many commentators on the military aspects of the plan assert that the changes Kennedy asked for in order to lower the political risks had the effect of increasing markedly the already serious risks of military failure. But Kennedy was apparently oblivious to those consequences, as were the members of his inner circle. And also, like others on his team, he grossly underestimated the likelihood that, despite having cut down on the noise level, the invasion would still be reported by the news media as a United States government operation and would elicit worldwide condemnation. (The planned invasion by Cuban refugees was already exposed as a CIA operation in the United States press during the week preceding the actual event.) There were also at least three other important potential risks that Kennedy and his team overlooked or seriously underestimated—the risk of instigating a prolonged civil war in Cuba with the loss of many lives, the risk of alienating Latin American countries, and the risk of pushing Castro toward a protective military alliance with the Soviet Union, culminating in Cuba becoming armed with Soviet missiles directed against the United States. (This third potential actually materialized and led to the Cuban missile crisis in 1962.)

Minimizing the major risks of an ill-conceived plan is a central feature of the *illusion of invulnerability*. When this diagnosis is made, it does not necessarily mean that those who share the illusion are totally oblivious to the risks of a very hazardous venture. Rather, it means that to some extent the major risks are being minimized on the basis of a preconscious assumption that *everything is going to work out all right because we are a special group*. When combat flyers in a cohesive air crew are assigned a hazardous target, their shared illusion of invulnerability does not take the form of denying the dangers of aircraft on the mission being shot down (such denial would be psychotic). Rather, it takes the form of a preconscious belief that "others on this dangerous mission are likely to be killed, *but not us*." Similarly, when statesmen in a cohesive policy-making group share an illusion of invulnerability in the face of a risky venture, their preconscious belief is "if others tried to do it they might fail, *but not us*." I surmise from all that has been reported about the exuberant confidence of Kennedy and his team, as well as their minimization of the major risks, that the leader, as well as members of the inner circle, shared an illusion of invulnerability of this kind.

When the members of a cohesive group share an illusion of invulnerability they tend to display a collusive tendency to exclude from their meetings anyone who is likely to challenge their overoptimism by calling attention to the serious risks that are being soft-pedaled. Kennedy did, in fact, exclude many potentially valuable advisers who might have been nay-sayers. On the one occasion when he invited a nay-sayer (Senator Fulbright) to present his political and moral objections at a formal meeting of his large group of advisers, he did not give the group an opportunity to discuss the objections that were being raised. Instead, he immediately called for a vote on the CIA plan. This was the meeting at which Rusk and other participants felt it was essential to "close ranks with the President." William Bundy told Wyden that at that meeting he felt that he and the other members of the executive branch of the Kennedy administration were expected "to stand with the President against Fulbright's arguments to back up the presidential effort at 'rallying the troops' to deal with the lone nay-sayer" (Wyden, p. 149). In this instance, although the leader did arrange to have the group exposed to an outsider's opposing viewpoint, he did not take the essential steps to encourage the members of the group to openly discuss and evaluate the outsider's challenge to their assumptions about the moral acceptability and the political soundness of the plan to sponsor an unprovoked military attack against a small neighboring nation.

Wyden points out that Kennedy generally took pains to avoid exposing himself and others on his team to all such challenges:

> Kennedy . . . filtered the information that went into his decision-making by stifling protest and potential resistance. Schlesinger was finally told by Bob Kennedy outright to shut up. Other nay-sayers—Bowles, Murrow, Hilsman, Meeker—were silenced by nonadmission into the inner circle. Influential potential nay-sayers—Ted Sorensen, Clark Clifford, Adlai Stevenson—were left ignorant because they were generalists or too intellectual and therefore presumably not action-minded. (Wyden, pp. 316–17)

It should be emphasized that at least three other members of the in-group participated actively in the process of excluding or silencing potential dissenters—Robert Kennedy (who silenced Schlesinger), Dean Rusk (who was responsible for preventing Bowles and Hilsman from presenting their objections to Kennedy and his team), and McGeorge Bundy (who told Edward R. Murrow, the director of the United States Information Agency, that his moral and political "objections were not without validity, but nothing could be done about them" [Wyden, p. 145]). If the various articulate nay-sayers mentioned in the above quotation from Wyden had not been silenced or excluded, the illusion of invulnerability shared-by Kennedy and the members of his in-group might well have been dispelled (and perhaps along with it their unexamined assumption of the morality of the planned act of aggression). Had that happened, Kennedy and the members of his in-group would most likely have engaged in a much more vigilant information search, which would have greatly increased their chances of discovering the major flaws in the basic assumptions of the ill-conceived plan.

3. Schlesinger's somewhat self-abasing confession about his failure to present his objections at the group meetings might be a symptom of persisting loyalty to the dead leader and to the group. He appears to be saying, in effect, "Don't put all the blame on President Kennedy or on the other leading members of our team." This theme is not apparent in other portions of Schlesinger's account of the Bay of Pigs fiasco, which level many serious criticisms against the Kennedy team and is far from a whitewash. Still, at present there is no way of knowing to what extent a protective attitude colors Schlesinger's description of how the CIA's invasion plan came to be accepted at the White House. The same problem arises, of course, for all accounts by pro-Kennedy authors, especially Sorensen (who has sought to gain political office on his record as a participant on the Kennedy team and his close personal ties with the Kennedy brothers). My only solution to the problem of subtle distortions and biased reporting is to take the position that *if* the facts reported by Schlesinger, Sorensen, and the other authors are essentially accurate, my analysis of the converging pattern of this "evidence" leads to the conclusion that the groupthink hypothesis helps to account for the deficiencies in the decision-making of the Kennedy team.

4. Bureaucratic political considerations might also have contributed to the group norm of trying to keep the two new members of the team happy. The President and his senior advisers may have realized that if they asked Dulles and Bissell too many embar-

rassing questions and appeared to be rejecting the work of their agency, the two chiefs of the CIA might be pushed in the direction of becoming allied with the military men in the Pentagon, who were already supporting them, rather than with the Kennedy team in the White House.

Another contributing factor might have been the President's personal receptivity to the idea of taking aggressive action against Castro. Although somewhat skeptical of the plan, Kennedy may have welcomed the opportunity to make good on his campaign pledge to aid the anti-Castro rebels. According to Sorensen, the opportunity to inflict a blow against Castro was especially appealing to the President: "He should never have permitted his own deep feeling against Castro (unusual for him) and considerations of public opinion— specifically, his concern that he would be assailed for calling off a plan to get rid of Castro—to overcome his innate suspicion" (Theodore Sorenson, *Kennedy* [New York: Bantam, 1966], p. 343.

Obviously, these ancillary political and psychological factors are not symptoms of groupthink. But they may have reinforced the group norms conducive to concurrence-seeking and thus could be regarded in the same general category as biased leadership practices—that is, as conditions that foster groupthink.

33

ERIK H. ERIKSON

On Followers

*F*OLLOWERS, too, deserve a diagram. Whatever motivation or conflict they may have in common as they join a leader and are joined together by him has to be studied in the full complementarity of the following.

	I *Moment*	II *Sequence*
1. INDIVIDUAL	the stage of life when they met the leader	lifelong themes transferred to the leader
2. COMMUNITY	their generation's search for leadership	traditional and evolving patterns of followership

From Erik H. Erikson, "On the Nature of Psycho-Historical Evidence: In Search of Gandhi," *Daedalus* 97, no. 3 (Summer 1968): 134. Reprinted by permission of *Daedalus*, journal of the American Academy of Arts and Sciences, Boston, Mass.

PART VI

IS THERE A LEADERSHIP FOR ALL SEASONS?

TODAY'S students of leadership—especially social scientists—consider it conventional wisdom that no single paradigm of leadership applies to all leaders in all circumstances. Good leadership is said to be the result of good fit between leaders and followers and between leaders and the tasks at hand. Put another way, it is generally agreed that no single individual, no matter how gifted a leader in one circumstance, can be equally effective in all circumstances.

Yet there have always been some students of political life who have reached a quite different conclusion. They argue that there is in fact a leadership for all seasons. As the following essays indicate, there is an intellectual tradition that maintains that certain leadership traits, styles, and behaviors are best, and that these are timeless and universal.

Plato's meditation on the ideal state led him to propose that leaders should be philosopher-kings, educated to rule according to certain principles of order and reason. Machiavelli, in contrast, took a hard look at the real world and decided that to insure us against the chaos to which humankind was inclined, leaders must have the capacity to rule with an iron hand. And in this century social scientista have tended to conclude on the basis of their empirical studies that democratic leadership is the most satisfactory, both for the individual and the group.

Our ideas about leadership grow out of our ideas about human nature. If I hold the Hobbesian view that life is nasty and brutish, and that without firm governmental controls we would be threatened by enduring anarchy, then I must inevitably reach certain conclusions both about the need for leadership, and the essential nature of that leadership. If, on the other hand, I have the

349

Rousseauian idea that humans in a state of nature are decent, good, and true, and that it is precisely "civilized" society that provokes us to uncivilized behavior, then I would, perforce, argue for an altogether different type of leadership, and indeed question the need for leadership altogether.

Similarly, our view of the ideal leader is shaped by what we deem most important. Do we consider it essential that everyone in the group be reasonably happy? Or should the accomplishments of the state take precedence over how people feel? Of course, the answers to these questions will depend to some extent on the immediate situation. But it is also true that those primarily concerned with how people feel will be inclined to place a premium on democratic leadership, while those who place relatively more importance on order and efficiency might tend to support a more authoritarian leadership style. In some circumstances, however, democratic leadership is demonstrably more conducive to task accomplishment than authoritarian leadership.

The excerpt from Plato's *Republic* concerns the guardians of the state, in particular statesmen (leaders) charged with protecting the public welfare. Plato had little interest in describing what exists; rather he sought to uncover the real nature of the state, or what it would be like if its full purpose were realized. Plato assumed that a rational order underlies all things on this earth, including the structure and practices of the state. Thus, the guardian-statesman, or philosopher-king, must be able above all to grasp the scheme of things, to grasp, that is, this underlying order. In Plato's view some men will be by nature more suited to the philosopher's role than others. But to be so inclined is not enough. The *Republic* alludes repeatedly to the importance of proper education and to the life-long habit of temperance and learning that will prepare the right candidates to become leaders in the prime of their adulthood.

One of the many pleasures of Plutarch is that he expresses his own likes and dislikes. Plutarch is almost gossipy in his predilection for writing about great men by describing their traits and habits, and then judging these according to his own opinion of what constitutes right and wrong and good and bad. The brief piece which compares two great Roman generals, Timoleon and Aemilius Paulus, is actually the coda of an in-depth profile of Aemilius Paulus, which tells in detail about his skill and heroism in war and his decency and honor in victory. For Plutarch, the leader is one who excels in battle and then capitalizes on his triumph to further the common good. A leader is also full of grace, as shown in this passage about Aemilius as host at a victory banquet:

> Then he celebrated all manner of shows and games, and sacrifices to the gods, and made great entertainments and feasts; the charge of all which he liberally defrayed out of the king's treasury; and showed that he understood the ordering and placing of his guests, and how every man should be received, answerably to their rank and

quality, with such nice exactness, that the Greeks were full of wonder, finding the care of these matters of pleasure did not escape him, and that though involved in such important business, he could observe correctness in these trifles. . . . And he told those that seemed to wonder at his diligence, that there was the same spirit shown in marshalling a banquet as an army.[1]

Finally, Plutarch's leader is a man of great dignity. Here is his description of how Aemilius Paulus grieved:

Aemilius had four sons . . . of whom [two] were adopted into other families; the other two, whom he had by a second wife, and who were yet but young, he brought up in his own house. One of these died at fourteen years of age, five days before his father's triumph; the other at twelve, three days after; so that there was no Roman without a deep sense of his suffering, and who did not shudder at the cruelty of fortune, that had not scrupled to bring so much sorrow into a house replenished with happiness, rejoicing, and sacrifices, and to intermingle tears and laments with songs of victory and triumph.

Aemilius, however, reasoning justly that courage and resolution was not merely to resist armor and spears, but all the shocks of ill-fortune, so met and so adapted himself to these mingled contrasting circumstances, as to outbalance the evil with the good, and his private concerns with those of the public; and thus did not allow any thing either to take away from the grandeur, or sully the dignity of his victory. [For as soon as he had buried his two sons] he gathered together an assembly of the people, and made an oration to them, not like a man that stood in need of comfort from others, but one that undertook to support his fellow-citizens in their grief for the sufferings he himself underwent.[2]

The Prince by Machiavelli has been described by Lester Crocker as a tract on the "fundamentals of government, of political relations of human nature, and of man as a political being."[3] Machiavelli wrote the book after having witnessed Italy's suffering from relentless and often brutal warfare; his solution was the competent autocrat, a ruler willing and able to act with the ruthlessness required to restore peace and maintain order.

Crocker observes that the great historical impact of *The Prince* derives from two crucial viewpoints. First, the author "treats all matters relating to politics and human behavior in general as purely natural phenomena, capable of objective analysis and control." Second, he considers "success in achieving one's goals, in the personal or interstate struggle for survival, to be the only real or meaningful criterion of acts."[4] Thus Machiavelli was prepared to recommend cruelty, but only under circumstances in which, in the long run, it would be kinder to be cruel than compassionate. The excerpt below indicates that such cruelty as Machiavelli did advocate was not arbitrary. For example, the prince who gains his title by the favor of his fellow citizens, rather than by treason and violence, is advised to pursue a steady course and even to endear himself to his subjects so that they will come to "feel the need of his authority."

Kurt Lewin's short essay on "The Consequences of Authoritarian and Democratic Leadership," written shortly after World War II, makes the case for democratic leadership. In particular, he argues that not only does the individual profit by having a democratic rather than authoritarian or laissez faire leader, but that the group is better off as well. "There was about thirty times as much hostile domination in the autocracy as in the democracy, more demands for attention and much more hostile criticism; whereas in the democratic atmosphere co-operation and praise of the other fellow was much more frequent." According to Lewin, a leadership for all seasons must certainly be democratic in character, and he therefore places rather less emphasis on the quality of the leader and more on the quality of life for the followers. In fact, one can conclude from his piece that in a democratic system the question of whether or not the leader is excellent is relatively unimportant.

The essay by Dennis F. Thompson is ostensibly not about leaders at all, but rather about "public officials." It is included here because many public officials *are* political leaders, and because Thompson draws a bottom line. At the very least, he claims, public officials should avoid making excuses for their failures. Instead, they ought to assume personal responsibility for their decisions and behaviors, for "personal responsibility in this way can lay a foundation for democratic accountability of the officials who make objectionable decisions and policies." For Thompson, all political leaders should, at a minimum, hold themselves publicly accountable for what they do.

Although James MacGregor Burns lists several different characteristics of authentic leadership in the selection from his book *Leadership*, in fact it is a single theme that sounds through all his writings on the subject: the equation of leadership with moral purpose. For Burns, leaders for all seasons must pass one ostensibly simple test: they must demonstrate a genuine commitment to the welfare of their followers.

NOTES

1. *Plutarch's Lives*, trans. John Dryden, ed. A. H. Clough (Philadelphia: The Nottingham Society, n.d.), vol. II, P. 124.
2. Ibid., p. 131.
3. Nicolo Machiavelli, *The Prince*, ed. Lester A. Crocker (New York: Washington Square Press, 1963), p. xxviii.
4. Ibid., p. xxii.

34

PLATO

The Philosopher King

So now, Glaucon, I said, our argument after winding a long and weary way has at last made clear to us who are the philosophers or lovers of wisdom and who are not.

Yes, he said, a shorter way is perhaps not feasible.

Apparently not, I said. I, at any rate, think that the matter would have been made still plainer if we had had nothing but this to speak of, and if there were not so many things left which our purpose of discerning the difference between the just and the unjust life requires us to discuss.

What, then, he said, comes next?

What else, said I, but the next in order? Since the philosophers are those who are capable of apprehending that which is eternal and unchanging, while those who are incapable of this, but lose themselves and wander amid the multiplicities and multifarious things, are not philosophers, which of the two kinds ought to be the leaders in a state?

What, then, he said, would be a fair statement of the matter?

Whichever, I said, appear competent to guard the laws and pursuits of society, these we should establish as guardians.

Right, he said.

Is this, then, said I, clear, whether the guardian who is to keep watch over anything ought to be blind or keen of sight?

Of course it is clear, he said.

Do you think, then, that there is any appreciable difference between the blind and those who are veritably deprived of the knowledge of the veritable being of things, those who have no vivid pattern in their souls and so cannot, as painters look to their models, fix their eyes on the

From Edith Hamilton and Huntington Cairns, eds., *The Collected Dialogues of Plato* (Princeton: Princeton University Press, 1961), *The Republic*, bk. 6, 484a–503d, pp. 720–39. Written ca. 375 B.C.

absolute truth, and always with reference to that ideal and in the exactest possible contemplation of it establish in this world also the laws of the beautiful, the just, and the good, when that is needful, or guard and preserve those that are established?

No, by heaven, he said, there is not much difference.

Shall we, then, appoint these blind souls as our guardians, rather than those who have learned to know the ideal reality of things and who do not fall short of the others in experience and are not second to them in any part of virtue?

It would be strange indeed, he said, to choose others than the philosophers, provided they were not deficient in those other respects, for this very knowledge of the ideal would perhaps be the greatest of superiorities.

Then what we have to say is how it would be possible for the same persons to have both qualifications, is it not?

Quite so.

Then, as we were saying at the beginning of this discussion, the first thing to understand is the nature that they must have from birth, and I think that if we sufficiently agree on this we shall also agree that the combination of qualities that we seek belongs to the same persons, and that we need no others for guardians of states than these.

How so?

We must accept as agreed this trait of the philosophical nature, that it is ever enamored of the kind of knowledge which reveals to them something of that essence which is eternal, and is not wandering between the two poles of generation and decay.

Let us take that as agreed.

And, further, said I, that their desire is for the whole of it and that they do not willingly renounce a small or a great, a more precious or a less honored, part of it. That was the point of our former illustration drawn from lovers and men covetous of honor.

You are right, he said.

Consider, then, next whether the men who are to meet our requirements must not have this further quality in their natures.

What quality?

The spirit of truthfulness, reluctance to admit falsehood in any form, the hatred of it and the love of truth.

It is likely, he said.

It is not only likely, my friend, but there is every necessity that he who is by nature enamored of anything should cherish all that is akin and pertaining to the object of his love.

Right, he said.

Could you find anything more akin to wisdom than truth?

Impossible, he said.

Then can the same nature be a lover of wisdom and of falsehood?

By no means.

Then the true lover of knowledge must, from childhood up, be most of all a striver after truth in every form.

By all means.

But, again, we surely are aware that when in a man the desires incline strongly to any one thing, they are weakened for other things. It is as if the stream had been diverted into another channel.

Surely.

So, when a man's desires have been taught to flow in the channel of learning and all that sort of thing, they will be concerned, I presume, with the pleasures of the soul in itself, and will be indifferent to those of which the body is the instrument, if the man is a true and not a sham philosopher.

That is quite necessary.

Such a man will be temperate and by no means greedy for wealth, for the things for the sake of which money and great expenditure are eagerly sought others may take seriously, but not he.

It is so.

And there is this further point to be considered in distinguishing the philosophical from the unphilosophical nature.

What point?

You must not overlook any touch of illiberality. For nothing can be more contrary than such pettiness to the quality of a soul that is ever to seek integrity and wholeness in all things human and divine.

Most true, he said.

Do you think that a mind habituated to thoughts of grandeur and the contemplation of all time and all existence can deem this life of man a thing of great concern?

Impossible, said he.

Hence such a man will not suppose death to be terrible?

Least of all.

Then a cowardly and illiberal spirit, it seems, could have no part in genuine philosophy.

I think not.

What then? Could a man of orderly spirit, not a lover of money, not illiberal, nor a braggart nor a coward, ever prove unjust, or a driver of hard bargains?

Impossible.

This too, then, is a point that in your discrimination of the philosophical and unphilosophical soul you will observe—whether the man is from youth up just and gentle or unsocial and savage.

Assuredly.

Nor will you overlook this, I fancy.

What?

Whether he is quick or slow to learn. Or do you suppose that anyone could properly love a task which he performed painfully and with little result from much toil?

That could not be.

And if he could not keep what he learned, being steeped in oblivion, could he fail to be void of knowledge?

How could he?

And so, having all his labor for nought, will he not finally be constrained to loathe himself and that occupation?

Of course.

The forgetful soul, then, we must not list in the roll of competent lovers of wisdom, but we require a good memory.

By all means.

But assuredly we should not say that the want of harmony and seemliness in a nature conduces to anything else than the want of measure and proportion.

Certainly.

And do you think that truth is akin to measure and proportion to disproportion?

To proportion.

Then in addition to our other requirements we look for a mind endowed with measure and grace, whose native disposition will make it easily guided to the aspect of the ideal reality in all things.

Assuredly.

Tell me, then, is there any flaw in the argument? Have we not proved the qualities enumerated to be necessary and compatible with one another for the soul that is to have a sufficient and perfect apprehension of reality?

Nay, most necessary, he said.

Is there any fault, then, that you can find with a pursuit which a man could not properly practice unless he were by nature of good memory, quick apprehension, magnificent, gracious, friendly, and akin to truth, justice, bravery, and sobriety?

Momus himself, he said, could not find fault with such a combination.

Well, then, said I, when men of this sort are perfected by education and maturity of age, would you not entrust the state solely to them?

And Adimantus said, No one, Socrates, would be able to controvert these statements of yours. But, all the same, those who occasionally hear you argue thus feel in this way. They think that owing to their inexperience in the game of question and answer they are at every question led astray a little bit by the argument, and when these bits are accumulated at the conclusion of the discussion mighty is their fall, and the apparent contradiction of what they at first said, and that just as by expert draughts players the unskilled are finally shut in and cannot make a move, so they are finally blocked and have their mouths stopped by this other game of draughts played not with counters but with words; yet the truth is not affected by that outcome. I say this with reference to the present case, for in this instance one might say that he is unable in words to contend against you at each question, but that when it comes to facts he sees that of those who turn to philosophy, not merely touching upon it to complete their education and dropping it while still young, but lingering too long in the study of it, the majority become cranks, not to say rascals, and those accounted the finest spirits among them are still rendered useless to society by the pursuit which you commend.

And I, on hearing this, said, Do you think that they are mistaken in saying so?

I don't know, said he, but I would gladly hear your opinion.

You may hear, then, that I think that what they say is true.

How, then, he replied, can it be right to say that our cities will never be freed from their evils until the philosophers, whom we admit to be useless to them, become their rulers?

Your question, I said, requires an answer expressed in comparison or parable.

And you, he said, of course, are not accustomed to speak in comparisons!

So, said I, you are making fun of me after driving me into such an impasse of argument. But, all the same, hear my comparison so that you may still better see how I strain after imagery. For so cruel is the condition of the better sort of relation to the state that there is no single thing like it in nature. But to find a likeness for it and a defense for them one must bring together many things in such a combination as painters mix when they portray goat stags and similar creatures. Conceive this sort of thing happening either on many ships or on one. Picture a shipmaster in height and strength surpassing all others on the ship, but who is slightly deaf and of similarly impaired vision, and whose knowledge of navigation is on a par with his sight and hearing. Conceive the sailors to be wrangling with one another for control of the helm, each claiming that it is his right to steer though he has never learned the art and cannot point out his teacher or any time when he studied it. And what is more, they affirm that it cannot be taught at all, but they are ready to make mincemeat of anyone who says that it can be taught, and meanwhile they are always clustered about the shipmaster importuning him and sticking at nothing to induce him to turn over the helm to them. And sometimes, if they fail and others get his ear, they put the others to death or cast them out from the ship, and then, after binding and stupefying the worthy shipmaster with mandragora or intoxication or otherwise, they take command of the ship, consume its stores, and, drinking and feasting, make such a voyage of it as is to be expected from such, and as if that were not enough, they praise and celebrate as a navigator, a pilot, a master of shipcraft, the man who is most cunning to lend a hand in persuading or constraining the shipmaster to let them rule, while the man who lacks this craft they censure as useless. They have no suspicion that the true pilot must give his attention to the time of the year, the seasons, the sky, the winds, the stars, and all that pertains to his art if he is to be a true ruler of a ship, and that he does not believe that there is any art or science of seizing the helm with or without the consent of others, or any possibility of mastering this alleged art and the practice of it at the same time with the science of navigation. With such goings on aboard ship do you not think that the real pilot would in very deed be called a stargazer, an idle babbler, a useless fellow, by the sailors in ships managed after this fashion?

Quite so, said Adimantus.

You take my meaning, I presume, and do not require us to put the comparison to the proof and show that the condition we have described is the exact counterpart of the relation of the state to the true philosophers.

It is indeed, he said.

To begin with, then, teach this parable to the man who is surprised that philosophers are not honored in our cities, and try to convince him that it would be far more surprising if they were honored.

I will teach him, he said.

And say to him further, You are right in affirming that the finest spirits among the philosophers are of no service to the multitude. But bid him blame for this uselessness, not the finer spirits, but those who do not know how to make use of them. For it is not the natural course of things that the pilot should beg the sailors to be ruled by him or that wise men should go to the doors of the rich. The author of that epigram was a liar.

But the true nature of things is that whether the sick man be rich or poor he must needs go to the door of the physician, and everyone who needs to be governed to the door of the man who knows how to govern, not that the ruler should implore his natural subjects to let themselves be ruled, if he is really good for anything. But you will make no mistake in likening our present political rulers to the sort of sailors we were just describing, and those whom these call useless and stargazing ideologists to the true pilots.

Just so, he said.

Hence, and under these conditions, we cannot expect that the noblest pursuit should be highly esteemed by those whose way of life is quite the contrary, But far the greatest and chief disparagement of philosophy is brought upon it by the pretenders to that way of life, those whom you had in mind when you affirmed that the accuser of philosophy says that the majority of her followers are rascals and the better sort useless, while I admitted that what you said was true. Is not that so?

Yes.

Have we not, then, explained the cause of the uselessness of the better sort?

We have.

Shall we next set forth the inevitableness of the degeneracy of the majority, and try to show if we can that philosophy is not to be blamed for this either.

By all means.

Let us begin, then, what we have to say and hear by recalling the starting point of our description of the nature which he who is to be a scholar and gentleman must have from birth. The leader of the choir for him, if you recollect, was truth. *That* he was to seek always and altogether, on pain of being an imposter without part or lot in true philosophy.

Yes, that was said.

Is not this one point quite contrary to the prevailing opinion about him?

It is indeed, he said.

Will it not be a fair plea in his defense to say that it was the nature of the real lover of knowledge to strive emulously for true being and that he would not linger over the many particulars that are opined to be real, but would hold on his way, and the edge of his passion would not be blunted nor would his desire fail till he came into touch with the nature of each thing in itself by that part of his soul to which it belongs to lay hold on that kind of reality—the part akin to it, namely—and through that approaching it, and consorting with reality really, he would beget intelligence and truth, attain to knowledge, and truly live and grow, and so find surcease from his travail of soul, but not before?

No plea could be fairer.

Well, then, will such a man love falsehood, or, quite the contrary, hate it?

Hate it, he said.

When truth led the way, no choir of evils, we, I fancy, would say, could ever follow in its train.

How could it?

But rather a sound and just character, which is accompanied by temperance.

Right, he said.

What need, then, of repeating from the beginning our proof of the necessary order of the choir that attends on the philosophical nature? You surely remember that we found pertaining to such a nature courage, grandeur of soul, aptness to learn, memory. And when you interposed the objection that though everybody will be compelled to admit our statements, yet, if we abandoned mere words and fixed our eyes on the persons to whom the words referred, everyone would say that he actually saw some of them to be useless and most of them base with all baseness— it was in our search for the cause of this ill repute that we came to the present question. Why is it that the majority are bad? And, for the sake of this, we took up again the nature of the true philosophers and defined what it must necessarily be?

That is so, he said.

We have, then, I said, to comtemplate the causes of the corruption of this nature in the majority, while a small part escapes, even those whom men call not bad but useless. And after that in turn we are to observe those who imitate this nature and usurp its pursuits, and see what types of souls they are that thus entering upon a way of life which is too high for them and exceeds their powers, but the many discords and disharmonies of their conduct everywhere and among all men, bring upon philosophy the repute of which you speak.

Of what corruptions are you speaking?

I will try, I said, to explain them to you if I can. I think everyone will grant us this point, that a nature such as we just now postulated for the perfect philosopher is a rare growth among men and is found in only a few. Don't you think so?

Most emphatically.

Observe, then, the number and magnitude of the things that operate to destroy these few.

What are they?

The most surprising fact of all is that each of the gifts of nature which we praise tends to corrupt the soul of its possessor and divert it from philosophy. I am speaking of bravery, sobriety, and the entire list.

That does sound like a paradox, said he.

Furthermore, said I, all the so-called goods corrupt and divert, beauty and wealth and strength of body and powerful family connections in the city and all things akin to them—you get my general meaning?

I do, he said, and I would gladly hear a more precise statement of it.

Well, said I, grasp it rightly as a general proposition and the matter will be clear and the preceding statement will not seem to you so strange.

How do you bid me proceed? he said.

We know it to be universally true of every seed and growth, whether vegetable or animal, that the more vigorous it is the more it falls short of its proper perfection when deprived of the food, the season, the place that suits it. For evil is more opposed to the good than to the not-good.

Of course.

So it is, I take it, natural that the best nature should fare worse than the inferior under conditions of nurture unsuited to it.

It is.

Then, said I, Adimantus, shall we not similarly affirm that the best endowed souls become worse than the others under a bad education? Or do you suppose that great crimes and unmixed wickedness spring from a slight nature and not from a vigorous one corrupted by its nurture, while a weak nature will never be the cause of anything great, either for good or evil?

No, he said, that is the case.

Then the nature which we assumed in the philosopher, if it receives the proper teaching, must needs grow and attain to consumate excellence, but, if it be sown and planted and grown in the wrong environment, the outcome will be quite the contrary unless some god comes to the rescue. Or are you too one of the multitude who believe that there are young men who are corrupted by the Sophists, and that there are Sophists in private life who corrupt to any extent worth mentioning, and that it is not rather the very men who talk in this strain who are the chief Sophists and educate most effectively and mold to their own heart's desire young and old, men and women?

When? said he.

Why, when, I said, the multitude are seated together in assemblies or in courtrooms or theaters or camps or any other public gathering of a crowd, and with loud uproar censure some of the things that are said and done and approve others, both in excess, with full-throated clamor and clapping of hands, and thereto the rocks and the region round about re-echoing redouble the din of the censure and the praise. In such case how do you think the young man's heart, as the saying is, is moved within him? What private teaching do you think will hold out and not rather be swept away by the torrent of censure and applause, and borne off on its current, so that he will affirm the same things that they do to be honorable and base, and will do as they do, and be even such as they?

That is quite inevitable, Socrates, he said.

And, moreover, I said, we have not yet mentioned the chief necessity and compulsion.

What is it? said he.

That which these "educators" and Sophists impose by action when their words fail to convince. Don't you know that they chastise the recalcitrant with loss of civic rights and fines and death?

They most emphatically do, he said.

What other Sophist, then, or what private teaching do you think will prevail in opposition to these?

None, I fancy, said he.

No, said I, the very attempt is the height of folly. For there is not, never has been, and never will be a divergent type character and virtue created by an education running counter to theirs—humanly speaking, I mean, my friend. For the divine, as the proverb says, all rules fail. And you may be sure that, if anything is saved and turns out well in the present condition of society and government, in saying that the providence of God preserves it you will not be speaking ill.

Neither do I think otherwise, he said.

Then, said I, think this also in addition.

What?

Each of these private teachers who work for pay, whom the politicians call sophists and regard as their rivals, inculcates nothing else than these opinions of the multitude which they opine when they are assembled and calls this knowledge wisdom. It is as if a man were acquiring the knowledge of the humors and desires of a great strong beast which he had in his keeping, how it is to be approached and touched, and when and by what things it is made most savage or gentle, yes, and the several sounds it is wont to utter on the occasion of each, and again what sounds uttered by another make it tame or fierce, and after mastering this knowledge by living with the creature and by lapse of time should call it wisdom, and should construct thereof a system and art and turn to the teaching of it, knowing nothing in reality about which of these opinions and desires is honorable or base, good or evil, just or unjust, but should apply all these terms to the judgments of the great beast, calling the things that pleased it good, and the things that vexed it bad, having no other account to render of them, but should call what is necessary just and honorable, never having observed how great is the real difference between the necessary and the good, and being incapable of explaining it to another. Do you not think, by heaven, that such a one would be a strange educator?

I do, he said.

Do you suppose that there is any difference between such a one and the man who thinks that it is wisdom to have learned to know the moods and the pleasures of the motley multitude in their assembly, whether about painting or music or, for that matter, politics? For if a man associates with these and offers and exhibits to them his poetry or any other product of his craft or any political service, and grants the mob authority over himself more than is unavoidable, the proverbial necessity of Diomedes will compel him to give the public what it likes, but that what it likes is really good and honorable, have you ever heard an attempted proof of this that is not simply ridiculous?

No, he said, and I fancy I never shall hear it either.

Bearing all this in mind, recall our former question. Can the multitude possibly tolerate or believe in the reality of the beautiful in itself as opposed to the multiplicity of beautiful things, or can they believe in anything conceived in its essence as opposed to the many particulars?

Not in the least, he said.

Philosophy, then, the love of wisdom, is impossible for the multitude.

Impossible.

It is inevitable, then, that those who philosophize should be censured by them.

Inevitable.

And so likewise by those laymen who, associating with the mob, desire to curry favor with it.

Obviously.

From this point of view do you see any salvation that will suffer the born philosopher to abide in the pursuit and persevere to the end? Consider it in the light of what we said before. We agreed that quickness in learning, memory, courage, and magnificence were the traits of this nature.

Yes.

Then even as a boy among boys such a one will take the lead in all things, especially if the nature of his body matches the soul.

How could he fail to do so? he said.

His kinsmen and fellow citizens, then, will desire, I presume, to make use of him when he is older for their own affairs.

Of course.

Then they will fawn upon him with petitions and honors, anticipating and flattering the power that will be his.

That certainly is the usual way.

How, then, do you think such a youth will behave in such conditions, especially if it happen that he belongs to a great city and is rich and wellborn therein, and thereto handsome and tall. Will his soul not be filled with unbounded ambitious hopes, and will he not think himself capable of managing the affairs of both Greeks and barbarians, and thereupon exalt himself, haughty of mien and stuffed with empty pride and void of sense?

He surely will, he said.

And if to a man in this state of mind someone gently comes and tells him what is the truth, that he has no sense and sorely needs it, and that the only way to get it is to work like a slave to win it, do you think it will be easy for him to lend an ear to the quiet voice in the midst of and in spite of these evil surroundings?

Far from it, said he.

And even supposing, said I, that owing to a fortunate disposition and his affinity for the words of admonition one such youth apprehends something and is moved and drawn toward philosophy, what do we suppose will be the conduct of those who think that they are losing his service and fellowship? Is there any word or deed that they will stick at to keep him from being persuaded and to incapacitate anyone who attempts it, both by private intrigue and public prosecution in the court?

That is inevitable, he said.

Is there any possibility of such a one continuing to philosophize?

None at all, he said.

Do you see, then, said I, that we were not wrong in saying that the very qualities that make up the philosophical nature do, in fact, become, when the environment and nurture are bad, in some sort the cause of its backsliding, and so do the so-called goods—riches and all such instrumentalities?

No, he replied, it was rightly said.

Such, my good friend, and so great as regards the noblest pursuit, is the destruction and corruption of the most excellent nature, which is rare enough in any case, as we affirm. And it is from men of this type that those spring who do the greatest harm to communities and individuals, and the greatest good when the stream chances to be turned into that channel, but a small nature never does anything great to a man or a city.

Most true, said he.

Those, then, to whom she properly belongs, thus falling away and leaving philosophy forlorn and unwed, themselves live an unreal and alien life, while other unworthy wooers rush in and defile her as an orphan bereft of her kin, and attach to her such reproaches as you say her revilers taunt her with, declaring that some of her consorts are of no account and the many accountable for many evils.

Why, yes, he replied, that is what they do say.

And plausibly, said I, for other manikins, observing that the place is unoccupied and full of fine terms and pretensions, just as men escape from prison to take sanctuary in temples, so these gentlemen joyously bound away from the mechanical arts to philosophy, those that are most cunning in their little craft. For in comparison with the other arts the prestige of philosophy even in her present low estate retains a superior dignity, and this is the ambition and aspiration of that multitude of pretenders unfit by nature, whose souls are bowed and mutilated by their vulgar occupations even as their bodies are marred by their arts and crafts. Is not that inevitable?

Quite so, he said.

Is not the picture which they present, I said, precisely that of a little bald-headed tinker who has made money and just been freed from bonds and had a bath and is wearing a new garment and has got himself up like a bridegroom and is about to marry his master's daughter who has fallen into poverty and abandonment?

There is no difference at all, he said.

Of what sort will probably be the offspring of such parents? Will they not be bastard and base?

Inevitably.

And so when men unfit for culture approach philosophy and consort with her unworthily, what sort of ideas and opinions shall we say they beget? Will they not produce what may in very deed be fairly called sophisms, and nothing that is genuine or that partakes of true intelligence?

Quite so, he said.

There is a very small remnant, then, Adimantus, I said, of those who consort worthily with philosophy, some wellborn and well-bred nature, it may be, held in check by exile, and so in the absence of corrupters remaining true to philosophy, as its quality bids, or it may happen that a great soul born in a little town scorns and disregards its parochial affairs, and a small group perhaps might by natural affinity be drawn to it from other arts which they justly disdain, and the bridle of our companion Theages also might operate as a restraint. For in the case of Theages all other conditions were at hand for his backsliding from the philosophy, but his sickly habit of body keeping him out of politics holds him back. My own case, the divine sign, is hardly worth mentioning—for I suppose it has happened to few or none before me. And those who have been of this little company and have tasted the sweetness and blessedness of this possession and who have also come to understand the madness of the multitude sufficiently and have seen that there is nothing, if I may say so, sound or right in any present politics, and that there is no ally with whose aid the champion of justice could escape destruction, but that he would be as a man who has fallen among wild beasts, unwilling to share their misdeeds and unable to hold out singly against the savagery of all, and that he would thus, before he could in any way benefit his friends or the state, come to an untimely end without doing any good to himself or others—for all these reasons I say the philosopher remains quiet, minds his own affair, and, as it were, standing aside under shelter of a wall in a storm and blast of dust and sleet and seeing others filled full of lawlessness, is content if in any way he may keep himself free from iniquity and unholy deeds through this life and take his departure with fair hope, serene and well content when the end comes.

Well, he said, that is no very slight thing to have achieved before taking his departure.

He would not have accomplished any very great thing either, I replied if it were not his fortune to live in a state adapted to his nature. In such a state only will he himself rather attain his full stature and together with his own preserve the commonweal. The causes and the injustice of the calumniation of philosophy, I think, have been fairly set forth, unless you have something to add.

No, he said, I have nothing further to offer on that point. But which of our present governments do you think is suitable for philosophy?

None whatever, I said, but the very ground of my complaint is that no polity of today is worthy of the philosophical nature. This is just the cause of its perversion and alteration; as a foreign seed sown in an alien soil is wont to be overcome and die out into the native growth, so this kind does not preserve its own quality but falls away and degenerates into an alien type. But if ever it finds the best polity as it itself is the best, then will it be apparent that this was in truth divine and all the others human in their natures and practices. Obviously then you are next going to ask what is this best form of government.

Wrong, he said. I was going to ask not that but whether it is this one that we have described in our establishment of a state or another.

In other respects it is this one, said I, but there is one special further point that we mentioned even then, namely, that there would always have to be resident in such a state an element having the same conception of its constitution that you the lawgiver had in framing its laws.

That was said, he replied.

But it was not sufficiently explained, I said, from fear of those objections on your part which have shown that the demonstration of it is long and difficult. And apart from that the remainder of the exposition is by no means easy.

Just what do you mean?

The manner in which a state that occupies itself with philosophy can escape destruction. For all great things are precarious and, as the proverb truly says, "fine things are hard."

All the same, he said, our exposition must be completed by making this plain.

It will be no lack of will, I said, but if anything, a lack of ability, that would prevent that. But you shall observe for yourself my zeal. And note again how zealously and recklessly I am prepared to say that the state ought to take up this pursuit in just the reverse of our present fashion.

In what way?

At present, said I, those who do take it up are youths, just out of boyhood, who in the interval before they engage in business and money-making approach the most difficult part of it, and then drop it—and these are regarded forsooth as the best exemplars of philosophy. By the most difficult part I mean discussion. In later life they think they have done much if, when invited, they deign to listen to the philosophical discussions of others. That sort of thing they think should be bywork. And toward old age, with few exceptions, their light is quenched more completely than the sun of Heraclitus, inasmuch as it is never rekindled.

And what should they do? he said.

Just the reverse. While they are lads and boys they should occupy themselves with an education and a culture suitable to youth, and while their bodies are growing to manhood take right good care of them, thus securing a basis and a support for the intellectual life. But with the advance of age, when the soul begins to attain its maturity, they should make its exercises more severe, and when the bodily strength declines and they are past the age of political and military service, then at last they should be given free range of the pasture and do nothing but philosophize, except incidentally, if they are to live happily, and, when the end has come, crown the life they have lived with a consonant destiny in that other world.

You really seem to be very much in earnest, Socrates, he said. Yet I think most of your hearers are even more earnest in their opposition and will not be in the least convinced, beginning with Thrasymachus.

Do not try to breed a quarrel between me and Thrasymachaus, who have just become friends and were not enemies before either. For we will spare no effort until we either convince him and the rest or achieve something that will profit them when they come to that life in which they will be born again and meet with such discussions as these.

A brief time your forecast contemplates, he said.

Nay, nothing at all, I replied, as compared with eternity. However, the unwillingness of the multitude to believe what you say is nothing surprising. For of the thing here spoken they have never beheld a token, but only the forced and artificial chiming of word and phrase, not spontaneous and accidental as has happened here. But the figure of a man "equilibrated" and "assimilated" to virtue's self perfectly, so far as may be, in word and deed, and holding rule in a city of like quality, that is a thing they have never seen in one case or in many. Do you think they have?

By no means.

Neither, my dear fellow, have they ever seriously inclined to hearken to fair and free discussions whose sole endeavor was to search out the truth at any cost for knowledge's sake, and which dwell apart and salute from afar all the subtleties and cavils that lead to nought but opinion and strife in courtroom and in private talk.

They have not, he said.

For this cause and foreseeing this, we then despite our fears declared under compulsion of the truth that neither city nor polity nor man either will ever be perfected until some chance compels this uncorrupted remnant of philosophers, who now bear the stigma of uselessness, to take charge of the state whether they wish it or not, and constrains the citizens to obey them, or else until by some divine inspiration a genuine passion for true philosophy takes possession either of the sons of the men now in power and sovereignty or of themselves. To affirm that either or both of these things cannot possibly come to pass is, I say, quite unreasonable. Only in that case could we be justly ridiculed as uttering things as futile as daydreams are. Is not that so?

It is.

If, then, the best philosophical natures have ever been constrained to take charge of the state in infinite time past, or now are in some barbaric region far beyond our ken, or shall hereafter be, we are prepared to maintain our contention that the constitution we have described has been, is, or will be realized when this philosophical Muse has taken control of the state. It is not a thing impossible to happen, nor are we speaking of impossibilities. That it is difficult we too admit.

I also think so, he said.

But the multitude—are you going to say?—does not think so, said I.

That may be, he said.

My dear fellow, said I, do not thus absolutely condemn the multitude. They will surely be of another mind if in no spirit of contention but soothingly and endeavoring to do away with the dispraise of learning you point out to them whom you mean by philosophers, and define as we recently did their nature and their pursuits so that the people may not suppose you to mean those of whom they are thinking. Or even if they do look at them in that way, are you still going to deny that they will change their opinion and answer differently? Or do you think that anyone is ungentle to the gentle or grudging to the ungrudging if he himself is ungrudging and mild? I will anticipate you and reply that I think that only in some few and not in the mass of mankind is so ungentle or harsh a temper to be found.

And I, you may be assured, he said, concur.

And do you not also concur in this very point that the blame for this harsh attitude of the many toward philosophy falls on that riotous crew who have burst in where they do not belong, wrangling with one another, filled with spite, and always talking about persons, a thing least befitting philosophy?

Least of all, indeed, he said.

For surely, Adimantus, the man whose mind is truly fixed on eternal realities has no leisure to turn his eyes downward upon the petty affairs of men, and so engaging in strife with them to be filled with envy and hate, but he fixes his gaze upon the things of the eternal and unchanging order, and seeing that they neither wrong nor are wronged by one another, but all abide in harmony as reason bids, he will endeavor to imitate them and, as far as may be, to fashion himself in their likeness and assimilate himself to them. Or do you think it possible not to imitate the things to which anyone attaches himself with admiration?

Impossible, he said.

Then the lover of wisdom associating with divine order will himself become orderly and divine in the measure permitted to man. But calumny is plentiful everywhere.

Yes, truly.

If, then, I said, some compulsion is laid upon him to practice stamping on the plastic matter of human nature in public and private the patterns that he visions there, and not merely to mold and fashion himself, do you think he will prove a poor craftsman of sobriety and justice and all forms of ordinary civic virtue?

By no means, he said.

But if the multitude become aware that what we are saying of the philosopher is true, will they still be harsh with philosophers, and will they distrust our statement that no city could ever be blessed unless its lineaments were traced by artists who use the heavenly model?

They will not be harsh, he said, if they perceive that. But tell me, what is the manner of that sketch you have in mind?

They will take the city and the characters of men, as they might a tablet, and first wipe it clean—no easy task. But at any rate you know that this would be their first point of difference from ordinary reformers, that they would refuse to take in hand either individual or state or to legislate before they either received a clean slate or themselves made it clean.

And they would be right, he said.

And thereafter, do you not think that they would sketch the figure of the constitution?

Surely.

And then, I take it, in the course of the work they would glance frequently in either direction, at justice, beauty, sobriety and the like as they are in the nature of things, and alternately at that which they were trying to reproduce in mankind, mingling and blending from various pursuits that hue of the flesh, so to speak, deriving their judgment from that likeness of humanity which Homer too called, when it appeared in men, the image and likeness of God.

Right, he said.

And they would erase one touch or stroke and paint it another until in the measure of the possible they had made the characters of men pleasing and dear to God as may be.

That at any rate would be the fairest painting.

Are we then making any impression on those who you said were advancing to attack us with might and main? Can we convince them that such a political artist of character and such a painter exists as the one we then were praising when our proposal to entrust the state to him angered them, and are they now in a gentler mood when they hear what we are now saying?

Much gentler, he said, if they are reasonable.

How *can* they controvert it? Will they deny that the lovers of wisdom are lovers of reality and truth?

That would be monstrous, he said.

Or that their nature as we have portrayed it is akin to the highest and best?

Not that either.

Well, then, can they deny that such a nature bred in the pursuits that befit it will be perfectly good and philosophical so far as that can be said of anyone? Or will they rather say it of those whom we have excluded?

Surely not.

Will they, then, any longer be fierce with us when we declare that, until the philosophical class wins control, there will be no surcease of trouble for city or citizens nor will the polity which we fable in words be brought to pass in deed?

They will perhaps be less so, he said.

Instead of less so, may we not say that they have been altogether tamed and convinced, so that for very shame, if for no other reason, they may assent?

Certainly, said he.

Let us assume, then, said I, that they are won over to this view. Will anyone contend that there is no chance that the offspring of kings and rulers should be born with the philosophical nature?

Not one, he said.

And can anyone prove that if so born they must necessarily be corrupted? The difficulty of their salvation we too concede, but that in all the course of time not one of all could be saved, will anyone maintain that?

How could he?

But surely, said I, the occurrence of one such is enough, if he has a state which obeys him, to realize all that now seems so incredible.

Yes, one is enough, he said.

For if such a ruler, I said, ordains the laws and institutions that we have described it is surely not impossible that the citizens should be content to carry them out.

By no means.

Would it, then, be at all strange or impossible for others to come to the opinion to which we have come?

I think not, said he.

And further that these things are best, if possible, has already, I take it, been sufficiently shown.

Yes, sufficiently.

Our present opinion, then, about this legislation is that our plan would be best if it could be realized and that this realization is difficult yet not impossible.

That is the conclusion, he said.

This difficulty disposed of, we have next to speak of what remains, in what way, namely, and as a result of what studies and pursuits, these preservers of the constitution will form a part of our state, and at what ages they will severally take up each study.

Yes, we have to speak of that, he said.

I gained nothing, I said, by my cunning in omitting heretofore the distasteful topic of the possession of women and procreation of children and the appointment of rulers—because I knew that the absolutely true and right way would provoke censure and is difficult of realization—for now I am nonetheless compelled to discuss them. The matter of the women and children has been disposed of, but the education of the rulers has to be examined again, I may say, from the starting point. We were saying, if you recollect, that they must approve themselves lovers of the state when tested in pleasures and pains, and make it apparent that they do not abandon this fixed faith under stress of labors or fears or any other vicissitude, and that anyone who could not keep that faith must be rejected, while he who always issued from the test pure and intact, like gold tried in the fire, is to be established as ruler and to receive honors in life and after death and prizes as well. Something of this sort we said while the argument slipped by with veiled face in fear of starting our present debate.

Most true, he said, I remember.

We shrank, my friend, I said, from uttering the audacities which have now been hazarded. But now let us find courage for the definitive pronouncement that as the most perfect guardians we must establish philosophers.

Yes, assume it to have been said, said he.

Note, then, that they will naturally be few, for the different components of the nature which we said their education presupposed rarely consent to grow in one, but for the most part these qualities are found apart.

What do you mean? he said.

Facility in learning, memory, sagacity, quickness of apprehension, and their accompaniments, and youthful spirit and magnificence in soul are qualities, you know, that are rarely combined in human nature with a disposition to live orderly, quiet, and stable lives, but such men, by reason of their quickness, are driven about just as chance directs, and all steadfastness is gone out of them.

You speak truly, he said.

And on the other hand, the steadfast and stable temperaments, whom one could rather trust in use, and who in war are not easily moved and aroused to fear, are apt to act in the same way when confronted with studies. They are not easily aroused, learn with difficulty, as if benumbed, and are filled with sleep and yawning when an intellectual task is set them.

It is so, he said.

But we affirmed that a man must partake of both temperaments in due and fair combination or else participate in neither the highest education nor in honors nor in rule.

And rightly, he said.

Do you not think, then, that such a blend will be a rare thing?

Of course.

35

PLUTARCH

Timoleon and Aemilius Paulus

Such being the story of these two great men's lives, without doubt in the comparison very little difference will be found between them. They made war with two powerful enemies; the one against the Macedonians, and the other with the Carthaginians; and the success was in both cases glorious. One conquered Macedon from the seventh succeeding heir of Antigonus; the other freed Sicily from usurping tryants, and restored the island to its former liberty. Unless, indeed, it be made a point on Aemilius's side, that he engaged with Perseus when his forces were entire, and composed of men that had often successfully fought with the Romans; whereas, Timoleon found Dionysius in a despairing condition, his affairs being reduced to the last extremity: or, on the contrary, it be urged in favor of Timoleon, that he vanquished several tryants, and a powerful Carthaginian army, with an inconsiderable number of men gathered together from all parts, not with such an army as Aemilius had, of well disciplined soldiers, experienced in war, and accustomed to obey; but with such as through the hopes of gain resorted to him, unskilled in fighting and ungovernable. And when actions are equally glorious, and the means to compass them unequal, the greatest esteem is certainly due to that general who conquers with the smaller power.

Both have the reputation of having behaved themselves with an uncorrupted integrity, in all the affairs they managed: but Aemilius had the advantage of being, from his infancy, by the laws and customs of his country, brought up to the proper management of public affairs, which Timoleon brought himself to by his own efforts. And this is plain; for at

From *Plutarch's Lives*, trans. John Dryden (Philadelphia: The Nottingham Society, n.d.), vol. II, pp. 136–38. Written ca. 100 A.D.

that time all the Romans were uniformly orderly and obedient, respectful to the laws and to their fellow-citizens: whereas it is remarkable, that not one of the Greek generals commanding in Sicily, could keep himself uncorrupted, except Dion, and of him many entertain a jealousy that he would establish a monarchy there, after the Lacedaemonian manner. Timaeus writes, that the Syracusans sent even Gylippus home dishonorably, and with a reputation lost by the unsatiable covetousness he displayed when he commanded the army. And numerous historians tell us of the wicked and perfidious acts committed by Pharax the Spartan, and Callippus the Athenian, with the view of making themselves kings of Sicily. Yet what were these men, and what strength had they, to entertain such a thought? The first of them was a follower of Dionysius, when he was expelled from Syracuse, and the other a hired captain of foot under Dion, and came into Sicily with him. But Timoleon at the request and prayers of the Syracusans, was sent to be their general, and had no need to seek for power, but had a perfect title, founded on their own offers, to hold it; and yet no sooner had he freed Sicily from her oppressors, but he willingly surrendered it.

It is truly worthy our admiration in Aemilius, that, though he conquered so great and so rich a realm as that of Macedon, yet he would not touch, nor see any of the money, nor did he advantage himself one farthing by it, though he was very generous of his own to others. I would not intend any reflection on Timoleon, for accepting of a house and handsome estate in the country, which the Syracusans presented him with; there is no dishonor in accepting; but yet there is greater glory in a refusal, and the supremest virtue is shown in not wanting what it might fairly take. And as that body is, without doubt, the most strong and healthful, which can the easiest support extreme cold and excessive heat in the change of seasons, and that the most firm and collected mind which is not puffed up with prosperity, nor dejected with adversity; so the virtue of Aemilius was eminently seen in his countenance and behavior continuing as noble and lofty upon the loss of two dear sons, as when he achieved his greatest victories and triumphs. But Timoleon, after he had justly punished his brother, a truly heroic action, let his reason yield to a causeless sorrow, and, humiliated with grief and remorse, forbore for twenty years to appear in any public place, or meddle with any affairs of the commonwealth. It is truly very commendable to abhor and shun the doing any base action; but to stand in fear of every kind of censure or disrepute, may argue a gentle and openhearted, but not an heroic temper.

36

NICCOLÒ MACHIAVELLI

The Prince

OF SUCH AS HAVE ACHIEVED
SOVEREIGNTY BY MEANS OF CRIMES

BUT as there are also two ways in which a person may rise from private station to sovereignty, and which can neither be attributed to fortune nor to valor, it seems to me they should not be left unnoticed; although one of these ways might be more fully discussed when we treat of republics. These two modes are, when one achieves sovereignty either by wicked and nefarious means, or when a private citizen becomes sovereign of his country by the favor of his fellow-citizens. I will explain the first by two examples, the one ancient and the other modern; and without entering otherwise into the merits of these cases, I judge they will suffice to any one who may find himself obliged to imitate them.

Agathocles, a Sicilian, rose to be King of Syracuse, not only from being a mere private citizen, but from the lowest and most abject condition. He was the son of a potter, and led a vicious life through all the various phases of his career. But his wickedness was coupled with so much moral and physical courage, that, having joined the army, he rose by successive steps until he became Praetor of Syracuse. Having attained that rank he resolved to make himself sovereign, and to retain by violence, and regardless of others, that which had been intrusted to him by public consent. For this purpose he came to an understanding with Hamilcar the Carthaginian, who was at that time carrying on war with his army in Sicily; and having one morning called an assembly of the people and the Senate of Syracuse, as though he wished to confer with them about public affairs, he made his soldiers, at a given signal, slay all the senators and the richest of the people, and then seized the sovereignty of that city without any resistance on the part of the citizens. Although afterward twice defeated by the Carthaginians, and finally besieged by them in Syracuse, he not only defended that city, but, leaving a portion of his forces to sustain the siege, he crossed the sea with the other part and attacked Africa, thus raising the siege of Syracuse in a short time, and driving the Carthaginians to the extremest necessity, compelling them to make terms with him, and to remain content with the possession of Africa, and leave Sicily to him.

Whoever now reflects upon the conduct and valor of Agathocles will find in them little or nothing that can be attributed to fortune; for, as I have said, he achieved sovereignty, nor by the favor of any one, but through his high rank in the army, which he had won by a thousand efforts and dangers, and he afterward maintained his sovereignty with great courage, and even temerity. And yet we cannot call it valor to massacre one's fellow-citizens, to betray one's friends, and to be devoid of good faith, mercy and religion; such means may enable a man to achieve empire, but not glory. Still, if we consider the valor of Agathocles in encountering and overcoming dangers, and his invincible courage in supporting and mastering adversity, we shall find no reason why he should be regarded inferior to any of the most celebrated captains. But with all this, his outrageous cruelty and inhumanity, together with his infinite crimes, will not permit him to be classed with the most celebrated men. We cannot therefore ascribe to either valor or fortune the achievements of Agathocles, which he accomplished without either the one or the other.

In our own times, during the pontificate of Alexander VI, Oliverotto da Fermo, having been left an orphan, was brought up by his maternal uncle, Giovanni Fogliani, and was in early youth placed in the military service under Paolo Vitelli; so that, after having been thoroughly trained and disciplined, he might attain prominent rank in the army. After the death of Paolo, he served under his brother Vitellozzo; and became in a very short time, by his intelligence, his bodily strength and intrepidity, one of the foremost men in the service. But deeming it servile to act under the command of others, he planned, together with some of the citizens of Fermo who preferred servitude to the liberty of their country, and with the concurrence of Vitellozzo, to seize Fermo and make himself lord of the same. With this object he wrote to his uncle, Giovanni Fogliani, that, having been absent from home for several years, he desired now to come to see him and his native city, and also to look up his patrimony; and that, having until then striven only to acquire honor, he desired to show his fellow-citizens that he had not labored in vain; and therefore he wished to come in splendid style, accompanied by one hundred cavaliers, friends of his. He begged his uncle, therefore, to be pleased to arrange that the inhabitants of Fermo should give him an honorable reception, which would be an honor not only to him but also to Giovanni, who was his near relative and had brought him up. Giovanni therefore omitted no courtesies due to his nephew, and caused the citizens of Fermo to give him an honorable reception, as well as lodgings in their houses for himself and all his retinue. After spending some days in Fermo, and arranging all that was necessary for the execution of his villainous design, Oliverotto gave a sumptuous entertainment, to which he invited his uncle Giovanni and all the principal citizens of Fermo. After the dinner and the other entertainments that are customary on such occasions, Oliverotto artfully started a grave discussion respecting the greatness of Pope Alexander VI and his son Cesare Borgia and their enterprises. When Giovanni and the others replied to his remarks, Oliverotto suddenly arose, saying that these things were only to be spoken of in private places, and withdrew to another room, whither Giovanni and the other citizens followed. No sooner had they seated themselves there, than some of Oliverotto's soldiers rushed out from concealment and massacred Giovanni and all the others.

After this murder Oliverotto mounted his horse, rode through the streets of Fermo, and besieged the supreme magistrates in the palace, who, constrained by fear, obeyed him, and formed a government of which Oliverotto made himself sovereign. And as all those who, as malcontents, might have injured him, had been put to death, Oliverotto fortified himself in his position with new institutions, both civil and military, so that for the space of a year, during which he held the sovereignty, he was not only secure in the city of Fermo, but had become formidable to all his neighbors; so that it would have been as difficult to overcome him as Agathocles, had he not allowed himself to be deceived by Cesare Borgia, when, as I have related, he entrapped the Orsini and the Vitelli at Sinigaglia, where Oliverotto was also taken and strangled, together with Vitellozzo, his master in valor and in villainy, just one year after he had committed parricide in having his uncle Giovanni Fogliani assassinated.

Some may wonder how it was that Agathocles, and others like him, after their infinite treason and cruelty, could live for any length of time securely in the countries whose sovereignty they had usurped, and even defend themselves successfully against external enemies, without any attempts on the part of their own citizens to conspire against them; while many others could not by means of cruelty maintain their state even in time of peace, much less in doubtful times of war, I believe that this happened according as the cruelties were well or ill applied; we may call cruelty well applied (if indeed we may praise evil) when it is committed once from necessity for self-protection, and afterward not persisted in, but converted as far as possible to the public good. Ill-applied cruelties are those which, though at first but few, yet increase with time rather than cease altogether. Those who adopt the first practice may, with the help of God and man, render some service to their state, as had been done by Agathocles; but those who adopt the latter course will not possibly be able to maintain themselves in their state. Whence it is to be noted that in taking possession of a state the conqueror should well reflect as to the harsh measures that may be necessary, and then execute them at a single blow, so as not to be obliged to renew them every day; and by thus not repeating them, to assure himself of the support of the inhabitants, and win them over to himself by benefits bestowed. And he who acts otherwise, either from timidity or from being badly advised, will be obliged ever to be sword in hand, and will never be able to rely upon his subjects, who in turn will not be able to rely upon him, because of the constant fresh wrongs committed by him. Cruelties should be committed all at once, as in that way each separate one is less felt, and gives less offence; benefits, on the other hand, should be conferred one at a time, for in that way they will be more appreciated. But above all a prince should live upon such terms with his subjects that no accident, either for good or for evil, should make him vary his conduct toward them. For when adverse times bring upon you the necessity for action, you will no longer be in time to do evil; and the good you may do will not profit you, because it will be regarded as having been forced from you, and therefore will bring you no thanks.

Of Civil Principalities

But let us come now to that other case, when a prominent citizen has become prince of his country, not by treason and violence, but by the favor of his fellow-citizens. This may be called a civil principality; and to attain it requires neither great courage and talent nor extraordinary good fortune, but rather a happy shrewdness. I say, then, that such principalities are achieved either by the favor of the people or by that of the nobles; for in every state there will be found two different dispositions, which result from the fact that the people dislike being ruled and oppressed by the nobles, while the nobles seek to rule and oppress the people. And this diversity of feeling and interests engenders one of three things: either a principality, or a government of liberty, or license. A principality results either from the will of the people or from that of the nobles, according as either the one or the other prevails and has the opportunity. For the nobles, seeing that they cannot resist the people, begin to have recourse to the influence and reputation of one of their own class, and make him a prince, so that under the shadow of his power they may give free scope to their desires. The people also, seeing that they cannot resist the nobles, have recourse to the influence and reputation of one man, and make him prince, so as to be protected by his authority. He who becomes prince by the aid of the nobles will have more difficulty in maintaining himself that he who arrives at that high station by the aid of the people. For the former finds himself surrounded by many who in their own opinion are equal to him, and for that reason he can neither command nor manage them in his own way. But he who attains the principality by the favor of the people stands alone, and has around him none, or very few, that will not yield him a ready obedience. Moreover, you cannot satisfy the nobles with honesty, and without wrong to others, but it is easy to satisfy the people, whose aims are ever more honest than those of the nobles; the latter wishing to oppress, and the former being unwilling to be oppressed. I will say further, that a prince can never assure himself of a people who are hostile to him, for they are too numerous; the nobles on the other hand being but few, it becomes easy for a prince to make himself sure of them.

The worst that a prince may expect of a people who are unfriendly to him is that they will desert him; but the hostile nobles he has to fear, not only lest they abandon him, but also because they will turn against him. For they, being more farsighted and astute, always save themselves in advance, and seek to secure the favor of him whom they hope may be successful. The prince also is obliged always to live with the same people; but he can do very well without the same nobles, whom he can make and unmake at will any day, and bestow upon them or deprive them of their rank whenever it pleases him. The better to elucidate this subject, we must consider the nobles mainly in two ways; that is to say, they either

shape their conduct so as to ally themselves entirely to your fortunes, or
they do not. Those who attach themselves to you thus, if they are not
rapacious, are to be honored and loved. Those who do not attach themselves to you must be regarded in two ways. Either they are influenced by
pusillanimity and a natural lack of courage, and then you may make use
of them, and especially of such as are men of intelligence; for in prosperity they will honor you, and in adversity you need not fear them. But if
they purposely avoid attaching themselves to you from notions of ambition, then it is an evidence that they think more of their own interests
than of yours; and of such men a prince must beware, and look upon
them as open enemies, for when adversity comes they will always turn
against him and contribute to this ruin.

Any one, therefore, who has become a prince by the favor of the
people, must endeavor to preserve their good will, which will be easy for
him, as they will ask of him no more than that he shall not oppress them.
But he who, contrary to the will of the people, has become prince by the
favor of the nobles, should at once and before everything else strive to win
the good will of the people, which will be easy for him, by taking them
under his protection. And as men, when they receive benefits from one of
whom they expected only ill treatment, will attach themselves readily to
such a benefactor, so the people will become more kindly disposed to
such a one than if he had been made prince by their favor. Now a prince
can secure the good will of the people in various ways, which differ with
their character, and for which no fixed rules can be given. I will merely
conclude by saying that it is essential for a prince to possess the good will
and affection of his people, otherwise he will be utterly without support in
time of adversity. Nabis, prince of Sparta, sustained the attacks of all
Greece, and of a victorious Roman army, and successfully defended his
country and his state against them; and when danger came, it was enough
for him to be assured of a few supporters, which would not have sufficed
if the people had been hostile to him. And let no one contravene this
opinion of mine by quoting the trite saying, that "he who relies upon the
people builds upon quicksand"; though this may be true when a private
citizen places his reliance upon the people in the belief that they will
come to his relief when he is oppressed by his enemies or the magistrates.
In such a case he will often find himself deceived; as happened in Rome
to the Gracchi, and in Florence to Messer Scali. But it being a prince
who places his reliance upon those whom he might command, and being
a man of courage and undismayed by adversity, and not having neglected
to make proper preparations, and keeping all animated by his own cou-

rageous example and by his orders, he will not be deceived by the people; and it will be seen that the foundations of his state are laid solidly.

Those princes run great risks who attempt to change a civil government into an absolute one; for such princes command either in person or by means of magistrates. In the latter case, their state is more feeble and precarious; for the prince is in all things dependent upon the will of those citizens who are placed at the head of the magistracy, who, particularly in times of adversity, may with great ease deprive him of the government, either by open opposition or by refusing him obedience. For when danger is upon him, the prince is no longer in time to assume absolute authority; for the citizens and subjects who have been accustomed to receive their commands from the magistrates will not be disposed to yield obedience to the prince when in adversity. Thus in doubtful times there will ever be a lack of men whom he can trust. Such a prince cannot depend upon what he observes in ordinary quiet times, when the citizens have need of his authority; for then everybody runs at his bidding, everybody promises, and everybody is willing to die for him, when death is very remote. But in adverse times, when the government has need of the citizens, then but few will be found to stand by the prince. And this experience is the more dangerous as it can only be made once.

A wise prince, therefore, will steadily pursue such a course that the citizens of his state will always and under all circumstances feel the need of his authority, and will therefore always prove faithful to him.

OF CRUELTY AND CLEMENCY, AND WHETHER IT IS BETTER TO BE LOVED THAN FEARED

Coming down now to the other aforementioned qualities, I say that every prince ought to desire the reputation of being merciful, and not cruel; at the same time, he should be careful not to misuse that mercy. Cesare Borgia was reputed cruel, yet by his cruelty he reunited the Romagna to his states, and restored that province to order, peace, and loyalty; and if we carefully examine his course, we shall find it to have been really much more merciful than the course of the people of Florence, who, to escape the reputation of cruelty, allowed Pistoia to be destroyed. A prince, therefore, should not mind the ill repute of cruelty, when he can thereby keep his subjects united and loyal; for a few displays of severity will really be more merciful than to allow, by an excess of clemency, disorders to occur, which are apt to result in rapine and murder; for these injure a whole community, while the executions ordered by the prince fall only upon a few individuals. And, above all others, the new prince will find it almost impossible to avoid the reputation of cruelty, because new states are generally exposed to many dangers. It was on this account that Virgil made Dido to excuse the severity of her government, because it was still new, saying, —

> "Res dura, et regni novitas me talia cogunt
> Moliri, et late fines custode tueri."[1]

A prince, however, should be slow to believe and to act; nor should he be too easily alarmed by his own fears, and should proceed moderately and with prudence and humanity, so that an excess of confidence may not make him incautious, nor too much mistrust make him intolerant. This, then, gives rise to the question "whether it be better to be beloved than feared, or to be feared than beloved." It will naturally be answered that it would be desirable to be both the one and the other; but as it is difficult to be both at the same time, it is much more safe to be feared than to be loved, when you have to choose between the two. For it may be said of men in general that they are ungrateful and fickle, dissemblers, avoiders of danger, and greedy of gain. So long as you shower benefits upon them, they are all yours; they offer you their blood, their substance, their lives, and their children, provided the necessity for it is far off; but when it is near at hand, then they revolt. And the prince who relies upon their words, without having otherwise provided for his security, is ruined; for friendships that are won by rewards, and not by greatness and nobility of soul, although deserved, yet are not real, and cannot be depended upon in time of adversity.

Besides, men have less hesitation in offending one who makes himself beloved than one who makes himself feared; for love holds by a bond of obligation which, as mankind is bad, is broken on every occasion whenever it is for the interest of the obliged party to break it. But fear holds by the apprehension of punishment, which never leaves men. A prince, however, should make himself feared in such a manner that, if he has not won the affections of his people, he shall at least not incur their hatred; for the being feared, and not hated, can go very well together, if the prince abstains from taking the substance of his subjects, and leaves them their women. And if you should be obliged to inflict capital punishment upon any one, then be sure to do so only when there is manifest cause and proper justification for it; and, above all things, abstain from taking people's property, for men will sooner forget the death of their fathers than the loss of their patrimony. Besides, there will never be any lack of reasons for taking people's property; and a prince who once begins to live by rapine will ever find excuses for seizing other people's property. On the other hand, reasons for taking life are not so easily found, and more readily exhausted. But when a prince is at the head of his army, with a multitude of soldiers under his command then it is above all things necessary for him to disregard the reputation of cruelty; for without such severity an army cannot be kept together, nor disposed for any successful feat of arms.

Among the many admirable qualities of Hannibal, it is related of him that, having an immense army composed of a very great variety of races of men, which he led to war in foreign countries, no quarrels ever occurred among them, nor were there ever any dissensions between them and their chief, either in his good or in his adverse fortunes; which can only be accounted for by his extreme cruelty. This, together with his boundless courage, made him ever venerated and terrible in the eyes of his soldiers; and without that extreme severity all his other virtues would not have sufficed to produce that result.

Inconsiderate writers have, on the one hand, admired his deeds, and, on the other, condemned the principal cause of the same. And the proof that his other virtues would not have sufficed him may be seen from the case of Scipio, who was one of the most remarkable men, not only of his own time, but in all history. His armies revolted in Spain solely in consequence of his extreme clemency, which allowed his soldiers more license than comports with proper military discipline. This act was censured in the Roman Senate by Fabius Maximus, who called Scipio the corrupter of the Roman soldiers. The tribe of the Locrians having been wantonly destroyed by one of the lieutenants of Scipio, he neither punished him for that nor for his insolence, — simply because of his own easy nature; so that, when somebody wished to excuse Scipio in the Senate, he said, "that there were many men who knew better how to avoid errors themselves than to punish them in others." This easy nature of Scipio's would in time have dimmed his fame and glory if he had persevered in it under the Empire; but living as he did under the government of the Senate, this dangerous quality of his was not only covered up, but actually redounded to his honor.

To come back now to the question whether it be better to be beloved than feared, I conclude that, as men love of their own free will, but are inspired with fear by the will of the prince, a wise prince should always rely upon himself, and not upon the will of others; but, above all, should he always strive to avoid being hated, as I have already said above.

In What Manner Princes Should Keep Their Faith

It must be evident to every one that it is more praiseworthy for a prince always to maintain good faith, and practice integrity rather than craft and deceit. And yet the experience of our own times has shown that those princes have achieved great things who made small account of good faith, and who understood by cunning to circumvent the intelligence of others; and that in the end they got the better of those whose actions were dictated by loyalty and good faith. You must know, therefore, that there are two ways of carrying on a contest; the one by law, and the other by force. The first is practiced by men, and the other by animals; and as the first is often insufficient, it becomes necessary to resort to the second.

A prince then should know how to employ the nature of man, and that of the beasts as well. This was figuratively taught by ancient writers, who relate how Achilles and many other princes were given to Chiron the centaur to be nurtured, and how they were trained under his tutorship; which fable means nothing else than that their perceptor combined the qualities of the man and the beast; and that a prince, to succeed, will have to employ both the one and the other nature, as the one without the other cannot produce lasting results.

It being necessary then for a prince to know well how to employ the nature of the beasts, he should be able to assume both that of the fox and that of the lion; for while the latter cannot escape the traps laid for him, the former cannot defend himself against the wolves. A prince should be a fox, to know the traps and snares; and a lion, to be able to frighten the wolves; for those who simply hold to the nature of the lion do not understand their business.

A sagacious prince then cannot and should not fulfill his pledges when their observance is contrary to his interest, and when the causes that induced him to pledge his faith no longer exist. If men were all good, then indeed this precept would be bad; but as men are naturally bad, and will not observe their faith toward you, you must, in the same way, not observe yours to them; and no prince ever yet lacked legitimate reasons with which to color his want of good faith. Innumerable modern examples could be given of this; and it could easily be shown how many treaties of peace, and how many engagements, have been made null and void by the faithlessness of princes; and he who has best known how to play the fox has ever been the most successful.

But it is necessary that the prince should know how to color this nature well, and how to be a great hypocrite and dissembler. For men are so simple, and yield so much to immediate necessity, that the deceiver will never lack dupes. I will mention one of the most recent examples. Alexander VI never did nor ever thought of anything but to deceive, and always found a reason for doing so. No one ever had greater skill in pledging his word, no one affirmed his pledges with greater oaths, and observed them less, than Pope Alexander; and yet he was always successful in his deceits, because he knew the weakness of men in that particular.

It is not necessary, however, for a prince to possess all the above-mentioned qualities; but it is essential that he should at least seem to have them. I will even venture to say, that to have and to practice them constantly is pernicious, but to seem to have them is useful. For instance, a prince should seem to be merciful, faithful, humane, religious, and upright, and should even be so in reality; but he should have his mind so trained that, when occasion requires it, he may know how to change to the opposite. And it must be understood that a prince, and especially one who has but recently acquired his state, cannot perform all those things which cause men to be esteemed as good; he being often obliged, for the sake of maintaining his state, to act contrary to humanity, charity, and religion. And therefore is it necessary that he should have a versatile mind, capable of changing readily, according as the winds and changes of fortune bid him; and, as has been said above, not to swerve from the good if possible, but to know how to resort to evil if necessity demands it.

A prince then should be very careful never to allow anything to escape his lips that does not abound in the above-named five qualities, so that to see and to hear him he may seem all charity, integrity, and humanity, all uprightness, and all piety. And more than all else is it necessary for a prince to seem to possess the last quality; for mankind in general judge more by what they see than by what they feel, every one being capable of the former, and but few of the latter. Everybody sees what you seem to be, but few really feel what you are; and these few dare not oppose the opinion of the many, who are protected by the majesty of the state; for the actions of all men, and especially those of princes, are judged by the result, where there is no other judge to whom to appeal.

A prince then should look mainly to winning, and to the successful maintenance of his state. The means which he employs for this will always be accounted honorable, and will be praised by everybody; for the common people are always taken by appearances and by results, and it is the vulgar mass that constitutes the world. But a very few have rank and station, while the many have nothing to sustain them. A certain prince of our time, whom it is well not to name, never preached anything but peace and good faith; but if he had always observed either the one or the other, it would in most instances have cost him his reputation or his state.

NOTE

1. "My cruel fate, / And doubts attending an unsettled state, / Force me to guard my coasts from foreign foes."—DRYDEN.

37

KURT LEWIN

Authoritarianism and Democratic Leadership

THE psychologist of today recognizes that there are few problems more important for the development of the child and the problem of adolescence than a study of the processes by which a child takes over or becomes opposed to the ideology and the style of living predominant in his social climate, the forces which make him belong to certain groups, or which determine his social status and his security within those groups.

A genuine attempt to approach these problems experimentally—for instance, that of social status or leadership—implies technically that one has to create different types of groups and to set up experimentally a variety of social factors which might shift this status. The experimental social psychologist will have to acquaint himself with the task of experimentally creating groups, creating a social climate or style of living. The sociologist I hope will therefore forgive him when he cannot avoid handling also the so-called sociological problems of groups and group life. Perhaps the social psychologist might prove to be even of considerable help to the sociologist. Frequently the investigation on the border line between two sciences has proved to be particularly fruitful for the progress of both of them.

Take, for instance, the concept "social group." There has been much discussion about how to define a group. The group often has been considered as something more than the sum of the individuals, something better and higher. One has attributed to it a "group mind." The opponents of this opinion have declared the concept of "group mind" to be mere

Kurt Lewin, "The Consequences of Authoritarian and Democratic Leadership," in Alvin W. Gouldner, ed., *Studies in Leadership* (New York: Harper & Brothers, 1950), pp. 409–17.

metaphysics and that in reality the group is nothing other than the sum of the individuals. To one who has watched the development of the concept of organism, whole or Gestalt, in psychology this argumentation sounds strangely familiar. In the beginning of Gestalt theory, at the time of Ehrenfels, one attributed to a psychological whole, such as a melody, a so-called Gestalt quality—that is, an additional entity like a group mind, which the whole was supposed to have in addition to the sum of its parts. Today we know that we do not need to assume a mystical Gestalt quality, but that any dynamical whole has properties of its own. The whole might be symmetric in spite of its parts being asymmetric, a whole might be unstable in spite of its parts being stable in themselves.

As far as I can see, the discussion regarding group versus individual in sociology follows a similar trend. Groups are sociological wholes; the unity of these sociological wholes can be defined operationally in the same way as a unity of any other dynamic whole, namely, by the interdependence of its parts. Such a definition takes mysticism out of the group conception and brings the problem down to a thoroughly empirical and testable basis. At the same time it means a full recognition of the fact that properties of a social group, such as its organization, its stability, its goals, are something different from the organization, the stability, and the goals of the individuals in it.

How, then, should one describe a group? Let us discuss the effect of democratic, autocratic and laissez-faire atmospheres at clubs which have been experimentally created by R. Lippitt, and by R. Lippitt and R. K. White, at the Iowa Child Welfare Research Station. Let us assume the club had five members and five observers were available. It might seem the simplest way always to assign one observer to one member of the club. However, the result at best would be five parallel micro-biographies of five individuals. This procedure would not yield a satisfactory record even of such simple facts of the group life as its organization, its sub-groups, and its leader-member relationship, not to speak of such important facts as the general atmosphere. Therefore, instead of assigning every observer to one individual, one observer was assigned to record from minute to minute the organization of the group into subgroups, another the social interactions, etc. In other words, instead of observing the properties of individuals, the properties of the group as such were observed.

In one additional point sociology may well profit from psychology. It is a commonplace that the behavior of individuals as well as groups depends upon their situation and their peculiar position in it. In my mind the last decade of psychology has shown that it is possible to give a clearly detailed description of the peculiar structure of a concrete situation and its dynamics in scientific terms. It can even be done in exact mathematical terms. The youngest discipline of geometry called "topology" is an excellent tool with which to determine the pattern of the life-space of an individual, and to determine within this life-space the relative positions which the different regions of activity or persons, or groups of persons, bear to each other. It has become possible to transform into mathematical terms such everyday statements as: "He is now closer to his goal of being a first-rate physician," "He has changed the direction of his actions," or "He has joined a group." In other words, it is possible to determine, in a geometrically precise manner, the position, direction, and distance within the life-space, even in such cases where the position of the person and the direction of his actions are not physical but social in nature. With this in mind let us return to the social experiment which was undertaken at the Iowa Child Welfare Research Station.

THE EXPERIMENTAL SETTING

It is well known that the amount of success a teacher has in the classroom depends not only on her *skill* but to a great extent on the *atmosphere* she creates. This atmosphere is something intangible; it is a property of the social situation as a whole, and might be measured scientifically if approached from this angle. As a beginning, therefore, Lippitt selected a comparison between a democratic and an autocratic atmosphere for his study. The purpose of his experiment was not to duplicate any given autocracy or democracy or to study an "ideal" autocracy or democracy, but to create set-ups which would give insight into the underlying group dynamics. Two groups of boys and girls, ten and eleven years of age, were chosen for a mask-making club from a group of eager volunteers of two different school classes. With the help of the Moreno test both groups were equated as much as possible on such qualities as leadership and interpersonal relations. There were eleven meetings of the groups, the democratic group meeting always two days ahead of the autocratic one. The democratic group chose its activities freely. Whatever they chose the autocratic group was then ordered to do. In this way the activities of the group were equated. On the whole, then, everything was kept constant except the group atmosphere.

The leader in both groups was an adult student. He tried to create the different atmospheres by using the following technique:

Democratic	*Authoritarian*
1. All policies a matter of group determination, encouraged and drawn out by the leader.	1. All determination of policy by the strongest person (leader).
2. Activity perspective given by an explanation of the general steps of the process during discussion at first meeting (clay mould, plaster of Paris, papier-mache, etc.). Where technical advice was needed, the leader tried to point out two or three alternative procedures from which choice could be made.	2. Techniques and steps of attaining the goal (completed mask) dictated by the authority, one at a time, so that future direction was always uncertain to a large degree.
3. The members were free to work with whomever they chose and the division of tasks was left up to the group.	3. The authority usually determined autocratically what each member should do and with whom he should work.
4. The leader attempted to be a group member in spirit and in discussion but not to perform much of the actual work. He gave objective praise and criticism.	4. The dominator criticized and praised individual's activities *without giving objective reasons*, and remained aloof from active group participation. He was always impersonal rather than outwardly hostile or friendly (a necessary concession in method).

During the meetings of the two groups, the observers noted the number of incidents and actions per unit of time. It was observed that the autocratic leader put forth about twice as much action toward the members as the democratic leader, namely, 8.4 actions as against 4.5. This difference is even greater if one takes into account only the initiated social approach, namely, 5.2 as against 2.1. Still greater is this difference in relation to ascendant or initiated ascendant behavior: the ascendant actions of the autocratic leader were nearly three times as frequent as those of the democratic leader.

In regard to submissive actions, the proportion was opposite, namely, more frequent by the democratic leader, although in both groups submissive actions of the leader were relatively rare. A similar relation held for the objective, matter-of-fact actions. Here too the democratic leader showed a higher frequency.

On the whole, then, there existed a much greater impact on the members of the group by the leader in autocracy than in democracy, and the approach was much more ascendant and less matter-of-fact.

When we attempt to answer the question "How does the leader compare with the ordinary member in an autocracy and a democracy?" we must refer to an ideal average member who is a statistical representation of what would happen if all activities were distributed equally among the members of the group, including the leader. In Lippitt's experiment the figures showed two facts clearly: first, in both groups the leader was really leading. The autocratic leader showed 118 percent more initiated ascendant acts than the average ideal member, and the democratic leader 41 percent more. Both leaders were less submissive than the average member, namely, the autocrat 78 percent, the democrat 53 percent. It was interesting to note that both showed also more matter-of-fact action than the average ideal member.

However, the difference between the ordinary member and the leader was much less pronounced in democracy than in autocracy, both in ascendant and submissive action. The democratic leader distinguished himself, also relatively, more by his greater matter-of-factness.

What do these figures indicate about the situation in which the autocratic and democratic group members find themselves? I can only mention a few aspects: In the autocratic group it is the leader who sets the policy. For instance, a child says: "I thought we decided to do the other mask." The leader answers: "No, this is the one *I* decided last time would be the best one." In dynamical terms such an incident means that the child would have been able to reach his own goal but the leader puts up a barrier against this locomotion. Instead he induces another goal for the child and a force in this direction. We are calling such goals, set up by the power of another person, an *induced* goal.

A parallel example in the democratic group might be this: A child asks, "How big will we make the mask? Are they out of clay or what?" The leader answers: "Would you like me to give you a little idea of how people generally make masks?" In other words, the leader in the democratic group, instead of hindering the children in getting to their own goal, bridges over whatever regions of difficulty might exist. For the democratic group, many paths are open; for the autocratic only one, namely, that determined by the leader. In an autocracy the leader determines not only the kind of activity but also who should work with whom. In our experimental democracy all work co-operation was the result of spontaneous sub-grouping of children. In the autocracy 32 percent of the work groups were initiated by the leader, as against 0 percent in the democracy.

On the whole, then, the autocratic atmosphere gives a much greater and more aggressive dominance of the leader, and a narrowing down of the free movement of the members, together with a weakening of their power fields.

EFFECTS ON THE GROUP

What is the effect of this atmosphere on the group life of the children? As measured by the observers the child-to-child relationship was rather different in the two atmospheres. There was about thirty times as much hostile domination in the autocracy as in the democracy, more demands for attention and much more hostile criticism; whereas in the democratic atmosphere co-operation and praise of the other fellow was much more frequent. In the democracy more constructive suggestions were made and a matter-of-fact or submissive behavior of member to member was more frequent.

In interpreting these data, we might say that the "style of living and thinking" initiated by the leader dominated the relations between the children. In the autocracy, instead of a co-operative attitude, a hostile and highly personal attitude became prevalent. This was strikingly brought out by the amount of group or "we" feeling as against "I" feeling: Statements which were "we-centered" occurred twice as often in the democracy as in the autocracy, whereas far more statements in the autocracy were "I-centered" than in the democracy.

So far as the relation of the children toward the leader was concerned, the statistical analysis revealed that the children in the autocratic group who were *less submissive* to each other were about twice as submissive to their leader, as the children in the democratic group. Initiated approaches to the leader in the democratic group were less frequent than in the autocratic group. In autocracy the action by the member toward the leader had more the character of a *response* to an approach of the leader. The approach to the leader in the autocracy was more submissive, or kept at least on a matter-of-fact basis.

On the whole, then, the style of living in both atmospheres governed the child-child relation as well as the child-leader relation. In the autocratic group the children were less matter-of-fact, less cooperative, and submissive toward their equals, but more submissive to their superior than in the democracy.

Behind this difference of behavior lie a number of factors. The tension is greater in the autocratic atmosphere, and the dynamic structure of both groups is rather different. In an autocratic group there are two clearly distinguished levels of social status: the leader is the only one having higher status, the others being on an equally low level. A strong barrier kept up by the leader prevents any one from increasing his status by acquiring leadership. In a democratic atmosphere the difference in social status is slight and there exists no barrier against acquiring leadership.

This has a rather clear effect on the amount of individuality. In our experiment every individual in the democracy showed a relatively greater individuality, having some field of his own in spite of the greater "we" feeling among them, or perhaps because of it. In the autocratic group on the contrary the children all had a low status without much individuality. The type of sub-grouping showed this difference even more clearly. In the autocracy, there was little "we" feeling and relatively little spontaneous sub-grouping among the children. If the work required the co-operation of four or five members, it was the leader who had to order the members to get together. In the democracy those groups came together spontaneously and they kept together about twice as long as in the autocracy. In the autocracy these larger units disintegrated much faster when left to themselves.

These group structures, in combination with the high tension in the autocracy, led in Lippitt's experiments to a *scapegoat* situation. The children in the autocratic group ganged together not against their leader, but against one of the children and treated him so badly that he ceased coming to the club. This happened to two different children during twelve sessions. Under autocratic rule any increase in status through leadership was blocked and the attempt to dominate was dictated by the style of living. In other words, every child became a potential enemy of every other one and the power fields of the children weakened each other, instead of strengthening each other by co-operation. Through combining in an attack against one individual the members who otherwise could not gain higher status were able to do so by violent suppression of one of their fellows.

One may ask whether these results are not due merely to individual differences. A number of facts rule out this explanation, although of course individual differences always play a role. Of particular interest was the transfer of one of the children from the autocratic to the democratic group, and of another from the democratic to the autocratic one. Before the transfer the difference between the two children was the same as between the two groups they belonged to, namely, the autocratic child was more dominating and less friendly and objective than the democratic one. However, after the transfer the behavior changed so that the previously autocratic child now became the less dominating and more friendly and objective child. In other words, the behavior of the children mirrored very quickly the atmosphere of the group in which they moved.

Later Lippitt and White studied four new clubs with other leaders. They included a third atmosphere, namely, that of laissez faire, and exposed the same children successively to a number of atmospheres. On the whole, the results bear out those of Lippitt. They show a striking difference between laissez faire and democracy very much in favor of democracy. They show further two types of reaction in the autocratic groups, one characterized by aggression, the second by apathy.

On the whole, I think there is ample proof that the difference in behavior in autocratic, democratic, and laissez-faire situations is not a result of individual differences. There have been few experiences for me as impressive as seeing the expression in children's faces change during the first day of autocracy. The friendly, open, and co-operative group, full of life, became within a short half-hour a rather apathetic-looking gathering without initiative. The change from autocracy to democracy seemed to take somewhat more time than from democracy to autocracy. Autocracy is imposed upon the individual. Democracy he has to learn.

38

DENNIS F. THOMPSON

Moral Responsibility of Public Officials

That many different officials contribute in many different ways to
decisions and policies in the modern state makes it difficult to
ascribe moral responsibility to any official. The usual responses to
this problem—based on concepts of hierarchial and collective
responsibility—distort the notion of responsibility. The idea of
personal responsibility—based on causal and volitional criteria—
constitutes a better approach to the problem of ascribing
responsibility to public officials. Corresponding to each of these
criteria are types of excuses that officials use in defending the
decisions they make. An analysis of the conditions under which the
excuses eliminate or mitigate responsibility provides a foundation for
accountability in a democracy.

PHILOSOPHERS and political scientists in recent years have begun to apply moral principles to public policy and to public officials.[1] None of these scholars supposes that moral principles can, without modification, be directly deployed in politics. Indeed, one of their preoccupations is the possibility that public life may require officials to act in ways that would be wrong in private life, raising the classic problem of "dirty hands"(Walzer 1973). But in a significant respect, their analyses are often apolitical: the official they portray agonizing over a moral dilemma seems a solitary figure, single-handedly gathering information and implementing decisions. This paradigm of the lonely leader obscures a pervasive feature of modern government—a feature that stands in the way of applying moral principles, whatever their content, to individual officials.

From Dennis F. Thompson, "Moral Responsibility of Public Officials: The Problem of Many
Hands," *American Political Science Review* 74 (1980): 905–16. Reprinted by permission.

Because many different officials contribute in many ways to decisions and policies of government, it is difficult even in principle to identify who is morally responsible for political outcomes. This is what I call the problem of many hands.

I shall argue that the two most common ways of ascribing responsibility to officials—the hierarchical and the collective models—do not adequately respond to this problem; and that personal responsibility, suitably interpreted, can be imputed to officials more often than these models suggest. The criteria for personal responsibility I adopt are common to wide range of moral theories; they hold us responsible for outcomes insofar as we cause them and do not act in ignorance or under compulsion. On these criteria we can say that one official is more or less responsible than another official without implying, as in the law, that degrees of fault correspond to proportionate shares of compensation or match the standard categories of criminal liability. Legal responsibility, though suggestive, is not a reliable guide to moral responsibility (see Hart 1968, 211–30; and Feinberg 1970, 24–54).

Corresponding to each of the criteria of personal responsibility are types of excuses officials use to eliminate or mitigate their responsibility for political outcomes.[2] Drawing examples from episodes in contemporary American government (chiefly the executive branch), I shall outline some of the conditions under which the excuses seem to be acceptable or unacceptable. From such an outline, we should not expect to derive anything so systematic as a general theory of excuses, but we should be able to develop a set of considerations based on a body of cases, more like traditional moral casuistry than modern ethical and political theory. In most political contests, this set of considerations will have to be supplemented by substantive principles of political ethics grounded in concepts such as justice and the public interest. But even by itself an analysis of excuses can serve to inform our judgments about those who govern us, and thus enrich our understanding of political responsibility.[3] Its use might even influence the conduct of public officials. Those who took the idea of personal responsibility seriously would perhaps make decisions with greater care, and if they did not, citizens or other officials could reinforce ascriptions of responsibility with sanctions, such as public criticism, dismissal from office, or exclusion from public office in the future. Whether personal responsibility could actually support democratic accountability in this way depends partly on the nature of the social and political structure in which citizens and officials act. But as important as it is to analyze this structure, the prior task, and the one on which I concentrate here, is to establish a framework for the discourse of responsibility.

HIERARCHICAL RESPONSIBILITY

According to the hierarchical model, responsibility for political outcomes falls on the person who stands highest in the (formal or informal) chain of authority. Weber provides the classic statement of the model. He holds, first, that modern government recognizes "fixed jurisdictional areas" and "office hierarchy" in which "there is a supervision of the lower offices by the higher ones" (Gerth and Mills 1958, 196–97). Second, he sharply distinguishes between administration and politics: administrators merely execute the policies set by politicians (pp. 95, 214–16). Finally, the administrator and the politician are therefore subject to "exactly the opposite principle of responsibility": "The honor of the civil servant is vested in his ability to execute conscientiously the order of the superior authority, exactly as if the order agreed with his own conviction. . . . The honor of the political leader . . . however, lies precisely in an exclusive personal responsibility for what he does, a responsibility he cannot and must not reject or transfer."[4]

Weber's model vastly simplifies the task of ascribing responsibility to public officials since it places most public officials most of the time beyond the province of moral responsibility. As long as they follow the orders of their superiors and the procedures of the organization, they are not responsible for any harmful results of their actions. We are of course still left with the chore of sorting out the responsibility of the various politicians who have a hand in making the policies that the administrators carry out, but because the hands are fewer and because the jurisdictions are well defined, the problem is much more tractable.

Weber's model, however, does not correspond to the portrait of politics that emerges from modern studies of the making of public policy. Instead of functioning within well-defined jurisdictions and settled lines of authority, officials act within overlapping "issue networks" whose membership is shifting and partially drawn from outside government (Heclo 1978, 87–124); they engage in a "bargaining game" where victory depends more on "skill and will in using [other] bargaining advantages" and "other players' perceptions" than on positions in a hierarchy (Allison 1971, 144–84). Instead of respecting a clear distinction between politics and administration, bureaucrats exercise discretionary authority either delegated to them, or simply assumed by them, to shape and often make policy; meanwhile, elected politicians concern themselves with the details of implementation (Altshuler 1977, 2–17; Lowi 1979, 92–126; and Rourke 1978, 253).

The empirical deficiencies of the hierarchical model do not necessarily defeat it as a normative standard. Weber himself anticipated some of the developments that impugn the model (pp. 232–33), and later writers continue to commend the model in spite of—or because of—the growth of administrative discretion and the dispersion of authority in the modern state (e.g., Lowi 1979, 295–313; and Krasner 1972, 160). But even if a more hierarchical structure of government is desirable, the hierarchical model is not a satisfactory basis on which to ascribe responsibility in the structure of government that now prevails—at least not where discretion and dispersion abound. Insofar as officials holding the top positions in a hierarchy cannot be expected to have control over political outcomes, hierarchical responsibility does not coincide with moral responsibility. To try to impute moral responsibility according to hierarchical position would in these circumstances violate a fundamental presupposition of morality, namely, that a person should be blamed only if he or she could have acted otherwise. The difficulty is not that it would be unfair to hold top officials responsible for failures beyond their control. Officials know in advance that they may lose their jobs because of events over which they could have had little or no influence, and they thus tacitly consent to the risk of this kind of political "punishment." Such risk, moreover, may be a useful feature in the design of political institutions, encouraging officials to take every possible precaution to avoid mistakes. But these considerations show only that strict liability in politics may be morally justifiable; they do not establish that such liability is equivalent to moral responsibility. Even when we hold officials strictly accountable in this way, we usually do not condemn them morally.

That hierarchical responsibility imparts scarcely any moral force explains why political leaders are often quite ready to declare themselves fully responsibile for some pernicious decision or policy. Taking responsibility becomes a kind of political ritual that has no negative effect on a leader. Indeed, leaders can often turn this ritual to their advantage (cf. Thompson 1961, 129–37; and Edelman 1964, 79). With regular incantations of "I accept full responsibility," an official strengthens his or her own political standing—by reassuring the public that someone is in charge and by projecting an image of a courageous leader who does not pass the buck. Also, as one becomes known as a leader who takes the blame for subordinates, one gains gratitude and thus greater obedience from those subordinates in the future. Most significantly, the ritual often quells public debate about a controversial decision or policy, effectively blocking further inquiry into the genuine moral responsibility of all of the officials involved, especially that of the leader. After the failure of the Bay of Pigs invasion, President Kennedy privately blamed the CIA, the Joint Chiefs, and just about everyone who knew about the invasion in advance. But publicly he accepted the "sole responsibility" and objected to anyone's "attempting to shift responsibility" away from him (Schlesinger 1965, 289–90). The hierarchical model, reinforcing this ritual taking of responsibility, in this case not only cut short public inquiry into other officials' responsibility for the failure of the invasion, but more importantly, also forestalled public debate about each officials' failure to consider whether subversion of this kind is morally justified at all. It seems, further, that the more personally blameworthy an official, the more strenuously the official is likely to insist on accepting hierarchical responsibility. In the spring of 1973, as Watergate intruded more and more into the office of the president itself, Nixon invoked the ritualistic formula of responsibility in almost its pure form:

> Who is to blame for what happened in this case? . . . The easiest course would be for me to blame those to whom I delegated the responsibility to run the campaign. But that would be a cowardly thing to do. . . . In any organization, the man at the top must bear the responsibility. That responsibility, therefore, belongs here in this office. I accept it. (Transcribed from tape of CBS broadcast of Nixon's address to the nation, April 30, 1973)

COLLECTIVE RESPONSIBILITY

The argument underlying the collective model begins by posing a version of the problem of many hands: many political outcomes are the product of the actions of many different people whose individual contributions may not be identifiable at all, and certainly cannot be distinguished significantly from other people's contributions. The second step is the claim that no one individual, therefore, can be morally blamed for these outcomes. At the final stage of the argument, its proponents reach two seemingly contradictory conclusions: one stating that every individual associated with the collectivity should be charged with the moral responsibility, the other holding that only the collectivity can be charged. But the conclusions are not so different since neither ascribes responsibility to persons on the basis of their specific and distinct connections to the outcome in question.

The first version of the collective model can be illustrated by Herbert Kaufman's effort to pin the blame for the (immoral as well as inefficient) consequences of bureaucratic "red tape": "It would not surprise me . . . if [public officers and employees] are merely scapegoats. . . . We may accuse them because, intuitively, we want to divert the guilt from the real cause: ourselves. No one element of the population is responsible for all red tape or even for most of it . . . we all have a hand in it."[5] W. H. Walsh (1970) has offered a general theoretical defense for this sort of dispersion of responsibility. Walsh rejects non-collective ideas of moral responsibility because they incorrectly assume that the individual is "self-contained and self-subsistent" (p. 4). We are morally responsible for the actions of people with whom we have any "special relationship" (p. 5); that includes all our fellow citizens, and even earlier generations, but fortunately does not encompass all humanity since we are not, Walsh concedes, culpable for the actions of Genghis Khan. While Walsh thus radically expands the responsibility of citizens, he drastically diminishes the responsibility of public officials. Because officials act as representatives, limited by the demands of citizens and bound by long-standing commitments their predecessors have made, their decisions are not fully voluntary, and, Walsh concludes, they are therefore not fully responsible for the decisions.

This version of the collective model, however, cannot account for many distinctions that we intuitively wish to draw in apportioning blame. We normally distinguish degrees of responsibility that citizens and officials bear for policies of the government or of the groups with which they are associated. For example, those who do not protest against an unjust policy are normally thought to be more responsible for it than those who do protest; and among those who do not protest, those who have greater resources with which to influence the policy are more responsible than those with fewer such resources. These and many other similar distinctions presuppose some form of the principle Walsh must reject (at least for citizens), namely, that responsibility for a policy depends in part on the contribution an individual actually made, or could have made, to the policy.

The second version of the collective model—blaming the collectivity rather than any specific member of it—is sometimes represented by the hypothetical example of the old-time train robbery (Feinberg 1970, 248). An armed bandit holds up a carful of passengers and escapes with all their money. All of the passengers, or even a few of them could have prevented the robbery, had they coordinated their actions. In this way the passengers were collectively responsible for their own losses, but since no passenger was obligated to resist the bandit, none was individually responsible. The fault lay not in individual actions or omissions, but in the structure of the group.[6]

Similarly, a political system may suffer from structural faults that block the efforts of all but the heroic bureaucrat or politician to accomplish morally respectable ends. An example appears in "The Blast in Centralia No. 5," the introductory case in a widely used casebook in public administration:

> Responsibility [for the mine disaster that killed 111 men] here transcends individuals. The miners at Centralia, seeking somebody who would heed their conviction that their lives were in danger, found themselves confronted with officialdom, a huge organism scarcely mortal. . . . As one strives to fix responsibility for the disaster, again and again one is confronted, as were the miners, not with any individual but with a host of individuals fused into a vast, unapproachable, insensate organism. Perhaps this immovable juggernaut is the true villain in the piece.[7]

However, the responsibility of the private and public officials in this case differs from that of the passengers in the train robbery example. Officials act in the context of an ongoing institution, not an isolated incident, and they or other officials therefore may be culpable for creating the structural faults of the institution, or for neglecting to notice them, or for making inadequate efforts to correct them. The responsibility of officials is no more temporally bounded than is the existence of the institutions in which they act.

Because both versions of the collective model distort the idea of responsibility, neither can serve as the foundation for judgments we wish to make about public officials. The first version blurs moral distinctions not only among various officials but also between officials and citizens. The second version recognizes no connection between structural faults and individual responsibility for making structural criticisms or changes. The hierarchical model has the advantage of locating responsibility in determinate positions, but it neglects the problem of many hands. Proponents of the collective model take that problem all too seriously, reproducing it in the model itself and as a result weakening democratic accountability. I do not want to deny that hierarchical position is relevant in imputing responsibility, or that collective responsibility sometimes makes sense. But I do wish to suggest that an approach that preserves a traditional notion of personal responsibility—with its advantages for democratic accountability—can accommodate many of the complexities of a political process in which many different officials contribute to policies and decisions.

PERSONAL RESPONSIBILITY

Ascribing responsibility to officials as persons rather than simply as occupants of certain offices or as members of a collectivity relies on two criteria of moral responsibility. An official is morally responsible for an outcome insofar as (1) the official's actions or omissions are a cause of the outcome; and (2) these actions or omissions are not done in ignorance or under compulsion. These are notoriously difficult ideas, and I can provide only a few general comments about them before turning to the excuses they underlie.

The criterion of causal responsibility, as I interpret it, is quite weak: it requires only that one be a cause of an outcome in the sense that the outcome would not have happened but for one's act or omission.[8] To say that a person is a cause merely connects his or her action with the outcome—along with the action of many other hands and the influence of many other forces. It does not establish that the person is the most important cause or even an agent on whom we should pin responsibility at all. If we wish to select an individual from among all the other causal factors in this "cone of causation," we have to invoke other moral and political considerations, chiefly the importance of the outcome in question and the formal and informal expectations of the individual's official role.

It might be objected that we should not use the causal criterion at all. Ladd (1970) argues that the part played by any single official is neither necessary nor sufficient to bring about an organizational decision; therefore, to require, as a necessary condition of responsibility, that an official be a cause of the decision is to "give aid and comfort to officials who want to avoid responsibility" (pp. 513–15). Ladd is surely correct in refusing to assimilate moral responsibility to causal responsibility: we should not want to say that an official is less responsible to the degree that he or she is less causally effective. But the weak causal criterion does not have this implication since it is not sufficient to determine moral responsibility, let alone degrees of moral responsibility. Yet unless an official's action is at least a causal factor of an outcome, it is hard to see why the question should arise of holding that official, rather than anyone or everyone else, responsible for it.

The second criterion—volitional responsibility—in its most general form stipulates that a person is reponsible for an action insofar as he or she could have done otherwise.[9] Inability to act otherwise takes many different forms, ranging from general incapacity (such as insanity) to specific defects in particular actions (such as inadvertence). Most relevant for assessing the actions of public officials are these specific faults, which may be considered under the traditional Aristotelian categories of ignorance and compulsion (Aristotle, 1109b-1111b; cf. Glover 1970, esp. 60–61; and Donagan 1977, 112–42). Ignorance of what one does (not knowing that a certain description applies to one's action) counts as an excuse only if the ignorance is not negligent. In the case of public officials, the standards of negligence depend on moral and political considerations, such as an assessment of the outcomes in question and the nature of the role of the official. So does the question of whether compulsion should count as an excuse. The compulsion that public officials cite to excuse their conduct is rarely the extreme physical and psychological kind that philosophers and lawyers usually discuss. When officials proclaim, "I had no choice," we seldom take them literally. They can usually be understood as implying that they did not choose the *range* of alternatives within which they made some decision. Like Aristotle's sea captain (1110a 8–15), they confront two undesirable options (jettisoning the cargo or sinking the ship); the duties of office conspire with the forces of nature to pose a choice between disagreeable alternatives. Limitations on the range of alternatives do not eliminate an official's responsibility, but they do warrant our specifying, in any ascription of praise or blame, what alternatives were realistically accessible.

CAUSAL EXCUSES

In "Centralia No. 5," one of the persons blamed for the deaths of the miners was Inspector Scanlan, who had the authority to close the mine he knew to be unsafe but failed to do so. Scanlan's defense (in part) was that "had he closed the Centralia mine, Medill [the Director of the Illinois Department of Mines and Minerals] simply would have fired him and appointed a more tractable inspector" (Stillman 1980, 33). This is an example of the excuse from alternative cause: "If I hadn't done it, someone else would have," or "If I don't do it, someone else will." The excuse is more common in official than in personal life because in organizations the empirical assumption on which it depends is more likely to be true; in organizations persons often are fungible.

In a general and unqualified form, the excuse seems incoherent. To relieve one person of responsibility, the excuse asserts that other people (the alternative causal agents) would be responsible for the action; but if the excuse is valid, each of the other people would be exonerated, seriatim, in the same way as the first person. In other words, if the excuse is valid, no one is responsible. In any case, the excuse evidently has not been accepted in civil or criminal law (Hart and Honoré 1959), 225–26), and moral judgment seems to agree with the law in this regard.

Nevertheless, the excuse may sometimes be acceptable in a modified form. One such form is as a criterion of causal relevance. Here an official claims not that someone else would have made the same mistake, but rather than someone else would have made a different mistake that would have been sufficient to cause the harmful outcome. The excuse is thus used to show that the respect in which the official's action is faulty is not a cause of the outcome.[10] In the political process, however, judgments about causal connections or their absence are often uncertain. Consider the case of an FDA official who permits a drug, which subsequently turns out to be unsafe, to be placed on the agency's list of substances "generally recognized as safe"—without ordering certain standard laboratory tests on the drug. We might perhaps not blame this official for any harm suffered by users of the drug if we believe that the technicians charged with performing the tests would have approved the drug anyhow. But to the extent that the causal relevance remains uncertain (e.g., we doubt that the technicians would have approved the drug), then other factors will influence our judgment about the validity of the excuse. Specifically, we will be more likely to accept the excuse if the fault is relatively minor (e.g., failing to order the tests because of overlooking some technicality rather than because of accepting a bribe), or if the consequences to which the fault allegedly contributed are relatively harmless. It is perhaps odd that these factors should affect our judgment at all, since in principle an official should be blamed only if his fault was a cause of the outcome, but given the inevitable uncertainty of causal connections in organizations, we may be justified, as a practical matter, in considering these other factors when assessing even causal excuses.

The excuse from alternative cause is also acceptable if it is combined with certain kinds of justifications. To the plea that someone else would have committed the wrong is added the claim that he or she would have

committed a worse wrong, or in some other way would have made the
consequences worse. This excuse comes most naturally to officials who
do not resign from a government that is pursuing an admittedly wrong
policy. During the Vietnam War, many officials,. including Hubert
Humphrey and Robert McNamara, privately told friends that they were
staying on to keep the escalation from getting worse; others, like Charles
Frankel (Assistant Secretary of State for Educational and Cultural Affairs)
pointed to benefits they could accomplish that in their judgment out-
weighed any effect their resignations might have on the war (Weisband
and Franck 1976, 92–93). We are right to be suspicious of such pleas; the
heady mixture of exercising power while believing oneself to be doing
good can easily forestall a sober assessment of the consequences of alternative courses of action. Still, the plea is sometimes surely acceptable.
Even when the government an official serves is utterly evil, resignation
may not be the most appropriate course. It has been argued that the S.S.
Officer Kurt Gerstein, by continuing in his post during the Second World
War, "prevented worse things from happening" (Friedlander 1969, 199).
In less extreme circumstances, the range of choice is usually greater, but
an argument based on the worse alternative may still seem plausible.
After Attorney General Elliot Richardson and then his deputy resigned
rather than carry out Nixon's order to fire the Watergate Special Prosecutor Archibald Cox, the Solicitor General Robert Bork decided to stay
on the job and dismiss Cox. Bork argued (in part) that he would be more
likely to protect the integrity of the Justice Department and the independence of any future Special Prosecutor than anyone Nixon would appoint
as his replacement (Lukas 1977, 592). In this way, the justifiability of
Bork's use of the argument from the worse alternative comes to depend on
his subsequent conduct.

    It might be argued that the validity of this sort of excuse-cum-
justification should not turn on simply a comparison of the consequences
of an official's actions and the consequences of the actions of alternative
causal agents. Bernard Williams (1973) maintains that this way of ascribing responsibility (which he associates with utilitarianism) ignores the
value of personal integrity (pp. 97–98). He argues that a young scientist
who opposes research on chemical and biological warfare should not take
a job in a government laboratory engaged in such research, even if as a
result another scientist will take the job and pursue the research much
more zealously. Agents should be primarily responsible for their own
"projects" (actions based on commitments that form part of their personal
character) and should not abandon them simply because the calculation

of general social utility dictates that they should (p. 116). While Williams may be correct in criticizing utilitarianism for permitting an impersonal perspective to dominate a personal one, his own account of personal integrity remains insufficiently developed to support the radically circumscribed responsibility he evidently favors. Acting to protect one's personal integrity, at the expense of avoidable and serious harm to other people, seems too close to moral self-indulgence; it could represent an effort to keep one's hands clean no matter what happens to the rest of society.

A second category of causal excuses comprises those pleas that would disconnect an official completely from the chain of events leading to a harmful outcome. These may be called excuses from null cause. Since it is often possible to cite as a cause almost any act or omission by an official in the organization that brings about the outcome, an official who uses the excuse must distinguish his or her act or omission from that of others. One way to do this is the familiar plea, "It's not my job." In this form the excuse is usually intended to cut short any argument about whether the official could have made any difference, or could make any difference in the future. Because the duties of the official's role do not concern the policy in question, failure to oppose the policy or to resign from the government that pursues it should not be considered a cause of its perpetuation. As George Ball said in an interview in 1973, "Why *should* I have resigned in protest over Vietnam policy just because I disagreed with it? My main responsibility . . . was Western Europe. Perhaps five percent of my time was spent on Vietnam. It simply wasn't my responsibility; . . . It wasn't as if I were the Honduras desk officer being put in the "position of having to approve a U.S. military action in Honduras" (quoted in Weisband and Franck 1976, 139). Ball is surely right to suppose that the nature of an office circumscribes an official's responsibility to some extent; one cannot be culpable for all the policies on which one could have had any influence. That Ball's "main responsibility" did not concern Vietnam at least counts as a reason for ascribing less responsibility to him than to those officials whose main duties did concern Vietnam. By the same token, as a high-ranking State Department official, Ball shares more blame than (say) an official in the Department of Health, Education and Welfare. The nature of the role of office, however, should not be understood rigidly. Contrary to the implication of Ball's reference to the Honduras desk officer, it is not enough to claim that one's role does not require specific positive decisions in the area in question. Omissions, acquiescence, tacit approval, even ritualized opposition—all may gain one a place in the causal chain.

Similarly, a narrowly technical definition of an office does not necessarily exonerate the person who holds that office. Scientific personnel, for
example, may be responsible for the uses others make of their work,
especially if the risks of harm from these uses are great. The case for
ascribing responsibility to scientists for their discoveries increases if, like J.
Robert Oppenheimer, they continue to have influence on how politicians use their discoveries. Defending himself in 1954, Oppenheimer
disclaimed any such responsibility: "I did my job . . . I was not in a
policy-making position" (U.S. Atomic Energy Commission 1971, 236).
But earlier he evidently accepted a rather extreme form of such responsibility. According to Truman, Oppenheimer in 1946 "came into my
office . . . and spent most of his time wringing his hands and telling me
that [they] had blood on them because of the discovery of atomic energy"
(Donovan 1977, 97). To say that scientists or other officials who are
engaged in technical work may be morally responsible for the consequences of their work is not necessarily to claim that they should not
perform the work when its use offends their conscience (they may have an
overriding duty to contribute their talents and skills to society in some
circumstances). But it does imply that their choice of whether to perform
the work is a moral one, and that they have a continuing obligation to
consider and question the uses to which their contributions are put. Even
if the duties of office do not require (or perhaps do not permit) an official
to do anything about an immoral policy, we may wish to criticize the
official for remaining in office as part of an immoral regime. But this
would be an accusation of complicity (claiming that one's association
with this regime is itself immoral or dishonorable), rather than an ascription of responsibility (asserting that by some act or omission, one actually
furthered specific immoral politics) (see Hill 1979, 83–102).

In another form of the excuse from null cause, an official cites a
novus actus interveniens—a subsequent act by another official who can
control whether the first official's action has any effect and therefore
supposedly bears the entire responsibility for any harmful consequences.
It is sometimes said, for example, that advisers are not responsible for the
results of policies since the person whom they advise is free to accept or
reject their counsel (e.g., Nelson 1968, 119). Hobbes put forward such a
view maintaining the innocence of advisers, but he recognized that it
makes sense only if advisers are understood as providing instrumental
counsel for achieving ends that are not in dispute (1962, 191–92). The
trouble is that beyond the boundaries of the Leviathan, ends usually are
controversial, and so then is the question of whether instrumental analy-

sis of means or advocacy of ends is the appropriate role for an adviser to assume. A report by a professional association (Operations Research 1971) criticizing six scientists for engaging in advocacy instead of analysis in the controversy over the Anti-Ballistic Missile System in 1969 itself generated further controversy. Reaction to the society's definition of the proper role of an adviser evidently depended on where one stood on the substance of the ABM issue (Doty 1972, 281).

In general, we assume that even an adviser who advocates a position bears less responsibility than the official who decides to follow the advice. However, this assumption depends on the personal relationship between the adviser and the advisee, and on the ways the adviser perceives the advice. If an official adopts a proposal mostly because he trusts the adviser personally—as President Kennedy was said to have decided for a blockade because those with whom he was "personally most compatible" recommended it (Allison 1971, 203–04)—we might want to say that the adviser should accept equal responsibility for the decision, or in some cases even more responsibility than the official who makes the decision. Similarly, in deciding whether to press the perspective of a particular office or to advocate a more general perspective, an adviser must assess how other people are likely to react—including how other advisers are performing their own jobs, and how the balance of advice is likely to come out. For this reason even devil's advocates, if their opposition begins to legitimize the course of action they oppose, may come to share some responsibility for it (cf. Hirschman 1970, 115–19). A *novus actus interveniens* therefore does not in general, and certainly not in any simple way, cancel an adviser's responsibility for the policies about which he or she offers counsel.

VOLITIONAL EXCUSES

Some theories of responsibility would obviate the problem of many hands by making officials responsible only for what they intend, not at all (or at least never as much) for what anyone else does as a result of their decisions. Kant expresses this view in its most absolute form. Kant insists, for example, that you must tell the truth even to a murderer who asks where your friend, his intended victim, is hiding (1949, 346–50). You are responsible for your own intentional act (truth telling or lying), and if you tell the truth you cannot be blamed for what other people do as a result of your honesty. The implausibility of this view in ordinary moral life is magnified in public life. Even if we deny that a public official should let utilitarian calculation determine whether he or she lies or commits other acts that are absolutely wrong on a Kantian view, we would surely hold the official morally responsible for failing to take precautions to avoid harmful consequences of others' responses to his or her decisions. Even a traditional morality, which otherwise disregards consequences, "commands" that we carefully consider "what bad consequences, flow from abiding by it" and "what dispositions [we] can make to avoid them" (Donagan 1977,206–07). To say that intention is not a necessary condition for charging an official with responsibility is not inevitably to embrace a consequentialism that holds that we are all "equally morally responsible for all consequences."[11] It is simply to recognize that, at least for public officials, the contours of responsibility are likely to be more irregular than the criterion of intention would draw. In tracing the bounds of responsibility, we shall also have to pay attention to other criteria, specifically those of ignorance and compulsion.

If ignorance in general were a valid excuse, the innocence of some public officials would be irreproachable. But the kind of ignorance relevant to the problem of many hands concerns an official's lack of specific knowledge about the actions of other officials. An official who admittedly contributes to an objectionable outcome may seek to excuse the contribution by claiming that he or she did not know, and should not have been expected to know, that other officials had acted wrongly or would act wrongly. When as UN Ambassador in 1961 Adlai Stevenson stated that the U.S. did not have anything to do with the invasion of Cuba, he could not have been expected to realize that his statement was false, and therefore escapes responsibility for any wrong that was committed (Muller 1967, 283–84). Whether Stevenson should have been told is another matter, but ambassadors, spokespersons and others in similar roles have to trust that they are being told the truth, or at least that they are being told everything they need to know about governmental activities within their purview.

At the other end of the causal chain, an official may sometimes be excused for consequences of a decision when he or she could not be expected to foresee the wrongs that other officials would commit in implementing the decision. President Truman, after the surrender of Germany, signed an order terminating the shipment of food, clothing and other goods that our allies had been receiving under Lend-Lease; the aburpt disruption of these supplies threatened significant hardship for many citizens in these countries until Truman rescinded the order. Truman defended himself by claiming that his aides had executed the order too literally (1955, 227–28). Such an excuse will not work when officials are the instruments of their own ignorance. They may, for example, encourage subordinates not to tell them about certain possibly objectionable plans so that they can deny knowledge of the plans if they go awry. Or officials may elicit misleading information from subordinates by indicating sometimes unwittingly, what kind of conclusions they wish to hear, as when Rusk and McNamara, considering an American intervention in the Dominican Republic in 1965, asked the acting U.S. Ambassador to the Dominican Republic if "he agreed with their view that a rebel victory would probably lead to a pro-Communist government" (Martin 1966, 659). Not surprisingly, the acting ambassador agreed.

To reject a plea of ignorance, we do not have to show that an official should have foreseen the specific act of some particular official (for example, that an aide would misinterpret an order in exactly this way). It is sufficient that the official should have realized that mistakes of the kind that occurred were likely. In bureaucracies, certain patterns of fault are common enough that we should expect any competent official to anticipate them and to take reasonable precautions to avoid them or at least to minimize their harmful consequences. During the early months of the Peace Corps, Sargent Shriver, disappointed in the small number of requests foreign governments had submitted for Corps programs, urged his "programmers" to seek out more requests. According to one account, those who failed to come back with programs "in their pockets" were fired or fell into disfavor; consequently, some programmers created fictitious programs. It has been argued that Shriver should bear some responsibility for those consequences since he should have foreseen that his own injunction could induce such behavior by some of his staff (Peters 1973, 22; for a different account, see Ashabranner 1971, 19–42). When a superior puts great pressure on subordinates to produce results and gives the impression that questionable practices to achieve these results will be condoned—as allegedly occurred in the army recruiting scandals reported in the fall of 1979—then the blame falls at least equally on the superior. Ignorance ceases even to mitigate responsibility.

But that an official apply pressure, even of the mild sort Shriver evidently exerted, is not a necessary condition for making an official responsible for the subsequent actions of others. An official who sets in motion bureaucratic routines cannot escape culpability for the consequences even if he or she is no longer involved in the process when the consequences occur. The system of double-bookkeeping that Henry Kissinger approved in 1969, supposedly to conceal a single bombing attack on Cambodia, persisted "by rote and without a special new decision" and led other officials in 1973 to give Congress false information (Kissinger 1979a, 7; 1979b, 239–54). Even if the initial bombing and secrecy could somehow be justified, Kissinger would not escape blame for the subsequent deception. Whether the bureaucratic routines are pathological or conventional (or both), that they have a life of their own, often roaming beyond their original purpose, is a fact of organizational behavior that officials should be expected to appreciate. The more that the consequences of a decision fit such bureaucratic patterns, the less an official can plausibly appeal to the excuse from ignorance.

Yet an official may still have an escape. Some of the most normal and expected patterns of behavior in bureaucracies are also the most difficult for anyone to change, and some of these may obligate an official to act in certain ways despite harmful consequences he or she may be able to foresee. Thus, just as the excuse from ignorance begins to falter, the excuse from compulsion comes to the rescue. Of the many kinds of constraints that officials cite to reduce their responsibility for decisions, those that derive from other officials' actions, rather than from forces of nature or reactions of the public, most directly bear on the problem of many hands.

The question of responsibility certainly arises when an official issues an explicit order to carry out some morally objectionable policy, but I pass over such cases because they are extensively discussed in the literature on war crimes (Walzer 1977, 287–327), and also because they are less prevalent in the workaday life of administrators in the modern bureaucracies. More common are cases where no explicit order has been given but a subordinate believes that a superior expects him or her to pursue what is seen as a morally dubious course of action. This is the gray area between command and discretion. When a superior relies on subordinates to know what to do without being told, the superior can no more escape responsibility for the subordinates' actions than they can. No one ordered the FBI Director L. Patrick Gray to destroy the incriminating files from E. Howard Hunt's safe, but, as Gray later testified "The clear implication . . . was that these two files were to be destroyed" (Congressonal Quarterly 1975, 226).

But perhaps an even more common constraint than orders from a superior, however implicit, is that of various practices and procedures established by other officials who may not be identifiable, or, for that matter, may no longer be alive. Such practices circumscribe an official's range of choices, and thus may mitigate his or her responsibility. Consider Mayor Beame's dilemma during the New York City fiscal crisis before the market for city securities collapsed in the spring of 1975 (Thompson 1981). Among other charges, critics accused Beame of misleading the public by failing to disclose the true state of the city's finances. Beame insisted that it was not his fault if the budget misrepresented the city's financial condition. He had inherited the questionable accounting practices ("gimmicks," the critics called them) that gave rise to any misrepresentation. Those practices that he knew about, he could neither change nor even publicize (he believed) without risking the bankruptcy of the city, and jeopardizing the welfare of millions of the city's residents and employees. For example, the budget overstated the amount of federal and state aid the city expected to receive because city officials recorded, as receivable, funds that federal and state authorities did not intend to allocate. Beame argued that if he removed the disputed receivables from the books, or even had conceded that they were in dispute, he would have significantly reduced the chances for collecting these funds from the federal and state governments. There were other such "gimmicks"— nearly all difficult to change and none of them of the mayor's making. We may be prepared to excuse Beame as mayor for the existence of these practices, and blame him less for any decisions constrained by these practices. We would normally impute more responsibility to the mayor's predecessors. But in this case there is a twist: Among his predecessors were Abe Beame, Controller, 1969–73, 1962–65; Abe Beame, Budget Director, 1952–61; and Abe Beame, Assistant Budget Director, 1946–52. Personal responsibility, unlike role responsibility, pursues officials through time.

Some bureaucratic practices, unobjectionable in intent, turn out to constrain the performances of officials in harmful ways. Such constraints particularly affect those officials who have been called "street-level bureaucrats"—social workers, policemen and the like, who deal frequently with citizens, and exercise considerable discretion in an uncertain environment (Lipsky 1980, 81–156). Because these officials face demanding standards of job performance and rarely have sufficient resources to meet them, they develop "bureaucratic mechanisms" to evade responsibility for their failures. For example, because the performance of officials in the Job Corps program was measured by the number of trainees who received a job after completing the program, officials tended to recruit those youths who already seemed disposed to succeed in a job; these turned out to be youths with more middle-class than lower-class orientations (Sjoberg et al., 1978, 42–43). A seemingly neutral procedure of evaluation thus gave rise to discriminatory bureaucratic conduct. In these circumstances, we would want to impute major responsibility to the higher-level officials who set up the procedures—if we can locate these officials.

But street-level bureaucrats themselves cannot be considered blameless no matter what they do. Even within the constraints of fixed routines, some officials perfrom worse than others; and these variations open some space for ascribing responsibility. A measure of actual variation—for example, an average performance—would not serve as a satisfactory base line from which to assess responsibility since all officials may be doing less well than they could, even given the constraints. We would need some criterion based on a hypothetical average performance—what the average official could reasonably be expected to do under the circumstances (a "reasonable bureaucrat" test?). Moreover, when these lower-level officials come to recognize how certain bureaucratic routines cause them to perform in morally questionable ways, they acquire, as do other officials who work within defective structures, a special responsibility to call attention to the defects, even if they cannot correct them.

CONCLUSION

The conditions under which excuses eliminate or mitigate the responsibility of a public official depend not only on factors to which the excuses refer directly (causality and volition) but also on factors that help interpret the excuses (the nature of the policy in question and the role the official holds). The interaction of these factors is best captured not by a general theory of responsibility but by a casuistic analysis of a range of exemplary cases. I have given reasons for rejecting the simpler approaches of the hierarchical and collective models, as well as for avoiding formulas (such as alternative cause) that would simplify the ascription of personal responsibility itself.

Insofar as we can locate those officials who are personally responsible and thus most closely connected with the policies and decisions that governments promulgate, we refine and fortify the praise and blame that, as democratic citizens, we direct toward public officials. Personal responsibility in this way can lay a foundation for democratic accountability of the officials who make objectionable decisions and policies. But it also supports accountability for harmful policies and decisions that are less attributable to any current officials as moral agents than to bureaucratic routines and structural defects of the organization in which the officials act. Because personal responsibility attaches to persons, not to office or collectivities, it follows an official wherever he or she goes. We can trace it through time—to the past when the mayor was the controller, or to the future when the solicitor general makes good on his claim that he was the least bad alternative. Moreover, our assessment of an official's responsibility for harmful decisions made within a defective structure, even if the official did the best job possible in face of the constraints imposed by this structure, depends on the efforts he or she makes to criticize and change those defects. The grounds for this extension of responsibility derive from the volitional criteria. Officials who operate within faulty machinery of government may be presumed to know more than others about its faults; the excuse of ignorance is usually less accessible to them. They are also often in the best position to refute or to fulfill the claim that they cannot do anything about the defects; hence, the excuse from compulsion becomes less plausible to the extent that an official fails to make efforts toward criticism or reform.

We can hardly expect to identify officials who are responsible for all, or perhaps even the worst, evils that governments visit upon their citizens; nor for that matter can we always identify officials who deserve credit for the good that governments occasionally accomplish. But the pursuit of personal responsibility provides the best foundation for understanding the role that human agency plays in good and bad government, and therefore, establishes some basis for initiating whatever political change may be necessary.

NOTES

I am grateful to Joel Feinberg, Amy Gutmann, Geoffrey Hawthorn, Albert Hirshman, and Marion Smiley for advice on earlier versions of this article. I am also indebted to the Institute for Advanced Study in Princeton, which provided a congenial environment in which to write the article.

1. E.g., Anderson 1979; Bok 1978; Hampshire 1979; Rohr 1978; and Walzer 1973. For a survey of the growing literature in this field, see Fleishman and Payne 1980.

2. Austin's classic essay (1956–57) is a valuable source on this topic, but more directly relevant are Hart and Honoré 1959; and Feinberg 1970.

3. Generally on the concept of political responsibility, see Pennock 1979, 260–308.

4. Gerth and Mills 1958, 95. This distinction does not depend on accepting Weber's further claim that the political leader should act on an "ethic of responsibility" rather than an "ethic of ultimate ends" (pp. 120–28).

5. Kaufman 1977, pp. 27–28. For discussion of similar arguments in the context of war crimes, see French 1972.

6. I put aside the question of whether it makes sense to hold a collectivity morally responsible. Even if it does, individual responsibility for collective faults is not necessarily or usually extinguished.

7. Stillman 1976, 34. For some other examples (drawn from the Vietnam War), see Weisband and Franck 1976, 79–80.

8. The interpretation of this statement is not only much more complex than I can indicate here, but it is also a chief point of controversy between the two best works in the theory of responsibility. Cf. Hart and Honoré 1959, 61–62, 103–22; and Feinberg 1970, 201–07, 184. My interpretation more closely follows Feinberg.

9. I hope that I will be excused for disregarding the relevant but complex metaphysical problems raised by this criterion. Two of the best contemporary discussions are: Frankfurt 1971; and Strawson 1968.

10. Feinberg 1979, 196, 207–12. In this form, then, the excuse from alternative cause becomes the basis of what I call below the excuse from null cause. Both kinds of excuse should be distinguished from the excuse from additional cause (see Hart and Honoré 1959, 216–25).

11. Fried 1978, 34–35. Fried himself defends a qualified version of the Kantian theory, conceding that we are morally responsible for some of the unintended consequences of our actions but insisting that we are "primarily" responsible for only what we intend in the sense that we may never do intentional harm in order to avoid greater unintended harm (pp. 21–22, 26, 28, 42, 168).

REFERENCES

Allison, Graham 1971. *Essence of Decision*. Boston: Little, Brown.

Altshuler, Alan A. 1977. "The Study of American Public Administration." In Alan A. Altshuler and Norman C. Thomas (eds.), *The Politics of the Federal Bureaucracy.* New York: Harper and Row.

Anderson, Charles W. 1979. "The Place of Principles in Policy Analysis." *American Political Science Review* 73:711–23.

Aristotle. 1963. Ethica Nicomachea. In W. D. Ross (ed.), *The Works of Aristotle*. Oxford: Oxford University Press.

Ashabranner, Brent. 1971. *A Moment in History*. Garden City, N. Y.: Doubleday.

Austin, J. L. 1956–57. "A Plea for Excuses." *Proceedings of the Aristotelian Society* 57: 1–30.

Bok, Sissela. 1978. *Lying*. New York: Pantheon.

Congressional Quarterly. 1975. *Watergate*. Washington, D.C.: Congressional Quarterly.

Donagan, Alan. 1977. *The Theory of Morality*. Chicago: University of Chicago Press.

Donovan, Robert J. 1977. *Conflict and Crisis*. New York: Norton.

Doty, Paul. 1972. "Can Investigations Improve Scientific Advice? The Case of the ABM." *Minerva* 10: 280–94.

Edelman, Murray. 1964. *The Symbolic Uses of Politics.*Urbana: University of Illinois Press.

Feinberg, Joel.1970. *Doing and Deserving.* Princeton, N.J.: Princeton University Press.

Fleishman, Joel, and Bruce Payne.*Ethical Dilemmas and the Education of Policymakers.* Hastings-on-Hudson, N.Y.: Hastings Center.

Frankfurt, Harry G. 1971. "Freedom of the Will and the Concept of a Person." *Journal of Philosophy* 68: 5–20.

French, Peter A., ed. 1972 *Individual and Collective Responsibility.* Cambridge, Mass.: Schenkman.

Fried, Charles. 1978. *Right and Wrong.* Cambridge, Mass.: Harvard University Press.

Friedlander, Saul. 1969. *Kurt Gerstein.* New York: Knopf.

Gerth, H. H., and C. Wright Mills. 1958. *From Max Weber.* New York: Oxford University Press.

Glover, Jonathan. 1970. *Responsibility.* London: Routledge and Kegan Paul.

Hampshire, Stuart, ed. 1978. *Public and Private Morality.*Cambridge, England: Cambridge University Press.

Hart, H. L. A. 1968. *Punishment and Responsibility.*New York and Oxford: Oxford University Press.

_____, and A. M. Honoré 1959. *Causation in the Law.* Oxford, England: Claredon Press.

Heclo, Hugh. 1978. "Issues Networks and the Executive Establishment." In Anthony King (ed.), *The New American Political System.* Washington, D.C.: American Enterprise Institute.

Hill, Thomas E. 1979. "Symbolic Protest and Calculated Silence." *Philosophy and Public Affairs* 9:83–102.

Hirshman, Albert O. 1970. *Exit, Voice, and Loyalty,* Cambridge, Mass.: Harvard University Press.

Hobbes, Thomas. 1962. *Leviathan.* New York: Collier.

Kant, Immanuel. 1949. "On a Supposed Right to Lie from Altruistic Motives." In L. W. Beck (ed.), *Critique of Practical Reason.* Chicago: University of Chicago Press.

Kaufman, Herbert. 1977. *Red Tape.* Washington, D.C.: Brookings.

_____. 1979b. *White House Years.* Boston: Little, Brown.

Krasner, Stephen D. 1972. "Are Bureaucracies Important? (Or Allison in Wonderland)." *Foreign Policy* 7: 159–79.

Ladd, John. 1970. "Morality and the Ideal of Rationality in Formal Organizations." *Monist* 54: 488–516.

Lipsky, Michael. 1980. *Street-Level Bureaucracy.* New York: Russell Sage.

Lowi, Theodore J. 1979. *The End of Liberalism,* 2d ed. New York: W. W. Norton.

Lukas, J. Anthony. 1977. *Nightmare.* New York: Bantam.

Martin, John Bartlow. 1966. *Overtaken by Events.* Garden City, N. Y.: Doubleday.

Muller, Robert J. 1967. *Adlai Stevenson,* New York: Harper and Row.

Nelson, William R., ed. 1968. *The Politics of Science* New York: Oxford University Press.

Operations Research Society of America. 1971. "Guidelines for the Practice of Operations Research." *Operations Research* 19: 1123–58.

Pennock, J. Roland. 1979. *Democratic Political Theory.* Princeton, N. J.: Princeton University Press.

Peters, Charles 1973. "The Culture of Bureaucracy." *Washington Monthly* 5: 22–24.

Rohr, John A. 1978. *Ethics for Bureaucrats.* New York and Basel: Dekker.

Rourke, Francis E., ed. 1978. *Bureaucratic Power in National Politics*, 3rd ed. Boston: Little, Brown.

Schlesinger, Arthur M., Jr. 1965. *A Thousand Days.* Boston: Houghton-Mifflin.

Sjoberg, Gedeon et al. 1978. "Bureaucracy and the Lower Class." In Francis E. Rourke (ed.), *Bureaucratic Power in National Politics.* Boston: Little, Brown.

Stillman, Richard J. 1980. *Public Administration: Concepts and Cases*, 2d ed. Boston: Houghton-Mifflin.

Strawson, P. F. 1968. "Freedom and Resentment." In Strawson (ed.), *Studies in the Philosophy of Thought and Action.* Oxford: Oxford University Press.

Thompson, Dennis. 1981. "Excuses Officials Use: Moral Responsibility and the New York City Fiscal Crisis." In Joel Fleishman et al. (eds.). *Ethics in Government.* Cambridge, Mass.: Harvard University Press, forthcoming.

Thompson, Victor. 1961. *Modern Organizations.* New York: Random House.

U.S. Atomic Energy Commision. 1971. *In the Matter of J. Robert Oppenheimer.* Cambridge, Mass.: MIT Press.

Walsh, W. H. 1970. "Pride, Shame and Responsibility." *Philosophical Quarterly* 20: 1–13.

Waltzer, Michael. 1973. "Political Action: The Problem of Dirty Hands." *Philosophy and Public Affairs* 2: 160–80.

———. 1977. *Just and Unjust Wars.* New York: Basic Books.

Weisband, Edward, and Thomas M. Franck. 1976. *Resignation in Protest.* New York: Penguin Books.

Williams, Bernard. 1973. "A Critique of Utilitarianism." In J. J. C. Smart and Bernard Williams, *Utilitarianism for and Against.* Cambridge: Cambridge University Press.

39

JAMES MACGREGOR BURNS

Leadership

THE calls for leadership, the uncertainties as to just what it is, the ambivalent attitudes toward moral leadership and principled leaders—all these, I think, reflect deep ambiguity and confusion over the place of leadership in political life—at least in the democracies where leaders are expected to lead the people while the people are supposed to lead the leaders. The confusion will continue as long as we fail to distinguish leadership from brute power, leadership from propaganda, leadership from manipulation, leadership from pandering, leadership from coercion. It has been contended in these pages that by clarifying the definition of leadership we can enormously broaden its utility as a tool for causal analysis and its potential for realizing modal values and end-values. It remains to put some of the characteristics of leadership so defined in summary form and to note some possible implications, practical and otherwise.

Leadership is collective. "One-man leadership" is a contradiction in terms. Leaders, in responding to their own motives, appeal to the motive bases of potential followers. As followers respond, a symbiotic relationship develops that binds leader and follower together into a social and political collectivity. Cadres form; hierarchies evolve; structure hardens. Responding to leaders' initiatives, followers address their hopes and demands to politicians who use their power resources relevant to those hopes and demands to satisfy them. Leaders seek to mobilize existing social collectivities, whether class, nationalistic, ethnic, or other.

From James MacGregor Burns, *Leadership* (New York: Harper & Row, 1978), pp. 452–57. Copyright © 1978 by James MacGregor Burns. Reprinted by permission of Harper & Row, Publishers, Inc.

419

A critical consideration is the form or structure that collective leader-follower relationships assume. The emotional connection between heroic leaders and the vast numbers of followers who relate to them in mass meetings or on television is a form of collective leadership. But the absence of "layers" of grass-roots activists, cadres, subleaders (save for the small circle of aides and advisers surrounding the charismatic leader) makes for imbalances between leaders' and followers' powers, a certain instability and precariousness in their relationships, and potential derangements of political and constitutional processes. Hence the vital necessity of political movements that metamorphose into the kind of political party that over the years helps leaders to satisfy peoples' valid needs. "The labor parties in Northwestern Europe," according to Gunnar Myrdal, "are . . . the final outcome of much more than a century of great and influential people's movements, the temperance movement, the non-conformist religious movements, the cooperative movement, the trade union movement, the adult education movement and the movement for general suffrage." The absence in the United States of a major party firmly based in a social movement has impaired the linkage between Americans and their leaders, especially the President.

Leadership is dissensual. The dynamo of political action, meaningful conflict, produces engaged leaders, who in turn generate more conflict among the people. Conflict relevant to popular aspirations is also the key democratizer of leadership. It causes leaders to expand the field of combat, to reach out for more followers, to search for allies. It organizes motives, sharpens popular demands, broadens and strengthens values. Much depends on the organization of conflict—whether, for example, the axis of conflict is shifted from national boundaries, or from regional boundaries within nations, to class or interest group or doctrinal cleavages *within* nations or regions.

Dissensus and conflict run up against the ethic of "unity" in many democracies. Political leaders call for harmony and cooperation, though they practice the opposite as they compete for office. In particular, party politics is supposed to "stop at the water's edge." Except perhaps in time of war, such calls for national unity can be a danger sign in a democracy. Vietnam for the Americans, Suez for the British, Pearl Harbor for the Japanese, demonstrated that party politics—that is, conflictive politics—should not stop short of *any* major concern of people. It would probably be better for most organizations, including corporations, unions, and university faculties, for dissensus to be built into their structures. A two-party or two-faction system could keep alive a kind of "loyal opposition" to the establishment, a goad to complacent doctrine, a steady drumfire of criticism. The scope and nature of this kind of conflict—which must not be allowed to override other kinds—would need to be spelled out in some type of charter.

The paramount question facing all the peoples of the world is the *global* organization and management of conflict—how to shift the axis of conflict so that needs and aspirations could be appealed to and aggregated on a worldwide basis, so that right-wing as well as socialistic and other left-wing parties could be organized on a world scale, and so that rival leaders of global parties and movements could build links among like-minded people across national boundaries. Conflict unifies people just as it divides them. The only long-run hope for world peace is to realign the foundations of political combat and consensus so that conflicts are managed peacefully within nations rather than by force between nations. This was the noble vision of the pre–World War I European socialists. It remains a utopian hope, given the political fragmentation of the globe.

Leadership is causative. True leadership is not merely symbolic or ceremonial, nor are "great men" simply the medium or mechanism through which social forces operate. The interaction of leaders and followers is not merely transactional or a process of exchange. The result of the interactive process is a change in leaders' and followers' motives and goals that produces a causal effect on social relations and political institutions. That effect ranges from the small and hardly noticed to the creative and historic. The small changes are more numerous, of course, and collectively and cumulatively they bring about the "gradual change" that permanently alters the course of history. The role of the leader may be differentiated between the event-full and event-making, in Sidney Hook's term, or between the Mosaic (calculating, bureaucratic) and the Alexandrian (heroic, revolutionary) in James Reichley's. Hook's event-making man is our transforming leader, provided that the event makers are moral leaders—that they are both responding to and elevating the wants and aspirations and values of those affected by the events.

The most lasting tangible act of leadership is the creation of an institution—a nation, a social movement, a political party, a bureaucracy—that continues to exert moral leadership and foster needed social change long after the creative leaders are gone. An institution, it is said, is but the lengthened shadow of a man, but it takes many men and women to establish lasting institutions. The establishment of a new system of government embracing a structure of divided and fragmented powers by the framers of 1787—and by their supporters and adversaries in the various states and by the political theorists who inspired them—was perhaps the most creative and durable act of political planning in modern history. It was ironic that such brilliant leadership would found a system that so hobbled leadership; yet it was a system that could meet, albeit partially and with all deliberate slowness, the moral challenge of slavery in the 1860s and that of black rights a century later.

The most lasting and pervasive leadership of all is intangible and noninstitutional. It is the leadership of influence fostered by ideas embodied in social or religious or artistic movements, in books, in great seminal documents, in the memory of great lives greatly lived.

Leadership is morally purposeful. All leadership is goal-oriented. The failure to set goals is a sign of faltering leadership. Successful leadership points in a direction; it is also the vehicle of continuing and achieving purpose. Where leadership is necessary, Philip Selznick writes, "the problem is always *to choose key values and to create a social structure that embodies them.*" Purpose may be singular, such as the protective and enhancement of individual liberty, or it may be multiple, in which case it will be expressed in a set of priorities. Both leaders and followers are drawn into the shaping of purpose. "Our dilemma, then, is not an absence of leaders," Benjamin Barber observes, "but a paucity of values that might sustain leaders; not a failure of leadership but a failure of followership, a failure of popular will from which leadership might draw strength. . . ." But the transforming leader taps the needs and raises the aspirations and helps shape the values—and hence mobilizes the potential—of followers.

Transforming leadership is elevating. It is moral but not moralistic. Leaders engage with followers, but from higher levels of morality; in the enmeshing of goals and values both leaders and followers are raised to more principled levels of judgment. Leaders most effectively "connect with" followers from a level of morality only one stage higher than that of the followers, but moral leaders who act at much higher levels—Gandhi, for example—relate to followers at all levels either heroically or through the founding of mass movements that provide linkages between persons at various levels of morality and sharply increase the moral impact of the transforming leader. Much of this kind of elevating leadership asks sacrifices *from* followers rather than merely promising them goods.

The most dramatic test in modern democracies of the power of leaders to elevate followers and of followers to sustain leaders was the civil rights struggle in the United States. Myrdal recognized presciently that this was a moral struggle, a struggle for the soul of America. There were those who pandered to the base instincts of persons—the very negation of leadership—but many more who appealed to the spirit of a "moral commitment of the American nation to high ideals," Myrdal said years later. "In spite of all the conspicuous and systematic gross failures of compliance, America of all countries I knew had come to have the most explicitly formulated system of general ideals in reference to human interrelations, shared, on one level of valuations, by all its citizens." Shared by all its citizens—that was the crux of the struggle. The battle was won at lunch counters, on highways, in classrooms, in front of courthouses by followers who had become leaders. On the other side of the globe, the pacific and egalitarian values taught by Mohandas Gandhi were proving to be an elevating force in an even harsher struggle for social justice.

On the other side of the world stands, too, the leadership heritage of Mao. For many years Westerners comfortably assumed that the choice of democratic leadership models lay between the British parliamentary system, with its emphasis on majority rule, cabinet (collective) leadership, and loyal opposition, and the American "presidential" system, with its provisions for presidential leadership, checks and balances, minority rights, and shifting majority and minority coalitions in legislatures and in elections. A kind of constitutional sweepstakes took place as partisans of either of the two forms watched anxiously to see which model the new nations of Africa or Asia would adopt. As it turned out, many of the developing nations that bothered to adopt either of the models created oligarchic structures behind the democratic forms. Most of their rulers were not leaders but power wielders (including a few despots); hence they taught us little about principled leadership except its vulnerability and disposability.

Mao's alternative looms as a far greater practical and moral challenge to the West, especially in its attraction for a new nations and for dissident Communists in Eastern Europe and perhaps even in Russia. That model is not one of the alternation of leadership projected into power by parties vying for election victories but of a leadership *that both renews and challenges its own institutions* by mobilizing the masses against their own bureaucracies in party and government. It is Jefferson's notion of the tree of liberty being watered by revolution every twenty years or so, transported to another culture. Like the commanders of a guerrilla army, Mao and his associates alternated between spurring the masses on to act, to seize power, and to extend democracy, and restraining the grass-roots activists and putting limits on mass action. They led a fluid, shifting coalition of leaders closely linked to followers, and they acted as brokers between the conflicting interests of the vast, multi-faceted constituencies that they had mobilized. To some it seemed that Mao and his associates were swinging back and forth like a pendulum, from left to right, from anarchy to order, from democracy to dictatorship. On closer analysis it appears that Mao's actions were dictated by his ideology, that his complicated, zig-zag course can be explained by his determination to chart an ideological and strategic course that at the same time incorporated *both* poles of the contradiction between centralism and diffusion of power.

His strategy was based solidly in Mao Tse-tung Thought with its theory of conflict—the "unity of opposites"—in every contradiction, its Leninist discipline and organization balanced by mass spontaneity and participation. The new constitution of the Communist party, adopted in 1969, called for "both centralism and democracy, both discipline and freedom, both unity of will and personal ease of mind and liveliness." To a large extent Mao failed to reshape the institutional means in order to achieve his ultimate aims. The People's Communes were repudiated, the tripartite revolutionary committees were awkward and undemocratic, and the reformed party was unable to eradicate bureaucratization and revisionism. The erosion of personal liberty and privacy was enormous. but he did succeed in fashioning another instrument, more intangible but more powerful, to move closer toward his goal—raising consciousness and transforming values on a vast scale, mobilizing the higher aspirations of the Chinese people, reconstructing political institutions, producing substantial and real change, the nature of which cannot yet be fully evaluated.

"Here I stand, I can do no other!" Luther cried. It is the power of a person to become a leader, armed with principles and rising above self-interest narrowly conceived, that invests that person with power and may ultimately transform both leaders and followers into persons who jointly adhere to modal values and end-values. A person, whether leader or follower, girded with moral purpose is a tiny principality of power. In all my observations of men of practical affairs making policy, I remember most vividly a meeting of men of "power" and a quixotic woman who was very much present though not there. She had opposed a construction project that, in her view, threatened environmental and aesthetic damage. Again and again the meeting returned to the question, what would Mrs. Lowell accept? She had armed herself with a moral issue—and with a power base in a band of mobilized followers. That impractical woman had turned out to be practicality itself.

PART VII

LEADERS ON LEADERSHIP

FOUR extraordinary and very different types of leaders wrote the works in this section: Woodrow Wilson was a democrat; Hitler a totalitarian; Lenin a revolutionary; and Gandhi a charismatic non-constituted leader. Each piece dates from a time before the author assumed power, illustrating the truism that they all had more time and inclination to reflect on leadership before they become leaders.

"Leaders of Men," delivered on June 17, 1890 is considered one of Wilson's most notable addresses. He had just accepted a professorship at Princeton, and twelve years later he would become the university's first lay president. Arthur S. Link, editor of the voluminous Wilson papers, has written of "Leaders of Men" that "in substance and style, it is poetic, emotional, and prophetic. It may have been the product of a flash of insight in which, in the relative euphoria that came from the growing success of 1889, Wilson's accumulated ideas and experiences became, as it were, fused."[1] Link points to the connections between "Leaders of Men" and earlier works by Wilson. For example, in an essay on William Gladstone, Wilson had written: "Great statesmen seem to direct and rule by a sort of power to put themselves in the place of the nation over whom they are set, and may thus be said to possess the souls of poets at the same time that they display the coarser sense and the more vulgar sagacity of practical men of business." Wilson, then, thought that leaders should be thinking men and, simultaneously, men of action. But most interesting, perhaps, for subsequent generations are Wilson's views on leadership and political compromise. Given his failure to lead America into the League of Nations, it would seem he was unable at the end of his life to heed his own earlier instruction that "there is and must be in politics a sort of pervasive sense of compromise."

Hitler wrote the first volume of *Mein Kampf* while he was in prison after his unsuccessful *putsch* of November 1923. He had two aims in mind: to establish himself as the undisputed founder and now center of the National Socialist movement, and to present the principles and strategies of his political program. Although the book has been called "a kind of Satanic Bible," what is most interesting in the context of this volume on political leadership are those sections that reveal Hitler as a pragmatist as well as an ideologue. The excerpt presented here is part of a long list of tactics designed to "accomplish the nationalization of the masses." The "movement" referred to is the National Socialist German Workers party (the Nazis), and the topic at hand is what Hitler calls the organizing principle of Germanic democracy: "The leader is elected, but then enjoys unconditional authority." Authority to do what? To "intolerantly impose [the organization's] will against all others."

What Is to Be Done, a pamphlet published some fifteen years before the Russian Revolution, while Lenin lived in Western Europe (in 1902 he moved from Munich to London), contains virtually all of the ideas on politics and political organization that have come to be known as Leninist. Like *Mein Kampf* it was addressed at least as much to those already in the movement as to those outside it, and like *Mein Kampf* a key question is what kinds of leadership and organization are necessary to transform a fledgling group into a vehicle capable of seizing and maintaining political power. Above all, Lenin argues that only a small, centralized, professional group will prove itself capable of correcting the sloppy practices that he believed had up to then characterized most Social Democratic collectives, and that this group must be headed by "a stable organization of leaders maintaining continuity." Of course, what this hierarchically structured band of professional revolutionaries would mean in practice was still hidden in the future.

The short essays by Mahatma Gandhi first appeared in *Young India*, one of two weekly newspapers he used during the 1920s to both educate and propagandize. Although the word *Satyagraha* was coined in South Africa to distinguish, as Gandhi notes, "the non-violent resistance of the Indians of South Africa from the contemporary 'passive resistance' of the suffragettes and others," it was in India finally that Satyagraha had its most dramatic impact. It was during the years 1920–22 that Gandhi first employed militant nonviolence to great effect; Indians began to seriously question British rule. (The tactic was used in the United States during the Civil Rights movement of the 1960s, under the leadership of Martin Luther King, Jr.)

Although the weapon of civil disobedience tends to be successfully employed only by leaders of extraordinary talent and skill—even these brief pieces reveal Gandhi to be both an intellectual leader and a brilliant political tactician—Gandhi's tactic was to play down the importance of the leader and to appear embarrassed by the reverential title of Mahatma that was bestowed upon him in the mid 1920s. His example reminds us of what we already know: that some of the greatest leaders in human history claimed no followers and taught that political office and power should be shunned.

NOTE

1. Arthur S. Link, ed., *The Papers of Woodrow Wilson*, vol. 6 (Princeton: Princeton University Press, 1969), p. 645.

40

WOODROW WILSON

Leaders of Men

Oₙₗy those are "leaders of men," in the general eye, who lead in action. The title belongs, if the whole field of the world be justly viewed, no more rightfully to the men who lead in action than to those who lead in silent thought. A book is often quite as quickening a trumpet as any made of brass and sounded in the field. But it is the estimate of the world that bestows their meaning upon words: and that estimate is not often very far from the fact. The men who act stand nearer to the mass of men than do the men who write; and it is at their hands that new thought gets its translation into the crude language of deeds. The very crudity of that language of deeds exasperates the sensibilities of the author; and his exasperation proves the world's point. He may be *back* of the leaders, but he is not the leader. In his thought there is due and studied proportion; all limiting considerations are set in their right places, as guards to ward off misapprehension. Every cadence of right utterance is made to sound in the careful phrases, in the perfect adjustments of sense. Translate the thought into action and all its shadings disappear. It stands out a naked, lusty thing, sure to rasp the sensibilities of every man of fastidious taste. Stripped for action, a thought must always shock those who cultivate the nice fashions of literary dress, as authors do. But it is only when thought does thus stand forth in unabashed force that it can perform deeds of strength in the arena round about which the great public sit as spectators, awarding the prizes by the suffrage of their applause.

Here, unquestionably, we come upon the heart of the perennial misunderstanding between the men who write and the men who act. The men who write love proportion; the men who act must strike out practicable lines of action, and neglect proportion. This would seem to explain the well-nigh universal repugnance felt by literary men towards Democracy. The arguments which induce popular action must always be broad and obvious arguments. Only a very gross substance of concrete conception can make any impression on the minds of the masses; they must get their ideas very absolutely put, and are much readier to receive a half truth which they can promptly understand than a whole truth which has too many sides to be seen all at once. How can any man whose method is the method of artistic completeness of thought and expression, whose mood is the mood of contemplation, for a moment understand or tolerate "the majority," whose purpose and practice it is to strike out broad, rough-hewn *policies,* whose mood is the mood of action? The great stream of freedom which

> broadens down
> from precedent to precedent, [1]

is not a clear mountain current such as the fastidious man of chastened taste likes to drink from: it is polluted with not a few of the coarse elements of the gross world on its banks; it is heavy with the drainage of a very material universe.

One of the nicest *tests* of the repugnance felt by the literary nature for the sort of leadership and action which commends itself to the world of common men you may yourself apply. Ask some author of careful, discriminative thought to utter his ideas to a *mass-meeting,* from a platform occupied by "representative citizens." He will shrink from it as he would shrink from being publicly dissected! Even to hear *some one else,* who is given to apt public speech, re-render his thoughts in oratorical phrase and make them acceptable to a miscellaneous audience, is often a mild, sometimes an accute, form of torture for him. If the world would really know his thoughts for what they are, let them go to his written words, con his phrases, join paragraph with paragraph, chapter with chapter: then, the whole form and fashion of his conceptions impressed upon their minds, they will know him as no platform speaker can ever make him known. Of course such preferences greatly limit his audience. Not many out of the multitudes who crowd about him buy his books.

But, if the few who can understand read and are convinced, will not his thoughts finally leaven the mass?

The true leader of man, it is plain, is equipped by lacking such sensibilities, which the literary man, when analyzed, is found to possess as a chief part of his make-up. He lacks that subtle power of sympathy which enables the men who write the great works of the imagination to put their minds under the spell of a thousand individual motives not their own but the living force in the several characters they interpret. No popular leader could write fiction. He could not conceive the "Ring and the Book," the impersonation of a half-score points of view. An imaginative realization of other natures and minds than his own is as impossible for him, as his own commanding, dominating frame of mind and character is impossible for the sensitive seer whose imagination can give life to a thousand separate characters. . . .

The competent leader of men cares little for the interior niceties of other people's characters: he cares much—everything for the external uses to which they may be put. His will seeks the lines of least resistance; but the whole question with him is a question *of the application of force.* There are men to be moved: how shall he move them? He supplies the power; others supply only the materials upon which that power operates. The power will fail if it be misapplied; it will be misapplied if it be not suitable both in kind and method to the nature of the materials upon which it is spent; but that nature is, after all, only its means. It is the *power* which dictates, dominates: the materials yield. Men are as clay in the hands of the consummate leader.

It often happens that the leader displays a sagacity and an insight in the handling of men in the mass which quite baffle the wits of the shrewdest analyst of *individual* character. Men in the mass differ from men as individuals. A man who knows, and keenly knows, every man in town may yet fail to understand a mob or a mass-meeting of his fellow-townsmen. Just as the whole tone and method suitable for a public speech are foreign to the tone and method proper in individual, face to face dealings with separate men, so is the art of leading different from the art of writing novels. . . .

I advance my explanation . . . another step. Society is not a crowd, but an organism; and, like every organism, it must grow as a whole or else be deformed. The world is agreed, too, that it is an organism also in this, that it will die unless it be vital in every part. That is the only line of reasoning by which we can really establish the majority in legitimate authority. This organic whole, Society, is made up, obviously, for the most part, of the majority. It grows by the development of its aptitudes and desires, and under their guidance. The evolution of its institutions must take place by slow modification and nice all-around adjustment. And all this is but a careful and abstract way of saying that no reform may succeed for which the major thought of the nation is not prepared: that the instructed few may not be safe leaders except in so far as they have communicated their instruction to the many—except in so far as they have transmuted their thought into a common, a popular thought.

Let us fairly distinguish, therefore, the peculiar and delicate duties of the popular leader from the not very peculiar or delicate misdemeanors of the demagogue. Leadership, for the statesman, is *interpretation*. He must read the common thought: he must test and calculate very circumspectly the *preparation* of the nation for the next move in the progress of politics. If he fairly hit the popular thought, when we have missed it, are we to say that he is a demagogue? The nice point is to distinguish the firm and progressive popular *thought* from the momentary and whimsical popular *mood*, the transitory or mistaken popular passion. But it is fatally easy to blame or misunderstand the statesman.

Our temperament is one of logic, let us say. We hold that one and one make two and we see no salvation for the people except they receive the truth. The statesman is of another opinion. "One and one doubtless make two," he is ready to admit, "but the people think that one and one make more than two and until they see otherwise we shall have to legislate on that supposition." This is not to talk nonsense. The Roman augurs very soon discovered that sacred fowls drank water and pecked grain with no sage intent of prophecy, but from motives quite mundane and simple. But it would have been a revolution to say so in the face of a people who believed otherwise, and executive policy had to proceed on the theory of a divine method of fowl appetite and digestion. The divinity that once did hedge a king, grows not now very high about the latest Hohenzollern;[2] but who that prefers growth to revolution would propose that legislation in Germany proceed independently of this accident of hereditary succession?

In no case may we safely hurry the organism away from its habit: for it is held together by that habit, and by it is enabled to perform its functions completely. The constituent habit of a people inheres in its thought, and to that thought legislation,—even the legislation that advances and modifies habit,—must keep very near. The ear of the leader must ring with the voices of the people. He cannot be of the school of the prophets; he must be of the number of those who studiously serve the slow-paced daily demand.

In what, then, does political leadership consist? It is leadership in *conduct*, and leadership in conduct must discern and strengthen the tendencies that make for development. The legislative leader must perceive the direction of the nation's permanent forces, and must feel the speed of their operation. There is initiative here, but not novelty. There are old *thoughts*, but a progressive *application* of them.

There is such initiative as we may conceive the man part of the mythical *centaur* to have exercised. Doubtless the centaur acted, not as a man, but as a horse, would act, the head conceiving only such things as were possible for the performance of its lower and nether equine parts. He never dared to climb where hoofs could gain no sure foothold: and we may be confident that he knew that there were four feet, not two, to be provided with standing-room. There must have been the caper of the beast in all his schemes. He would have had as much respect, we may suppose, for a blacksmith as for a haberdasher. He must have had the standards of the stable rather than the standards of the drawing-room. The headship of the mind over the body is a like headship for all of us: it is observant of possibility and of physical environment.

The inventing mind is impatient of such restraints: the aspiring soul has at all times longed to be loosed from the body. But such are the conditions of organic life that if the body is to be put off dissolution must be endured. As the conceiving mind is tenant of the body, so is the conceiving legislator tenant of that greater body, Society. Practical leadership may not beckon to the slow masses of men from beyond some dim unexplored space or some intervening chasm: it must daily feel under its own feet the *road* that leads to the goal proposed, knowing that it is a slow, a very slow, evolution to wings, and that for the present, and for a very long future also, Society must *walk*, dependent upon practicable paths, incapable of scaling sudden, precipitous heights, a road-breaker, not a fowl of the air. In the words of the master, Burke, "to follow, not to force, the public inclination,—to give a direction, a form, a technical dress, and a specific sanction, to the general sense of the community, is the true end of legislature." That general sense of the community may wait to be aroused, and the statesman must arouse it; may be inchoate and vague, and the statesman must formulate and make it explicit. But he cannot and he should not do more. The forces of the public thought may be blind: he must lend them sight; they may blunder: he must set them right. He can do something, indeed, to *create* such forces of opinion; but it is a creation of forms, not of substance:—and without such forces at his back he can do nothing effective.

This function of interpretation, this careful exclusion of individual origination it is that makes it difficult for the impatient original mind to distinguish the popular statesman from the demagogue. *The demagogue* sees and seeks *self-interest* in an acquiescent reading of that part of the public thought upon which he depends for votes; the *statesman*, also reading the common inclination, also, when he reads aright, obtains the votes that keep him in power. But if you will justly observe the two, you will find the one trimming to the inclinations of the moment, the other obedient only to the permanent purposes of the public mind. The one adjusts his sails to the breeze of the day; the other makes his plans to ripen with the slow progress of the years. While the one solicitously watches the capricious changes of the weather, the other diligently sows the grains in their seasons. The one ministers to himself, the other to the race.

To the literary temperament leadership in both kinds is impossible. The literary mind conceives images, images rounded, perfect, ideal; unlimited and unvaried by accident. It craves outlooks. It handles such stuff as dreams are made of. It is not guided by principles, as statesmen conceive principles, but by conceptions. Principles, as statesmen conceive them, are threads to the labyrinth of circumstances; principles, as the literary mind holds them, are unities, instrumental to nothing, sufficient unto themselves. Throw the conceiving mind, habituated to contemplating wholes, into the arena of politics, and it seems to itself to be standing upon shifting sands, where no sure foothold and no upright posture are possible. Its ideals are to it more real and more solid than any actuality of the world in which men are managed.

The late Mr. Matthew Arnold was wont now and again to furnish excellent illustration of these points. In the presence of the acute political crisis in Ireland, he urged that no radical remedy be undertaken,— except the *very* radical remedy of changing the character of the English people. What was needed was not home rule for Ireland but a sounder home conscience and less Philistinism in England. "Wait," he said, in effect, "don't legislate. Let me talk to these middle classes a little more, and then, without radical measures of relief, they will treat Ireland in the true human spirit." Doubtless he was right. When America was discontented, and, because England resisted home *rule*, began to clamour for home *sovereignty*, peradventure the truest remedy would have been, not revolution, but the enlightenment of the English people. But the process of enlightenment was slow; while the injustice was pressing: and revolution came on apace. Unquestionably culture is the best cure for anarchy; but anarchy is swifter than her adversary. Culture lags behind the practicable remedy.

There is a familiar anecdote that belongs just here. The captain of a
Mississippi steamboat had made fast to the shore because of a thick fog
lying upon the river. The fog lay low and dense upon the surface of the
water, but overhead all was clear. A cloudless sky showed a thousand
points of starry light. An impatient passenger inquired the cause of the
delay. "We can't see to steer," said the captain. "But all's clear overhead,"
suggested the passenger, "you can see the North star." "Yes," replied the
officer, "but we are not going that way." Politics must follow the actual
windings of the channel: if it steer by the stars it will run aground.

You may say that if all this be truth: if practical political thought may
not run in straight lines, but must twist and turn through all the sinuous
paths of various circumstance, then compromise is the true gospel of
politics. I cannot wholly gainsay the proposition. But it depends almost
altogether upon how you conceive and define compromise whether it
seem hateful or not, — whether it *be* hateful or not. I understand the
biologists to say that all *growth* is a process of compromise: a compromise
of the vital forces within the organism with the physical forces without,
which constitute the environment. Yet growth is not dishonest. Neither
need compromise in politics be dishonest, — if only it be progressive. Is
not compromise the law of society in all things? Do we not in all dealings
adjust views, compound differences, placate antagonisms? Uncompromising thought is the luxury of the closeted recluse. Untrammelled
reasoning is the indulgence of the philosopher, of the dreamer of sweet
dreams. We make always a sharp distinction between the literature of
conduct and the literature of the imagination. "Poetic justice" we recognize as being quite out of the common run of experience.

Nevertheless, leadership does not always wear the harness of compromise. Once and again one of those great Influences which we call a
Cause arises in the midst of a nation. Men of strenuous minds and high
ideals come forward, with a sort of gentle majesty, as champions of a
political or moral principle. They wear no armour; they bestride no
chargers; they only speak their thought, in season and out of season. But
the attacks they sustain are more cruel than the collisions of arms. Their
souls are pierced with a thousand keen arrows of obloquy. Friends desert
and despise them. They stand alone: and oftentimes are made bitter by
their isolation. They are doing nothing less than defy public opinion, and
shall they convert it by blows? Yes. Presently the forces of the popular
thought hesitate, waver, seem to doubt their power to subdue a half score
stubborn minds. Again a little while and those forces have actually

yielded. Masses come over to the side of the reform. Resistance is left to the minority, and such as will not be convinced are crushed.

What has happened? Has it been given to a handful of men to revolutionize by the foolishness of preaching the whole thought of a nation and of an epoch? By no means. None but Christian doctrine was ever permitted to dig entirely new channels for human thought, and turn that thought rapidly about from its old courses: and even Christianity came only in "the fulness of time," and has had a triumph as slow-paced as history itself. No cause is born out of time. Every successful reform movement has had as its efficient cry some principle of equity or morality already *accepted* well-nigh universally, but not yet universally applied in the affairs of life. Every such movement has been the awakening of a people to see a new field for old principles. These men who stood alone at the inception of the movement and whose voices then seemed as it were the voices of men crying in the wilderness, have in reality been simply the more sensitive organs of Society—the parts first awakened to consciousness of a situation. With the start and irritation of a rude and sudden summons from sleep, Society at first resents the disturbance of its restful unconsciousness, and for a moment racks itself with hasty passion. But, once completely aroused, it will sanely meet the necessities of conduct revealed by the hour of its awakening.

Great reformers do not indeed *observe* times and circumstances. Theirs is not a service of opportunity. They have no thought for occasion, no capacity for compromise. But they are none the less *produced* by occasions. They are early vehicles of the Spirit of the Age. They are born of the very times that oppose them: their success is the acknowledgement of their legitimacy. For how many centuries had the world heard single, isolated voices summoning it to religious toleration before that toleration became inevitable, because not to have had it would have been an anomaly, an anachronism. It was postponed until it should fit into the world's whole system,—and only in this latter time did its advocates become leaders. Did not Protestantism come first to Germany, which had already unconsciously drifted very far away from Rome? Did not parliamentary reform come in England only as the tardy completion of tendencies long established and long drilled for success? Were not the Corn Laws repealed because they were a belated remnant of an effete system of economy and politics? Did not the abolition of slavery come just in the nick of time to restore to a system sorely deranged the symmetry and wholeness of its original plan? Take what example you please, and in every case what took place was the destruction of an anomaly, the wiping out of an anachronism. Does not every historian of insight perceive the *timeliness* of these reforms? Is it not the judgement of history that they were the products of a period, that there was laid upon their originators, not the gift of creation, but in a superior degree the gift of insight, the spirit of the age? It was theirs to hear the inarticulate voices that stir in the night-watches, apprising the lonely sentinal of what the day will bring forth. . . .

And yet it seems to me that these phenomena of conduct which so disturb us are but further illustrations of the principles of leadership upon which I have most insisted. There is and must be in politics a sort of pervasive sense of compromise, an abiding consciousness of the fact that there is in the general growth and progress of affairs no absolute initiative for any one man, but that each must both give and take. If I am so strenuous in every point of belief and conduct that I cannot meet those of opposite opinions in good fellowship wherever and whenever conduct does not tell immediately upon the action of the state, you may be sure that when you examine my schemes you will find them impracticable, — impracticable, that is, to be *voted* upon. You may be sure that I am a man who must have his own way wholly or not at all. Of course there is much in mere everyday association. Men of opposite parties, seeing each other every day, are enabled to discover that there are no more tails and cloven hoofs on one side in politics than on the other. But it is not all the effect of use and companionship. More than that, it is the effect of openness of mind to impressions of the general opinion, to the influences of the whole situation as to character and strategy. Now and again their [there] arises the figure of a leader silent, reserved, intense, uncompanionable, shut in upon his own thoughts and plans; and such a man will oftentimes prove a great force; but you will find him generally useful for the advancement of but a single cause. He holds a narrow commission, and his work is soon finished. He may count himself happy if he escape the misfortune of being esteemed a fanatic.

What a lesson it is in the organic wholeness of Society, this study of leadership! How subtle and delicate is the growth of the organism, and how difficult initiative in it! Where is rashness? It is excluded. And raw invention? It is discredited. How, as we look about us into the great maze of Society, see its solidarity, its complexity, its restless forces surging amidst its delicate tissues, its hazards and its exalted hopes, — how can we but be filled with awe! Many are the functions that enter into its quick, unresting life. There is the lonely seer, seeking the truths that shall stand permanent and endure; the poet, tracing all perfected lines of beauty, sounding full-voiced all notes of love or hope, of duty or gladness; the toilers in the world's massy stuffs, moulders of metals, forgers of steel, refiners of gold; there are the winds of commerce; the errors and despairs of war; the old things and the new; the vast things that dominate and the small things that constitute the world; passions of men, loves of women; the things that are visible and which pass away and the things that are invisible and eternal. And in the midst of all stands the leader, gathering, as best he can, the thoughts that are completed, that are perceived, that have told upon the common mind; judging also of the work that is now at length ready to be completed; reckoning the gathered gain; perceiving the fruits of toil and of war, — and combining all these into words of progress, into acts of recognition and completion. Who shall say that this is not an exalted function? Who shall doubt or dispraise the titles of leadership?

Shall we wonder, either, if the leader be a man open at all points to all men, ready to break into coarse laughter with the Rabelaisian vulgar; ready also to prose with the moralist and the reformer; with an eye of tolerance and shrewd appreciation for life of every mode and degree; a sort of sensitive dial registering all the forces that move upon the face of Society? I do not conceive the leader a *trimmer*, weak to yield what clamour claims, but the deeply human man, quick to know and to do the things that the hour and his people need.

NOTES

The notes are by Arthur S. Link. [BK]

1. From Tennyson's "You Ask Me Why."
2. Wilhelm II, who had acceded to the throne on June 15, 1888, and had dismissed Bismarck on March 18, 1890.

41

ADOLF HITLER

Mein Kampf

IN little as well as big things, the movement advocates the principle of a Germanic democracy: the leader is elected, but then enjoys unconditional authority.

The practical consequences of this principle in the movement are the following:

The first chairman of a local group is elected, but then he is the responsible leader of the local group. All committees are subordinate to him and not, conversely, he to a committee. There are no electoral committees, but only committees for work. The responsible leader, the first chairman, organizes the work. The first principle applies to the next higher organization, the precinct, the district or county. The leader is always elected, but thereby he is vested with unlimited powers and authority. And, finally, the same applies to the leadership of the whole party. The chairman is elected, but he is the exclusive leader of the movement.[1] All committees are subordinate to him and not he to the committees. He makes the decisions and hence bears the responsibility on his shoulders. Members of the movement are free to call him to account before the forum of a new election, to divest him of his office in so far as he has infringed on the principles of the movement or served its interests badly. His place is then taken by an abler, new man, enjoying, however, the same authority and the same responsibility.

It is one of the highest tasks of the movement to make this principle determining, not only within its own ranks, but for the entire state.

From Adolf Hitler, *Mein Kampf*, trans. Ralph Manheim (Boston: Houghton Mifflin, 1971), pp. 244–51. Copyright 1943 and © renewed 1971 by Houghton Mifflin Company. Reprinted by permission of Houghton Mifflin Company and Century Hutchinson, Ltd. First published in 1925.

Any man who wants to be leader bears, along with the highest unlimited authority, also the ultimate and heaviest responsibility.

Anyone who is not equal to this or is too cowardly to bear the consequences of his acts is not fit to be leader; only the hero is cut out for this.

The progress and culture of humanity are not a product of the majority, but rest exclusively on the genius and energy of the personality.

To cultivate the personality and establish it in its rights is one of the prerequisites for recovering the greatness and power of our nationality.

Hence the movement is anti-parliamentarian, and even its participation in a parliamentary institution can only imply activity for its destruction, for eliminating an institution in which we must see one of the gravest symptoms of mankind's decay.

(10) The movement decisively rejects any position on questions which either lie outside the frame of its political work or, being not of basic importance, are irrelevant for it. Its task is not a religious reformation, but a political reorganization of people. In both religious denominations it sees equally valuable pillars for the existence of our people and therefore combats those parties which want to degrade this foundation of an ethical, moral, and religious consolidation of our national body to the level of an instrument of their party interests.

The movement finally sees its task, not in the restoration of a definite state form and in the struggle against another, but in the creation of those basic foundations without which neither republic nor monarchy can endure for any length of time. Its mission lies not in the foundation of a monarchy or in the reinforcement of a republic, but in the creation of a Germanic state.

The question of the outward shaping of this state, its crowning, so to speak, is not of basic importance, but is determined only by questions of practical expediency.

For a people that has once understood the great problems and tasks of its existence, the questions of outward formalities will no longer lead to inner struggle.

(11) The question of the movement's inner organization is one of expediency and not of principle.

The best organization is not that which inserts the greatest, but that which inserts the smallest, intermediary apparatus between the leadership of movement and its individual adherents. For the function of organization is the transmission of a definite idea—which always first arises from the brain of an individual—to a larger body of men and the supervision of its realization.

Hence organization is in all things only a necessary evil. In the best case it is a means to an end, in the worst case an end in itself.

Since the world produces more mechanical than ideal natures, the forms of organization are usually created more easily than ideas as such.

The practical development of every idea striving for realization in this world, particularly of one possessing a reform character, is in its broad outlines as follows:

Some idea of genius arises in the brain of a man who feels called upon to transmit his knowledge to the rest of humanity. He preaches his view and gradually wins a certain circle of adherents. This process of the direct and personal transmittance of a man's ideas to the rest of his fellow men[2] is the most ideal and natural. With the rising increase in the adherents of the new doctrine, it gradually becomes impossible for the exponent of the idea to go on exerting a personal, direct influence on the innumerable supporters, to lead and direct them. Proportionately as, in consequence of the growth of the community, the direct and shortest communication is excluded, the necessity of a connecting organization arises: thus, the ideal condition is ended and is replaced by the necessary evil of organization. Little sub-groups are formed which in the political movement, for example, call themselves local groups and constitute the germ-cells of the future organization.

If the unity of the doctrine is not to be lost, however, this subdivision must not take place until the authority of the spiritual founder and of the school trained by him can be regarded as unconditional. The geopolitical significance of a focal center in a movement cannot be overemphasized. Only the presence of such a place, exerting the magic spell of a Mecca or a Rome, can in the long run give the movement a force which is based on inner unity and the recognition of a summit representing this unity.

Thus, in forming the first organizational germ-cells we must never lose sight of the necessity, not only of preservng the importance of the original local source of the idea, but of making it paramount. This intensification of the ideal, moral, and factual immensity of the movement's point of origin and direction must take place in exact proportion as the movement's germ-cells, which have now become innumerable, demand new links in the shape of organizational forms.

For, as the increasing number of individual adherents makes it impossible to continue direct communication with them for the formation of the lowest bodies, the ultimate innumerable increase[3] of these lowest organizational forms compels in turn creation of higher associations which politically can be designated roughly as county or district groups.

Easy as it still may be to maintain the authority of the original center toward the lowest local groups, it will be equally difficult to maintain this position toward the higher organizational forms which now arise. But this is the precondition for the unified existence of the movement and hence for carrying out an idea.

If, finally, these larger intermediary divisions are also combined into new organizational forms, the difficulty is further increased of safeguarding, even toward them, the unconditional leading character of the original founding site, its school, etc.

Therefore, the mechanical forms of an organization may only be developed to the degree in which the spiritual ideal authority of a center seems unconditionally secured. In political formations this guaranty can often seem provided only by practical power.

From this the following directives for the inner structure of the movement resulted:

(a) Concentration for the time being of all activity in a single place: Munich. Training of a community of unconditionally reliable supporters and development of a school for the subsequent dissemination of the idea. Acquisition of the necessary authority for the future by the greatest possible visible sucesses in this one place.

To make the movement and its leaders known, it was necessary, not only to shake the belief in the invincibility of the Marxist doctrine in one place for all to see, but to demonstrate the possibility of an opposing movement.

(b) Formation of local groups only when the authority of the central leadership in Munich may be regarded as unquestionably recognized.

(c) Likewise the formation of district, county, or provincial groups depends, not only on the need for them, but also on certainty that an unconditional recognition of the center has been achieved.

Furthermore, the creation of organizational forms is dependent on the men who are available and can be considered as leaders.

This may occur in two ways:

(a) The movement disposes of the necessary financial means for the training and schooling of minds capable of future leadership. It then distributes the material thus acquired systematically according to criteria of tactical and other expediency.

This way is the easier and quicker; however, it demands great financial means, since this leader material is only able to work for the movement when paid.

(b) The movement, owing to the lack of financial means, is not in a position to appoint official leaders, but for the present must depend on honorary officers.

This way is the slower and more difficult.

Under certain circumstances the leadership of a movement must let large territories lie fallow, unless there emerges from the adherents a man able and willing to put himself at the disposal of the leadership, and organize and lead the movement in the district in question.

It may happen that in large territories there will be no one, in other places, however, two or even three almost equally capable. The difficulty that lies in such a development is great and can only be overcome in the course of years.

The prerequisite for the creation of an organizational form is and remains the man necessary for its leadership.

As worthless as an army in all its organizational forms is without officers, equally worthless is a political organization without the suitable leader.

Not founding a local group is more useful to the movement when a suitable leader personality is lacking than to have its organization miscarry due to the absence of a leader to direct and drive it forward.

Leadership itself requires not only will but also ability, and a greater importance must be attached to will and energy than to intelligence as such, and most valuable of all is a combination of ability, determination, and perseverance.

(12) The future of a movement is conditioned by the fanaticism, yes, the intolerence, with which its adherents uphold it as the sole correct movement, and push it past other formations of a similar sort.

It is the greatest error to believe that the strength of a movement increases through a union with another of similar character. It is true that every enlargement of this kind at first means an increase in outward dimensions, which to the eyes of superficial observers means power; in truth, however, it only takes over the germs of an inner weakening that will later become effective.

For whatever can be said about the like character of two movements, in reality it is never present. For otherwise there would actually be not two movements but one. And regardless wherein the differences lie— even if they consisted only in the varying abilities of the leadership—they exist. But the natural law of all development demands, not the coupling of two formations which are simply not alike, but the victory of the stronger and the cultivation of the victor's force and strength made possible alone by the resultant struggle.

Through the union of two more or less equal political party formations momentary advantages may arise, but in the long run any success won in this way is the cause of inner weaknesses which appear later.

The greatness of a movement is exclusively guaranteed by the unrestricted development of its inner strength and its steady growth up to the final victory over all competitors.

Yes, we can say that its strength and hence the justification of its existence increases only so long as it recognizes the principle of struggle as the premise of its development, and that it has passed the high point of its strength in the moment when complete victory inclines to its side.

Therefore, it is only profitable for a movement to strive for this victory in a form which does not lead to an early momentary success, but which in a long struggle occasioned by absolute intolerance also provides long growth.

Movements which increase only by the so-called fusion of similar formations, thus owing their strength to compromises, are like hothouse plants. They shoot up, but they lack the strength to defy the centuries and withstand heavy storms.

The greatness of every mighty organization embodying an idea in this world lies in the religious fanaticism and intolerence with which, fanatically convinced of its own right, it intolerantly imposes its will against all others. If an idea in itself is sound and, thus armed, takes up a struggle on this earth, it is unconquerable and every persecution will only add to its inner strength.

NOTES

The notes are by Ralph Mannheim.[BK]

1. This is one of the few passages the sense of which has been radically changed in the second edition. By the time of the appearance of the second edition, Hitler had emerged victorious from the factional conflicts within the party. His authority was now uncontested. In the second edition the passage reads:

"The young movement is in its nature and inner organization anti-parliamentarian; that is, it rejects in general and in its own inner structure, a principle of majority rule in which the leader is degraded to the level of a mere executant of other people's will and opinion. In little as well as big things, the movement advocates the principle of unconditional authority of the leader, coupled with the highest responsibility. . . ."

2. *"die andere Mitwelt."*

3. *"die zahllose Vermehrung."*

42

V. I. LENIN

What Is to Be Done?

"EVERYONE agrees" that it is necessary to develop the political consciousness of the working class. The question is, *how* that is to be done and what is required to do it. The economic struggle merely "impels" the workers to realise the government's attitude towards the working class. Consequently, *however much we may try to* "lend the economic struggle itself a political character," we *shall never be able to* develop the political consciousness of the workers (to the level of Social-Democratic political consciousness) by keeping within the framework of the economic struggle, for that *framework* is too narrow. . . . It is only natural to expect that for a Social-Democrat whose conception of the political struggle coincides with the conception of the "economic struggle against the employers and the government," the "organisation of revolutionaries" will more or less coincide with the "organisation of workers." This, in fact, is what actually happens; so that when we speak of organisation, we literally speak in different tongues. I vividly recall, for example, a conversation I once had with a fairly consistent Economist, with whom I had not been previously acquainted.[1] We were discussing the pamphlet, *Who Will Bring About the Political Revolution?* and were soon of a mind that its principal defect was its ignoring of the question of organisation. We had begun to assume full agreement between us; but, as the conversation proceeded, it became evident that we were talking of different things. My interlocutor accused the author of ignoring strike funds, mutual benefit societies, etc., whereas I had in mind an organisation of revolutionaries as an essential factor in "bringing about" the political revolution. As soon

From "What Is to Be Done?" in Robert C. Tucker, ed., *The Lenin Anthology* New York: Norton, 1975), pp. 49, 67–68, 72–73, 76–77. First published in 1902.

as the disagreement became clear, there was hardly, as I remember, a single question of principle upon which I was in agreement with the Economist!

What was the source of our disagreement? It was the fact that on questions both of organisation and of politics the Economists are forever lapsing from Social-Democracy into trade-unionism. The political struggle of Social Democracy is far more extensive and complex than the economic struggle of the workers against the employers and the government. Similarly (indeed for that reason), the organisation of the revolutionary Social-Democratic Party must inevitably be of *a kind different* from the organisation of the workers designed for this struggle. The workers' organisation must in the first place be a trade union organisation; secondly, it must be as broad as possible; and thirdly, it must be as public as conditions will allow (here, and further on, of course, I refer only to absolutist Russia). On the other hand, the organisation of the revolutionaries must consist first and foremost of people who make revolutionary activity their profession (for which reason I speak of the organisation of *revolutionaries*, meaning revolutionary Social-Democrats). In view of this common characteristic of the members of such an organisation, *all distinctions as between workers and intellectuals*, not to speak of distinctions of trade and profession, in both categories, *must be effaced*. Such an organisation must perforce not be very extensive and must be as secret as possible. . . .

A small, compact core of the most reliable, experienced, and hardened workers, with responsible representatives in the principal districts and connected by all the rules of strict secrecy with the organisation of revolutionaries, can, with the widest support of the masses and without any formal organisation, perform *all* the functions of a trade union organisation, in a manner, moreover, desirable to Social-Democracy. Only in this way can we secure the *consolidation* and development of a *Social Democratic* trade union movement, despite all the gendarmes.

It may be objected that an organisation which is so *lose* that it is not even definitely formed, and which has not even an enrolled and registered membership, cannot be called an organisation at all. Perhaps so. Not the name is important. What is important is that this "organisation without members" shall do everything that is required, and from the very outset ensure a solid connection between our future trade unions and socialism. Only an incorrigible utopian would have a *broad* organisation of workers, with elections, reports, universal suffrage, etc., under the autocracy.

The moral to be drawn from this is simple. If we begin with the solid foundation of a strong organisation of revolutionaries, we can ensure the stability of the movement as a whole and carry out the aims both of Social-Democracy and of trade unions proper. If, however, we begin with a broad workers' organisation, which is supposedly most "accessible" to the masses (but which is actually most accessible to the gendearmes and makes revolutionaries most accessible to the police), we shall achieve neither the one aim nor the other. . . .

"A dozen wise men can be more easily wiped out than a hundred fools." This wonderful truth (for which the hundred fools will always applaud you) appears obvious only because in the very midst of the argument you have skipped from one question to another. You began by talking and continued to talk of the unearthing of a "committee," of the unearthing of an "organisation," and now you skip to the question of unearthing the movement's "roots" in their "depths." The fact is, of course, that our movement cannot be unearthed, for the very reason that it has countless thousands of roots deep down among the masses; but that is not the point at issue. As far as "deep roots" are concerned, we cannot be "unearthed" even now, despite all our amateurism, and yet we all complain, and cannot but complain, that the *"organisations"* are being unearthed and as a result it is impossible to maintain continuity in the movement. But since you raise the question of *organisations* being unearthed and persist in your opinion, I assert that it is far more difficult to unearth a dozen wise men than a hundred fools. This position I will defend, no matter how much you instigate the masses against me for my "anti-democratic" views, etc. As I have stated repeatedly, by "wise men," in connection with organisation, I mean *professional revolutionaries*, irrespective of whether they have developed from among students or working men. I assert: (1) that no revolutionary movement can endure without a stable organisation of leaders maintaining continuity; (2) that the broader the popular mass drawn spontaneously into the struggle, which forms the basis of the movement and participates in it, the more urgent the need for such an organisation, and the more solid this organisation must be (for it is much easier for all sorts of demagogues to side-track the more backward sections of the masses); (3) that such an organisation must consist chiefly of people professionally engaged in revolutionary activity; (4) that in an autocratic state, the more we *confine* the membership of such an organisation to people who are professionally engaged in revolutionary activity and who have been professionally trained in the art of combating the political police, the more difficult will it be to unearth the organisation; and (5) the *greater* will be the number of people from the working class and from the other social classes who will be able to join the movement and perform active work in it.

NOTE

The note is by Robert C. Tucker. [BK]

1. This apparently refers to Lenin's first meeting with A. S. Martynov in 1901.

43

M. K. GANDHI

Satyagraha

Satyagraha, Civil Disobedience, Passive Resistance, Non-co-operation

SATYAGRAHA is literally holding on to Truth and it means, therefore, Truth-force. Truth is soul or spirit. It is, therefore, known as soul-force. It excludes the use of violence because man is not capable of knowing the absolute truth and, therefore, not competent to punish. The word was coined in South Africa to distinguish the non-violent resistance of the Indians of South Africa from the contemporary "passive resistance" of the suffragettes and others. It is not conceived as a weapon of the weak.

Passive resistance is used in the orthodox English sense and covers the suffragette movement as well as the resistance of the Non-conformists. Passive resistance has been conceived and is regarded as a weapon of the weak. Whilst it avoids violence, being not open to the weak, it does not exclude its use if, in the opinion of a passive resister, the occasion demands it. However, it has always been distinguished from armed resistance and its application was at one time confined to Christian martyrs.

Civil Disobedience is civil breach of unmoral statutory enactments. The expression was, so far as I am aware coined by Thoreau to signify his own resistance to the laws of a slave State. He has left a masterly treatise on the duty of Civil Disobedience. But Thoreau was not perhaps an out and out champion of non-violence. Probably, also Thoreau limited his reach of statutory laws on the revenue law, i.e., payment of taxes.

From M. K. Gandhi, *Satyagraha (Non-Violent Resistance)*, ed. Bharatan Kumarappa (Ahmedabad: Navajivan, 1951), pp. 3–4, 68–69, 82–84. Reprinted by permission of the Navajivan Trust. First published 1921–31.

Whereas the term Civil Disobedience as practised in 1919 covered a breach of any statutory and unmoral law. It signified the resister's outlawry in a civil, i.e., non-violent manner. He invoked the sanctions of the law and cheerfully suffered imprisonment. It is a branch of Satyagraha.

Non-co-operation predominantly implies withdrawing of cooperation from the State that in the non-co-operator's view has become corrupt and excludes Civil Disobedience of the fierce type described above. By its very nature, non-co-operation is even open to children of understanding and can be safely practised by the masses. Civil Disobedience presupposes the habit of willing obedience to laws without fear of their sanctions. It can, therefore, be practised only as a last resort and by a select few in the first instance at any rate. Non-co-operation, too, like Civil Disobedience is a branch of Satyagraha which includes all non-violent resistance for the vindication of Truth.[1]

MY POLITICAL PROGRAMME

[Some American friends sent Gandhiji a gift of 145 dollars to be spent on that part of his work which appealed to them most, viz. anti-untouchability and Hindu-Muslim unity, and said that they knew too little about his political programme to wish to help in that part of his work also. In reply, Gandhiji wrote as follows: —Ed.]

My political programme is extremely simple. If the donors had added the spinning wheel to untouchability and unity, they would have practically completed it. My opinion is becoming daily more and more confirmed that we shall achieve our real freedom only by effort from within, i.e., by self-purification and self-help, and therefore, by the strictest adherence to truth and non-violence. Civil Disobedience is no doubt there in the background. But Civil Disobedience asks for and needs not a single farthing for its support. It needs and asks for stout hearts with faith that will not flinch from any danger and will shine the brightest in the face of severest trial. Civil Disobedience is a terrifying synonym for suffering. But it is better often to understand the terrible nature of a thing if people will truly appreciate its benignant counterpart. Disobedience is a right that belongs to every human being and it becomes a sacred duty when it springs from civility, or, which is the same thing, love. The anti-untouchability reformers are offering Civil Disobedience against entrenched orthodoxy. Protagonists of Hindu-Muslim unity are resisting with their whole soul those who will divide classes and sects. Just as there may be this resistance against those who will hinder the removal of untouchability or promotion of unity, so must there be resistance against a rule that is stunting India's manhood. It is daily grinding down the starving millions of this vast country. Heedless of future consequences the rulers are pursuing a course of conduct regarding intoxicating drinks and drugs that must, if it remains unchecked, corrupt the toilers of the land and make posterity ashamed of us who are making use of this immoral source of revenue for educating our children. But the condition of this terrible resistance—resistance against orthodoxy, resistance against enemies of unity, and resistance against Government—is possible of fulfilment only by a strong, and if need be, a long course of self-purification and suffering.[2]

POLITICAL POWER V. SATYAGRAHA

If I want political power it is for the sake of the reforms for which the Congress stands. Therefore when the energy to be spent in gaining that power means so much loss of energy required for the reforms, as threatens to be the case if the country is to engage in a duel with the Mussalmans or Sikhs, I would most decidedly advise the country to let the Mussalmans and Sikhs take all the power and I would go on with developing the reforms.

If we were to analyse the activities of the Congress during the past twelve years, we would discover that the capacity of the Congress to take political power has increased in exact proportion to its ability to achieve success in the constructive effort. That is to me the substance of political power. Actual taking over of the Government machinery is but a shadow, an emblem. And it could easily be a burden if it came as a gift from without, the people having made no effort to deserve it.

It is now perhaps easy to realize the truth of my statement that the needful can be "gained more quickly and more certainly by Satyagraha than by political power." Legislation in advance of public opinion has often been demonstrated to be futile. Legal prohibition of theft in a country in which the vast majority are thieves would be futile. Picketing and the other popular activities are therefore the real thing. If political power was a thing apart from these reforms, we should have to suspend the latter and concentrate on the former. But we have followed the contrary course. We have everywhere emphasized the necessity of carrying on the constructive activities as being the means of attaining Swaraj. I am convinced that whenever legal prohibition of drinks, drugs and foreign cloth comes, it will come because public opinion had demanded it. It may be said that public opinion demands it today but the foreign Government does not respond. This is only partly right. Public opinion in this country is only now becoming a vital force and developing the real sanction which is Satyagraha.[3]

For "Followers"

A friend sends me the following:

"It will be very helpful if you will kindly guide your followers about their conduct when they have to engage in a political controversy. Your guidance on the following points is particularly needed:
(a) Vilification so as to lower the opponent in public estimation:
(b) Kind of criticism of the opponent permissible:
(c) Limit to which hostility should be carried;
(d) Whether effort should be made to gain office and power.

I have said before in these pages that I claim no followers. It is enough for me to be my own follower. It is by itself a sufficiently taxing perform- ance. But I know that many claim to be my followers. I must therefore answer the questions for their sakes. If they will follow what I endeavour to stand for rather than me they will see that the following answers are derived from truth and *ahimsa*.

(a) Vilification of an opponent there can never be. But this does not exclude a truthful characterization of his acts. An opponent is not always a bad man because he opposes. He may be as honourable as we may claim to be and yet there may be vital differences between him and us.

(b) Our criticism will therefore be if we *believe* him to be guilty of untruth to meet it with truth, of discourtesy with courtesy, of bullying with calm courage, of violence with suffering, of arrogance with humil- ity, of evil with good. "My follower" would seek not to condemn but to convert.

(c) There is no question of any limit to which hostility may be carried. For there should be no hostility to persons. Hostility there must be to acts when they are subversive of morals or the good of society.

(d) Office and power must be avoided. Either may be accepted when it is clearly for greater service.[4]

NOTES

1. *Young India,* 23–3–21.
2. *Young India,* 1–4–26.
3. *Young India,* 2–7–31. *Swaraj* is political independence. [BK]
4. *Young India,* 7–5–31. *Ahimsa* is the Hindu doctrine of refraining from causing injury or death to animal life. [BK]

BIOGRAPHICAL NOTES

THEODOR ADORNO (1903–1969) was a German born musicologist, sociologist, literary and cultural critic, and philosopher. In the early 1930s he began his long collaboration with Max Horkheimer, director of the Frankfurt Institute for Social Research. The "Frankfurt School" of sociologists and psychologists concentrated on the study of Marxist theory and counted among its associates such major figures as Erich Fromm, Herbert Marcuse, Walter Benjamin, and Franz Neumann. Because of the Nazis, several members of the Frankfurt Institute emigrated to America. Between 1944 and 1949 Adorno served as co-director and theoretician of the most famous of the institute's American projects: the Research Project on Social Discrimination. A team of Berkeley psychologists and institute personnel interviewed some two thousand Americans, seeking to establish which traits and backgrounds characterized those with antidemocratic views. It was this study that was published in 1950 as *The Authoritarian Personality*.

HANNAH ARENDT (1906–1975) arrived in the United States in 1940, a political refugee. Before emigrating, she had received her Ph.D. in philosophy from the University of Heidelberg where she studied under Karl Jaspers. When Hitler came to power in 1933, Arendt fled from Germany to France. There she continued to study and write. She also worked in Paris for a Jewish relief organization responsible for the placement of Jewish orphans in Palestine. In the United States, Arendt served in the late 1940s as editor of Schocken Books where she was credited with the publication of several classics including the Max Brod edition of the Kafka diaries. Arendt's reputation as a thinker and scholar was firmly established with the publication of *The Origins of Totalitarianism*, which examined the institutions, organizations, and functioning of totalitarian movements and governments—especially Nazism and Soviet Communism.

CRANE BRINTON (1898–1968), an historian, was an authority on the history of ideas and an expert on the theory of revolution. He spent his entire academic career at Harvard University, using Cambridge, Mass., and Peacham, Vermont, as bases from which to write his many books.

JAMES MACGREGOR BURNS is a Pulitzer Prize winning historian and political scientist. Best known perhaps for his definitive two-volume biography of Franklin Roosevelt, Burns has written extensively on American government and politics, on the roles of political parties and political leaders, and on the impact of leadership on America past and present. Throughout his professional life—during which Burns has played the role of activist as well as academic—his interest in leadership has been reflected in the view that the United States needs strong leadership sustained by centralized and disciplined political parties.

JOSEPH CAMPBELL was a member of the literature faculty of Sarah Lawrence College between 1934 and 1972—although his own work fused literature with anthropology and psychology. Campbell's special interest has been in the impact on our lives of religion and myth. These interests were explored in *The Hero with a Thousand Faces* and a four-volume work, *The Masks of God*.

THOMAS CARLYLE (1795–1881) was a Scottish writer and leading literary figure. He held the controversial views that might and right are the same, that a few people are innately superior to all the others, that democracy is absurd, and that nations should be under the control of one great man. Among his books are *The French Revolution*, *The Life of Schiller*, and *Oliver Cromwell's Letters and Speeches*.

ERIK H. ERIKSON is best known for extending the tenets of psychoanalytic theory beyond infancy and early childhood to early, middle, and even late adulthood. Born in Germany in 1902, Erikson lived as a young man in Vienna, where he began his analysis with Anna Freud (Sigmund Freud's daughter), and studied psychoanalysis at the Vienna Psychoanalytic Society. After emigrating to the United States in the 1930s, Erikson was affiliated with several institutions including Harvard, Yale, the University of California, and the Austin Riggs Center. By focusing on individual psychosexual development within the context of a particular society, Erikson made at least two major contributions: first he challenged Freud's notion that personality is decisively formed in the earliest years of life; and second he demonstrated how individuals are shaped not only by their personal histories, but by the broader sociocultural and political contexts as well. This fusion between the person and the historical moment is brilliantly realized in Erikson's pathbreaking psychobiographies, or psychohistories, *Young Man Luther* (1958) and *Gandhi's Truth* (1969).

JOHN R. P. FRENCH, JR. is retired from the Institute for Social Research at the University of Michigan.

SIGMUND FREUD (1856–1939) has been called "the Copernicus of the Mind." In developing a new method of treating mentally disturbed patients, a method known as psychoanalysis, Freud hypothesized that human behavior is determined in large part by unconscious motives. According to Freud, these motives originate in infancy and early childhood experiences and act later as determinants of adult behavior. Freud also uncovered our propensity for transference, for projecting figures from the past onto figures in the present.

ERICH FROMM (1900–1980) was a psychoanalyst and social philosopher who emigrated from Nazi Germany to the United States in the 1930s. The overall theme in Fromm's writings is the impact of the individual on society. In particular, he applied psychoanalytic insights to the problems of cultural neurosis. *Escape from Freedom* examines the tendency of modern emancipated men and women to take refuge from the dehumanization of contemporary culture in totalitarian movements. The book manifestly struck a responsive chord: twenty-five years after publication it was in its twenty-fifth printing.

MOHANDAS K. GANDHI (1869–1948) was the Hindu nationalist leader and social reformer credited with gaining India's independence from England.

ALEXANDER L. GEORGE is Professor of International Relations at Stanford University. He is co-author, along with Juliette George, of the pathbreaking psychological biography, *Woodrow Wilson and Colonel House: A Personality Study* (1956). Although still debating the genesis of Wilson's adult persona (in *Political Psychology*, June 1983) George has in recent years turned his attention to the study of U.S.-Soviet relations. Among his books in this general area are *Deterence in American Foreign Policy* and *Presidential Decisionmaking in Foreign Policy*.

FRED I. GREENSTEIN is Professor of Politics at Princeton University. He has written widely on political socialization, personality and politics, and leadership in the American presidency. His most recent books are *The Hidden-Hand Presidency: Eisenhower as Leader* and *The Reagan Presidency: An Early Assessment* (editor).

ALEXANDER HAMILTON (1757–1804) was an American statesman and first secretary of the treasury. In an energetic effort to have the Constitution of 1887 ratified in his home state of New York, Hamilton began writing a series of essays explaining and defending the document. He was helped in this work by two equally eminent advocates of a new and vigorous national government: John Jay and James Madison. Originally appearing in the newspapers under the shared pseudonym Publius, together the collected essays constitute *The Federalist Papers*. A summary of *The Federalist Papers* by Clinton Rossiter reads: "No happiness without liberty, no liberty without self-government, no self-government without constitutionalism, no constitutionalism without morality—and none of these great goods without stability and order."

ADOLF HITLER (1889–1945) was dictator of Nazi Germany from 1933 to 1945.

SIDNEY HOOK is a leading twentieth-century philosopher and author who was one of the major interpreters of John Dewey. An early interest in Marxism was followed by disenchantment with the Soviet model and subsequent warnings against communist attempts to dominate intellectual and cultural life in America in the 1940s and 1950s. Hook continues to write on a wide variety of social, philosophical, educational, and political topics.

WILLIAM JAMES (1842–1910) was a distinguished American psychologist and philosopher. By serving as one of the principal interpreters of the modern worlds of science, education, and technology, he helped raise psychology to the rank of a full-fledged science. The 1890 publication of his two-volume work, *Principles of Psychology*—still considered to be original, learned, and beautifully written— brought him international attention. In his later volume on Pragmatism, James advocated that we accept only what can be proved in action or practical effect.

IRVING JANIS has been a member of the Department of Psychology at Yale since 1947. He has written extensively on psychological stress, attitude change, and decision making.

HAROLD LASSWELL (1902–1978) was one of this century's foremost political scientists. He pioneered in the application of the insights of modern psychology—especially Freudian psychology—to the study of politics. Of *Psychopathology and Politics* one reviewer wrote: "Here is an honest attempt to answer the root problem of politics: How to direct into healthy channels the neurotic lust for domination."

VLADIMIR ILYICH LENIN (1870–1924) was the leader of the Bolshevik revolution in Russia in 1917. He was the first premier of the Soviet Union (1917–1924).

KURT LEWIN (1890–1947) was an emigre to the United States from Nazi Germany. While still in Europe he analyzed the phenomenon of self-hatred among members of minority groups. Later, he became known for his ideas on "field theory" and "life space," both of which pertain to the notion that individuals can be understood only in the context of all the events—past, present and future— that pertain to them. During his last decade, Lewin became especially interested in group processes. At his untimely death he was director of research in group dynamics at the Massachusetts Institute of Technology.

EUGENE LEWIS received his Ph.D. in political science from Syracuse University. Since 1967 he has been affiliated with Hamilton College and New College of the University of South Florida.

NICCOLÒ MACHIAVELLI (1469–1527) was an Italian statesman and philosopher who drew on his profound understanding of politics to produce masterpieces of political analysis. From the age of twenty-nine he held a series of important government posts, some of which exposed him to the politics of Germany and France as well as Italy. In his early thirties, Machiavelli witnessed the exploits of Cesare Borgia, whose ruthlessness and ambition had enabled him to conquer a dominion for himself within a few short months. Borgia provided Machiavelli with the model for a "new prince" who would provide the answer to Italy's desperate political problems. Certain blunt maxims in Machiavelli's works combined with a tragic sense of evil in the world gave his writings a reputation—both contemporaneously and posthumously—for being immoral and even diabiolical. Although such a reputation is as undeserved as it is simplistic, it is true that in his best known work, *The Prince*, Machiavelli argues that in order to establish and maintain authority the ends justify the means, and that the most dastardly acts of the ruler are justified by the wickedness and treachery of the ruled.

BRUCE MAZLISH, an historian, has been at the Massachusetts Institute of Technology since 1950. Within the last fifteen years, Mazlish has written books on Richard Nixon, James and John Stuart Mill, Henry Kissinger, and (with Edwin Diamond) Jimmy Carter. His interest in leadership is also realized in *The Revolutionary Ascetic*, in which he explores why some of the great revolutionary leaders were austere "puritans" with few emotional ties.

ROBERT MICHELS (1876–1936) became a radical socialist while teaching at the University of Marburg in the early 1900s. His personal involvement with German revolutionary causes gave him insights into the political behavior of intellectual elites and the problems of power and its abuse. *Political Parties* drew on Michels's experience with prewar German socialism. He concluded that even organizations intent on promoting democratic values inevitably develop strong oligarchic tendencies, and that even the best-intentioned leaders will be compelled to rely on bureaucracies to centralize their authority. Michels called this theory the "iron law of oligarchy."

STANLEY MILGRAM was, at his untimely death in 1984, Professor of Psychology at the City University of New York. He remained best known for his controversial experiments on obedience to authority.

TALCOTT PARSONS (1902–1979), one of America's foremost sociologists, sought to create a single theoretical framework within which all aspects of society could be systematically classified. In this he resembled European theorists who emphasized the broad conceptual outlook rather than American academics who concerned themselves with narrower empirical studies. Parsons taught at Harvard for most of his professional life. The Department of Social Relations—of which he was the first chairman—offered instruction in sociology, social psychology, and social anthropology in order to facilitate the study of men and women within the context of the society in which they live.

PLATO (c. 427–c. 347 B.C.) is considered one of the supremely great philosophical genuises of all time. His early ardor for politics was dampened when his friend and mentor, Socrates, was tried and executed for political reasons. As a consequence, and in vindication of Socrates, Plato entered a life of research and writing that centered on the creation of thirty-five dialogues, a style which reflects his conviction that learning can best be achieved through discussion and shared inquiry. Most of the dialogues featured Socrates although, over time, Socrates became the mouthpiece of Platonic rather than Socratic doctrines. It is impossible to overestimate Plato's influence on Western thought. As twentieth-century philosopher Alfred North Whitehead put it: Western philosophy is but a "footnote to Plato."

PLUTARCH (c. 46–c. 120 A.D.), Greek historian, biographer and philosopher, commenced his higher education in Athens in 66. His most enduring work, *Parallel Lives*, contains a gallery of fifty portraits of the great Greek and Roman characters of the ages preceding his own. The *Lives* are monuments of great historical and literary value, in part because they are based on lost records. Plutarch adheres throughout the biographies to his professed purpose; portraits of character. He only touches on his subjects' distinguished careers, preferring instead to illuminate the natures of great men by an incident, word, or jest.

BERTRAM H. RAVEN is Professor of Psychology at the University of California in Los Angeles.

JOSEPH SCHUMPETER (1883–1950) is widely considered one of the great economists of the twentieth century. Educated in Vienna, Schumpeter was a professor of economics at the University of Graz. Later he served briefly as Austrian minister of finance and as president of a private bank. He returned to academic life when the bank failed, finally emigrating to the United States where he became a member of the faculty of Harvard University. Schumpeter's *Theory of Economic Development* (1912) focused on the "entrepreneur-innovator" as the key figure in capitalist society. His massive two-volume *Business Cycles* (1930) also stressed the importance of innovators and creators in economic growth. In perhaps his most widely known book, *Capitalism, Socialism, and Democracy* (1942), Schumpeter predicted that as pure types both capitalism and communism were doomed, and that they would gradually merge into a form of socialism. His last work, *History of Economic Analysis*, published posthumously, is considered a giant among studies of economic thought.

GEORG SIMMEL (1858—1918) was a German sociologist and philosopher who in many ways was the quintessential marginal man. Rather than following a single academic discipline, Simmel pursued an unorthodox amalgam of subjects, provoking Ortega y Gasset to compare him to a philosophical squirrel, gracefully acrobatic in leaping from one branch of knowledge to another. Simmel did not see society as a thing or an organism, nor as a convenient label for something that did not have "real" existence. Rather, according to his view, society "is merely the name for a number of individuals, connected by interaction."

HERBERT SPENCER (1820–1903) attempted to work out a philosophy based on the scientific discoveries of his day. In his masterly ten-volume work, *Synthetic Philosophy*, Spencer applied the idea of gradual development, or evolution, to biology, psychology, sociology, and other fields. Later, still stressing the scientific approach to all phenomena in opposition to the prevailing religious or metaphysical approach, Spencer studied politics and society, again in terms of evolutionary theory.

DENNIS F. THOMPSON received his Ph.D. in political science from Harvard. He has served since 1968 as a member of the Politics Department at Princeton.

ROBERT C. TUCKER is Professor Emeritus of Politics at Princeton University. He specializes in the study of the Soviet Union. His many books include *The Soviet Political Mind*, *The Marxian Revolutionary Idea*, and *Stalin as a Revolutionary*. Currently he is working on volume two of a projected three-volume biography of Stalin.

MAX WEBER (1864–1920) was a German social scientist widely considered to be one of the founders of modern social thought. He wrote important works on social organization, the nature of the modern state, jurisprudence and ethics, authority and leadership, and the relationship between religion and capitalist economies. Preoccupied with the growth and development of rationalism in Western civilization, Weber sought to understand this movement through in-depth analyses of the Eastern religions, including Buddhism, Confucianism, Hinduism, and Taoism, and also ancient Judaism. It was this course of study that convinced Weber of the tie between Protestantism, which encourages individual enterprise, and capitalism, which encourages the private accumulation of capital. Although best known for the objectivity of his sociological analyses, one of his colleagues, the esteemed sociologist Reinhard Bendix, drew attention to the moral dimension of Weber's work: "Weber sought to safeguard the great legacy of the Enlightenment after fully exploring the historical preconditions of that legacy."

FRED H. WILLHOITE, JR. teaches Political Science at Coe College, in Cedar Rapids, Iowa.

ANN RUTH WILLNER is Professor of Political Science at the University of Kansas. She has served as a foreign affairs analyst for the U.S. Congress, and as political science editor of the *International Encyclopedia of the Social Sciences*.

WOODROW WILSON (1856–1924) was the twenty-eighth president of the United States (1913–1921).

E. VICTOR WOLFENSTEIN teaches in the Department of Political Science at the University of California at Los Angeles.

PITT SERIES IN POLICY AND INSTITUTIONAL STUDIES
BERT A. ROCKMAN, EDITOR